剑桥应用语言学年度评论 2005
Annual Review of Applied Linguistics

应用语言学概述
A Survey of Applied Linguistics

主编 〔美〕Mary McGroarty

导读 孙迎晖

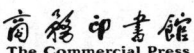

2016年·北京

Originally published by Cambridge University Press in 2005. This reprint edition is published with the permission of the Syndicate of the Press of the University of Cambridge, Cambridge, England.

原书由英国剑桥大学出版社于 2005 年出版。

本版经英国剑桥大学出版社授权出版。

This edition is licensed for sale in the People's Republic of China only (excluding Hong Kong SAR, Macao SAR and Taiwan Province). No part of this publication may be reproduced or distributed by any means, or stored in a database or retrieval system, without the prior written permission of the publisher.

本版仅限在中华人民共和国境内（不包括香港特别行政区、澳门特别行政区及台湾）销售。未经出版者书面许可，不得以任何方式复制或发行本书的任何部分。

剑桥应用语言学年度评论专家委员会

主　任	胡壮麟
副主任	田贵森　朱永生
委　员	曹　进　何　伟　靳　琰　赖良涛　李战子
	彭宣维　齐振海　孙迎晖　王振华　辛志英
	杨信彰　于　晖　张　辉　张　琳　张　薇
	郑　萱

CONTENTS

总　序 ··· 胡壮麟　1
导　读 ··· 孙迎晖　11

EDITOR'S INTRODUCTION
·· Mary McGroarty　i

FUNDAMENTAL ISSUES IN LANGUAGE LEARNING

1. CROSSLINGUISTIC INFLUENCE AND CONCEPTUAL TRANSFER: WHAT ARE THE CONCEPTS?
   ·· Terence Odlin　3
2. LONGITUDINAL RESEARCH IN SECOND LANGUAGE ACQUISITION: RECENT TRENDS AND FUTURE DIRECTIONS
   ························· Lourdes Ortega and Gina Iberri-Shea　32
3. APTITUDE AND SECOND LANGUAGE ACQUISITION
   ·· Peter Robinson　58

RESEARCH ON LANGUAGE LEARNING PROCESSES

4. IMPACT OF LITERACY ON ORAL LANGUAGE PROCESSING: IMPLICATIONS FOR SECOND LANGUAGE ACQUISITION RESEARCH
   ······························· Elaine Tarone and Martha Bigelow　95
5. CURRENT APPROACHES TO RESEARCHING SECOND LANGUAGE LEARNER PROCESSES[1]
   ·· Gillian Wigglesworth　121

6. LANGUAGE LEARNING STRATEGY INSTRUCTION: CURRENT ISSUES AND RESEARCH
.... Anna Uhl Chamot 138

LITERACY STUDIES

7. PROGRESS AND PROCRASTINATION IN SECOND LANGUAGE READING
.... Elizabeth Bernhardt 165

8. CRITICAL LITERACIES AND LANGUAGE EDUCATION: GLOBAL AND LOCAL PERSPECTIVES
.... Brian Morgan and Vaidehi Ramanathan 186

9. CONTEXT AND LITERACY PRACTICES
.... Stephen Reder and Erica Davila 209

10. TECHNOLOGIES FOR SECOND LANGUAGE LITERACY
.... Denise E. Murray 232

RESEARCH IN LANGUAGE ASSESSMENT

11. TRENDS IN ASSESSMENT SCALES AND CRITERION-REFERENCED LANGUAGE ASSESSMENT
.... Thom Hudson 251

12. TRENDS IN COMPUTER-BASED SECOND LANGUAGE ASSESSMENT
.... Joan Jamieson 279

13. RESEARCH INTO THE ASSESSMENT OF SCHOOL-AGE LANGUAGE LEARNERS
.... Penny McKay 298

CONTRIBUTOR BIODATA

总　　序

自 2013 年 8 月起，商务印书馆与剑桥大学出版社开始商洽在大陆出版《应用语言学年度评论》(Annual Review of Applied Linguistics)事宜，至 2014 年春末签约。此后，商务印书馆英语编辑室领导栾奇和马浩岚并责任编辑杨子辉博士先后来访，约我办三件事，一是代为组织国内学者为各卷写导读，二是承担导读的审稿任务，三是为商务版《应用语言学年度评论》写一个总序。作为对我的照顾，同意我邀请复旦大学朱永生教授[①]和北京师范大学田贵森教授[②]参加导读审定工作。就总序而言，多次思考之后，想谈以下四个方面。

一、刊物方针

《应用语言学年度评论》(以下简称《年度评论》)是美国应用语言

[①] 朱永生：复旦大学教授、博导，杭州师范大学钱塘学者，高校功能语言学研究会副会长，高校语篇分析研究会副会长，Linguistics and Human Sciences 编委及《中国外语》等杂志编委。曾任苏州大学外语系主任、复旦大学外文系主任和国际文化交流学院院长、国际系统功能语言学研究会执委、国务院学科评议组成员、全国高校外语教学指导委员会委员等职务。著有《系统功能语言学多维思考》《系统功能语言学再思考》《语境动态研究》《系统功能语言学概论》等。

[②] 田贵森：北京师范大学外文学院教授、博导，中国功能语言学学会常务理事、中国社会语言学学会理事。1976 年河北师范大学外语系毕业后留校任教，1987 年北京外国语大学硕士，1991 年纽约市立大学硕士，1997 年北京大学博士。曾任河北师大外国语学院院长，河北省高校外语教学研究会会长，中国教育学会外语教学专业委员会副理事长。著有《禁忌语的功能研究》《英语专业毕业论文写作教程》《新编英语词汇学教程》等。

学学会（American Association for Applied Linguistics，简称 AAAL）主办的一部书刊结合的出版物，自1980年起每年一卷，至2014年已出版34卷。该刊最初由 Newbury House 出版社出版，自第5卷起改为剑桥大学出版社出版，延续至今。美国南加州大学美国语言研究所主任 Robert B. Kaplan 教授筹划第1卷《年度评论》时，邀请犹他州布里格姆-扬大学日耳曼语系 Randall L. Jones 教授和华盛顿大学应用语言学中心主任 G. Richard Tucker 教授三人合作主编。在他们领导下的编委会对办刊宗旨确定这样一个基本认识：尽管1941年美国密执安大学率先成立了将语言学理论应用于语言教育的英语学院，1956年英国爱丁堡大学成立了应用语言学系，1959年美国华盛顿大学建立了应用语言学中心，1966年 TESOL Quarterly 出版，1977年美国应用语言学学会成立，《年度评论》编委会无意选定其中之一作为应用语言学界共同遵循的蓝图，而是决定走自己的路。在此基础上编委会确定的方针有如下特点：(1)《年度评论》不是杂志，因为它一年只出一本；它又被看作是一本杂志，因为它由出版社的杂志部负责编辑、发行事务。① (2) 该出版物不对应用语言学做面面俱到的报道，而是对应用语言学学科的现状进行专题评论、综述和文献式的归纳。(3) 应用语言学具有高度的跨学科性，因此该刊重点结合双语教育、语言教育学、心理语言学和社会语言学四个方面进行选题。考虑到这四个学科枝叶蔓生，年刊会对一个学科的某一领域做全面的综述和评论。(4) 即使上述四个学科也不是应用语言学的唯一研究领域，因为该刊遵循美国应用语言学学会所倡导的功能导向，着眼于具体应用更甚于理论。(5) 所有的文章由编委会组织某一领域的专家撰写，不转载已在其他刊物上发表的文章，也不采用在某个学术会议上已经宣读的论文，更不对某一部具体的学术著作进行评论。因此，《年度评论》的主要任务是收集和突出被学术界很少报道或研究的领域，不重复已有工作，更不企图贬低某一

---

① 《应用语言学年度评论》问世后，受到国际学术界的高度重视，被权威的《社会科学引文索引》（SSCI）、《艺术和人文科学引文索引》（AHCI）和《科学引文索引》（SCI）所收录。

个方面，或对本学科内某项研究的价值进行排队。这样，《年度评论》对二语习得和语言干扰等内容谈得不多，因为这方面的研究成果已经发表很多。反之，微语言学、符号语言学、计算机辅助教学等受到重视。（6）《年度评论》本身应当正确面对来自不同领域实践者的认同或挑战。[①][②] 鉴于上述情况，《年度评论》每卷都有一个主题，如"语言和语言教育政策"（卷2）、"书面话语"（卷3）、"读写教育"（卷4）等。这些选题均具有学术性、实用性、时代性和独特性。与此同时，该刊每隔四五年会有一卷就应用语言学的整体研究从不同方面进行总结式的调研和讨论，内容涉及语言学习和教学、话语分析、教学创新、二语习得、计算机辅助教学、职场语境下的语言用途、社会语言学、语言政策和语言评估（如卷1、5、10、15、19等）。每年向读者提供500多个新的文献，以帮助本学科教学科研人员能深入掌握情况，点面结合。《年度评论》原计划的第1卷在1980年出版，由于组稿和印刷的原因，实际上在1981年问世。这一脱节现象直到1994年第14卷才得到扭转，即每卷标明的年度与出版年度取得一致。[③]

二、主编更迭

三十多年来，《年度评论》的总主编大约十年更换一次。美国南加利福尼亚大学美国语言研究所主任Robert B. Kaplan教授从创刊起任总主编，连续十年。Kaplan曾任美国应用语言学会会长、英语作为第二语言教

---

① Rota, A. (1982). ANNUAL REVIEW OF APPLIED LINGUISTICS (ARAL). Robert B. Kaplan (Gen. Ed.); Randall L. Jones and G. Richard Tucker (Co-Eds.). *TESOL Quarterly*, *16*, 398–404.
② Kaplan, Robert B. (1980). Introduction. *Annual Review of Applied Linguistics*, *1*, vii–xi.
③ Kaplan, Robert B. and William Grabe. (2000). Applied Linguistics and the Annual Review of Applied Linguistics. in *Annual Review of Applied Linguistics*, *20*, 3–17. Cambridge University Press.

学学会会长、《牛津应用语言学手册》总主编、《国际语言学百科全书》编委等。① 在 Kaplan 主编的《牛津应用语言学手册》中,他认为应用语言学家至少应该具备以下领域的一些知识:人类学、社会学、经济学、政治学、教育学、老年人学、历史学、国际关系、语言学习和教学、词典编纂学、政策研究、心理学和神经科学、公共管理、教师培训和文本生成等。此外,每一位应用语言学家都应精于计算机使用,能够对数据进行统计分析。②③

自第 11 卷起,William Grabe 任主编。Grabe 是美国北亚利桑那州大学负责科研的副校长,曾先后在该校英语系和应用语言学系任教。Grabe 认为应用语言学的核心是"试图解决人们在日常生活中遇到的与语言相关的问题",是一种"研究现实世界语言问题的、实践驱动的学科"。④ 鉴于这个原因,应用语言学必然是一个交叉学科,涉及许多其他领域。这可见之于他对每卷的选题,如"读写教育"(卷 12)、"二语教学"(卷 13)、"语言政策和规划"(卷 14)、"技术和语言"(卷 16)、"多语现象"(卷 17)、"二语教育基础"(卷 18)、"应用语言学的学科性"(卷 19,20)。Grabe 任总主编至 2000 年卸任。在他最后一次负责的第 20 卷,他和 Robert Kaplan 合写了一篇回顾应用语言学和《年度评论》发展历程的总结性文章。

自 2001 年起任总主编的是北亚利桑那大学英语系的 Mary McGroarty 教授。她主要研究双语现象、语言政策、语言教育和课堂研究、社会语言学、二语教学的文化影响等。由于第一次出任主编,McGroarty 邀请了美

---

① Bruthiaux, Paul, Dwight Atkinson, William G. Egginton, William Grabe, Viadehi Ramanathan. Eds. (2005). *Directions in Applied Linguistics in Honour of Robert B. Kaplan.* Clevedon: Multilingual Matters Ltd.
② Kaplan, Robert B. (1999). *The Oxford Handbook of Applied Linguistics.* Edinburgh: Edinburgh University Press.
③ 刘海涛. 从比较中看应用语言学. 北华大学学报(社会科学版),2007,8(2):4.
④ Grabe, William. (2000). Introduction. *Annual Review of Applied Linguistics, 20,* 1–2. Cambridge University Press.

国著名外语教学法专家 Wilga M. Rivers 为第 21 卷"语言和心理学"写序，题为"沿着记忆巷道的漫长旅程"。此后，McGroarty 在她任期内主编了"话语和对话"（卷 22）、"语言接触和演变"（卷 23）、"语言教育学的进展"（卷 24）和"通用语语言"（卷 26）。《年度评论》第 27 和 28 卷的主题分别为"语言与科技"和"神经语言学和认知语言处理"，但未见到这两卷本应由总主编执笔的引言，在目录中也未出现，原因不详。作为总主编的 McGroarty 在第 29 卷"语言政策和语言评估"中再次出现，不过她邀请了著名学者 Bernard Spolsky 作为客座主编。Spolsky 教授长期在以色列的 Bar-Ilan 大学任教，曾任该校人文学院院长，并创建语言政策研究中心。在编辑业务方面，他曾任国际刊物 *Language Policy*（《语言政策》）的总主编，*Asia TEFL*（《亚洲英语作为外语教学》）杂志的出版部主任和总编辑。Spolsky 的专著都与语言政策和语言教育有关，如《教育语言学导论》(1978)、《二语学习的条件》(1991)、《社会语言学》(1998)、《以色列诸语言：政策、意识和实践》(1999)、《语言政策》(2004)、《语言管理》(2009)等。[①] 由此看来，Spolsky 无力全心投入《年度评论》的编辑工作，这次只是扮演一次客串角色而已。

自第 30 卷起，总主编一职由美国密执安州立大学的 Charlene Polio 教授担任。Polio 的主要研究领域为二语写作、二语习得、外语课堂话语、新技术和有经验教师之间的行为差异。她在编辑工作上有较多经验，除接受《年度评论》的总主编任务外，也是 *Modern Language Journal*（《现代语言杂志》）的编辑，此前曾为 *Journal of Second Language Writing*（《二语写作杂志》）和 *TESOL Quarterly* 杂志编委会委员。[②] Polio 为《年度评论》各卷确定的选题为"应用语言学专题"（卷 30）、"第二语言教育研究"（卷 31）、"公式化语言研究"（卷 32）、"多语现象研究"（卷 33）、"研究方法专题"（卷 34）。这体现了她作为总主编延续了该刊创办时的主导思

---

① Spolsky, Bernard. Homepage. http://www.biu.ac.il/faculty/spolsky/. 2015.1.3.
② Polio, Charlene. http://www.wsu.edu/~oikui/. 2015.1.5.

想,即每卷的稿子都是就某一领域的特定问题而精选的。

为《年度评论》写稿的作者中不乏名人,如 Henry G. Widdowson、James R. Martin、Bernard Spolsky、Alan Davies 等都是国际著名语言学家。

三、国人参与

我国大陆、港台地区和国际华人圈对《应用语言学年度评论》很为重视。

台湾学者郑锦全(Chan-chuan Cheng)在第 7 卷上发表"语言和计算机"一文。郑当时任台湾师范大学华语文教学研究所讲座教授、台湾地区研究院语言所研究员和人文社会科学研究中心通信研究员(Cheng, 2014)。[①]另一位是台湾清华大学培养的许静芬(Ching-fen Hsu)博士,现在台湾华梵大学人文学院师资培养研究中心工作,专攻威廉姆斯综合征(Williams Syndrome)发育障碍的语言习得研究,是第 28 卷"威廉姆斯综合征:基因型和认知表型描述"一文的第一作者。[②]香港教育学院语言教学研究中心主任的李楚成(David C. S. Li)教授在第 26 卷上发表"作为大中华通用语的汉语"一文。[③]在《年度评论》第 30 卷独立发表有关传承语学习的社会文化维度一文的何纬芸(Agnes Weiyun He)教授,早期毕业于北京外国语大学,现为 Stony Brook 大学应用语言学和亚洲研究专业的教授,筹建了该校多语和跨文化交际中心。何纬芸主要研究语言语境和语篇的结合,人们如何通过日常互动逐步构建和重构概念、社团和文化。近十年来,她专门研究不同时期和不同背景下汉语作为传承语的社会化。[④]在《年度评论》第 27 卷与 John Flowerdew 联名发表"多语制和二语写作在电

---

① Cheng, Chan-chuan(郑锦全). http://doc88.com/P-795557797523.html. 2014.12.9.
② Hsu, Ching-fen(许静芬). http://www.docin.com/p-2898691.html & key. 2015.1.5.
③ Li, David, C. S.(李楚成). http://dfl.shufe.edu.cn/structure/xueshu-com-142410-1.htm. 2014.12.9.
④ He, Agnes Weiyun(何纬芸). http://www.stonybrook.edu/commcms/asian/PROGRAMS.html. 2014.12.9.

子时代的关系"一文的李咏燕博士（Yongyan Li）任教于香港大学教育学院英语教育系，其研究范围包括专业写作、多语学者的研究和发表实践、言而有据的写作、科学文章的整篇抄袭现象、在职教育等。① 令人瞩目的是，上述学者与大陆高校和研究单位保持良好的学术联系，如郑锦全教授曾担任四川大学文学与新闻学院兼职教授、厦门大学嘉庚学院中文系兼职教授、北京大学汉语语言学研究中心兼职研究员；李楚成教授曾在上海财经大学举行关于中国外语学习者和使用者常见错误的纠正讲座；何纬芸教授与上海交通大学苗瑞琴副教授合作编写了"继承语之习得及其社会化"一文。②

大陆学者对《年度评论》也做出了应有的反应和贡献。早在1981年《年度评论》第1卷问世后，我国学者左焕琪教授便在国内语言学权威刊物《当代语言学》上作了报道，既介绍了编者 Kaplan 的背景，也对该卷四个部分作了近似导读的介绍。作者当时就以敏锐的眼光指出这是"近年来美国应用语言学领域引人瞩目的新刊物"。③ 较近的可举2012年方秀才的"程式语面面观介绍"一文，对《年度评论》第32卷从认知视角、教学应用、社会学进展和未来展望四个部分深入介绍。作者特别注意到，为了从多种视角讨论程式语这一主题，总主编没有限定程式语的定义、内涵，也没有统一术语，让每篇文章的作者采用自己认同的术语和定义，④ 这表明《年度评论》并没有因为总主编的变动而放弃原有的风格。

行文至此，有必要提一下以 Charlene Polio 为首的新编委会所作的一个重大决定，那就是她代表编委会聘请了我国广东外语外贸大学王初明教授从第31卷起任《年度评论》顾问委员会的委员。这是对我国应用语言

---

① Li, Yongyan（李咏燕）. http://www_researchgate.net/profile/Yongyan_Li/publications. 2014.12.9.
② 何纬芸, 苗瑞琴. 继承语之习得及其社会化. 载姬建国, 蒋楠主编：应用语言学（西方人文社会科学前沿述评）. 北京：中国人民大学出版社, 2007. 239–255.
③ 左焕琪. 应用语言学年度评述（1980）.《国外语言学》, 1983,（3）：46–49.
④ 方秀才.《程式语面面观》介绍.《当代语言学》, 2013, 15（4）：492–495.

学研究发展和水平的肯定。我与王初明教授结识于1995年9月，当时我是香港中文大学的访问学者，他是英语系的博士生。我们经常一起讨论学术问题。长江后浪推前浪，2011年我从北京外国语大学中国外语教育研究中心学术委员会主任退下后，他接替了此职。王初明教授现在的学术兼职有国务院学位委员会外国语言文学学科评议组成员、中国高等教育学会外语教学研究分会副会长。他的主要研究方向为第二语言习得研究及其在外语教学中的应用，主要学术创见有外语写长法、语境补缺假说、外语语音学习假设、外语学习的学伴用随原则、读后续写的理论和应用价值。

四、"商务"特色

除保留剑桥版《应用语言学年度评论》的原有特色外，商务版《应用语言学年度评论》有它自己的特色。

商务版《年度评论》从第20卷开始，而不是从第1卷开始。我认为商务印书馆此举着眼于让读者以更多的精力把握应用语言学在新世纪的发展，急读者之所急。我们还应该看到，《年度评论》第20卷实际上起到承前启后的作用。在该卷中，为上世纪创刊时立下汗马功劳的Robert Kaplan、William Grabe和G. Richard Tucker分别对应用语言学和《年度评论》在二十年中的发展作了系统的总结，帮助读者对前二十年有个总体了解，又寄厚望于这门新学科在新世纪、新千年的发展，把握前进的方向。其次，商务版《年度评论》增加了满足中国读者需求的新内容，那就是每卷都有一篇1.5万字左右的中文导读。这便于帮助读者掌握每卷的基本内容和背景材料，特别是汉语界的教师、研究者和学生。

参与此任务的导读作者有国内外语界著名学者，也有新生代的中青年学者。这些专家学者对自己撰写的内容比较熟悉。作为此项目的组织者，我没有向他们摊派任务，而是让各位学者根据自己熟悉的领域自由选题。对各位作者的努力我在此谨表谢意。如前所述，导读初稿完成后均由上海复旦大学朱永生教授和北京师范大学田贵森教授分别先行审读。对两位教授退休后仍能不辞辛苦、鼎力相助的感激之情,难以言表。

由于《年度评论》涉及多个学科和领域,各卷原版的体例不全相同,而各位导读作者的学术生涯也不尽相同,我们对导读编写体例上只作大致要求,不强调绝对统一。总的印象是,每位导读作者对本卷各章内容都能做提纲挈领的介绍和解释,帮助读者理解和抓住要点,这是共同的优点。导读作者各自的特色则表现在:(1)能在正文之前对本卷的总主编、客座编辑做介绍,并对总主编的引言深入分析,起到画龙点睛的作用;(2)对本卷主题进行了解释;(3)对有关主题在20世纪的研究状况或《年度评论》已经发表过的专辑作必要回顾;(4)对每卷论文内容进行归纳,指出其特点;(5)坦率指出某卷内容的不足之处;(6)结合国内现状进行讨论,并进行反思;(7)在讨论中,引入当代先进理论;(8)向我国学界和领导部门提出今后有待深入展开研究的问题。

在结束本序之际,再次感谢各位导读作者,以及永生教授和贵森教授的共同努力,使本项艰巨任务得以顺利完成;祝贺商务版《应用语言学年度评论》正式出版;祝愿商务印书馆今后在应用语言学和理论语言学等领域为外语教育界和学术界做出更多更大贡献!

北京大学蓝旗营寓所

2015年元月

导　读

孙迎晖[①]

一、引言

　　"应用语言学"自 20 世纪中叶在英美国家诞生以来，发展迅速、日趋成熟，对世界范围内语言学诸领域的研究，尤其是在以语言教学为主的应用领域，影响巨大。欧美学者就应用语言学学科著书立说，成果丰硕。既有经典专著，例如：Halliday、McIntosh 和 Strevens 在英国出版的《语言科学与语言教学》(*The Linguistic Sciences and Language Teaching*, 1964) 和 Wilga Rivers 在美国出版的《心理学家与外语教师》(*The Psychologist and the Foreign Language Teachers*, 1964)。还有一些经典词典，例如：《朗文语言教学及应用语言学词典》(*Longman Dictionary of Language Teaching & Applied linguistics*)，《应用语言学百科词典：语言教学手册》(*Encyclopedia Dictionary of Applied Linguistics: A Handbook for Language Teaching*) 等。这些成果不仅方便读者的学习、使用，也极大地促进了应用语言学在世界范围内的传播及相关研究。

　　20 世纪 80 年代，中国学者开始了应用语言学的相关研究，几十年间，涌现出一批享有盛誉的学者和学术著述，对我国语言教学，尤其是外语教学的发展起到了重要的引领和推动作用。就应用语言学的概念、在国内外的发展历程、学科特点、卓越贡献、研究现状及存在的问题及挑战，不少专家及

---

① 孙迎晖：北京师范大学外文学院教授，博士，博士生导师。研究领域为应用语言学，功能语言学及英语语言教学。

学者有详细的论述，具体内容可参见 Richards, Platt & Platt, 2000; Johnson & Johnson, 2001; 胡壮麟, 2001; 桂诗春, 2000, 2010; Kramsch, 2012。

半个世纪以来，英美国家不仅组织了国际应用语言学年会，还出现了多个以"应用语言学"命名的专业学术期刊，比较著名的有《应用语言学》(*Applied Linguistics*)，《国际应用语言学评论》(*The International Review of Applied Linguistics*)以及本刊《应用语言学年度评论》(*Annual Review of Applied Linguistics*)。

作为一门解决实际语言及教学问题的新型学科，应用语言学一直处于不断发展中，研究内容极其丰富，新成果层出不穷。为了帮助读者了解最新研究成果，厘清一些重要话题的发展过程及今后走向，很有必要每隔一段时间对前期研究进行一次"调研"。本书是剑桥《应用语言学年度评论》(*Annual Review of Applied Linguistics*)第25卷（2005年出版），书名为《应用语言学概述》(*A Survey of Applied Linguistics*)，是对2005年以前应用语言学研究成果的一次回顾和讨论。本书包括四部分内容，分别为：语言学习中的基本议题；语言学习过程研究；读写能力研究；语言评价研究。每部分由三至四篇文章组成，除了该期刊主编 Mary McGroarty 在开篇对本书的介绍外，共有13篇文章。为了便于读者理解，我们将就本书的主要内容、重要概念及特色做一简单的介绍。

二、本卷主要内容及重要概念介绍 [①]

第一部分：语言学习中的基本议题

第一部分有三篇文章，内容涉及：跨语言(cross-linguistic)影响及概念迁移(conceptual transfer)，二语习得跟踪研究(longitudinal research)，和语言禀赋(aptitude)与二语习得的关系。

---

① 在本节内引用的学者和论著请参阅各篇文章的英语原文末尾的参考文献。

1. 跨语言影响及概念迁移

本文回顾了语言迁移相关的最新研究,重点描述二语习得和语言相对性(linguistic relativity)研究的交叉部分,即概念迁移。作者 Terence Odli 在概述语言迁移最新研究成果的基础上,重新审视语言相关性理论,即语言和思维的影响关系,重点探讨第一语言对二语学习的影响关系。

作者首先简述了语言迁移研究主要涉及的内容,包括语音学和音系学、言语感知(speech perception)、词汇研究、阅读、语用学、句法结构,还涉及到语言接触领域、三语和多语迁移以及双向迁移(bidirectional transfer)等等。

接着作者又界定了几个重要概念,首先是语言相对性。此观点认为,语言影响人们感知外部世界的方式,人们看待世界的方法部分或者完全地受本族语的制约。语言影响思维的观点最初由德国人类文化学家洪堡特(1767—1835)提出,美国人类语言学家萨丕尔和沃尔夫大力提倡,因此又称为萨丕尔-沃尔夫假说(Sapir-Whorf hypothesis),他们认为语言不仅影响第一语言的理解和输出,也影响第二语言的理解和输出,涉及到第二语言的语言影响思维的情况都可以称为概念迁移。来自母语的语义和语用意义对其他语言学习的影响称为意义迁移(meaning transfer)。文中区分了意义迁移和概念迁移,指出所有概念迁移都包含意义迁移,但并不是所有意义迁移都包含概念迁移,也就是说概念迁移只是意义迁移的一个子集。

作者还讨论了洪堡特和沃尔夫对于语言相对性的研究以及他们观点的异同,然后简述了语言相对性研究的争议和进展。洪堡特和沃尔夫都认为概念迁移是语言相对性的体现。洪堡特认为学习一门新语言意味着在自己已有世界观的基础上获得一种新的世界观,但新观念的习得并不是彻底的,因为已有的语言和观念总会或多或少的影响对新的语言和观念的习得。沃尔夫也认为母语对于新语言的学习具有约束力量(binding power),但他认为这种约束力量是因为学习者对母语的语言知识是无意识的,一旦学习者的意识被唤起,母语的约束力量就能够被克服。近年来语言相对性的研究取得了很大进展,同时也引起了很多争议。一些学者提出了一些反面证据,另外,一些哲学家和文学理论家也提出了语言相对性理论的不足。

最后作者回顾了有关空间意义(spatial meaning)迁移、时间意义(temporal meaning)迁移和情感意义(effective meaning)迁移的研究。

(1)空间意义迁移。直到最近,大家普遍认为虽然在不同语言中,空间的语法体现不同,但是所有人对空间概念的理解是一致的。然而沃尔夫认为人们对空间的理解受语言影响。文中引用Levinson的研究,表明不同母语的被试对物体位置的记忆方式是不一样的。如澳大利亚人习惯用基于东西南北的绝对位置的记忆方式,然而日本人则习惯用基于左右的相对位置记忆方式。另外,Carroll的研究也证明,在二语习得中,是存在空间意义迁移的。

(2)时间意义迁移。对于时间意义迁移的研究主要围绕情状体假设(Aspect Hypothesis)展开。情状体假设认为,学习者对于时态和体的学习,主要基于对动词形式和动词本身的内在含义之间的联系的理解,这种联系在不同语言中的体现是不同的。Rocca的研究证明,二语学习者在建立了这种联系后,会尝试把母语中的联系运用到第二语言的学习中,因此会产生时间意义迁移。

(3)情感意义迁移。对于情感意义迁移的研究主要围绕语义空间(semantic space)和焦点结构(focus construction)展开。Moore的研究说明,不同母语的人对于语义空间的划分是不同的,母语的语义空间会影响学习者对第二语言语义空间的判断。Odlin关于分裂句(cleft sentence)的研究证明,母语的焦点结构会影响第二语言的学习。

2. 二语习得跟踪研究:近期研究及未来发展方向

二语学习是一个复杂的过程,具有历时长的特点,因此,时间是二语习得研究中不可或缺的一项考量条件。对个体或群体跟踪一段时期,即追踪同一组学习者在一段时间内的语言习得进程,观察他们语言能力如何随着时间增长而发生变化的跟踪研究方法(longitudinal study),应该是观察学习者语言学习过程的理想方法。但是，正是由于时间跨度长，二语研究中多采用横面研究（cross-sectional approaches），即比较某一给定时间相同或不同组别学习者语言的方法，但这种方法无疑对研究结论的可信度产生一些不利影响。本文的两位作者 Lourdes Ortega 和 Gina Iberri-Shea 注意到这一长期存在于二语习得研究方法中的局限性，将讨论的焦点放在二语习得跟踪研究及其相关成果上。

本文通过电子和手动检索方式搜集了 2002—2004 年共 38 篇有关二语习得（second language acquisition, SLA）领域跟踪研究的论文，划分了四种方法，为未来的 SLA 跟踪研究提供了发展思路。四种跟踪研究方法分别为：(1) 二语学习发展中描述-定量的跟踪研究方法；(2) 基于二语学习项目结果的跟踪研究；(3) 二语教学有效性的跟踪研究；(4) 质性-跟踪研究。

跟踪研究存在不少难点，其主要特点是历时长，但是最佳时间长度是多少不好确定，多数研究持续 3、4 个月至 6 年。作者建议无论是从生物机制出发还是按照惯例出发，都应该考虑社会环境下的重要事件和转折点。由于跟踪研究持续时间长，要收集多方数据，所以要综合研究的总长度，样本量大小等因素来决定合适的收集数据的频次。除此之外，数据的可比性是个难点，因为有些数据根据不同的任务，有些根据不同的话题。解决这个问题的小技巧是建立周期导出计划。

当前跟踪研究中存在许多缺陷，研究数据通常依赖推论统计（inferential statistics），例如 T 检验（t-test），多变量分析（multivariate analysis）。将来的跟踪研究中需要研究者使用创新的数据分析选择方法。跟踪研究的两个目标，一是捕捉随着时间的变化，二是建立不同阶段间变化之间的关系。人种志研究方法可以提供具有较强说服力的证据和观察结果，因此跟踪研究方法还需在今后研究中进一步加强。

3. 语言禀赋（aptitude）与二语习得的关系

本文作者为 Peter Robinson。他认为，语言禀赋，即一个人天生具有的语言学习能力，是各种语言能力的综合，包括辨识一门新语言语音模式的能力、识别句子单词的不同语法功能的能力、记忆能力及推断语言规则的能力。人们认为,在相同条件下,语言禀赋强的人,较之语言禀赋弱的人,学得更快。本文对语言禀赋与二语习得的关系进行了详细的阐述。文章不仅讨论了语言能力测量手段,如用于确定最有可能成功学习者的语言禀赋测试(aptitude test),以及相关的基本议题,还探讨了语言禀赋与学生认知能力发展中的其他重要因素的关系,包括课堂教学的设计策略等。

语言禀赋一直被认为是二语学习者的一种优势,学习者需要利用这种学习能力去处理不同情境和不同学习阶段下的信息。语言禀赋研究常采用两种方式,一种是自上而下,从信息处理的认知能力到个体差异研究;另一种是自下而上,研究二语习得过程中的认知能力和信息处理能力,以及语言禀赋和其他因素是如何共同致力于二语学习的。

本文还探讨了语言禀赋的测量方式。传统的二语语言禀赋测试用来预测不同二语学习阶段学习者学习效率的差异,只着眼于初学阶段,忽视了高水平阶段。当代研究则弥补了传统研究的不足,着眼于研究传统方法能否预测高水平成就,能否预测二语学习中偶然习得的能力,如果不能,则研究用什么方法能弥补。

和语言禀赋相关的一个课题是研究不同学习背景下的认知能力发展情况。DeKeyser发现包含元语言认知和指导的显性学习和在复杂刺激环境下的隐性学习一样有效;de Graaff、Robinson和Williams发现个人语言禀赋差异和记忆能力影响隐性和显性学习成效。研究表明,除偶然习得外,语言禀赋与各种情况下的学习都呈正相关。

第二部分:语言学习过程研究

第二部分聚焦语言学习过程的研究,有三篇文章,分别是:读写能力(literacy)对口头语言处理能力影响的研究、二语学习者学习过程研究方法,以及语言学习策略教学研究综述。

4. 读写能力对口头语言处理能力影响的研究

由 Elaine Tarone 和 Martha Bigelow 合作完成的本文报告了读写能力和口头语言处理能力关系的一系列研究，包括拼音文本读写能力对口头语言处理能力的影响、读写能力的构建、没有读写能力的个人与口头语言处理关系方面的相关研究。研究表明，不具有读写能力的成人与具有读写能力的成人因其对语言意识程度不同，在口头处理任务中的表现非常不同。对拼音文本解码能力的习得，能够改变个体在某些认知任务中口头语言的处理方式。文章从两个方面梳理了读写能力和口头语言处理能力的关系，分别是：儿童读写与口头语言处理能力；不具有读写能力的成人与口头语言处理能力。研究表明，拼音文本解码技巧导致了认知过程的差异。不同领域、相互独立的儿童语言习得研究和成人认知过程的研究却得出了相似结论：拼音文本读写能力习得与人类口头语言处理之间有着紧密联系。

上述研究对于应用语言学理论、母语教学以及二语教学等方面有重要启示作用。文章谈到"注意"(noticing) 对二语习得的影响。Schmidt 的"注意"假说认为，"注意"是输入变成吸收的必要条件。如果二语学习者不具有读写能力，他们将不会有意识地"注意"二语口语输入的语言成分，因此，学习者将不会习得二语。另外，读写能力和口头语言处理能力方面的研究对以下方面也有启示：输入和反馈对二语核心句法结构习得的影响；拼音文本读写能力对二语词汇习得的影响。

作者认为，将不具有读写能力的成年人作为二语习得研究的一部分具有重要意义。不具有读写能力的成人在口头语言处理过程中有其显著特点，因此，教师在二语口语和读写教学中，应考虑这些特点，才能有效地进行教学；要对不具有读写能力的成人进行语言培训，帮助他们建立口头语言与书面媒介之间的联系；教师还可以通过给学生大声朗读多种体裁语篇，帮助学习者更好地理解语篇意义、目的、语境。

5. 二语学习者学习过程研究方法

Gillian Wigglesworth 撰写的第五篇论文重点讨论了研究学习者认知

发展的三种方法，即有声思维（think-aloud protocols）、对话交流（talk aloud）以及任务规划效果（planning effects）。第一种是让学生在完成某项任务时叙述自己的思维过程，研究人员录下学生所言，并对录音材料进行分析，由此追踪学习者的思维过程以及所采用的学习策略。第二种是通过研究人员与学习者对话的方式收集语料。研究人员通过询问使学生说出自己的构思经过，从而了解学生的思维过程。第三种方法是通过不同类型的任务规划，观察学习者在任务实施过程中语言的使用情况。

三种研究方法分别从不同视角对二语学习过程开展研究，作者在详细阐述了相关研究成就的同时指出，每种方法各有优缺点。例如，"有声思维方法"是了解学习者大脑认知过程的最直接方法，但并不适合所有群体的二语学习者，尤其是不适合低水平的学习者，因为他们的语言能力过于薄弱，还不能够自如地表达自己的想法。"对话交流方法"虽然能够按照研究人员的思路进行，但也不能保证学习者能够提供真实的想法。"任务规划"对于了解学习者的差异具有一定的优势，但却不如前两种方法更能直接地了解学习者的思维过程。

本文共包括四个部分。第一部分主要描述了学习者的学习过程在二语习得研究中的重要地位。语言学习者对他们自身语言学习情况的意识程度一直是众多研究的主题。Krashen 认为习得是一个无意识的过程，而其他学者如 Schmidt 则将其视为一个有意识的过程。本部分简要介绍了三种研究方法，从不同的方面对学习者处理语言的方式进行研究，并指出三种方法的共同之处，那就是分析学习者的会话产出。

第二部分深入描写了语言记录（verbal protocol）这一研究方法。通常把语言记录法分为三种类型：有声思维记录（think-aloud protocol）、反思记录（introspective protocol）、以及回顾记录（retrospective protocol）。前两种方法依赖工作记忆（working memory），并且数据是在学习者执行任务过程中收集的；回顾记录则趋向于记录学习者短时间提供的可用信息。有声思维法是在学习者执行与语言有关的任务时开展的，说话内容将被随之记录。有声思维法内在的思维是：语流是自发的、未解释的，并直接从工作记忆中所获得的。

第三部分详细描写了第二种研究方法,即学习者在对话交流时的情况。学习者话语为研究者提供了探究语言学习过程是如何实现的数据来源。此方法的前提在于,互动对于成功的二语习得十分重要,课堂练习设计应该是最大限度地给予学习者观察、假设、接受、内化和反馈的机会。本部分还详细讲述了一个研究案例,此案例运用第二种研究方法探究两种类型的反馈,即校正(editing)和重述(reformulation),看哪一种方法能使学习者更关注语言本身。结果表明,绝大部分二语言学习者倾向于选择校正这一反馈方式,而且对来自老师的校正反馈抱有期待。本论文对此项研究进行了较为深入的延伸思考,指出不同的反馈方式、学习者具体的说话情况与语言内化处理的种种关系。

第四部分运用了"话语测量"(discourse measures)研究"计划影响",并且对"话语测量"和"计划影响"进行了详细的综述性描写。据报道,Yuan 和 Ellis 研究了任务前计划(pre-task planning)、在线式计划(online planning)以及无计划(no planning)对口语和书面语篇的影响,任务者是对一系列的图片进行描述。研究表明,在线式计划的参与者在口语和写作上都给出了更精确的产出,任务者说话语速更慢,对语言使用了更多的自我修正(self-repairs)。而任务前计划中的参与者的语言内容胜过语言形式。数据表明,在线式计划和任务前计划的参与者都给予了语言本身更多的关注,而无计划的参与者则由于时间限制对内容的安排更加关注。

总的来说,文中谈到的三种研究方法为我们提供了学习者处理语言的不同视角。有声思维记录法是最直接的方法,但并非适用于所有情况,特别是在针对水平较低的第二语言学习者的时候。交流对话(dialogic interchanges)没有那么直接,也不能够完全保证能够获取我们关注的学习过程。第三种计划影响方法的直接性相对更低,而且还要考虑在计划时间内,学习者的反馈或许受到较大的个人差异影响。因此,三种方法都还需要进一步完善。

6. 语言学习策略教学研究综述

语言教育界对语言学习策略的研究时间不长，不过三四十年的历史，相关研究也是断断续续。20世纪80及90年代曾出现过大量关于学习策略的研究，这期间的研究多以描述性研究为主。在随后的一段时间，人们对学习策略的研究又失去兴趣。直到最近，对学习策略的研究又重新出现。本文作者 Anna Uhl Chamot 跟踪语言学习策略的研究发展及焦点问题，重点讨论了学习策略的课堂指导模式及应用。作者认为，研究学习策略的意义有两点：一是通过学习策略的使用，了解学习者语言学习过程中元认知、认知、社会以及情感诸方面的参与情况；二是可以通过策略培训，提高学习者（尤其是学习能力差的）的学习效果。相关研究表明，成功的学习者与不成功的学习者在学习策略的使用上存在明显差异。前者能够根据不同的学习任务，采用恰当的学习策略，并能够根据问题的难易程度，调整策略；而后者常常缺乏元认知知识，因而不能对学习策略做出正确的选择。

论文首先阐述了学习策略的定义和重要性。学习策略是学习过程的一个步骤，通常认为是有意识、有目标驱动的，尤其是在刚开始接触一项不熟悉的语言任务时。学习策略在第二语言学习中占有重要地位，通过对学习者语言策略的探究，可以了解语言学习中的元认知发展以及情感过程；对于不太优秀的语言学习者来说，学习策略的实施可以帮助他们成为更好的学习者。

论文接着描述了识别学习者策略的方法，即通过多样的自我汇报（self-report）形式进行。自我汇报的具体方法又分为追溯性访谈（retrospective interviews）、刺激回顾式访谈（stimulated recall interviews）、问卷、书面日记或文章以及完成某学习任务时的有声思维记录法（think-aloud protocols）。

论文第三章描述了语言学习策略研究的历史进程，并探讨了优秀语言学习者的定义及其特点。优秀语言学习者指的是积极的学习者，能够较为全面地理解语言，并运用语言进行沟通交流；能够利用先前的语言和通用知识，使用多样的记忆工具学习语言。相关研究表明，优秀学习者擅长将适当的策略与学习任务相匹配,而其他学习者因缺乏元认知能力,不能很好地了解任务需要,因而不能选择合适的学习策略。

第四章描述了语言学习策略指导下的课堂研究。任何一项干预性研究都需要对许多变量进行严格的操控,自然课堂中都较难实施,因此,课堂语言策略研究相对较少。此部分针对一个具有代表性的课堂研究展开讨论,并从听力理解、口语表达、阅读理解、词汇策略、写作策略等方面对研究结果进行了探究。

最后,论文讲述了学习策略指导的方法论问题(methodological issues)以及其他实际应用问题。作者详细阐述了外显式和整合式的学习策略指导、学习任务和学习者语境不同对研究的影响、元认知的模型、如何发展教师的专业性等方面的内容。最后文章指出了语言策略研究的发展趋势,并对学习策略研究提出了指导建议。

第三部分:读写能力发展研究

第三部分综述读写能力发展研究,由四篇文章组成:第二语言阅读研究、批判性读写能力与语言教育、语境与读写实践以及技术在发展第二语言读写能力中的作用。这四篇文章分别从不同的视角梳理了读写研究的最新进展,讨论了影响读写发展的重要因素。

7. 第二语言阅读研究

第七篇文章的作者 Elizabeth Bernhardt 首先对二语阅读的研究作了简要的梳理。作为应用语言学研究中的一个重要领域,二语阅读研究以惊人的速度发展,已不再是对一语研究模式的简单模仿。20世纪七八十年代的二语阅读研究主要受到图式理论(schema theory)和心理语言学理论的影响,90年代,二语阅读研究受语言与读写能力相互依赖假说(interdependence of language and literacy hypothesis)和阈限假说(threshold hypothesis)的影响较大。阈限假说是由 Cummins 首次提出的,该假说认为在学习第二语言时,学生的熟练程度必须达到某一最低阈限才能听懂用该语言讲授的功课，上课才能学到东西。Cummins 把这一假设与发展性相互依赖假设联系起来，后者认为第二语言水平的发展取决于学童开始大量接触第二语言时第一语言已经达到的水平（Richards, Platt & Platt, 2000:477）。

在梳理二语阅读研究的基础上，Bernhardt 指出二语阅读模式包括以下必要成分：一语读写水平，二语知识水平，背景知识，语言处理策略，词汇水平，一语和二语之间的同源（cognate）和非同源(non-cognate)现象，读者自身的情况，如是初学者还是成年读者等内容。其中，同源是指历史上与另一语言或语言形式是同一来源的语言或语言形式。例如，西班牙语、意大利语、法语、葡萄牙语是"同源语"（戴维·克里斯特尔，2002:63）。一种语言中的一个单词和另一有关系的语言中的一个单词相似，两个单词称为同源词。例如，英语中的 *brother* 与德语中的 *bruder* 同源（Richards, Platt & Platt, 2000:73）。

在以上讨论的基础上，作者提出了较为满意的当代二语阅读补偿模式。这一模式本质上是三维的，内容包括目前关于读写知识的知识基础；语言知识，尤其词汇知识；正在研究中的知识维度。

虽然二语阅读研究取得很大进展，但是仍遇到一些困难，阻碍了阅读研究的发展，即"延迟"现象。表现在以下方面：一是没有较多的研究者研究英语语言以外的语言阅读；二是读写水平测试。作者指出一语读写是一个很重要的变量，但是在大多数研究中，一语读写水平只是简单地被重复测试，而没有揭示与二语阅读有关的任何可靠信息。作者最后总结二语阅读研究是应用语言学研究中的一个重要领域。尽管二语阅读面临一些阻碍，但研究前景光明。

8. 批判性读写能力与语言教育

鉴于学科中越来越多的批判性转向，Brian Morgan 和 Vaidehi Ramanathan 两位作者讨论了批判性读写（critical literacy）和语言教育这一严肃主题。"批判性"指的是读写文本中隐藏的权势关系和意识形态，学习过程中不能只关注语言形式，而应充分关注文本的社会阐释，如思想意识、政治问题等等。本文作者 Morgan 和 Ramanathan 梳理了学术英语和全球化这两大主要领域与批判性读写之间关系的研究。研究表明，批判性读写与学术英语和全球化这两大主要领域有很大相关性。

作者认为读写是一种社会实践，根植于社会结构，与社区和机构中权力的不平等分配等问题有关。21世纪政治、经济和文化的全球化大环境要求我们根据新的全球数字化技术和信息系统重新定义未来学校、工作、公共生活和传统读写等概念。因此，教育者提倡多元读写，使学生通过印刷字体、声音、图像、身势、空间和各种模态整合等方式理解更大范围的语篇。批判性读写是一种读写策略，能够帮助学生提高批评性意识。本文对学术英语批评性读写提供了一些具体的建议。这些建议包括：(1)使用叙述/自传将个人经验与社会历史、机构权力联系起来；(2)通过质问或反驳广为接受的学科知识使语篇再语境化；(3)将主流文化语码和历史表征语码多元化和非自然化；(4)使用多模态、符号策略。作者最后讨论了全球化、批判性读写和语言教育之间的关系。

9. 语境与读写实践

本文也由两位作者合作完成。Stephen Reder 和 Erica Davila 探讨了语境和读写实践之间的关系，重点梳理了读写作为文化情景实践系统和作为书面语言系统这两者关系的最新进展。文章首先回顾了关于读写能力的辩论。"大分界"读写理论(Great Divide theories of literacy)认为，具有读写能力的社会和个体与不具有读写能力的社会和个体之间存在着很大的认知差异。20世纪80年代早期，"大分界"理论受到了多方面的攻击。因为"大分界"理论过于简单化，过于夸大差异，产生了错误的二分法。

在这个背景下，Brandt 和 Clinton 主张采用"新读写理论研究"方法(New Literacy Studies)来理解读写的发展、习得和使用。这一方法基于两条原则：一、语境是理解读写的基础；二、取消口语和读写之间的界限。新读写研究从原来对社会政治、经济的考察转变为对具体的、局部的读写使用的考察。对此，Reder 和 Davila 提出，发展这一领域理论的要点之一是追溯具体交际实践的发展与写作的关系，把社会学理论和技术应用到读写理论的研究中。他们最后讨论了语境和读写理论在教育政策研究和实践中的应用，表现在以下方面：第一，为教育者提供宝贵视角，即将读写实践放在课堂和家庭双重语境去研究。第二，帮助教育者发展新的语言和读写教学新模式。

10. 技术在发展第二语言读写能力中的作用

本文是对第二语言读写能力中信息和交流技术（ICT）使用情况的讨论。ICT 在语言课堂中使用已有二十多年了。在这期间，ICT 在课堂上的使用经历了从句型操练、课文处理、单词讲解到现在互动性和交际性更强的交际方式，如 e-mail 和基于网络的教学和学习项目等发展过程。本文作者 Denise E. Murray 围绕 ICT 的使用讨论了两个问题：（1）新技术如何发展二语读写能力？（2）在日益增长的数字化世界，学习者需要什么样的二语读写能力？在作者看来，ICT 具有两种基本功能：提供人与人、人与机器交流的语境；提供信息产生、传递和分享的语境。

文章介绍了多种新技术读写形式，如数字读写、电子读写、网页读写、信息读写、电脑读写等。电脑读写是各种新技术读写中最基本的读写形式。作者从互动、身份形成与合作三个方面重点讨论了以电脑为媒介的读写形式。作者指出，网络为学习者接触真实的目标语提供了机会，然而，根据学习者接触的目标语水平是否过高、语类是否熟悉、信息来源是否可靠等方面的问题，这种真实性也可能变成学习难点。

第四部分：语言测试研究

最后的第四部分探讨语言测试研究，由三篇文章组成：测试量表与标准参照语言测试的发展趋势，计算机辅助二语测试，在校生语言学习者评估研究。这三篇文章分别从测试标准、计算机辅助测试和语言学习者评估方面论述了二语测试的新发展和新问题。

11. 测试量表与标准参照语言测试的发展趋势

本文作者 Thom Hudson 以《加拿大语言标准》《欧洲语言共同参考框架》和《语言行为评估》为例，谈论了语言评估领域中语言水平测试的等级量表（scale）与标准参照行为评估（criterion-referenced performance assessment）的发展趋势。本文涉及以下重要概念。

标准参照测试用于评估学习者所掌握的某领域知识范围，其核心是以参照量表为标准，根据特定领域行为反映应试者的能力。参照量表是标准参照测试的核心，它有不同的分类，例如命名量表、顺序量表、间隔量表等。量表说明应试者掌握语言能力的广度和深度，例如大小、多少、强度、重要性、等级等。语言测试中，量表主要用来描述行为水平，为评阅者提供指引，为测试提供具体说明，其组成成分取决于评估目的。

成绩测试和水平测试的量表分为两类：内容与语境相独立的量表和具体语境中基于行为的量表。顾名思义，内容与语境相独立的量表是确定去语境化的语言能力和水平的参照，例如 Bachman（1990）提出的语用能力量表。该量表从词汇和衔接角度考核语用能力，共分为 0-4 五个档次，每个档次都有具体的评分说明。但是，该量表评分说明不详细，而且缺少具体的语境和内容。

基于行为的量表根据真实语境中的行为描述应试者的语言水平。它包括不同类型：行为锚定等级评价（BARS）；行为总结评价（BSS）；行为观察评价（BOS）。目前广为使用的行为量表是《加拿大语言标准》、《欧洲语言共同参考框架》和《语言行为测试》。这三个量表都以交际能力为基础，分别从语言能力、策略能力、社会文化能力和语篇能力等方面制定相应的等级量表。

《加拿大语言标准》是基于任务的评估标准，是加拿大用来考核移民英语水平的标准。该语言标准以语言功能、语言使用和语言水平为导向的多功能标准为参照，其功能包括交际水平及其标准、交际能力和行为任务、教学计划和评估的参照框架、英语作为外语的国家标准。包括听、说、读、写四种语言能力和 12 个级别，每个级别首先简要描述体现学习者总体语言能力的语言行为,然后提供实现语言能力所需的具体交际条件,最后是能力结果和标准。然而,该标准过于宽泛,不适用于英语本族语者,而且缺少实证有效性。

《欧洲语言共同参考框架》是由欧洲理事会文化合作教育委员会制订的交际语言能力框架。它是制订教学大纲、设置课程、编写教材、研发考试等方面的重要参考。其纵向维度对语言能力水平分为三等六级:A等(A1和A2),基础使用者;B等(B1和B2),独立使用者;C等(C1和C2),熟练使用者。此框架的横向维度包括语言交际活动、交际策略、交际语言能力三个范畴。语言交际活动中的交际环境分为个人生活、公共生活、工作、学习。语言交际活动与交际策略密不可分。各项语言能力量表为教学和评估提供了一个全面、透明和一致的参考框架,目的是促进和提高欧盟各国教育机构的合作,为欧盟各国语言相互认同奠定基础,为学习者、教师、课程制定者、教育主管部门、测试机构等提供必要的帮助。然而,该框架仍有不完善之处,例如:它没有囊括语言使用的所有方面,如文学欣赏、语用和策略能力等。该框架的量表开发的初衷是以行为为导向,量表的具体制定者后来没有实际测试并重新校对语言能力等级。

《语言行为测试》是由美国夏威夷大学制定的,用来考核学习者语言能力和交际行为的参照框架。它以完成现实生活中的任务作为判断学习者表现的参照,而语言只是行为测试中完成任务的载体。学习者的语言能力与任务完成情况没有必然的因果关系,学习者高水平的语言运用能力并不意味着成功地完成相应的任务。通常情况下,语言行为测试中的任务难度根据语言复杂度,认知复杂度和交际难度进行分类。测试者使用依赖任务和独立任务两套量表为学习者打分,按照不能完成、能完成和熟练完成等五个等级评价学习者的任务完成情况和语言交际能力。实证研究结果表明,该框架中的两个量表具有一定的相关性,而且任务难度与任务表现也高度相关。虽然语言行为测试从多维角度评价学习者的能力,但是该量表对于独立任务量表中的能力描述不清,而且缺乏相应的评价标准。

12. 计算机辅助二语测试

本文论述了计算机辅助二语测试的发展历史和未来趋势，作者 Joan Jamieson 把计算机二语测试的发展归为以下几个主要阶段：

发展阶段 1：传统的测试项目和构念运用到计算机测试系统

传统测试词汇，语法和阅读理解的多选题和填空题率先实现了计算机测试。语言测试专家建立各具特色的测试网站，例如 Quiz Center、forumeducation.net、wordskills.com、Churchill House、netlanguages.com 等。在二语评估领域，韩国首尔国立大学的英语水平测试实现了机考与快速成绩报告。但是，一些实际问题也引起了众多测试专家的热烈讨论，例如机考对于测试效度的潜在威胁，机考与笔考对于应试者成绩产生的差异等。

发展阶段 2：增加机器评估权重

众多语言测试程序中，增加机器评估权重的方法是引入计算化调适性语言测试。理论上，它要实现给予适合应试者语言能力的测试项目，使得测试更加有趣和准确。然而，计算化调适性语言测试不能盲目地进行。事先测试者要决定题目内容和评估试题难度、区分度等。为了题目的稳定性，题目要在具有代表性的应试者中进行前测。

计算机化调适性语言测试有多方面的优势，例如应试者及时做出反应、自动成绩报告，自动生成应试者文件，并且随着测试的进行不断更新文件。但仍需进一步完善，例如应试者以相同的顺序同时进行相同题目的测试，口语测试的计算机自动评分，应试者测验题目"适应"选择，个体语言学习者的"适应"测试，交际语言能力测试的操作等。

发展阶段 3：语言观的新认识

语言测试受到技术的驱动，而不是技术为语言测试服务。技术引领语言测试走向前人从未走过的路。暂且不论计算机技术创新，测试新模式促使我们对于语言任务和测试成绩形成新的认识。语言领域中计算机技术的应用不仅反映了测试的真实性，也体现了语言使用的情境性。计算机技术促使语言测试项目与语言使用紧密结合，这使语言测试项目和内容更加具体和真实。

机考也促使评估方式发生新变化。例如 ACT 的 COMPASS/ESL，学生在电脑上按照自己的速度答题，电脑自动监控学生的反映时间，同时学生的测试时间也是衡量成绩的考虑因素之一。电脑除了自动等级评分以外，它还自动生成应试者的语言能力发展报告，说明学生的语言能力发展情况。

未来发展：电脑评分系统和新题型开发

目前，测试领域已经开发四套电脑评分系统。虽然每个系统还不是十分完善，但都有各自的特点，评分维度相对全面。未来电脑评分还要加大力度开发口语评分系统。机考的测试题目还要进一步开发，例如把视频资料应用到机考试题中，增加测试内容分的真实性和情境性。

13. 在校生语言学习者评价研究

本文作者 Penny McKay 从五个方面探讨了在校学生二语和外语学习的评价研究，分述如下：

（1）标准化行动（standards movement）对二语学习者和教师的影响

这里说的"标准化"指基于成果的课程大纲（outcomes-based curricula）、成绩水平（attainment levels）、等级（bandscales）等，用于描述课程结果或者学习发展阶段，包含内容标准和行为标准。前者指学生掌握学习内容的程度，后者指学生的行为水平。

现行的政府主导制定和实施的标准充满了浓郁的行政和商业色彩，有很多弊端和不足。美国和澳大利亚的教育工作者极力反对政府主导的无视公平的标准，提倡平等的教育和评估方式，众多二语教育工作者提出开发和实施针对二语学习者的具体标准。但由于受到教师经历、理解程度和态度等因素影响，标准的解释也因人而异，教师在相关标准的制订方面所发挥的作用也微乎其微。

（2）应对大规模测试对二语学习者的负面影响

美国联邦政府通过法案，要求所有学生进行基于学科内容知识的大规模测试。然而，该法案没有考虑到二语学习者的实际情况，众多的测试研究者对此颇有微词，例如什么时间给二语学习者测试合适？什么时间获取内容测试所反馈的二语学习者的学习信息？如何保证教育平等？测试专家对上述问题也提出了一些解决措施，例如使用母语测试、使用其他测试取代内容测试等。尤其是测试方法方面，测试专家提倡多维度的测试方式，例如基于教师的测试（teacher-based assessment）。

（3）二语环境下学术语言水平的评价

弄清楚什么是"学术语言水平"是评估二语学习者的学术语言水平至关重要的问题。目前，大量的基于课堂、教材、文献等方面的实证研究试图提炼出学术语言水平的精确定义。学术语言水平对于教育工作者、决策者等至关重要，它决定了课堂中使用什么样的语言、如何组织测试、教授二语学习者什么样的语言等等。

（4）二语/外语学习的课堂评价

目前，课堂评价的主要方法是形成性评价。然而，在二语/外语环境中，由于缺少学生的参与和评价方式等因素影响，形成性评价的信度和效度也遭受质疑，有些问题还需进一步解释清楚，例如形成性评价的性质，是否为学习者创造学习机会，语言学习的证据，外语环境中教师是否能够区分语言学习需求、特殊教育需求和课程内容需求等。针对上述问题，语言测试专家提出了不同的形成性评价模式，例如 Rea-Dickins 的评价循环（the cycles of assessment）、Morris 等的高风险评价（high stakes assessment）、形成性评价与终结性评价结合等。

（5）儿童语言学习者评价

目前，儿童语言学习评价仍处于探索阶段，对儿童语言水平的认识还没达成共识。尽管如此，这一领域还是值得语言测试工作者的高度关注，尤其是儿童语言学习者的社会和认知发展、二语读写发展、评价的原理与实践等。

三、本书主要特色

本书特色突出表现在以下两个方面：

第一,总主编 Mary McGroarty 对本书话题进行了精心的选择。具体说来,本书各篇讨论的内容涉及应用语言学领域近期的核心议题、重要议题、容易忽略的议题、特别是新的科技发展对语言研究和教学带来的挑战和课题,时效性强,有很强的学科引领和应用价值。

应用语言学学科的研究范围有两个方向,一个是微观的,主要针对语言教学研究,包括第一语言、第二语言和外语教学。一个是宏观的,针对实际问题而进行的语言及语言学研究,如词典学、翻译、言语病理学等。其中微观的内容是应用语言学研究的核心内容。本卷前两个板块以语言学习的基本议题及语言学习过程相关研究成果为标题内容,直接针对二语及外语教学,探讨了应用语言学的研究成就及焦点问题。在二语及外语教学诸核心议题中,本卷所选择的具体话题又是极具语言学价值的重要话题。例如本书开篇选择的跨语言的影响(crosslinguistic influence)话题一直是语言研究的重要内容,不仅对应用语言学中二语习得研究有重要意义,对语言接触(language contact)研究也有重要意义。(参见戴维·克里斯特尔,2002:81)。语言接触指语言或方言之间因地理上相邻接或社会上相邻近而互相影响的研究(如借词增多现象、音系和语法模式的演变、语言形式的混合以及各种双语现象等等),而本卷的第三、第四板块的"读写能力研究"和"语言测试研究"更是语言学和应用语言学领域长期致力研究的重要议题。

语言测试属于跨学科领域,它以语言学与应用语言学为理论指导,以心理测量为科学手段,以计算机为技术支持。它既涉及语言学、应用语言学、心理测量、计算机等多学科的知识与技术,又自成体系,有其自身的理论体系,研究方法,研究对象和研究内容,其研究成果对以上诸领域都有着重要的影响作用。

本卷内容极其重视读写能力研究。在本卷的 13 篇文章中,有 5 篇文章涉及此话题(分别为第 4、7、8、9、10 篇文章),内容丰富。既有传统读写能力自身的研究(如第 7 篇的阅读能力研究),也有新视角下的读写能力的释解与研究(如第 8 篇的批判性读写能力概念及其与语言教育的关系）；既有对读写能力影响因素的研究（如第9篇的语境与读写实践关系的研究，和第10篇现代技术对读写能力影响的研究），也有读写能力对其他语言技能的影响（如第4篇，对口头语言处理能力影响的研究）。文章从不同的视角梳理了读写研究的最新进展，讨论了影响读写发展的重要因素。文章还分析了对未来读写课程设计、读写教学方法、读写研究方法、读写实践和读写政策制定等的启示。

本卷也很重视一些非常重要却常常被忽视的研究议题。例如，关于语言学习策略的研究，以往的研究多集中在探讨学习者个体差异及其对学习效果的影响，但针对课堂教学中学习策略指导的研究没有引起足够的重视。顾永琦（2011，序，第IV页）认为，多年来对学习策略的研究成果并没有对一线教师和学习者带来"实实在在的用处"，原因是"多数研究基本停留在探索性阶段"，"对于学习策略到底怎样用才好，以及教师应该怎样帮助学生更好地运用学习策略等问题则很少涉及。"本书第二板块中的"语言学习策略教学研究综述"一文以课堂教学中语言学习策略的指导为研究议题，报告了相关研究成果，并对焦点问题进行了讨论。

本卷重视新科技研究手段下的研究。随着信息技术的发展，计算机辅助为测试者和应试者带来诸多便利，如更省时的测试，更快捷地报告分数，为应试者提供更便利的考试次数，以及更精确地测试应试者的语言能力水平。因此，二语测试与评估的未来将朝向计算机辅助评估语言发展。本卷的第12篇文章以计算机辅助下的二语测试发展趋向为话题，正是抓住了这一能反映最新发展动向的话题。

第二，重视对研究方法的研究。

研究方法是应用语言学研究中不可或缺的内容，选择是否恰当，直接影响研究成果的质量。国内外不少书籍专门介绍相关研究方法（例如：Dörnyei, 2007; Larsen-Freeman & Long, 2010; Nunan, 1992; Seliger & Shohamy,1989; 刘润清，胡壮麟，1999；文秋芳，俞洪亮，周维杰，2004），详细地介绍语言学习及二语习得过程中采用的诸如质性研究方法、量性研究方法、课堂数据收集及分析方法、实验研究方法等多渠道研究手法。但是,长期以来,人们一直将研究方法作为一项"幕后"辅助手段,而作为科研内容开展的探讨还比较少见。

本卷包含的13篇文章中,有两篇文章(第2篇和第5篇)以研究方法为话题,分别是二语习得中的跟踪研究方法和二语学习过程研究的研究方法。其他文章也有不少篇幅介绍相关研究方法的选择、操作方法,内容翔实。例如,第六篇文章"语言学习策略教学研究综述"详细地讨论了学习策略研究中"自我报告"(self-report)这一研究手段的具体操作方法。作者谈到,学习者"自我报告"的手段包括访谈、问卷调查、学习日记、自声思维方法等。访谈、问卷调查应紧接在任务完成以后来做,这样可以使学习者能够准确地反映策略的使用情况。记学习日记可以帮助学生发展元认知能力,如规划能力及评价能力,通过学习日记,学习者记录下自己的学习体验以及学习问题的解决方法。自声思维方法是在让学生完成某项任务的过程中口述自己大脑的思维过程。这种方法常常伴随着研究者的随机采访,例如,研究人员可以随时打断学习者,提出诸如"你现在是如何考虑的?""你刚才为什么停下了又重新开始?"等等问题,这种方法在于了解学生的即时思维过程。除此之外,作者还对研究方法的优缺点进行了评析。例如,本文提到的"自我报告",作者谈到,虽然此方法有不尽人意之处,但对于探究学习者大脑内容的思维过程,恐怕没有别的更好的办法了。

四、结语

随着语言学及其他社会科学理论的深入及实践范围的扩展,应用语言学所涵盖的内容也在不断地丰富和发展。除了以语言学理论为基础,以语言教学包括二语和外语教学为核心内容,应用语言学还从社会学、心理学、人类学及信息理论等学科汲取知识,应用于诸如言语矫正、语言规划、文体学研究等等实际问题的研究。由此可见,应用语言学涉及范围大,其研究内容除了包括语言教学、读写能力、语言教学大纲的设计、二语习得、语言教师职前培训、教师发展、课程大纲研制等基本议题外，还包括以下诸多方面内容：双语学习研究、语料库语言学、法律语言学、语言接触研究、语言测试、语言口笔语翻译、专业语境中的语言使用、词汇学等。

  正如本书主编 Mary Mcgroarty 在开篇时所言，应用语言学是一门动态学科，一直在不断地变化、发展，通过一本小册子来囊括应用语言学的所有议题是不可能的事情。对于应用语言学所涉及的话题来说，本卷只能算是"有选择地"进行综述，但每一篇都针对应用语言学研究的核心议题。本书在对一些重点议题进行系统描述和深度探究的同时，也不乏对本领域基本理论、具体概念以及研究方法的介绍。本书阐述的研究成果对语言教学及研究有着重要的启示作用，也为下一步的研究指明了方向。

参考文献

Bachman, Lyle, F. (1990). *Fundamental Consideration in Language Testing.* Oxford: Oxford University Press.

Dörnyei, Zoltán. (2007). *Research Methods in Applied Linguistics.* Oxford: Oxford University Press.

Johnson, Keith & Johnson, Helen. (2001). *Encyclopedia Dictionary of Applied Linguistics: A Handbook for Language Teaching.* Beijing: Foreign Language Teaching and Research Press.

Kramsch, Claire. (2012). Applied linguistic theory and second/foreign language education. Van Deusen-scholl, Nelleke & Hornberger, Nancy H. (eds.) *Second and Foreign Language Education.* Shanghai: Shanghai Foreign Language Education Press.

Larsen-Freeman, Diane & Michael H. Long. (2010). *An Introduction to Second Language Acquisition Research.* Beijing: Foreign Language Teaching and Research Press.

Nunan, David. (1992). *Research Methods in Language Learning.* Cambridge: Cambridge University Press.

Richards, Jack, C., Platt, John & Platt, Heidi. *Longman Dictionary of Language Teaching & Applied Linguistics.* Beijing: Foreign Language Teaching and Research Press.

Seliger, Herbert & Elana Shohamy. (1989). *Second Language Research Methods.* Shanghai: Shanghai Foreign Language Education Press. 1992.

戴维·克里斯特尔著，沈家煊译，《现代语言学词典》（第四版）．北京：商务印书馆，2002．

顾永琦，胡光伟，张军，白蕊．《英语教学中的学习策略培训：阅读与写作》．北京：外语教学与研究出版社，2011．

桂诗春."20世纪应用语言学评述".《外语教学与研究》,2000,(1):2—7.
桂诗春."应用语言学思想:缘起、变化和发展",《外语教学与研究》,2010,(3):163—169.
胡壮麟.《应用语言学百科词典:语言教学手册》导读.北京:外语教学与研究出版社,2001.
刘润清,胡壮麟.《外语教学中的科研方法》.北京:外语教学与研究出版社,1999.
文秋芳,俞洪亮,周维杰.《应用语言学研究方法与论文写作》.北京:外语教学与研究出版社,2004.

EDITOR'S INTRODUCTION

Mary McGroarty

It is a sign of overweening ambition if not hubris to think that all of applied linguistics can fit between two covers. Dynamic even when the *Annual Review of Applied Linguistics* (*ARAL*) began publication in 1981, applied linguistics has continued to change, grow, and redefine its areas of coverage, even as many other journals have emerged in the intervening 25 years. Writing in the 20th anniversary issue of *ARAL*, my editorial predecessors, Robert Kaplan and William Grabe, provide the historical context for the establishment of *ARAL* and show how it came to fit into the context of applied linguistics as the field evolved from the mid-20th century to the beginning of the 21st. They summarize the key notions that characterize applied linguistics and remark that it "commonly includes a core set of issues and practices that are readily identified as work done by many applied linguists (language teaching, language teacher preparation, and language curriculum development)" along with "several further identifiable subfields of study: bilingual studies, corpus linguistics, forensic linguistics, language contact studies, language testing, language translation and interpretation, language use in professional contexts, lexicography and dictionary making, literacy, second language acquisition, and second language writing research" (Kaplan & Grabe, 2000, p. 5). The variety and diversity of these subfields defy attempts to gather them into a single volume (although some useful recent handbooks have done so; see, for example, Davies & Elder, 2004; Kaplan, 2002); furthermore, at present, topics in applied linguistics are commonly addressed through entire handbooks for particular subfields (Bhatia & Ritchie, 2004; Doughty & Long, 2003; Spolsky, 1999) or even in multivolume sets such as the *Encyclopedia of Language and Education* (Corson, 1997). Hence, this year's volume should perhaps be labeled a 'selective' survey, or even a sampling of the field, rather than an exhaustive inventory of all possible endeavors that warrant inclusion within applied linguistics. The present volume features research on some of the perennial concerns of applied linguistics, akin to Kaplan and Grabe's 'core issues.'

That important qualification noted, the themes discussed herein offer insights into those aspects of language, language learning, literacy, and assessment of language that continue to serve as foci of research, draw attention at scholarly conferences, appear in specialized publications refereed by experts in the field, and affect issues of language learning, teaching, and use in multiple real-world settings, academic and otherwise. Each chapter helps to illuminate connections between the existing state of knowledge and the many questions that invite (and often require) additional investigation to advance the field. In serving as a major source of bibliographical guidance for specialist readers, this volume of *ARAL*, like the previous 24, aims to illuminate the most promising directions for theory building and research in the areas covered.

Chapters in the first section address some of the fundamental issues in the nature of language learning. Terence Odlin reconsiders the important questions of crosslinguistic and conceptual transfer, and shows that recent research has led to a reconsideration and amplification of the phenomena that may profitably be studied in these domains. In discussing longitudinal research in second language acquisition, Lourdes Ortega and Gina Iberri-Shea note that some of the chronic limitations of second language research, typically restricted to cross-sectional approaches, have begun to be addressed through use of alternative designs, but that much remains to be done to better describe the temporal course of language acquisition. They describe some recent investigative trends in attempts to capture temporal changes appropriately, though in very different ways. Peter Robinson offers a reevaluation of the definitions and operationalization of aptitude as related to second language acquisition and provides a comprehensive model that reflects multiple streams of research in cognitive psychology, psycholinguistics, and applied linguistics, offering several productive avenues for future investigations.

Papers in the second section relate directly to questions of the psycholinguistic processes implicated in second language learning. Elaine Tarone and Martha Bigelow argue that a near-exclusive focus in applied linguistics on the second language acquisition of highly literate participants has failed to address several key aspects of language learning and set out possibilities for related research, including recent studies done by them and their colleagues, to help fill the gap. The self-report methods most often used as the basis for inferences about language learning processes are reviewed by Gillian Wigglesworth, who shows that typical think-aloud methods, still prevalent, are now usefully complemented by research on learners' task-related discourse and planning strategies, thus bringing activity theory to bear. The recent trajectory of research on language learning strategies is traced by Anna Chamot; her discussion of contemporary investigations shows that, although instruction in language learning strategies remains attractive to many, sound research requires continued careful descriptive study in many different instructional contexts and demands that constraints such as learner goals, proficiency level, and nature of task must be clearly identified to shape pedagogical applications intelligently.

The third section includes four chapters that suggest the breadth of applied linguistics attention to literacy. Reviewing research on acquisition of second language literacy skills, Elizabeth Bernhardt proposes a model of second language reading that includes interactions between background knowledge, processing strategies, and level of second language proficiency as well as the often neglected assessment of first language literacy levels. Brian Morgan and Vai Ramanathan examine the many possible definitions of critical literacy, particularly those related to the study of English for academic purposes and globalization, and consider what provision of critical literacy instruction might mean in a variety of instructional settings. Tensions between conceptions of literacy as a universal system that transcends individual and local contexts versus those that define literacy as a system of locally situated cultural practices are also discussed by Stephen Reder and Erica Davila; they indicate that current scholarship is making efforts to establish new theoretical ground to recognize these tensions and devise socially responsible models of literacy capable of accounting for intellectual commonalities. Denise Murray surveys recent work on the contribution of computer technology to acquisition of second language literacy and considers implications for the varieties of literacies needed by learners in other domains, making the key point that use of new information technologies facilitate collaboration and autonomy only if instruction is carefully planned to provide related opportunities.

The fourth section addresses language assessment, a topic prominently featured in several past volumes of *ARAL*, and sets out some of the emerging trends. Thom Hudson provides a detailed consideration of issues related to the use of performance scales and criterion-referenced assessment, developments that reflect recognition of the complexity of language use and the need to make test results readily observable; through discussion of three major related initiatives that have used criterion-referenced approaches, he shows that, precisely because of the effort to mirror the complexity of language use, such approaches must also come to grips with sources of variability unrelated to language skill. Reviewing trends in the application of computer technology to language assessment, Joan Jamieson shows that increasing technological power along with more sophisticated conceptions of test quality have created an environment favorable to support progress not only in the efficiency but in the authenticity of language assessments. Penny McKay's overview of language assessment for school-age learners offers examples from several countries of studies on the effects of the standards movement, content-based assessment, definitions of academic language proficiency, new approaches to classroom assessment, and language assessment for young learners.

The chapters in this volume on second language research, language and literacy learning processes, and language assessment, all matters with substantial individual and societal impact, attest to the vibrancy of applied linguistics and its relevance to a range of real world issues. In 2000, Kaplan and Grabe observed that disciplinary acceptance of applied linguistics would only emerge "to the extent that applied linguistics responds to wider societal needs and its expertise is valued by people beyond the professional field" (2000, p. 3). In the tradition of the journal, I hope that these chapters will illuminate important trends and suggest promising directions to investigators who will pursue and eventually publish related research, thus contributing to the currency, coherence, and acceptance of applied linguistics as a discipline.

Procedural Notes

Each year, *ARAL* aims to provide specialist readers with a useful research tool that will assist them in locating and evaluating current research on the topics covered. A 10-year Contributor Index, listing authors, titles, and initial page numbers for Volumes 15–24 appears at the end of this volume. A five-year Author Citation Index for Volumes 20–24 and 10-year Subject Index for Volumes 15–24 are available on the *ARAL* section of the Cambridge Journals Web site: http://journals.cambridge.org/jid_APL. The publisher and editor hope that these multiple channels of access to current sources will assist *ARAL* readers in identifying appropriate sources on topics of interest.

Acknowledgments

Once again, it is a great pleasure to recognize the many people whose expertise and assistance makes publication of this volume possible. Thanks go first to the authors, all busy scholars and teachers, who have provided timely reviews of research in each area and, without exception, have been prompt and cooperative during the course of manuscript preparation and bibliographic checking. The advice of the Editorial Directors shapes the themes of each volume and helps to identify prospective contributors. Each aspect of planning is invaluable, and I am grateful for their generosity in sharing ideas.

In the academic world, good ideas build on each other and sometimes include prior related work. For permission to use previously published figures appearing in contributions to this volume, I would like to acknowledge Hodder Arnold for use of Figure 1 in the McKay chapter, which first appeared in *Language Testing*; and Lawrence Erlbaum Associates for use of Figure 1 in the Bernhardt chapter, which first appeared in Volume III of the *Handbook of Reading Research*.

At Cambridge University Press, North America, *ARAL* benefits greatly from the support of Ed Barnas, Journals Manager; Mark Zadrozny, Journals Editor; Ed Carey, Production Manager; and Susan Soule, Journals Marketing Manager; and the staff members who assist them. Their collective efforts enable *ARAL* to be planned, published, and distributed worldwide. Northern Arizona University provides in-kind support for the planning and production of *ARAL*, and I am grateful to Susan Fitzmaurice, Dean of the College of Arts and Letters, and Jean Boreen, Chair of the English Department, for their continued interest in the work. The reference staff members at Cline Library have offered timely and often tenacious assistance in resolving bibliographic discrepancies.

The work of producing *ARAL* each year owes an enormous debt to Beth Yule, who works meticulously with all manuscripts and indexes to ready them for production, and to Julie McCormick, who performs the page layout and incorporation of graphics for final publication. Preparation of the volume would be impossible without the extraordinary competence and adaptability of these two key individuals. Coordination of manuscript preparation and page layout has been greatly facilitated by the server set up by Marc Lord; Patrick Deegan has provided courier service when needed. The thorough proofreading of Teresa Barensfeld at Cambridge and Federica Barbieri, Brad Horn, and Nicole Tracy at Northern Arizona University has enhanced the accuracy of the volume. (I take responsibility and apologize to authors and readers in advance for any remaining errors.) Sincere thanks to all who work with and for *ARAL*.

Mary McGroarty
Flagstaff, Arizona
March 2005

REFERENCES

Bhatia, T., & Ritchie, W. (Eds.). (2004). *The handbook of bilingualism.* Malden, MA: Blackwell.

Davies, A., & Elder, C. (Eds.). (2004). *The handbook of applied linguistics.* Malden, MA: Blackwell.

Corson, D. (Gen. ed.). (1997). *Encyclopedia of language and education* [8 vols.]. Dordrecht: Kluwer.

Doughty, C., & Long, M. (Eds.). (2003). *The handbook of second language acquisition.* Malden, MA: Blackwell.

Kaplan, R. B. (Ed.). (2002). *The Oxford handbook of applied linguistics.* New York: Oxford University Press.

Kaplan, R. B., & Grabe, W. (2000). Applied linguistics and the *Annual Review of Applied Linguistics*, 20, 3–17.

Spolsky, B. (Ed.). (1999). *Concise encyclopedia of educational linguistics.* Amsterdam: Elsevier Science.

FUNDAMENTAL ISSUES IN
LANGUAGE LEARNING

1. CROSSLINGUISTIC INFLUENCE AND CONCEPTUAL TRANSFER: WHAT ARE THE CONCEPTS?

Terence Odlin

This chapter surveys recent work on language transfer and focuses on the intersection of second language acquisition (SLA) and linguistic relativity in what is often termed *conceptual transfer*. The two most famous exponents of relativity, Wilhelm von Humboldt and Benjamin Lee Whorf, developed their ideas largely from their study of Kawi and Hopi respectively, and both scholars viewed crosslinguistic influence as a manifestation of the "binding power" (to use Whorf's characterization) of language on thought. The views of von Humboldt and Whorf diverge in some ways, and the difference is relevant not only to issues in SLA such as ultimate attainment but also to theories of linguistic relativity. Indeed, some recent work on conceptual transfer indicates that even highly proficient learners may never free themselves entirely of the "binding power" of L1. The research reviewed also includes work with native speakers of different languages, suggesting real cognitive differences related to language in, for example, spatial concepts. The importance of distinguishing concepts from meanings is emphasized, as is the difference between meaning transfer and conceptual transfer. The chapter discusses in detail research on transfer involving spatial, temporal, and affective meanings, with some of the studies being interpreted as evidence of conceptual transfer.

Researchers have long used the terms *crosslinguistic influence* and *language transfer* interchangeably, a practice which assumes that some kind of influence is essential to the phenomenon of "transfer." This chapter considers the notion of influence not only in second language acquisition (SLA) but also in a field sometimes considered tangential to SLA: linguistic relativity. Recent investigations indicate that the two fields do indeed have some common concerns, especially in regard to what some second language researchers have called conceptual transfer.

Before considering conceptual transfer, however, a survey of recent studies of crosslinguistic influence will give a sense of the many dimensions of contemporary transfer research. Some investigations of L2 phonetics and phonology have foregrounded the role of crosslinguistic influence (e.g., Aoyama, Flege, Guran, Akathane-Yamoda, & Yamoda, 2004; Hancin-Bhatt, 2000; McAllister, Flege, & Piske, 2002), as has some work on speech perception (e.g., Flege & MacKay, 2004). Some lexical studies have likewise emphasized the importance of transfer (e.g., Jiang, 2002; Singleton, 2004; Zimmerman, 2004), and some have looked at transfer in morphology (e.g., De Angelis & Selinker, 2001; Herwig, 2001). There have also been studies of transfer in reading (e.g., Upton & Lee-Thompson, 2001) and pragmatics (e.g., Kwon, 2003; Tamanaha, 2003; Yu, 2004).

Syntactic structures have also been investigated in relation to crosslinguistic influence, as in a study of relative clauses by Matthews and Yip (2003), as well as a look at a wider range of structures where influence from the L1 seems evident (Chan, 2004). There have likewise been several studies within the framework of Universal Grammar where the possible influence of the L1 gets attention (e.g., Hertel, 2003; Juffs, 2002; White, 2003).

Several studies of various structures have offered especially convincing evidence of transfer, as with one of causatives by Helms-Park (2001), another by her of copular verbs (2003), one of grammatical gender by Sabourin (2001), two of lexis by Ringbom (2001, 2004) as well as one by Cenoz (2001), one of morphological awareness (Koda, 2000), one of L1 orthographic influence on L2 (Wang, Koda, & Perfetti, 2003), and one of the grammatical marking of topic continuity by Nakahama (2003). The nine studies just cited are especially convincing because all employ a methodology where the learners studied do not all speak the same L1 (cf. Jarvis, 2000). In the case of the Nakahama study, for example, the target language is Japanese and the native languages are Korean and English. A variant on such methodological rigor is seen in a study by Collins (2002) of the use of the English perfect by speakers of French. Although Collins studied only one native language group, she used the same tests already developed by Bardovi-Harlig and Reynolds (1995).

Crosslinguistic influence is an important topic not only for SLA research but also for studies of language contact, which usually emphasize the sociohistoric product of an acquisition process. Two notable creolist studies with important implications for transfer in SLA are one of serial verbs by Migge (2002) and one of pronouns by Schwegler (2002). The study by Helms Park (2003) of serial verbs makes an explicit connection to creolist research, and a similar connection between transfer in SLA and in creolistics is made by Siegel (2003). Apart from creolist research, some language contact investigations have also focused on substrate influence, as in a detailed historical investigation of the Gaelic-influenced *"after perfect"* in Irish English (McCafferty, 2004).

Although SLA discussions of transfer most often consider the question of the influence of L1 on L2, researchers have given increasing attention to trilingual and multilingual situations where, for example, L2 can influence L3 in ways that L1 does not. A volume edited by Cenoz, Hufheisen, and Jessner (2001) offers many perspectives on such cases, as do studies by Gabrys-Barker (2004), Odlin and Jarvis (2004), and Odlin, Alonso Alonso, and Alonso-Vázquez (2004). Still another dimension of transfer research is the study of bidirectional transfer. Rocca (2003), for instance, looks at the effects of L1 Italian on L2 English and of L1 English on L2 Italian. In a different kind of bidirectional study, Pavlenko and Jarvis (2002) consider the effects of L2 English on L1 Russian along with the effects of L1 on L2 (cf. Cook, 2003). Pavlenko and Jarvis reflect further on the notion of conceptual transfer, a focus of earlier as well as more recent work (e.g., Pavlenko, 1999, 2002). Work by von Stutterheim (2003) and Carroll, Murcia-Serra, Watorek, and Berdiscioli (2000) likewise investigates conceptual transfer although these investigators use somewhat different terms and frameworks.

Several of the studies already mentioned (and also studies not yet mentioned) will be described in more detail in the following sections. Before discussing the most recent research, however, it will help to consider definitions and also some earlier work.

Definitions

Along with the particular studies of transfer cited so far, there have appeared review articles of transfer (Odlin, 2001, 2002, 2003) focusing on research that appeared since earlier book-length treatments of crosslinguistic influence (Odlin, 1989; Ringbom, 1987). All of these studies discuss problems of defining transfer and related terms, and interested readers may consult those discussions. In this chapter, however, just three terms will be considered: *linguistic relativity*, *conceptual transfer*, and *meaning transfer.*

Linguistic relativity is often defined as the hypothesized influence of language on thought. Such influence might affect either comprehension or production, and such influence could, of course, affect comprehension or production in a second language (or a third, a fourth, etc.); moreover, the influence might be where the L1 is influenced by the L2. *Conceptual transfer* can accordingly be defined as those cases of linguistic relativity involving, most typically, a second language.

Caution is necessary in analyzing the connection between transfer and relativity. Cases of influence from the semantics or pragmatics of the native language (or a second in L3 acquisition) constitute what can be called *meaning transfer* (a term neutral between semantic and pragmatic influence). However, not all cases of meaning transfer involve linguistic relativity. One clear instance showing the need to distinguish meaning transfer and conceptual transfer is seen in an interlanguage English pronoun in Poland. Polish uses a first-person plural ending (*-my*) in some cases with a singular referent as in the following example:

Wczoraj byliśmy z bratem w teatrze
Yesterday were-1st PL with brother-INS at theatre LOC
= My brother and I went to the theatre yesterday.
(INS = instrumental; LOC = locative)

The byliśmy suggests more than one referent, but speakers of Polish often construe the meaning as a singular in some discourse contexts. Thus a possible transfer error would be *We were at the theater with my brother yesterday* when the first-person referent is singular. In fact, the Polish sentence (*Wczoraj byliśmy*) is discussed in a Polish textbook that goes on to make the following observation in ellipsis:

You may notice Poles who speak otherwise excellent English carrying this pattern over into English. You are told that 'we' did something with someone else. . . and then a character in a story seems to go missing. That is because 'We. . . with X' should really have been 'X and I.'(Gotteri & Michalak-Gray, 1997, pp. 180–181)

The "carrying over" clearly involves semantic as well as pragmatic transfer, but it would be absurd to claim that Poles do not conceptually distinguish singular and plural referents.

The Polish example thus warrants the following generalization: All conceptual transfer involves meaning transfer but not all meaning transfer involves conceptual transfer. In effect, conceptual transfer is a subset of meaning transfer. The generalization squares with other arguments such as one of Levinson (1997) that "semantic representations" must be theoretically distinct from "conceptual representations," and the same likely holds true of pragmatic representations, although Levinson does not address that issue. If meaning and thought were theoretically equivalent notions, any relativistic claim about language influencing thought would be tautological. Much of this chapter will examine types of meaning transfer that may or may not also be cases of conceptual transfer. Before examining such cases, however, a look at the history of relativity in relation to transfer will provide some useful background.

Von Humboldt, Whorf, and Subsequent Empirical Work

In the study of linguistic relativity the two best-known theorists are the German Wilhelm von Humboldt (1767–1835) and the American Benjamin Lee Whorf (1897–1941). Both von Humboldt and Whorf developed their interest in relativity largely as a result of their study of other languages, and in fact both regarded conceptual transfer as one manifestation of relativity even though their views on transfer differed somewhat.

Von Humboldt's most detailed discussion of relativity is a book-length preface (1836/1960, 1836/1988) that he wrote for his three-volume linguistic and cultural study of Kawi, a literary language in Java (von Humboldt, 1836–1839). Although obviously fascinated with the East Indies (which he never actually visited), von Humboldt has little specific to say about Kawi in the preface and instead foregrounds the diversity of human languages and the implications he sees in that diversity for the relation between mind and language. In the ninth chapter of the preface, he views the learning of a foreign language as the attainment of a new perspective in one's existing world-view (*Weltansicht*, p. 75). In fact he sees second language acquisition as the only way an individual may escape from the conceptual world of the native language. Yet the escape is never, in the view of von Humboldt, completely successful: because "one always more or less carries over (*hinüberträgt*) one's own world-, indeed one's own language-view (*Welt-...Sprachansicht*), this success will not be felt [to be] pure and complete" (1836/1960, p. 75, my translation). The verb *hinüberträgt* is an early use of the metaphor of *transfer* (the Latin source of which likewise means carrying over), and the use of *Welt-...Sprachansicht* shows that von Humboldt considered the transfer to be both conceptual and linguistic (cf. Dechert, 2004).

Whorf's views resemble von Humboldt's in some respects, but not in all. One characteristic of the mind/language relation that Whorf emphasizes is how most linguistic knowledge is unconscious. In one article, (Whorf, 1940/1956) he notes the difficulties of a typical English-speaking learner of French who is unaware of native language patterns which continue to inhibit learning. Whorf then optimistically says of the learner,

> if, however, he is so fortunate as to have his elementary French taught by a theoretic linguist, he first has the patterns of the English formula explained in such a way that they that become semiconscious, with the result that they lose their binding power over him which custom has given them, though they remain automatic as far as English is concerned. Then he acquires the French patterns without inner opposition, and the time for attaining command of the language is cut to a fraction ... (1940/1956, pp. 224–225).

Unlike von Humboldt, Whorf believed that consciousness raising can overcome inhibiting influences of the native language. However, Whorf took seriously the likelihood that the "binding power" of the native language could also affect the metalanguage used to characterize the structures of a language being studied. In another article Whorf writes: "We tend to think in our own language in order to examine the exotic language" (1941/1956, p. 138). His own experience with Hopi shows how he became aware of the analytical dangers of metalinguistic transfer (Odlin, 2004a). In the mid-1930s he analyzed Hopi as a language with three tenses: "factual or present-past, future, and generalized or usitative" (Whorf, 1936/1956, p. 51). However, his reanalysis of about two years later held that the verb system was not based in tense but in categories of evidentiality ("reportive," "expective," and "nomic"), which are, as he put it, "distinct realms of validity" (Whorf, 1938/1956, p. 113) that are "mutually exclusive" (p. 115). The experience of revising his analysis made him aware of the danger of spurious interlingual identifications: "Hopi categories are just enough like Indo-European ones to give at first a deceptive impression of identity" (p. 112).

For Whorf as for von Humboldt, the influence one's language extends beyond metalanguage:

> By 'habitual thought' and 'thought world' I mean more than simply language, i.e. than the linguistic patterns themselves. I include all the analogical and suggestive value of the patterns (e.g., our 'imaginary space' and its distant implications), and all the give-and-take between language and culture as a whole, wherein is a vast amount that is not linguistic but yet shows the shaping influence of language (1941/1956, p. 147).

His notion of "habitual" thought might sound behaviorist, but elsewhere he made his skepticism about behaviorism clear, and indeed his ideas seem more consonant with recent ones framed within the theoretical concept of "automaticity" (e.g., Dewaele, 2001; Hammarberg, 2001; Segalowitz, 2003).

Whorf's ideas and those of other relativists have generated many controversies. Some doubts about relativity arise from empirical concerns, as in the detailed analysis of Hopi by Malotki (1983) which calls into question Whorf's later belief that the Hopi verb is "timeless." Another skeptic (Pinker, 1994) cites a range of psycholinguistic studies that he sees as counterevidence to relativistic claims. Other objections go beyond empirical issues; as Lakoff (1987) notes, "conceptual relativism is often confused with moral relativism, and therefore any relativism is seen as the denial of the possibility of universal standards of ethical conduct" (p. 326). Certain philosophers and literary theorists (e.g., Battersby, 1992; Davidson, 1984) have pointed to shortcomings in some relativistic approaches in their fields. For example, one literary determinist (Fish, 1985) would have it "that the interpreter sees and hears *within* and as an extension of those [socially constructed] interpretive systems—he cannot choose for or against them because they constitute the limits of his consciousness" (p. 125, emphasis in the original). Fish assumes that individuals can belong to one and only one interpretive community, but the existence of bilingual and multilingual communities shows such an assumption to be wrong. Moreover, acquiring a second language can affect one's native language, as a great deal of research from Weinreich (1953/1968) to Cook (2003) has shown.

Despite the problems noted by skeptics such as Pinker and despite the dogmatism of determinists such as Fish, empirical work on relativism has made considerable progress in the last two decades. Work by John Lucy (1992) offered convincing evidence of certain differences between speakers of English and Yucatec with regard to how people categorize and remember certain kinds of objects, and how characteristics of the grammar of noun phrases in each language affect those differences in cognition, and recent work by Lucy and Gaskins (2003) on Japanese and English offers further support for the Whorfian notion of habitual thought. In a similar vein, research by Pederson et al. (1998) found that speakers of typologically different languages performed quite differently in a communication task designed to explore how speakers interpret spatial arrays, and the performances covaried with the type of locational system in the native language. Thus whereas speakers of Dutch used their deictically based system of left and right to recall the location of objects, speakers of Arandic (an Australian language) used their language's system of absolute locations (comparable to the cardinal points of north, south, etc.) to recall the same objects. Speakers of languages relying on absolute systems such as Arandic were found to have more accurate recall of the location of objects in comparison with speakers of languages such as Dutch. One of the members of the Pederson research team, Stephen Levinson, has organized similar research projects which will be discussed in the next section.

In second language acquisition there has long been an awareness of the possible significance of relativism, as seen in discussions in the mid-20th century by Lado (1957) and Kaplan (1966/1984), as well as in very recent discussions (e.g., Kramsch, 2004). Over the years there have been various empirical attempts to demonstrate the influence of L1 concepts, as in a study of putative effects of grammatical gender on the acquisition of English (Clark, Losoff, McCracken, & Still, 1981). One study, especially interesting because of its methodology (Ijaz,

1986), considered cases where meaning transfer from two native languages, Urdu and German, affected the use of spatial prepositions in English; in some cases, learners agreed in their prepositional choices but in others, diverging choices by the two groups reflected differences between the native languages. Ijaz assumed that meaning transfer was the same as conceptual transfer, and as the discussion in the preceding section suggests, such an assumption is mistaken. Furthermore, the cloze tests Ijaz used cannot really show the influence of a linguistic system on nonverbal cognition. Recent research discussed in the next section avoids this methodological problem by using elicitation devices such as picture description.

In the 1990s, the interest in conceptual transfer intensified. Slobin (1993) emphasized the fact that different languages make certain kinds of meaning more salient than others, and he viewed first language acquisition as a process of children developing varied routines of "thinking for speaking;" the outcome of the process is, in Slobin's view, an L1-specific world view likely to affect the subsequent acquisition of another language. The similarity of Slobin's approach to von Humboldt's is not accidental: He cites the German philosopher on this very point. Kellerman (1995) coined the phrase "transfer to nowhere" for cases of learners attempting to use an L1 meaning category that is not highly congruent with an L2 conceptual category (cf. Odlin, 2003). Although he did not invoke Whorf, Kellerman also stressed the unconscious nature of L1 categories involved in "transfer to nowhere."

Relativistic ideas also informed the empirical studies of Jarvis (1998) and Pavlenko (1999). In a comparison of transfer patterns in the English of L1 Finnish and L1 Swedish speakers, Jarvis found the two groups often differing in verb and prepositional choices to describe motion events and spatial relations. Jarvis interpreted such differences as rooted in L1-based conceptual differences, with the native language inducing different patterns of cognizing the events that learners described. Pavlenko likewise attributed to L1-based manners of cognizing the differences she observed in the descriptions of events by speakers of Russian and English. There will be further discussion of these as well other studies in the next section.

Recent Work

Not all meaning transfer should be seen as conceptual transfer, as the Polish English example discussed earlier shows. Even so, some cases of semantic or pragmatic transfer seem to overlap with conceptual transfer, even if it proves difficult to determine the overlap in some particular cases. Three areas of meaning transfer have gotten considerable recent attention: meanings related to space, time, and affect. In each of the three following subsections, issues of transfer will be discussed in relation to possible universals as well to relativity. Although relativism and universalism are sometimes viewed as incompatible theories, the soundest approaches to the study of human diversity have never rejected the notion of a fundamental unity of the human species (and in fact neither von Humboldt nor Whorf rejected such a unity). By the same token, the study of conceptual transfer and universals should be seen as interdependent (Odlin, 2002).

Spatial Meanings

Until recently there were few challenges to the belief that human beings represent spatial meanings in the same way even though the grammatical realizations vary considerably across languages. One fairly recent universalist stance is evident in a paper of Clark (1973), who developed a neo-Kantian phenomenology of space based on the canonical orientation of the upright human, and several other linguists have relied on this anthropomorphic approach (e.g., Levelt, 1989, Lyons, 1977). Even Whorf conceded some universality to the experience of space: "probably the apprehension of space is given substantially in the same form by experience irrespective of language" (1941/1956, p. 158). Nevertheless, he distinguished between the "apprehension" (i.e., perception) of space and conceptions of space, which he did view as somewhat language-specific.

Much of the recent relativistic work has looked in detail at how nonlinguistic spatial cognition covaries with crosslinguistic differences in linguistic structure. For example, Levinson, Meira, and The Language and Cognition Group (2003) found little crosslinguistic uniformity in the semantics of the adpositions used by speakers of nine typologically distinct languages, all of whom had been given a picture description task designed to be cross-culturally neutral. In a book-length study, Levinson (2003) expands on the findings of Pederson et al. (1998), reporting follow-up work with larger groups of individuals, with a larger sample of languages, with more kinds of experimental tasks, and with procedures to distinguish possible environmental influences only indirectly related to language (e.g., type of schooling). The results proved consistent with those of the Pederson et al. study. Speakers of languages such as the Austronesian language Longgu and the Mayan language Tzeltal performed very similarly on tasks which tested recall and recognition memory of the spatial arrangement of objects, both groups preferring a locational strategy of absolute coordinates (comparable to north, south, etc.). In contrast, speakers of both Dutch and Japanese preferred a relative locational strategy (based on right/left deictic orientations).

The Levinson team has confined itself largely to investigations of monolinguals' conceptions of space. However, other work has considered what occurs with people who have acquired or are acquiring a second language. Carroll, Murcia-Serra, Watorek, and Bendiscioli (2000) have inferred differences in spatial cognition in native speakers of German, on the one hand, and in English and Spanish speakers and their L2 German on the other, this inference coming from the results of picture-description tasks. For example, although the L2 users' morphosyntactic production of most structures in German was formally accurate, they produced (in contrast with a group of native speakers) few coadverbials such as *daneben* (beside there) as in *Auf dem Platz ist ein Kiosk; daneben is[t] ein Farbandständer* (On the square is a kiosk; beside there is a bicycle stand). The *da* in *daneben* is historically cognate with English *there*, and in fact some German coadverbials such as *dazu* and *darin* have Germanic cognates in English as in *thereto* and *therein;* even so, the German system plays a much larger role in native speakers' linguistic representation of space. The less productive English coadverbials may offer some positive transfer: on some spatial tasks English speakers approximated the German norms more closely than did a group of speakers of Spanish, a language considered by Carroll et al. to be like English its spatial system. Nevertheless, the English as well as the Spanish groups' underproduction of coadverbials supports von Humboldt's surmise about how difficult it is to fully adopt a new *Welt-...Sprachansicht* (world and language view).

The picture description task of Carroll et al. resembles that of Levinson et al. (2003) and offers a more promising approach to study conceptual transfer than does the kind of test used by Ijaz, described earlier. A film used by Jarvis (1997, 1998) and other researchers provides similar methodological advantages. Like the Carroll team, Jarvis studied native as well as nonnative spatial representations, and he identified some consistent differences between L1 Finnish and L1 Swedish speakers in their English narrations of events in a Charlie Chaplin film. For instance, Jarvis found that the L1 Swedish group often chose the prepositional verb *run on* whereas the L1 Finnish group did so much less often (and all those who did were learners who had also studied Swedish). The use or nonuse of *run on* concurs with the lexical preferences in L1 narrations of the film in Swedish and Finnish. Furthermore, Jarvis and Odlin (2000) found a comparable difference in some prepositional choices in the same narratives: in a scene showing Chaplin and Paulette Goddard on a lawn, the phrase sat *to the grass* was chosen by several Finnish speakers but not by any Swedish speakers.

All the second language research discussed so far has focused on linguistic representations of space, but paralanguage is another option that speakers can and do use. In a study of gestures used with speech, Kellerman and van Hoof (2003) identify what seem to be clear cases of transfer of L1 Spanish gestures (as seen among native speakers who were videotaped) in speakers' use of L2 English spatial descriptions of events in a story presented in pictures. Not all the results that Kellerman and van Hoof obtained were so straightforward, however. As the authors observe, there was little if any L1 transfer in other groups studied (L1 English speakers using Dutch, and L1 Dutch speakers using English). Kellerman and van Hoof candidly admit that they cannot explain the inconsistency of their results. One problem may be in their typological assumptions, which are also those of Slobin, who used a typological framework developed by Talmy (1985). In that framework, languages such as Dutch and English resemble each other more closely than does Spanish. Readers may recall, however, that the research of Carroll et al. (2000) posited a greater typological similarity in spatial representation between English and Spanish than between English and German (the latter being a language not very different from Dutch). Despite the discrepancies (which obviously call for a closer look at the typologies), some results of the gesture study are consistent with relativistic claims of Kellerman (1995, 2001), and will likely lead to further work.

Temporal Meanings

There have been several attempts to construct theoretical frameworks for the meanings of tense and aspect (e.g., Chung & Timberlake, 1985; Comrie, 1985, 1976), but the ideas having the greatest impact on second language acquisition are formulated in the Aspect Hypothesis (Andersen & Shirai 1996; Bardovi-Harlig, 2000). Owing much to analyses of Vendler (1967) and Dowty (1979), the Aspect Hypothesis maintains that the evolution of learners' use of tense and aspect reflects their associations between the forms marking tense/aspect and the inherent lexical aspect of the verbs that they use. For example, the hypothesis predicts that learners of English will tend to mark atelic (i.e., unbounded) meanings with progressive forms (e.g., *We're working on the project*) and to mark punctual meanings with past forms (e.g., *We finished the project yesterday*). According to the hypothesis, cognitive simplicity and prototypicality underlie such associations.

Empirical work on the Aspect Hypothesis has shown an impressive if not total consistency in studies of learners of many different language backgrounds. Proponents of the hypothesis have not usually denied the possibility of transfer involving tense and aspect, but as Shirai and Nishi (2003) observe, the emphasis of such research has been on universality, and "not much attention has been paid to the cross-linguistic differences in how these aspectual notions are lexicalised across languages" (p. 267). Their own paper is not an empirical study so much as a contrastive analysis of Japanese and English, which they naturally see as a preliminary for a study of actual transfer. As Shirai and Nishi suggest, there are real differences in how languages code temporal meanings. In fact, there are also some convincing studies of transfer effects involving such differences.

Some of the clearest evidence comes from a study by Collins (2002). As mentioned earlier, Collins studied only one native language group (French speakers), but she used the same cloze tests of English verb forms that Bardovi-Harlig and Reynolds (1995) had employed to investigate the use of the English tense and aspect by speakers of other languages. Most significantly, Collins found that the use of the perfect by French speakers was very different from that of the other groups. Unlike those groups, the Francophone learners often chose a perfect as an alternative to past simple marking of telic verbs, a result which Collins attributes to the *passé composé* of French. Even so, she interprets her results as support for the Aspect Hypothesis because the perfect was not common except among learners who had already started using past forms to mark telic verbs.

Rocca (2003) likewise finds support for the Aspect Hypothesis in her longitudinal study of bidirectional transfer. Looking at the acquisition of L2 Italian by English-speaking children and of L2 English by Italian-speaking children, she stresses, like Collins, the criterion of developmental readiness: Transfer of tense or aspect does not arise until learners show considerable progress in making the canonical associations predicted by the Aspect Hypothesis (e.g., progressive forms with atelic verbs). Once they have made such associations, however, learners then may tailor the Aspect Hypothesis to correspondences between the L1 and L2 where, for example, Italian children appear to seek a correspondence between a past imperfective form such as *voleva* (was wanting) and a one-word progressive such as *wanting* as in *Bunny wanting to catch the little devil*.

Both the Collins and Rocca studies emphasize the role of crucial similarity as expounded by earlier researchers such as Wode (1983), who recognized the importance of developmental readiness as a prerequisite for transfer. Yet also significant is the likelihood that interlanguage forms often encode meanings of the L1 more than of the L2. In the *Bunny wanting* sentence, the verb may indicate past tense as well as imperfective aspect in the child's own interlanguage semantics because one-word verb forms of Italian such as *voleva* code tense as well as aspect. Wenzell (1989) came to a similar conclusion about the alternation of past and nonpast forms in the interlanguage of Russian learners of English who seemed to be making interlingual identifications of past forms in English with perfective ones in Russian and non-past forms with imperfective ones. Something analogous also appears in the results obtained by Klee and Ocampo (1995) in a study of Spanish verb forms used by speakers of Quechua. Although present and past perfect forms appeared frequently in the Spanish of these bilinguals, the forms often did not mark tense but rather the modal category of evidentiality.

The studies of temporal meanings discussed up to this point do not offer clear evidence of conceptual transfer even though they do indicate some meaning transfer. However, von Stutterheim (2003) sees conceptual transfer at work in a study using film narration as the elicitation device. Native speakers of German tend to frame the events in the film with end points that give closure to the events whereas native speakers of English tend not to use such endpoints. For example, native speakers of English often said *Two nuns are walking down a road* in contrast to German speakers, who often gave an end point as in *Zwei Nonnen laufen auf einem Feldweg Richtung eines Hauses* (Two nuns walk along a lane towards a house), where the house is the endpoint of the event frame. The L1 English pattern of framing seems to be transferable. English speakers often did not state an endpoint in their German sentences as *in Zwei Nonnen laufen auf der Strasse lang* (Two nuns walk the street along), where the house is not mentioned. The framing difference is linked, according to von Stutterheim, to the grammatical importance of progressive aspect in English; in contrast, progressive aspect in German is not prominent. She argues that the typological difference has cognitive implications, where the prominence of progressive aspect in English induces speakers to frame events more analytically, whereas German speakers represent such events more holistically. If von Stutterheim is correct, the English progressive plays a role in such transfer but only an indirect one. She stresses that such crosslinguistic influence does not involve grammatical or semantic errors but rather differences in cognizing that persist even among very advanced learners.

Affective Meanings

The terms *affective, emotional, and attitudinal* are roughly synonymous, although the third term often indicates mental states that do not always involve emotion, including, for example, epistemic and deontic modality. In any case, affect permeates much of what speakers consider to be "meaning" —itself a highly ambiguous notion, as semanticists such as Lyons (1977) have often stressed, and the importance of affective meanings (as opposed to referential meanings) has been foregrounded by Ogden and Richards (1923) among others. Even though affect is not always deemed to be a cognitive phenomenon, several researchers (e.g., Lazarus, 1991; Ortony, Clore, & Collins, 1988; Schumann, 1997) see it so.

Affect has gotten recent attention from linguists interested in conceptual transfer (e.g., Pavlenko, 2002). Less studied has been the possible universality in human language of some emotions. Darwin (1872/1998) was intrigued by the idea of pan-cultural patterns of emotional expression shared to some extent with other species, and in more recent times a lively debate has arisen about universals and relativity in affect (e.g., Ekman, Levenson, & Friesen, 1983; Lutz & White, 1986; Wierzbicka, 1999). Some empirical work has attempted to detail culturally-specific readings of emotional states (e.g., Matsumoto et al., 2002) whereas other work has focused on possible pan-cultural affective associations (e.g., Moore, Ranney, Hsia, & Rusch, 1999). The anthropological study of the Moore team used word association tasks to develop statistical models of semantic space for emotion words of speakers of Chinese, English, and Japanese. They found similar lexical distances among all three groups. For example, the English words *tired*, *bored*, and *lonely* were adjacent to one another in contrast to the words *love*, *happy*, and *excitement*, which were in term clustered rather tightly. Similar results obtained for the semantic spaces of corresponding words in Chinese and Japanese. Despite the similar patterns of clustering, there were language-specific differences, as Moore et al. note. Moreover, the results from bilinguals in their study indicated that the L1-specific semantic space influenced L2 judgments, and a dissertation by Rusch (1996) that focused on Japanese-English bilinguals showed similar evidence of transfer. Neither investigation looked much at all at the literature on bilingualism or SLA, and both studies seem naïve in certain linguistic assumptions. Nevertheless, their results constitute a serious look at a likely pan-cultural basis for the interlingual identifications that learners can sometimes make in the emotion vocabulary of an L1 and L2.

Whatever universality there may be, it does not make the people's emotional lives identical. Speech communities vary in how they code the affective meanings that permeate languages, and the linguistic differences can induce conceptual as well as meaning transfer. Pavlenko (1999, 2002) has detailed a variety of forms of L1 Russian influence on L2 English and L2 English influence on L1 Russian involving affect. For example, some Russian speakers use idioms based in L1 to describe personal feelings as in *she is deep inside herself*, which was said of a woman in a film who appeared to be deep in thought (with the English words clearly a calque on the Russian *byt' w sebe* (to be inside oneself). In contrast to monolingual Russians, those who were bilingual talked about emotions differently in their L1 where, for instance, the former often used the verb *stanovitsa* (become, get) with adjectives of emotion such as *serieznoe* (serious) whereas monolinguals used emotive verbs instead of verb + emotive adjective collocations like those of English.

Although such cases might be interpreted as meaning transfer yet not conceptual transfer, other findings in Pavlenko's research make a compelling case for a relativistic interpretation. In comparison with monolingual English speakers, Russian monolinguals more frequently referred to body parts (face, hands, etc.) to assess the emotional states of characters, and bilinguals using their L2 English and L1 Russian likewise frequently referred to body parts. Moreover, Pavlenko found the Russian of bilinguals who had lived in the United States to be different from that of monolinguals in that the former but not the latter conceived of some events in a film as an invasion of *personal space* or of *privacy*, an affective concept that Pavlenko views as having no close translation equivalent in Russian. Work on compliment behavior by Yu (2004) shows a similar pragmatnic influence of the L2 on L1.

The problem of translating affect arises in grammar as well as in lexis, and focus constructions offer many examples of the elusiveness of cross-linguistic equivalence. Focus and emphasis are notoriously difficult constructs to define, yet their role in affective expression is well documented in some speech communities (e.g., Irvine, 1990; Odlin, 1998, 1997), and they appear again and again in the grammatical descriptions of countless languages (Odlin, 2004b). A study by Schmid (1999) offers many examples where a structure-preserving translation from English to German is difficult if the translator's goal is to preserve the attitude of the speaker or writer. The difficulty is especially significant because the two languages share many of the formal devices conveying focus and emphasis, including inversion, left dislocation, and cleft sentences while yet they differ in their reliance on specific devices in specific contexts (cf. Doherty, 1999).

Bilinguals who are professional translators may err in their assessments of the pragmatics of affect in a source text, and the challenges for second language learners are certainly greater. They may judge as unacceptable translations that native speakers actually approve of, or they may overrely on some structures and show "syntactic conservatism," not using the range of word order patterns licensed by the pragmatics of the target language (Aronsson, 2001; Håkansson, Pienemann, & Sayehli 2002, Plag & Zimmerman, 1998). As Callies (2002) suggests, even advanced learners do not always have the competence to use target language structures in pragmatically appropriate ways even when the crosslinguistic similarities between the L1 and L2 are considerable.

The discussion in the preceding paragraph might seem to imply that there exists a strong constraint on the transfer of focus constructions. However, several studies show that the focus patterns of the native language often influence interlanguage patterns. In some cases, the transfer is partly negative as in an attempted cleft sentence noted by Odlin (2004b): *He* [Chaplin] *say it were he som take the bred*. This and other uses of *som* as a relative pronoun in a cleft structure occur in the writing of some Swedish learners of English but not in the English of L1 Finns (Odlin & Jarvis, 2004). Moreover, the same kind of cleft pattern with *som* occurred in the L1 writing of a Swedish control group. In some cases the transfer may be positive, as in the study of Aronsson (2001), who found frequent accurate uses of clefts by L1 Swedish speakers writing in English. Other studies of Scandinavian language contact likewise indicate transfer of word order and cleft patterns (Rosén, 2001; Westergaard, 2003). The discrepancies between the findings of these studies and those where transfer was not evident show the complexities of the issues and also the importance of methodology (cf. Callies, 2002).

The focus studies reviewed here look mainly at production and related metalinguistic behaviors such as translation and acceptability judgments. Speakers and writers of different languages may vary in what they judge important or how they speak or write their judgment, and such variations are relevant to the problem of conceptual transfer. No less crucial, however, is what listeners or readers understand of target language discourse, yet comprehension, the silent partner of production, has gotten less attention in studies of affect in conceptual transfer. However, a study by Graham, Hamblin, and Feldstein (2001) indicates that native and nonnative speakers differ in how they assess the emotions in the voices of English speakers, and the two groups of nonnative speakers (Spanish and Japanese) did not closely resemble each other. Such results thus indicate transfer involving comprehension. It is conceivable that similar kinds of receptive transfer will some day be documented in lexis and focus constructions.

Conclusion

The review here of crosslinguistic influence in spatial, temporal, and affective meanings does not argue that all cases of meaning transfer involve conceptual transfer. However, meaning transfer is the natural starting point for considering what contributions SLA may make to the study of linguistic relativity. The research reviewed indicates the power of L1 semantics and pragmatics to influence the construction of meaning in language contact settings, and a number of these studies can also be interpreted as preliminary evidence of language influencing a person's cognitive capacities to notice, to categorize, or to recall the content of a picture, for example, or the events in a film. Such preliminary evidence thus offers support for the beliefs of von Humboldt, who saw the native language as a cognitive inhibition, and of Whorf, who likewise described transfer as a "binding power."

Yet the binding power of transfer is far from absolute. Whether or not learners can fully succeed in overcoming the influence of L1 (or perhaps L2 in the case of L3 acquisition), they often do become highly successful users of the target language. Furthermore, their success in acquiring the target can influence the use of their native language and perhaps restructure somewhat their cognitive capacities, as seen, for example, in the differences between how monolingual and bilingual Russian speakers cognize emotion in Pavlenko's research.

Although studies of meaning transfer are not new, intensive work on conceptual transfer has begun only in the last ten years or so, and despite the achievements of the studies to date, they are still more exploratory than thorough examinations of the issues. Clearly one priority for future research is to see if some of the cases of meaning transfer here also qualify as conceptual transfer. For instance, the Quechua/Spanish bilinguals studied by Klee and Ocampo make interlingual identifications between the perfect tenses of Spanish and the evidential categories of Quechua verbs, and such identifications might have subtle but real consequences for how events are remembered.

Conceptual transfer intersects with some other key issues in second language acquisition such as the question of ultimate attainment (e.g., Han, 2004; Long, 2003). Whereas some studies (e.g., Jarvis, 1998) have focused on transfer at earlier stages of proficiency, others (e.g., von Stutterheim, 2003) have looked at the capacities of highly proficient bilinguals and found significant differences between their capacities and those of native speakers. If von Humboldt's surmise was correct, the cognitive framework laid out with L1 is to some extent unalterable, yet if Whorf was correct, consciousness raising may eliminate the binding power. Whichever view eventually proves to be more accurate, SLA researchers would not be exaggerating to say that any theory of linguistic relativity will fall short unless it is compatible with the evidence of conceptual transfer.

ANNOTATED BIBLIOGRAPHY

None of the following studies is recent, and each therefore might be thought of as a classic even though some of them are not often cited by second language researchers.

Olshtain, E. (1983). Sociocultural competence and language transfer: The case of apology. In S. Gass & L. Selinker (Eds.), *Language transfer in language learning* (pp. 232–249). Rowley, MA: Newbury House.

Although some other studies in contrastive pragmatics also show good methodology (e.g., Tamanaha, 2003), the Olshtain investigation is one of the very few that compares two native language groups (English and Russian) in terms of transfer patterns in a speech act in the target language: in this case, apologies in Hebrew.

Orr, G. (1987). *Aspects of the second language acquisition of Chichewa noun class morphology.* Unpublished Ph.D. dissertation, University of California, Los Angeles.

Like the Olshtain study, this one has two NL groups (Ngoni and Gujarati), and it focuses on the acquisition of a target language rarely mentioned in SLA research: Chichewa. As a Bantu language, Chicchewa grammar employs a complex prefixation system in its noun phrases, and Orr's thesis simultaneously examines a typological feature not widely found outside of Africa and the transfer of bound morphology (often claimed—wrongly—to be impossible).

Rickford, J., & Rickford, A. (1976). Cut-eye and suck-teeth: African words and gestures in New World guise. *Journal of American Folklore, 89*, 294–309.

This study will appeal to many SLA researchers interested in the interaction of language and paralanguage, especially since it convincingly details how idioms and facial expressions from African languages have found their way into African-American English speech. It is also one of the most interesting studies of affective transfer available.

Sabban, A. (1982). *Gälisch-Englischer Sprachkontakt.* [Gaelic-English language contact]. Heidelberg: Julius Groos.

The author looked closely at the sociohistorical setting of bilingual region in the Scottish Hebrides, and provided a very detailed analysis of Gaelic-influenced features in the English of older speakers, who were contrasted with the younger generation. The widespread patterns of transfer involving verb phrases warrant a close look by anyone interested in transfer in relation to the Aspect Hypothesis.

Weinreich, U. (1953/1968). *Languages in contact*. The Hague: Mouton.

The ample bibliography alone would make this work a must-read, yet its insights on bilingualism and transfer remain poignant even now. Looking at L1 influence on L2, L2 influence on L1, as well as at social and historical contexts that can affect crosslinguistic influence, Weinreich showed a strong appreciation of the complexities of the phenomenon of transfer.

OTHER REFERENCES

Andersen, R., & Shirai, Y. (1996). The primacy of aspect in first and second language acquisition: The pidgin-creole connection. In W. Ritchie (Ed.), *Handbook of second language acquisition* (pp. 527–570). New York: Academic Press.

Aoyama, K., Flege, J., Guron, S., Akahane-Yamada, R., & Yamada, T. (2004).Perceived phonetic dissimilarity and L2 speech learning: The case of Japanese /r/ and English /l/ and / r/. *Journal of Phonetics, 32*, 233–250.

Aronsson, M. (2001). *It*-clefts and pseudo-clefts in Swedish advanced learner English. *Moderna Språk, 95*, 16–23.

Bardovi-Harlig, K. (2000). *Tense and aspect in second language acquisition: Form, meaning and use*. Oxford: Blackwell.

Bardovi-Harlig, K., & Reynolds, D. (1995). The role of lexical aspect in the acquisition of tense and aspect. *TESOL Quarterly, 29*, 107–131.

Battersby, J. (1992). Professionalism, relativism, and rationality. *PMLA: Publications of the Modern Language Association of America, 107*, 51–64.

Callies, M. (2002, September). Information structure and discourse-pragmatics in German-English interlanguage. Paper presented at Conference on the Pragmatics of Interlanguage English, Munster, Germany.

Carroll, M., Murcia-Serra, J., Watorek, M., & Bendiscioli, A. (2000). The relevance of information organization to second language acquisition studies: The descriptive discourse of advanced adult learners of German. *Studies in Second Language Acquisition, 22*, 441–466.

Cenoz, J. (2001). The effect of linguistic distance, L2 status, and age on crosslinguistic influence in third language acquisition. In J. Cenoz, B. Huyfeisen, & U. Jessner (Eds.), *Cross-linguistic influence in third language acquisition: Psycholinguistic perspectives* (pp. 8–20). Clevedon, UK: Multilingual Matters.

Cenoz, J., B. Hufeisen, B., & Jessner, U. (Eds.) (2001). *Cross-linguistic influence in third language acquisition: Psycholinguistic perspectives*. Clevedon, UK: Multilingual Matters.

Chan, A. (2004). Syntactic transfer: Evidence from the interlanguage of Hong Kong Chinese ESL Learners. *Modern Language Journal, 88*, 56–74.

Chung, S., & Timberlake, A. (1985). Tense, aspect, and mood. In T. Shopen (Ed.), *Syntactic description and linguistic typology* (pp. 202–258). Cambridge: Cambridge University Press.

Clark, H. H. (1973). Space, time, semantics, and the child. In T.E. Moore. (Ed) *Cognitive development and the acquisition of language.* (pp. 27–63). New York: Academic Press.

Clarke, M., Losoff, A., McCracken, M., & Still, J. (1981). Gender perception in Arabic and English. *Language Learning, 31*, 159–169.

Collins, L. (2002). The roles of L1 influence and lexical aspect in the acquisition of temporal morphology. *Language Learning, 52*, 43–94.

Comrie, B. (1976). *Aspect.* Cambridge: Cambridge University Press.

Comrie, B. (1985). *Tense.* Cambridge: Cambridge University Press.

Cook, V. (Ed.). (2003). *Effects of the second language on the first.* Clevedon, UK: Multilingual Matters.

Darwin, C. (1872/1998). *The expression of emotion in man and animals.* Oxford: Oxford University Press.

Davidson, D. (1984). *Inquiries into truth and interpretation.* Oxford: Oxford University Press.

De Angelis, G., & Selinker, L. (2001). Interlanguage transfer and competing linguistic systems in the multilingual mind. In J. Cenoz, B. Hufeisen, & U. Jessner (Eds.), *Cross-linguistic influence in third language acquisition: Psycholinguistic perspectives* (pp. 42–58). Clevedon, UK: Multilingual Matters.

Dechert, H. (2004). On the ambiguity of the notion "transfer." Forthcoming in D. Gabryś-Barker (Ed.), *Cross-linguistic influence in the second language lexicon.* Clevedon, UK: Multilingual Matters.

Dewaele, J. M. (2001). Activation or inhibition? The interaction of L1-L2-and L3 on the language mode continuum. In J. Cenoz, B. Hufeisen, & U. Jessner (Eds.), *Cross-linguistic influence in third language acquisition: Psycholinguistic perspectives* (pp. 69–89). Clevedon, UK: Multilingual Matters.

Doherty, M. (1999). Clefts in translation between English and German. *Target, 11*, 289–315.

Dowty, D. (1979). Word meaning and Montague Grammar. Dordrecht: Reidel.

Ekman, P., Levenson, R. W., & Friesen, W. V. (1983). Autonomic nervous system activity distinguishes among emotions. *Science, 221*, 1208–1210.

Fish, S. (1985). Anti-professionalism. *New Literary History, 17*, 89–127.

Flege, J., & MacKay, I. (2004). Perceiving vowels in a second language. *Studies in Second Language Acquisition, 26*, 1–34.

Gotteri, N., & Michalak-Gray, J. (1997). *Polish.* London: Teach Yourself Books.

Gabryś-Barker, D. (2004). The interaction of languages in the lexical search of multilingual language users. Forthcoming in D. Gabryś-Barker (Ed.), *Cross-linguistic influence in the second language lexicon.* Clevedon, UK: Multilingual Matters.

Graham, C.R., Hamblin, A., & Feldstein, S. (2001). Recognition of emotion in English voices by speakers of Japanese, Spanish and English. *IRAL, 39,* 19–37.

Håkansson, G., Pienemann, M., & Sayehli, S. (2002). Transfer and typological proximity in the context of second language processing. *Second Language Research, 18,* 250–273.

Hammarberg, B. (2001). Roles of L1 and L2 in L3 production and acquisition. In J. Cenoz, B. Hufeisen, & U. Jessner (Eds.), *Cross-linguistic influence in third language acquisition: Psycholinguistic perspectives* (pp. 21–41). Clevedon, UK: Multilingual Matters.

Han, Z. (2004). *Fossilization in second language acquisition.* Clevedon, UK: Multilingual Matters.

Hancin-Bhatt, B. (2000). Optimality in second language phonology: Codas in Thai ESL. *Second Language Research, 16,* 201–232.

Helms-Park, R. (2001). Evidence of lexical transfer in learner syntax: The acquisition of English causatives by speakers of Hindi-Urdu and Vietnamese. *Studies in Second Language Acquisition, 23,* 71–102.

Helms-Park, R. (2003). Transfer in SLA and creoles: The implications of causative serial verbs in the interlanguage of Vietnamese ESL learners. *Studies in Second Language Acquisition, 25,* 211–244.

Hertel, T. (2003). Lexical and discourse factors in the L2 acquisition of Spanish word order. *Second Language Research, 19,* 273–304.

Herwig, A. (2001). Plurilingual lexical organisation: Evidence from lexical processing in L1-L2-L3-L4 translation. In J. Cenoz, B. Hufeisen, & U. Jessner (Eds.), *Cross-linguistic influence in third language acquisition: Psycholinguistic perspectives* (pp. 115–137). Clevedon, UK: Multilingual Matters.

Humboldt, W. von. (1836/1960). Über die Verschiedenheit des menschlichen Sprachbaues und ihren Einfluss auf die geistige Entwickelung des Menschengeschlechts. [On the diversity of human language construction and its influence on human development]. Bonn: Dümmler.

Humboldt, W. von. (1836–1839). *Über die Kawi-sprache auf der insel Java.* [On the Kawi language on the island of Java]. Berlin: Royal Academy of Science.

Humboldt, W. von. (1836/1988). *On language.* Cambridge: Cambridge University Press.

Ijaz, I. H. (1986). Linguistic and cognitive determinants of lexical acquisition in a second language. *Language Learning, 36,* 401–451.

Irvine, J. (1990). Registering affect: Heteroglossia in the linguistic expression of emotion. In C. Lutz & L. Abu-Lughod (Eds.), *Language and the politics of emotion* (pp. 126–161). Cambridge: Cambridge University Press.

Jarvis, S. (1997). *The role of L1-based concepts in L2 lexical reference.* Unpublished Ph.D. dissertation, Indiana University, Bloomington, IN.

Jarvis, S. (1998). *Conceptual transfer in the interlanguage lexicon*. Bloomington: Indiana University Linguistics Club.

Jarvis, S. (2000). Methodological rigor in the study of transfer: Identifying L1 influence in the interlanguage lexicon. *Language Learning, 50*, 245–309.

Jarvis, S., & Odlin, T. (2000). Morphological type, spatial reference, and language transfer. *Studies in Second Language Acquisition, 22*, 535–556.

Jiang, N. (2002). Form-meaning mapping in vocabulary acquisition in a second language. *Studies in Second Language Acquisition, 24*, 617–637.

Juffs, A. (2002). Formal linguistic perspectives on SLA. In R. Kaplan (Ed.), *Oxford handbook of applied linguistics* (pp. 87–103). New York: Oxford University Press.

Kaplan, R. (1966/1984). Cultural thought patterns and inter-cultural education. In S. McKay (Ed.), *Composing in a second language*, (pp. 43–62). Rowley, MA: Newbury House.

Kellerman, E. (1995). Crosslinguistic influence: Transfer to nowhere? *Annual Review of Applied Linguistics, 15*, 125–150.

Kellerman, E. (2001). New uses for old language: Cross-linguistic and cross-gestural influence in the narratives of non-native speakers (pp. 170–191). In J. Cenoz, B. Hufeisen, & U. Jessner (Eds.), *Cross-linguistic influence in third language acquisition: Psycholinguistic perspectives* (pp. 59–68). Clevedon, UK: Multilingual Matters.

Kellerman, E., & van Hoof, M. (2003). Manual accents. *IRAL, 41*, 251–269.

Klee, C., & Ocampo, A. (1995). The expression of past reference in Spanish narratives of Spanish-English bilingual speakers. In C. Silva-Corvalán (Ed.), *Spanish in four continents* (pp. 52–70). Washington, DC: Georgetown University Press.

Koda, K. (2000). Crosslinguistic variations in L2 morphological awareness. *Applied Psycholinguistics, 21*, 297–320.

Kramsch, C. (2004). Language, thought, and culture. In A. Davies & C. Elder (Eds.), *Handbook of applied linguistics* (pp. 235–261). Oxford: Blackwell.

Kwon, (2003). *Pragmatic transfer and proficiency in refusals of Korean EFL learners*. Unpublished Ph.D. dissertation, Boston University.

Lado, R. (1957). *Linguistics across cultures*. Ann Arbor: University of Michigan Press.

Lakoff, G. (1987). *Women, fire, and dangerous things: What categories reveal about the mind*. Berkeley: University of California Press.

Lazarus, R. (1991). Progress on a cognitive-motivational-relational theory of emotion. *American Psychologist, 46*, 819–834.

Levelt, W. (1989). *Speaking: From intention to articulation*. Cambridge, MA: MIT Press.

Levinson, S. (1997). From outer to inner space: Linguistic categories and non-linguistic thinking. In J. Nuyts & E. Pederson (Eds.), *Language and linguistic categorization* (pp. 13–45). Cambridge, UK: Cambridge University Press.

Levinson, S. (2003). *Space in language and cognition.* Cambridge: Cambridge University Press.

Levinson, S., Meira, S., & The Language and Cognition Group (2003). "Natural concepts" in the spatial topological domain—adpositional meanings in crosslinguistic perspective: An exercise in semantic typology. *Language, 79*(3), 485–516.

Long, M. (2003). Stabilization and fossilization in interlanguage development. In C. Doughty & M. Long (Eds.), *Handbook on second language acquisition* (pp. 487–535). Oxford: Blackwell.

Lucy, J. (1992). *Grammatical categories and cognition.* Cambridge: Cambridge University Press.

Lucy, J., & Gaskins, S. (2003). Interaction of language type and referent type in the development of nonverbal classification preferences. In D. Gentner & S. Godlin-Meadow (Eds.), *Language in mind* (pp. 465–492). Cambridge, MA: MIT Press.

Lutz, C., & White, G. (1986). The anthropology of emotions. *Annual Review of Anthropology, 15*, 405–436.

Lyons, J. (1977). *Semantics, Vols. I-II.* Cambridge: Cambridge University Press.

Malotki, E. (1983). *Hopi time: A linguistic analysis of the temporal concepts in the Hopi language.* Berlin: Mouton.

Matsumoto, D., Consolacion, T., Yamada, H., Suzuki, R., Franklin, B., Sunita, P., Ray, R., & Uchida, H. (2002). American-Japanese cultural differences in judgements of emotional expressions of different intensities. *Cognition and Emotion, 16*, 721–747.

Matthews, S., & Yip, V. (2003). Relative clauses in early bilingual development: Transfer and universals. In A. Giacalone Ramat (Ed.), *Typology and second language acquisition* (pp. 39–81). Berlin, Germany: Mouton de Gruyter.

McCafferty, K. (2004). Innovation in language contact. *Diachronica, 21*, 113–160.

McAllister, R., Flege, J., & Piske, T. (2002). The influence of L1 on the acquisition of Swedish quantity by native speakers of Spanish, English and Estonian. *Journal of Phonetics, 30*, 229–258.

Migge, B. (2002). The origins of the copulas *(d/n)a* and *de* in the Eastern Maroon Creole. *Diachronica 19*, 81–133.

Moore, C., Romney, K., Hsia, T., & Rusch, C. (1999). Universality of the semantic structure of emotion terms: Methods for the study of inter and intracultural variability. *American Anthropologist, 101*, 529–546.

Nakahama, Y. (2003). *Cross-linguistic influence on the development of referential topic management in L2 Japanese oral narratives.* Unpublished Ph.D. dissertation, Georgetown University.

Odlin, T. (1989). *Language transfer.* Cambridge: Cambridge University Press.

Odlin, T. (1997). Bilingualism and substrate influence: A look at clefts and reflexives. In J. Kallen (Ed.), *Focus on Ireland* (pp. 35–50). Amsterdam: John Benjamins.

Odlin, T. (1998). On the affective and cognitive bases for language transfer. In R. Cooper. (Ed.), *Compare or contrast?* (pp. 81–106). Tampere, Finland: University of Tampere.

Odlin, T. (2001). Language transfer and substrate influence. In R. Mesthrie (Ed.), *Concise encyclopedia of sociolinguistics* (pp. 499–503). Amsterdam: Elsevier.

Odlin, T. (2002). Language transfer and cross-linguistic studies: Relativism, universalism, and the native language. In R. Kaplan (Ed.), *The Oxford handbook of applied linguistics* (pp. 253–261). New York: Oxford University Press.

Odlin, T. (2003). Crosslinguistic influence. In C. Doughty & M. Long (Eds.), *Handbook of second language acquisition* (pp. 436–486). Oxford: Blackwell.

Odlin, T. (2004a). Thinking about linguistic relativity and Benjamin Lee Whorf as a language learner. Universidad de Castilla-la Mancha, Cuenca Campus, Spain, February 25, 2004.

Odlin, T. (2004b). Could a contrastive analysis ever be complete? Forthcoming in D. Gabry's-Barker (Ed.), *Cross-linguistic influence in the second language lexicon.* Clevedon, U.K.: Multilingual Matters.

Odlin, T., & Jarvis, S. (2004). Same source, different outcomes: A study of Swedish influence on the acquisition of English in Finland. *The International Journal of Multilingualism* (in press).

Odlin, T., Alonso Alonso, R., & Alonso-Vázquez, C. (2004). Fossilization in L2 and L3. Forthcoming in Z. Han & T. Odlin (Eds.), *Studies of fossilization in second language acquisition.* Clevedon, UK: Multilingual Matters.

Ogden, C. K., & Richards, I. A. (1923). *The meaning of meaning: A study of the influence of language upon thought and of the science of symbolism.* New York: Harcourt, Brace and World.

Ortony, A., Clore, G. L., & Collins, A. (1988). *The cognitive structure of emotions.* Cambridge: Cambridge University Press.

Pavlenko, A. (1999). New approaches to concepts in bilingual memory. *Bilingualism, Language and Cognition, 2*, 209–230.

Pavlenko, A. (2002). Bilingualism and emotions. *Multilingua, 21*, 45–78.

Pavlenko, A., & Jarvis, S. (2002). Bidirectional transfer. *Applied Linguistics, 23*, 190–214.

Pederson, E., Danziger, E., Wilkins, D., Levinson, S., Kita, S. & Senft, G. (1998). Semantic typology and spatial conceptualization. *Language, 74*, 557–589.

Pinker, S. (1994). *The language instinct: How the mind creates language.* New York: Morrow.

Plag, I., & Zimmermann, R. (1998). "Wortstellungsprobleme in der Lernersprache Englisch—Frontierung und Inversion" [Word order problems in learner English: Fronting and inversion]. In W. Börner & K. Vogel, (Eds.), *Kontrast und Äquivalenz: Beiträge zu*

Sprachvergleich und Übersetzung, [Contrast and equivalence: Contributions to language comparison and translation], (pp. 208–232). Tübingen: Narr.

Ringbom, H. (1987). *The role of the first language in foreign language learning*. Clevedon, UK: Multilingual Matters.

Ringbom, H. (2001). Lexical transfer in L3 production. In J. Cenoz, B. Hufeisen, & U. Jessner (Eds.), *Crosslinguistic influence in third language acquisition: Psycholinguistic perspectives* (pp. 59–68). Clevedon, UK: Multilingual Matters.

Ringbom, H. (2004). The importance of different types of similarity in transfer studies. Forthcoming in D. Gabryś-Barker (Ed.), *Cross-linguistic influence in the second language lexicon*. Clevedon, UK: Multilingual Matters.

Rocca, S. (2003). Lexical aspect in child second language acquisition of temporal morphology: A bidirectional study. In R. Salaberry & Y. Shirai (Eds.), *The L2 acquisition of tense–aspect morphology* (pp. 249–284). Amsterdam: John Benjamins.

Rosén, C. (2001). Deutsch als Fremdsprache: Zur Informationsstruktur schwedischer Deutschstudierender [German as a foreign language: On the information structure of Swedish learners of German]. *Moderna Språk, 95*, 49–61.

Rusch, C. (1996). *The effects of bilingualism on cognitive semantic structure in the subjective lexicon: The case of emotions in Japanese and English*. Unpublished Ph.D. dissertation, University of California, Irvine.

Sabourin, L. (2001). L1 effects on the processing of grammatical gender in L2. *EUROSLA Yearbook, 1*, 159–169.

Schmid, M. (1999). *Translating the elusive: Marked word order and subjectivity in English-German translation*. Amsterdam: Benjamins.

Schumann, J. (1997). *The neurobiology of affect in language*. Malden, MA : Blackwell.

Schwegler, A. (2002). On the (African) origins of Palenquero subject pronouns. *Diachronica, 19*, 273–332.

Selinker, L. (1992). *Rediscovering interlanguage*. London: Longman.

Segalowitz, N. (2003). Automaticity. In C. Doughty & M. Long (Eds.), *Handbook of second language acquisition* (pp. 382–408). Oxford: Blackwell.

Shirai, Y., & Nishi, Y. (2003). Lexicalisation of aspectual structures in English and Japanese. In A. Giacalone-Ramat (Ed.), *Typology and second language acquisition* (pp. 267–290). Berlin: Mouton de Gruyter.

Siegel, J. (2003). Substrate Influence in creoles and the role of transfer in second language acquisition. *Studies in Second Language Acquisition, 25*, 185–209.

Singleton, D. (2004). Lexical transfer: Interlexical or intralexical? Forthcoming in D. Gabry's-Barker (Ed.), *Cross-linguistic influence in the second language lexicon*. Clevedon, UK: Multilingual Matters.

Slobin, D. (1993). Adult language acquisition: A view from child language study. In C. Perdue (Ed.), *Adult language acquisition: Cross-linguistic perspectives. Volume II: The results*, (pp. 239–252). Cambridge: Cambridge University Press.

Stutterheim, C. von. (2003). Linguistic structure and information organization: The case of very advanced learners. *EUROSLA Yearbook, 3*, 183–206.

Talmy, L. (1985). Lexicalization patterns: Semantic structure in lexical forms. In T. Shopen (Ed.), *Language typology and syntactic description*, Vol. 3 (pp. 57–149). Cambridge University Press.

Tamanaha, M. (2003). *Interlanguage speech act realization of apologies and complaints: The performances of Japanese L2 speakers in comparison with Japanese L1 and English L1 speakers*. Unpublished Ph.D. dissertation, University of California, Los Angeles.

Upton, T., & Lee-Thompson, L. (2001). The role of the first language in second language reading. *Studies in Second Language Acquisition, 23*, 469–495.

Vendler, Z. (1967). Verbs and times. In Z. Vendler (Ed.), *Linguistics in philosophy* (pp. 97–121). Ithaca, NY: Cornell University Press.

Wang, M., Koda, K., & Perfetti, C. (2003). Alphabetic and nonalphabetic L1 effects in English word identification: A comparison of Korean and Chinese English L2 learners. *Cognition, 87*, 129–149.

Weinreich, U. (1953/1968). *Languages in contact.* The Hague: Mouton.

Wenzell, V. (1989). Transfer of aspect in the English oral narratives of native Russian speakers. In H. Dechert & M. Raupach (Eds.), *Transfer in language production* (pp. 71–97). Norwood, NJ: Ablex.

Westergaard, M. (2003). Unlearning V2: Transfer, markedness, and the importance of input cues in the acquisition of word order in English by Norwegian children. *EUROSLA Yearbook, 2003, 3*, 77–101.

Wierzbicka, A. (1999). *Emotions across languages and cultures: Diversity and universals.* Cambridge, UK: Cambridge University Press.

Whorf, B. L. (1956). *Language, thought, and reality*, J. Carroll (Ed.). Cambridge, MA: MIT Press.

White, L. (2003). On the nature of interlanguage representation: Universal Grammar in the second language. In C. Doughty & M. Long (Eds.), *Handbook of second language acquisition* (pp. 19–42). Blackwell.

Wode, H. (1983). On the systematicity of L1 transfer in L2 acquisition. In H. Wode (Ed.), *Papers on language acquisition, language learning and language teaching* (pp. 144–149). Heidelberg: J. Groos.

Yu, M. (2004). Interlinguistic variation and similarity in second language speech act behavior. *Modern Language Journal, 88*, 102–119.

Zimmerman, R. (2004). Metaphorical transferability. Forthcoming in D. Gabryś-Barker (Ed.), *Cross-linguistic influence in the second language lexicon*. Clevedon, UK: Multilingual Matters.

2. LONGITUDINAL RESEARCH IN SECOND LANGUAGE ACQUISITION: RECENT TRENDS AND FUTURE DIRECTIONS

Lourdes Ortega and Gina Iberri-Shea

>Both common sense and expert knowledge tell us that learning a language other than the mother tongue is a complex process that happens through and over time. Time, indeed, is a construct implicated in many of the problems that second language acquisition researchers investigate. The purpose of this chapter is to survey longitudinal SLA research published in the last three years and to offer a critical reflection of best current longitudinal practices and desirable directions for future longitudinal SLA research. We highlight recent trends in longitudinal SLA research, paying particular attention to broad design choices and foci of research organized around four trends in SLA longitudinal investigation, and we describe key exemplary studies under each trend. We close by reflecting on some of the challenges and opportunities that await these longitudinal research programs in the future.

Both common sense and expert knowledge tell us that learning a language other than the mother tongue (a second, foreign, or heritage language; henceforth, an L2) is a complex process that happens through and over time. Indeed, it can be argued that many, if not all, fundamental problems about L2 learning that SLA researchers investigate are in part problems about "time," and that any claims about "learning" (or development, progress, improvement, change, gains, and so on) can be most meaningfully interpreted only within a full longitudinal perspective. It is, therefore, unfortunate that the bulk of disciplinary discussions within the field favors a cross-sectional view of language learning and, as a consequence, discussions about longitudinal research are scarce. For example, in Hatch and Lazaraton (1991), readers will find four pages devoted to time-series research, followed by an incidental remark that this is a special type of longitudinal design. No other specific discussion of longitudinal issues can be found in this 628-page compendium of applied linguistics research methods, now out of print. An inspection of more recent research methods textbooks confirms this state of affairs. SLA researchers who would like to pursue longitudinal research programs can find little guidance about questions such as: What problems about the development of L2 competencies have SLA researchers investigated longitudinally? and What unique challenges and strengths does the longitudinal investigation of L2 learning entail?

This chapter seeks to begin to address these questions. We survey longitudinal SLA research published in recent years and offer a critical reflection of best current longitudinal practices and desirable directions for future longitudinal SLA research.[1] In addressing the general purpose of *ARAL*, we hope this discussion of trends alerts specialist readers to recent cutting-edge longitudinal studies of L2 learning. Given the dearth of methodological discussions about longitudinal research in applied linguistics, another goal we set ourselves is to offer useful considerations for SLA researchers and graduate students who plan to conduct, or are in the process of reporting on, longitudinal studies, and to suggest to them critical areas in need of attention.

The Centrality of Time in SLA

Why is longitudinal research essential to advancement of knowledge in the field of SLA? The simple but uncontestable answer is that many questions concerning second language learning are fundamentally questions of time and timing. A cursory look at some central SLA research areas can easily show this.

For one, fundamental questions related to time concern biological time at the onset of learning, including not only "at what age" but also "for how long" L2 learning should occur, in contexts where near-native success is the desired outcome. These time-related questions have inspired basic research about maturational constraints for L2 learning and the critical periods hypothesis (Hyltenstam & Abrahamsson, 2003; Scovel, 1988). They have also been central in evaluating the research base for educational policy decisions regarding early or late exit from transitional bilingual education programs in the United States (Collier, 1989), and in evaluations of early versus late start of French immersion school education in Canada (Harley & Hart, 1997).

Even in SLA domains where the preponderance of studies favors cross-sectional practices, longitudinal claims are often implicitly posited. Task-based language learning proposals, for example (see Ellis, 2003; Robinson, 2001; Skehan, 2002), make theoretical inferences about competence-related changes that are posited to deploy over time, but they do so on the empirical foundation of static snapshots of learner's capacity for action in the L2 at a given point in time. The same is true of many other areas of instructed SLA research. For example, time issues are central in the empirical determination of ideal lengths and intensities of instruction in a given curriculum, once again, if the goal is to foster advanced L2 capacities: How much instructional time is optimal in a given school curriculum, overall, and how intensively packed into the institutional schedule should it be (Collins, Halter, Lightbown, & Spada, 1999)? Questions about the timing of instruction and how instructional intensity moderates L2 learning outcomes are implicated as well, if perhaps at a more abstract level, in the oft-lamented problem of articulation from high school to college in foreign language education in the United States (Lally, 2001). They also underlie characterizations of the crisis of FL collegiate education in North American universities, which many blame at least in part on the dichotomization of programs into lower-division language courses, where time is devoted to the basics of language learning alone, and upper-division content courses, where students experience discontinuity at a turning point when instructional time is suddenly devoted to the exclusive learning of literature and cultural studies (Byrnes, 2002).

Many broader SLA questions could be posed that require answers mustered in longitudinal evidence: What do we know about the pace and pattern of development in second language and literacy, throughout the lifetime of L2 learners? What critical transition points in L2 development need to be taken into account when planning and evaluating educational policy and practice for specific L2 learner populations? Ultimately, it is through cumulative longitudinal findings that the SLA research community would be able to contribute meaningful characterizations of the gradual process of attaining advanced second language and literacy competencies across various contexts. Given the centrality of time in SLA research programs, then, more attention to longitudinal research practices and to findings gleaned from longitudinal studies is desirable.

Methodology for the Present Review

Although we make no claim to exhaustion or completeness in this review, the themes we present emerged from strategies for systematic synthesis of primary research domains (Cooper & Hedges, 1994; Light & Pillemer, 1984). We conducted electronic searches to uncover longitudinal SLA studies published during 2002 and 2003 across 20 major applied linguistics journals. This was supplemented with hand searches of 2004 journal issues that were available at the time of this writing. The search yielded 38 longitudinal studies that focused on L2 learning (including second, foreign, and heritage language learning). A little fewer than half of these studies investigated some aspect of L2 learning by young adult students enrolled in institutions of higher education, whereas about 20% investigated high school or middle school contexts. Even fewer studies addressed adult learners in nonuniversity contexts or preschool or elementary-school-aged children. Broadly speaking, then, recent longitudinal research in SLA is consistent with the focus on college-level populations that is typical of applied linguistics research in general.

We located and read these studies and discussed main methodological features. We also recorded the extent to which studies defined and documented "change over time" (quantitatively, qualitatively, or both), and we evaluated the strengths and weaknesses of each study, noting any longitudinal challenges explicitly discussed in the primary reports. This process compelled us to refine and broaden our working definition of "longitudinal" SLA research, as we realized the study of second language and literacy development over time has been undertaken from a number of distinct epistemological traditions, including quantitative descriptive studies of linguistic features and qualitative interpretive studies of sociocognitive and sociocultural dimensions of multilingual development. In the remainder of this chapter, we characterize four broad trends in recent longitudinal SLA research. We conclude with a methodological discussion that we hope is useful for SLA researchers and graduate students who plan to conduct, or are in the process of reporting on, longitudinal studies.

Descriptive-Quantitative Longitudinal Studies of L2 Development

Many longitudinal SLA studies published in the last three years have adopted a descriptive (that is, nonexperimental), quantitative design. Such studies focus on quantifiable variables, but without researcher's manipulation and without random sampling or random assignment of participants to conditions or to contexts for learning. They are characterized by multiwave data collection from the same individuals over a relatively long period of time, which typically spans anywhere between four months and four years. Although the longitudinal data in these studies are quantified, the number of participants is far too small to warrant the use of inferential statistics. For this reason, descriptive statistics displayed in the form of frequencies, percentages, and proportions, and other analytical tools, such as visual displays and implicational scaling, are favored.

The research focus is often strictly linguistic, following up on the tradition of early SLA longitudinal studies that have become classics (e.g., Huebner, 1983; Sato, 1990; Schumann, 1978; but see Schmidt, 1983, for a broader linguistic focus). Although the early interlanguage work involved intense case studies of usually one or two participants only, more recent studies increasingly tend to involve multiple participants, although still typically small groups. For example, Perdue, Benazzo, and Giuliano (2002) charted the development of finiteness in the spoken production of five adult Italian and Spanish immigrant workers in Europe during 30 months of naturalistic exposure to English or French, and Bardovi-Harlig (2002) investigated the development of future tense as evinced in the written production by 16 college ESL learners during 7 to 17 months of study in a university's English Language Program (this is the same sample and longitudinal corpus previously studied in Bardovi-Harlig, 1994). Well established descriptive-quantitative longitudinal lines of SLA research to the present day concentrate on L2 morphology, as the studies just mentioned illustrate, and on L2 phonology (e.g., Abrahamsson, 2003; Hansen, 2004).

Descriptive-quantitative longitudinal SLA research draws on linguistic theories, often of a functional bent, and seldom includes nonlinguistic variables. These stable trends notwithstanding, it is interesting to note that in other recent SLA studies employing this type of design there has been a broadening not only of the linguistic focus but also of the epistemological approach to language development. This is the case of a longitudinal study conducted within a Vygotskian sociocultural framework by Belz and Kinginger (2002). The researchers documented critical incidents that contributed to the learning of indexical politeness (specifically, the use of *tu/vous* and *Du/Sein*) by two fourth-semester foreign language students at a U. S. university. The participants were involved in a telecollaboration project that afforded them the opportunity to establish a personal relationship with a native-speaking peer in France and Germany, respectively. The critical incidents were defined by the researchers a priori as instances in which a student chose the formal *you* during an e-mail exchange in the L2, causing the peer interlocutor to focalize overtly on the inappropriateness of this choice. The researchers argue that solidarity (for the French student) and even intimacy (for the German student) developed between cross-site partners, and that this personal investment infused the choice of term of address with special significance. In sum, the personal communicative investment enabled by the telecollaboration assignment outside of the classroom made choice of address term functionally salient for these students, whereas it also afforded them fine-tuned and timely assistance from their native-speaking peer.

The descriptive-quantitative type of design discussed here corresponds closely with traditional definitions of "longitudinal" research in a number of fields. Its main strength, according to the canon of statisticians (Johnson, 2001), is that it provides evidence for time relationships among variables, thus helping not only to describe phenomena and association among variables, but also to begin to explain causes and effects by looking at antecedent-consequent relationships (e.g., the co-occurrence of critical incidents and systematic shifts in the use of indexical politeness documented by Belz and Kinginger, 2002). In the social sciences, the longitudinal tradition of life-course studies is based on this descriptive, quantitative approach, and has contributed massive panel studies as well as more developmentally oriented studies, in both cases involving hundreds or thousands of participants followed over what is some times several decades of their lives (Phelps, Furstenberg, & Colby, 2002). However, the longitudinal SLA tradition, with its small samples and short-span lengths of investigation, is much closer to the spirit of longitudinal research in the feeder field of first language acquisition (e.g. Karmiloff-Smith & Karmiloff-Smith, 2001). Here, detailed case studies are the norm, and the chronological frame of several months up to five or six years is well established as sufficient for any given study, because this is the biological time scale naturally needed to capture the object of inquiry in child first language acquisition.

Longitudinal Research on L2 Program Outcomes

A very different kind of longitudinal design has been adopted more rarely in recent SLA studies, which we would like to call, in lieu of a better term, "programmatic" longitudinal research. By comparison to the descriptive-quantitative longitudinal design discussed in the previous section, the programmatic longitudinal design is used for evaluation of L2 curricular options, employs relatively large samples, and focuses on longer periods of observation scaled on institutional time (typically four to six years), coupled with fewer data collection waves spaced along wider time gaps (there are often one or two collection points per year). Although this longitudinal design has been infrequently employed in SLA, it addresses questions of utmost importance for policies and practices in L2 programs, such that an increase of longitudinal investigations of this kind would be a positive development in future instructed SLA research. In this section we discuss two representative studies: Lightbown, Halter, White, and Horst (2002) and Klapper and Rees (2003).

The participants in Lightbown et al. (2002) were a cohort of 73 French-speaking school students in the Canadian province of Nouveau-Brunswick who had received all their English L2 instruction via a self-access, comprehension-only experimental curriculum (that is, the program was entirely based on self-paced reading and listening activities). This cohort's overall proficiency in English was mapped during six years of comprehension-based instruction, with data points on the students' first year of English study (in grade 3), their last year of primary school (in grade 6), their first year of secondary school (in grade 7), and a year later (in grade 8). In addition, the cohort's L2 competencies were also compared to a group of 27 students from the same province who studied English under the traditional (audiolingual) curriculum and—for grades 6, 7, and 8 only—with another group of 14 traditional program students. The fact that these learners were followed for six years makes this one of the longest periods of observation investigated in any longitudinal SLA study focusing on group, rather than individual, performance. The analyses based on second-wave observations in grade 6 (the last year of primary school) yielded data that supported a no-difference interpretation. An inspection of the evidence over the longer period of six years, however, revealed a similar-sized improvement in reading and listening abilities for the experimental and the traditional curriculum samples, but a clear advantage in productive skills (particularly L2 writing, including the use of verbal morphology) for the traditional curriculum groups.

Klapper and Rees (2003) undertook a four-year comparison between two groups of university students (a total of 57 learners) in the same German department in the United Kingdom, who experienced a traditional grammar instruction curriculum (mostly grammar and grammar-translation courses for 2 to 3 hours a week in a major degree concentration) or a focus-on-form curriculum (mostly content-and task-based courses for 2 to 3 hours a week in a minor degree concentration). The two groups began their programs with comparable scores and received near identical amounts of instructional time during the first two years of study. Both groups' programs were enriched with a one-year study abroad component on the third year of the four-year college curriculum. Klapper and Rees examined changes on a grammar test and a test of general academic language proficiency, both administered in three waves, yearly, for years 1 through 3 of the program. The comparisons also included one-time indicators of academic ability and success (an IQ test at the beginning of the program; final exams and degree marks at completion of the program in year 4). Klapper and Rees concluded that the pace of development of the focus-on-forms and focus-on-form cohorts was different, but the final outcomes were comparable. Specifically, the focus-on-forms group showed large increases in grammar and proficiency test scores during the first two years of the program, whereas the focus-on-form group showed stagnation during the same period but similarly large progress after the one-year study abroad experience on the third year. In essence, then, the two groups had started equal and finished equal as well, but they exhibited interesting differences in the pace of development within the four-year observation period. Notably, these differences were eventually equalized by the turning-point experience of study abroad.

Despite rather large differences in L2 learning context and in instructional focus, these two programmatic longitudinal studies share strong design similarities. They are similar in the quantitative orientation of the analyses, the sampling of rather large groups, the comparison of broad curricular programmatic options, and the unusual length of the observation span, which was scaled on institutional time, coupled with infrequent, year-spaced data collection waves. Perhaps these shared features are responsible in part for the fact that in both studies the findings changed radically when the length of observation was doubled, from three to six years in Lightbown et al. and from two to four years in Klapper and Rees. Had the research teams in either study decided that three or two years was "long enough," this choice would have led them to the conclusion, erroneous in a fuller longitudinal perspective but consistent with the first available waves of data, that there was no difference between the two programs compared, in one case (Lightbown et al.), or that there was a difference, in the other (Klapper & Rees). Thus, these two programmatic SLA studies attest to the tremendous value of taking a very long view on L2 development in SLA research.

The Longitudinal Investigation of L2 Instructional Effectiveness

A third recent, noteworthy trend is the gradual emergence of what could eventually give rise to a longitudinal design tradition in effectiveness of L2 instruction research. For one, there is a pronounced tendency in recent quasi-experimental studies of instruction to feature longer-lasting interventions (eight weeks seems to be a favored choice) and to include delayed posttests (often only a month after instruction, some times up to three months later). This, for example, can be found in the designs adopted by Han (2002) and Lyster (2004). This is a valuable improvement over the prevalent practices in this research domain up until 1998 reported by Norris and Ortega (2000). Of the 49 studies included in that meta-analysis, the majority (30 or 61%) featured short duration treatments of a maximum of two hours, and only 22 (or 45%) included a delayed posttest. Although the presence of long-lasting interventions and delayed post-tests does not amount to longitudinal research per se, when data are collected and analyzed across multiple waves to document gains on several posttests, some times even repeatedly during the treatment period as well, the process of learning is presented in longitudinal perspective to some extent.

Moreover, some recent studies have implemented true longitudinal intervention designs, although they cannot be characterized as fully quasi-experimental because no control or comparison group was employed. A representative case in this category is an investigation of instruction by Kim and Hall (2002). These researchers, like Belz and Kinginger (2002), sought to document L2 pragmatic learning through the study of Vygotskian microgenetic change, taking a close look at the process of change throughout the history of a learning event. More specifically, their purpose was to investigate the benefits of interactive book sessions that took place between the teacher-researcher and four third-grade Korean students who had been learning English for a year at the time of the study. The interactive book reading sessions (the instructional 'treatment') took place over four months in 30-minute biweekly meetings, during which seven age-appropriate English books were read. One book was read per session during the first month, and then the same seven-book cycle was repeated each successive month. After 20 minutes of interactive reading, the last 10 minutes in each session were typically devoted to the children's role playing of some aspect of the story. This role play was identified as the ideal "testing" context, from the viewpoint of microgenesis. Pragmatic L2 development was operationalized as increases during these role play events in mean number of words, mean number of utterances, average use of moves that served to manage talk (that is, initiations, elaborations, conclusions, and formulaic expressions), and average use of moves that served to manage meaning (that is, self-and other-corrections). The researchers found clear improvement in the four children's EFL pragmatic competencies in terms of all dependent variables but one (the meaning management moves) over the four-month period.

Although the research trends in effectiveness of instruction discussed so far are clearly encouraging and take a longer view of instructed L2 development, little progress seems to have occurred regarding the use of time-series designs in SLA research. Time-series design constitutes the single best formal strategy for investigating effects of instruction longitudinally. The principles for this design were clearly and forcefully laid out as a promising longitudinal experimental research option in SLA by Mellow, Reeder, and Forster (1996). After nearly a decade since the publication of that article, we were able to uncover only one study of L2 instruction adopting a time-series longitudinal experimental design, Ishida (2004).

Ishida investigated whether a regime of intensive recasts on the aspectual Japanese form–*te i-(ru)* delivered over four 30-minute, biweekly tutorial sessions would have lasting effects on the oral accuracy exhibited on this form by four second-and third-year semester students. The time-series design was operationalized as two waves of data collection that established a baseline for all four participants (on week 1), followed by four more waves in which the treatment was delivered and immediate effects were documented (on weeks 2 and 3), and two final waves that served as posttest (on week 4) plus a final wave of data collection seven weeks later (on week 11 of the study) that provided delayed posttest observations. Ishida found that the intensive recasting treatment exerted an immediate effect, as shown in learners' more accurate use of -*te i-(ru)* immediately after the onset of the treatment. The accuracy gains were sustained on each successive wave of observation up until week 11. These results, together with those reported by Han (2002), offer longitudinal evidence that intensive, focused recasting is likely to be causally associated with higher levels of accuracy. When these findings are compared to those reported by Lyster (2004), the converging evidence suggests that recasts under tutoring conditions, but not in larger classroom settings, can be an effective means to promote long-term formal accuracy in a second language.

A longitudinal view on L2 instructional effectiveness is not only useful to establish the durability of effects, but it also helps elucidate effects that deploy unevenly and nonlinearly over time (cf. Mellow et al., 1996). A recent meta-analysis by Keck, Iberri-Shea, Tracy, and Wa-Mbaleka (forthcoming) yielded findings that underscore this point. These researchers synthesized 14 quasi-experimental studies (published between 1994 and 2003) that tested the direct link between interaction and acquisition of L2 forms. When they aggregated and compared effect sizes on immediate versus delayed posttests, they uncovered a systematic association between the timing of the posttests and the magnitude of effects for the two design features of task-essentialness and task usefulness (see Loschky & Bley-Vroman, 1993). Namely, aggregated effect sizes yielded by immediate posttests suggested no difference between task essential and task useful interaction treatments, as both were equally effective; but when effect sizes from delayed posttests were inspected, a trustworthy (that is, statistically significant) and large difference was noted, as groups who had experienced L2 forms through task essential treatments, rather than task useful treatments, were able to demonstrate more knowledge of the given forms on delayed post-tests ($d=1.66$ versus $d=.76$, respectively). Keck et al. were able to capture this important effect for task-essentialness, which was theoretically postulated first by Loschky and Bley-Vroman (1993) but had not been investigated in any single primary study, thanks to the meta-analysis methodology, but also because 10 of the 14 interaction studies synthesized featured delayed post-tests, scheduled as soon as seven days and as late as sixty days after the treatment.

In sum, we wish to reiterate the importance of this overall move towards a more longitudinal view on instructional effectiveness in SLA research. Even though quasi-experimental, cross-sectional designs have been predominant in this research domain, issues of intensity, timeliness, duration, and durability are hotly debated (see Doughty & Williams, 1998; Mellow et al., 1996; Norris & Ortega, 2000; Spada, 1997). Because the theoretical and educational claims implied in L2 instructional studies are tantamount with claims about change that unfolds gradually (but not linearly) over time and that is long-lasting, they will ultimately demand longitudinal evidence from researchers working in this SLA domain.

Recent Qualitative Longitudinal SLA Research

A fourth noticeable trend is the gradual accumulation of longitudinal research that employs primarily qualitative methodologies. These qualitative longitudinal studies are usually framed within Vygotskian sociocultural theory (Lantolf & Thorne, forthcoming), or within a socialization theory perspective (Kramsch, 2002; Watson-Gegeo, 2004), and they sometimes draw from both. Accumulation is only gradual, however, because the focus in these longitudinal studies is far from homogeneous.

Sociocultural SLA Longitudinal Studies

Recent qualitative longitudinal studies framed within a Vygostkian sociocultural perspective range from microanalysis of paralinguistic aspects of interaction (e.g., in the 15-week study of gesture development by a Taiwanese EFL student reported in McCafferty, 2002), to qualitative observation of classroom life and the contingencies of motivation (e.g., in the account of a summer experience with Chinese as a foreign language classroom learning presented by Lantolf & Genung, 2002), to autobiographical longitudinal accounts of the relationship between pronunciation and identity in foreign language learning (Marx, 2002). We will examine in some detail this last study, because of its unique and promising approach to mapping longitudinal change qualitatively.

Marx (2002) offers a detailed autobiographical chronicle of the development of identity that she underwent over three years of living in Germany, and as her accent in her second foreign language (German, which she had learned after French) became a site of identity (trans)formation. She frames this chronicle theoretically by positing six longitudinal stages originally proposed by Pavlenko (1998). When Marx arrived in Germany and was identified as "American" because of her English-accented German, she felt displaced and defined herself for the first time as "Canadian," in opposition to the American identity (understood as "from the United States") that her German interlocutors attributed to her. In a second stage after four months in the target environment, she developed a French accent in her German. This accent, which implied a loss of her Canadian identity, nevertheless allowed her to be identified by German interlocutors as "anything but American." After one year immersed in the L2 setting, stage three emerged as Marx consciously attempted to develop a native-like accent that would allow her to pass for a German native speaker. After two years, stage four was reached: the construction of her L2 identity, and with it her native-like accent, had consolidated, while her L1 began to experience signs of loss through the emergence of a British accent that in fact was truly "foreign" for her. After three years in Germany, Marx reentered the L1 context. This fifth stage lasted for about three months and was characterized by a strong British or German accented English. This foreign accent allowed her to position herself as "not just Canadian," that is, as someone who has been transformed by the experience of being a foreigner and a nonnative speaker. After three months, however, the final sixth stage of learner identity formation emerged. That is, her Canadian identity was finally reconstructed and her foreign accent in English subsided.

The autobiographical methodology that Marx (2002) adopted, together with her theoretical framework for identity transformation through participation in and out of L1 and L2 communities, makes this study unique as a three-year longitudinal account. It provides valuable theoretical and psychological insights into learner agency and identity negotiation, in ways that highlight, from the privileged vantage point of the agent, the dynamic development of multicompetence (Cook, 2002) as a learner transits through chronological and social time.

Ethnographies of L2 Learners

Socialization theory has also begun to contribute increasingly large numbers of longitudinal studies that chart the development of academic literacies in a second language. These studies tend to adopt a case study methodology and employ a rich mixture of qualitative approaches, including microanalysis of discourse and ethnographic observation and interviews. An illustrative case is Kobayashi (2003), who studied two undergraduate students from Japan during their preparation outside of class for their first group oral presentation in their first semester of study abroad, in a Canadian university. Although the preparation for the academic oral assignment was confined to a short cycle of five days, Kobayashi draws his insights from wider ethnographic data of the entirety of this Japan-Canada exchange program, which involved one academic year and a total of eighty undergraduate Japanese students. He uncovers a preparation process comprised of three stages spread over five days of meetings and group work. During the first stage, the students negotiated task content and assignment expectations, often using their shared L1 (Japanese) and drawing on their collaborative interpretation of written class documents. At a second stage, they collaborated to generate the language of the oral presentation. This stage was characterized by L1-L2 code-switching and by reliance on multiple modalities (speech and writing), supported by the use of technological literacy involving Powerpoint. A strong sense of audience and genre was also captured in the second-stage group data. The third and final preparation stage was devoted to rehearsal of the presentation, and favored the use of the L2 (English) and peer coaching, often through theatrical appropriation of the teacher voice by members of the group who acted as critics of each member's rehearsed contribution. Kobayashi invokes Rogoff's (1995) notion of "participatory appropriation" to acknowledge that true longitudinal data would be necessary to ascertain whether the preparation practices uncovered eventually contributed to the students' development of oral presentation skills in their future academic endeavors.

It is indeed surprising that many longitudinal qualitative studies adopting a case study or ethnographic approach end up reporting on only a small subset of the richer longitudinal data, making readers wait on a promised larger study that may take years (and several other shorter-spanned reports drawn out of the larger study) to appear in print. This trend is no doubt in part explained by the academic pressure to produce publications at a rate that works against multiple-year engagement with the same site and participants (this same pressure may also discourage dissertators from choosing longitudinal methodologies). However, even when considering ethnographic studies, a more fundamental issue emerges as well. Namely, we repeatedly encountered cases where an ethnographic report spanned long enough to be considered longitudinal in its own right, yet it was unclear whether it should be considered longitudinal because the results were presented with little attention to illuminating change over time. For example, Gebhard (2002) collected data from third and fourth graders at a magnet school in California for over two years. She motivated her focus on these grades during elementary school as "important turning points" in the academic trajectories of children at this age. She contextualized her findings against a four-year longitudinal perspective on the changing demographic, curricular, and material landscape of the school. Jackson (2002) drew her insights about classroom oral participation from a three-year ethnography of Chinese undergraduate students majoring in business at a Hong Kong university. She carefully triangulated a survey approach with systematic and in-depth observations and interviews over a 14-week semester. Similarly, Leki (2001) documented six English L2 students' semester-long experiences during group projects across university classes, but drew on a fuller longitudinal perspective and even richer data on the same informants over their total university life experience, which lasted for five years. In light of such features, all three ethnographic studies could be considered indeed "longitudinal." Yet, all three turn out to present a thick but relatively static description of the problems they sought to understand. The goal of these researchers in each case seems to have been, rather than to document and understand change over time, to capture continuity and to achieve deep understanding of roles, interrelationships, and intentionalities in ecologies of second language learning that are viewed as stable over time. We will return to this observation in our discussion in the next section.

Future Directions

The studies reviewed in this chapter, together with many other longitudinal studies of L2 learning and learners that have accumulated over the years since the inception of SLA, point at many implicit observations and questions regarding the unique benefits and the special challenges of investigating second language and literacy development over time, from a truly longitudinal perspective. One generalization that should serve SLA researchers well is that longitudinal research can be as diverse as the epistemological approaches that inspire it. This diversity is likely to continue in the future, and we hope it will also encourage longitudinal research that capitalizes on the strengths of mixed methods designs (see Johnson & Onwuegbuzie, 2004; Tashakkori & Teddlie, 2002). The following are some of the more persistent issues that we saw emerging across studies and authors.

How Long is "Longitudinal" ? Time Scales and Turning Points

A main definitional feature of longitudinal research is its long time span. Yet, little is known about the optimal length of observation for the longitudinal study of bilingual and biliterate development. When the focus is on linguistic development, there are often as many arguments to call for studies that span a few months to capture the phenomenon of interest (e.g., an observation period of about a year was enough for the development of English past perfect to be mapped in 10 of the 16 learners in Bardovi-Harlig, 1994), as there are to posit the entire life time of a learner as the right time frame for longitudinal SLA investigations (e.g., a 16-year observation span may not be sufficient evidence in the case of fossilization; Han, 2004). Yet few SLA researchers have acknowledged this challenge or discussed related methodological choices explicitly in their longitudinal reports. Most recent longitudinal SLA studies span anywhere between three or four months and up to six years. This seems related to two factors: (a) the influence of child first language acquisition studies, where longitudinal research is scaled on biological time; and (b) the convenient scaling of other studies on institutional time, particularly the one-semester and four-year periods widely meaningful in tertiary education, where many SLA studies are conducted. Thus, decisions about how long is long enough for the longitudinal study of L2 development are implicitly made in SLA research by recourse to biological and institutional time scales.

A main caveat to consider is that SLA researchers lack the certainty afforded by a biological scale such as that intrinsically given in child first language acquisition. Institutional schedules, on the other hand, may be at odds with social and developmental chronologies experienced by the L2 learners (for a useful discussion of such cases in educational longitudinal research, see Entwisle, Alexander, and Olson, 2002). We would like to suggest that, whether biological or institutional scales are chosen for longitudinal SLA research, they can be better motivated when key events and turning points in the social or institutional context investigated are considered. Indeed, such crucial turning points can be essential in motivating the appropriate length of observation.

When it comes to charting the developmental evolution (arguably, from emergence to mastery) of a given L2 linguistic feature, a strategic option would be to center on defining the time scale of the specific learning phenomenon under inquiry, rather than on the biological chronology of the subjects. Such strategy lies behind Belz and Kinginger's (2002) operationalization of the Vygostkian concept of microgenesis, which offers guidance for establishing the organic length of observation needed to map out the history of a learning event. Namely, these researchers collected a large longitudinal corpus of electronic communication transcripts (contextualized with a wealth of quantitative and qualitative data collected during the implementation of their three-year project). They then undertook "a thorough review of the interactions in the database, arranged chronologically, to select cases" (p. 196) of critical incidents involving the use of *tu/vous* and *Du/Sein* and decided to go as far before and after the incident in the data as was needed to trace the history of the phenomenon longitudinally. Aided by this inspection process, Belz and Kinginger determined an observation window around the critical events of 60 days (for the French student) and 49 days (for the German student) and they sampled data at five and nine observation points, respectively, within that window. Although rather short by traditional longitudinal methodological standards, this was precisely the organic length of observation needed to map out the history of the two critical incidents.

Notably, Belz and Kinginger (2002) had engaged in a wider three-year longitudinal study during which they had collected a substantial longitudinal corpus representative of the full length of the telecollaboration project. The availability of such a rich (and longer spanning) longitudinal corpus was therefore crucial in enabling the microgenetic method to study critical incidents, and allowed the researchers to identify the appropriate length of observation. In future studies using this microgenetic approach, an improvement could be to further inspect data recorded for the same participants in the full longitudinal corpus. This would allow researchers to trace evidence for the long-term impact of the critical incidents on learners' overall development of the L2 aspect under study, in effect enabling them to address Rogoff's (1995) longitudinal construct of "participatory appropriation."

Programmatic longitudinal SLA studies, which often scale study length on institutional time, also attest to the usefulness of considering turning points. For Lightbown et al. (2002), this meant including a long enough period of observation that would allow researchers to look at the transition from elementary to secondary school; for Klapper and Rees (2003), it meant documenting the turning point of the study abroad experience. In the future, it will also be useful to situate individual change over time against institutional and even sociopolitical and historical time. We also hope the field engages in explicit discussion of the relative merits of various criteria and rationales for determining the appropriate length for investigating specific SLA research questions longitudinally.

Multiwave Data Collection: How Many Waves, and How Comparable?

Another constitutive feature of longitudinal research is multiwave data, because data are collected repeatedly and usually more than twice to map change and growth over time. Thus, associated with the question of appropriate overall study length is that of optimal timing (frequency and spacing) of measurements. Our discussion about scales and turning points is equally relevant when making the decision of how often participants need to be observed and data collected, in that the estimated chronological scope of biological and institutional key events should help determine appropriate frequency and total number of observation points (see Entwisle et al., 2002). In addition, there is a likely trade-off in longitudinal SLA research among three factors: the overall length of study, the size of the sample, and the frequency of data collection waves. Finally, we would like to stress that the frequency of data collection is in part a matter of grain size of the phenomenon under investigation. It would certainly be impossible to attain the level of detail needed to chart many L2 developmental phenomena without striving for frequent data collection waves. For example, Bardovi-Harlig (1994) collected all classroom assignment products over six seven-week terms, for a total study length of slightly under one and a half years. She divided the language samples into two-week periods and sampled three texts per learner from each period. Consequently, her analyses of L2 development of past perfect are truly developmental and longitudinal, as they reflect individual growth data consisting of 34 waves in the best individual cases. In this sense, the case-study in depth approach chosen by descriptive-quantitative SLA researchers, which is modeled on first language acquisition research, represents a strength. For other longitudinal SLA research programs, however, it may be more appropriate to choose yearly or biannual data collection waves, as is the case with programmatic SLA longitudinal studies.

A special challenge with multiple data collection points that is likely to arise in any longitudinal SLA designs is the comparability of observations. The problem is that when different tasks and topics are employed over the length of a longitudinal study, it is difficult to disentangle time-induced and topic-or task-induced variability. Such topic-specific effects were found, for example, by Kim and Hall (2002), who reported large amounts of book-induced variability, as some books elicited much briefer role plays from the children than other books did, regardless of the time period at which the data were collected. This problem could be minimized logically by keeping elicitation techniques and content as similar as possible across waves. On the other hand, however, this may not always be the best strategy. For one, if SLA researchers were to repeat exactly the same tasks and the same topics over long periods of longitudinal study, the potential for diminished interest (and even demotivation or boredom), as well as practice effects, among participants would be a clear danger to the validity of the data. Further, it is possible that certain tasks are inappropriate at early points of development (because they require knowledge of the L2 that is not in place yet) or for the initial waves of data collection (because the participants, for example, are too young in the beginning of the study to be able to understand the task instructions). Such constraints were likely to be a consideration in Lightbown et al. (2002), for example, because what third graders and eighth graders can do with and in their L2 (and their L1) looks rather different. Thus, enhancing the equatability of data collection points is a formidable challenge in SLA longitudinal research.

At least for studies in which learners' general cognitive and linguistic abilities are not posited to change dramatically over the course of a lengthy investigation, a good strategy to deal with the multiwave comparability problem is to build in a cyclical elicitation schedule. Although it is unclear whether Kim and Hall (2002) planned this by design, they were able to compare four points of data for each of the seven books employed during the treatment, precisely because each book remained constant for four data collection waves, all four being equidistant in time over four months. In essence, then, in this study the longitudinal data analyses on each new book can be taken as seven cases of four-month long replications in search for reliable evidence of instruction-induced change over time. Even better would be the planning of cyclical elicitation points where similar tasks or content are employed over equally-spaced waves, interspersed with a range of dissimilar tasks, also spaced at equal intervals over the length of the study. This would ensure anchored points of comparison as well as strategic points of more varied performance that would not only improve participants' engagement but also enhance the richness of the longitudinal corpus available for study. Other creative strategies will need to be developed (and this problem discussed more explicitly) by longitudinal researchers so as to preserve the comparability of observations while ensuring participant affective, cognitive, and linguistic investment in the tasks and tests used.

Innovative Use of Analytical Options for Quantitative Longitudinal SLA Research

We found a general methodological shortcoming in current practices among longitudinal SLA researchers who draw on quantitative data, particularly in those studies that focused on program or instruction effects, because in these cases the number of participants and the quasi-experimental designs call for the use of inferential statistical analyses. Namely, none of these studies have benefited from advances in longitudinal quantitative analysis that began in the 1970s and that have been recently updated and presented in a comprehensive fashion by Singer and Willett (2003). Instead, SLA longitudinal data are often analyzed by recourse to the same inferential statistics that are employed in cross-sectional research (t-tests, multivariate analysis, and so on). Moreover, the larger-sized studies are often less about longitudinal change of a group (and much less so of individuals within the group), and more about comparing cohorts at repeated intervals of time. That is, often these multiwave between-groups comparisons are conceptually cross-sectional, and only indirectly longitudinal (e.g., Klapper & Rees, 2003; Lightbown et al., 2002). This tendency to recast longitudinal change through the analytical lens of repeated cross-sectional comparisons partly explains the absence of analysis of magnitude of longitudinal change in longitudinal SLA studies (in the form of repeated-measures effect sizes; see Ortega, 2003). In the future more SLA researchers may seek to map the L2 developmental path of a cohort transiting through curricular and instructional time with key turning points, different phases of stagnation and differently-paced development, and nonlinear progress. If this is the case, and more large-size longitudinal quantitative studies are conducted in SLA, it will be important to train ourselves in the use of statistical analytical options that are available specifically for use with longitudinal designs and data.

Strengthening Longitudinal Qualities of Ethnographic Studies

As mentioned earlier, when it comes to ethnographic qualitative studies of L2 learners, what counts as "longitudinal" is not easily decided. Sheer length of study and multiwave data collection are definitional features of longitudinal research in the social sciences, but so are two research goals: to capture change over time and to establish antecedent and consequent relations (cf. Phelps, Furstenberg, & Colby, 2002). Although the feature of prolonged engagement undeniably makes ethnographies of L2 learners "longitudinal" in one sense, ethnographers of L2 learning do not always appear to enter the multiple-year study with longitudinal research goals explicitly formulated. This does not need to be the case, however, as qualitative and specifically ethnographic studies can provide the most convincing evidence for fine-grained conceptualizations of change and growth and even for richly contextualized antecedent and consequent relations (for how qualitative research can do the latter and address causality in addition to description, see Maxwell, 2004).

Some L2 ethnographies in the past have successfully embodied all definitional features of longitudinal research. For example, Peirce (1995) ethnographically documented shifts and changes in five immigrant women's motivation and investment to learn and use English. From the recently published literature, an excellent example is Vavrus (2002), who reports on an in-depth and longitudinal investigation of high school students' changing views of the benefits of English-medium instruction versus vernacular education in Tanzania. Vavrus collected her ethnographic data over six years and three waves of surveys and focus groups with enrolled students who eventually became graduates from five high schools in the same Kilimanjaro area. Studies such as these reflect the best features of qualitative research drawing on ethnographic techniques and adopting a complex longitudinal view on L2 learners' lives. They strive to produce thick descriptions as much as depictions of change and growth over long periods of time.

Concluding Remarks

Research practices and disciplinary discussions in SLA typically favor a cross-sectional view of language learning and, in spite of much lip service, discussions about longitudinal research are scarce. In this review, we have highlighted recent trends in longitudinal SLA research, paying particular attention to broad design choices and foci of research organized around four trends of SLA longitudinal investigations, with key exemplary studies described for each trend. We have also reflected on some of the challenges and opportunities afforded by these longitudinal research programs.

We hope more explicit discussions will ensue in the future regarding what makes a study "longitudinal" and what the unique benefits and challenges of doing longitudinal SLA research are. We also hope SLA researchers will increasingly seek to look at second language and literacy development longitudinally. Ultimately, longitudinal findings can have a central place in advancing our SLA theories and research programs. We are hopeful that the diversity and accumulation of recent and future longitudinal research will help chart the development of advanced L2 capacities and help us understand the appropriate timing, duration, and content of optimal educational practices for L2 learning across educational settings and multilingual contexts.

Note

1. We are indebted to *ARAL* editor, Mary McGroarty, for her comments on an earlier version of this paper. This article is based on findings from a larger synthesis of longitudinal research in applied linguistics, funded by a National Academy of Education/Spencer Postdoctoral Fellowship to the first author and a research assistantship to the second author. We would like to thank the National Academy of Education and the Spencer Foundation for their generous support of this work over the period of 2003–2005. The views expressed here are not necessarily those of either supporting entity.

REFERENCES

Abrahamsson, N. (2003). Development and recoverability of L2 codas: A longitudinal study of Chinese-Swedish interphonology. *Studies in Second Language Acquisition, 25*, 313–349.

Bardovi-Harlig, K. (1994). Reverse-order reports and the acquisition of tense: Beyond the principle of chronological order. *Language Learning, 44*, 243–282.

Bardovi-Harlig, K. (2002). A new starting point? Investigating formulaic use and input in future expressions. *Studies in Second Language Acquisition, 24*, 189–198.

Belz, J. A., & Kinginger, C. (2002). The cross-linguistic development of address form use in telecollaborative language learning: Two case studies. *The Canadian Modern Language Review, 59*, 189–214.

Byrnes, H. (2002). Toward academic-level foreign language abilities: Reconsidering foundational assumptions, expanding pedagogical options. In B. L. Leaver & B. Shektman (Eds.), *Developing professional-level language proficiency* (pp. 34–58). New York: Cambridge University Press.

Collier, V. P. (1989). How long? A synthesis of research on academic achievement in a second language. *TESOL Quarterly, 23*, 509–531.

Collins, L., Halter, R. H., Lightbown, P. M., & Spada, N. (1999). Time and the distribution of time in L2 instruction. *TESOL Quarterly, 33*, 655–680.

Cook, V. (Ed.). (2002). *Portraits of the L2 user.* Clevedon, UK: Multilingual Matters.

Cooper, H., & Hedges, L. V. (Eds.). (1994). *The handbook of research synthesis.* New York: Russell Sage Foundation.

Doughty, C., & Williams, J. (1998). Pedagogical choices in focus on form. In C. Doughty & J. Williams (Eds.), *Focus on form in classroom second language acquisition* (pp. 197–261). New York: Cambridge University Press.

Ellis, R. (2003). *Task-based language learning and teaching.* New York: Oxford University Press.

Entwisle, D. R., Alexander, K. L., & Olson, L. S. (2002). Baltimore Beginning School study in perspective. In E. Phelps, F. F. J. Furstenberg, & A. Colby (Eds.), *Looking at lives: American longitudinal studies of the twentieth century* (pp. 167–193). New York: Russell Sage Foundation.

Gebhard, M. (2002). Fast capitalism, school reform, and second language literacy practices. *The Canadian Modern Language Review, 59*, 15–52.

Han, Z.-H. (2002). A study of the impact of recasts on tense consistency in L2 output. *TESOL Quarterly, 36*, 543–572.

Han, Z.-H. (2004). *Fossilization in adult second language acquisition.* Clevedon, UK: Multilingual Matters.

Hansen, J. G. (2004). Developmental sequences in the acquisition of English L2 syllable codas: A preliminary study. *Studies in Second Language Acquisition, 26,* 85–124.

Harley, B., & Hart, D. (1997). Language aptitude and second-language proficiency in classroom learners of different starting ages. *Studies in Second Language Acquisition, 19,* 379–400.

Hatch, E., & Lazaraton, A. (1991). *The research manual: Design and statistics for applied linguistics.* New York: Harper Collins/Newbury House.

Huebner, T. (1983). *A longitudinal analysis of the acquisition of English.* Ann Arbor, MI: Karoma.

Hyltenstam, K., & Abrahamsson, N. (2003). Maturational constraints in SLA. In C. Doughty & M. H. Long (Eds.), *Handbook of second language acquisition* (pp. 539–588). Malden, MA: Blackwell.

Ishida, M. (2004). Effects of recasts on the acquisition of the aspectual form-te i-(ru) by learners of Japanese as a foreign language. *Language Learning, 54,* 311–394.

Jackson, J. (2002). Reticence in second language case discussions: Anxiety and aspirations. *System, 30,* 65–84.

Johnson, B. (2001). Toward a new classification of nonexperimental quantitative research. *Educational Researcher, 30* (2), 3–13.

Johnson, R. B., & Onwuegbuzie, A. J. (2004). Mixed methods research: A research paradigm whose time has come. *Educational Researcher, 33* (7), 14–26.

Karmiloff-Smith, K., & Karmiloff-Smith, A. (2001). *Pathways to language: From foetus to adolescent.* Cambridge, MA: Harvard University Press.

Keck, C., Iberri-Shea, G., Tracy, N., & Wa-Mbaleka, S. (forthcoming). Investigating the empirical link between interaction and acquisition: A quantitative meta-analysis. In J. M. Norris & L. Ortega (Eds.), *Synthesizing research on language learning and teaching.* Philadelphia, PA: John Benjamins.

Kim, D., & Hall, J. K. (2002). The role of an interactive book reading program in the development of second language pragmatic competence. *The Modern Language Journal, 86,* 332–348.

Klapper, J., & Rees, J. (2003). Reviewing the case for explicit grammar instruction in the university foreign language learning context. *Language Teaching Research, 7,* 285–314.

Kobayashi, M. (2003). The role of peer support in ESL students' accomplishment of oral academic tasks. *The Canadian Modern Language Review, 59,* 337–368.

Kramsch, C. (Ed.) (2002). *Language acquisition and language socialization: Ecological perspectives.* London: Continuum.

Lally, C. G. (Ed.) (2001). *Foreign language program articulation: Current practice and future prospects.* Westport, CT: Bergin & Garvey.

Lantolf, J. P., & Genung, P. B. (2002). "I'd rather switch than fight" : An activity-theoretic study of power, success, and failure in a foreign language. In C. Kramsch (Ed.) *Language acquisition and language socialization: Ecological perspectives* (pp. 175–196). London: Continuum.

Lantolf, J. P. & Thorne, S. L. (forthcoming). *Sociocultural theory and the sociogenesis of second language development.* New York: Oxford University Press.

Leki, I. (2001). "A narrow thinking system:" Non-English-speaking students in group projects across the curriculum. *TESOL Quarterly, 35*, 39–67.

Light, R., & Pillemer, D. (1984). *Summing up: The science of reviewing research.* Cambridge, MA: Harvard University Press.

Lightbown, P., Halter, R., White, J., & Horst, M. (2002). Comprehension-based learning: The limits of "do it yourself." *The Canadian Modern Language Review, 58*, 427–464.

Loschky, L., & Bley-Vroman, R. (1993). Grammar and task-based methodology. In G. Crookes & S. Gass (Eds.), *Tasks and language learning* (pp. 123–167). Clevedon, UK: Multilingual Matters.

Lyster, R. (2004). Differential effects of prompts and recasts in form-focused instruction. *Studies in Second Language Acquisition, 26*, 399–432.

Marx, N. (2002). Never quite a "native speaker:" Accent and identity in the L2-and the L1. *The Canadian Modern Language Review, 59*, 264–281.

Maxwell, J. A. (2004). Causal explanation, qualitative research, and scientific inquiry in education. *Educational Researcher, 33* (1), 3–11.

McCafferty, S. (2002). Gesture and creating zones of proximal development for second language learning. *The Modern Language Journal, 86*, 192–203.

Mellow, D., Reeder, K., & Forster, E. (1996). Using time-series research designs to investigate the effects of instruction on SLA. *Studies in Second Language Acquisition, 18*, 325–350.

Norris, J. M., & Ortega, L. (2000). Effectiveness of L2 instruction: A research synthesis and quantitative meta-analysis. *Language Learning, 50*, 417–528.

Ortega, L. (2003). Syntactic complexity measures and their relationship to L2 proficiency: A research synthesis of college-level L2 writing. *Applied Linguistics, 24*, 492–518.

Pavlenko, A. (1998). Second language learning by adults: Testimonies of bilingual writers. *Issues in Applied Linguistics, 9* (1), 3–19.

Peirce, B. N. (1995). Social identity, investment, and language learning. *TESOL Quarterly, 29*, 9–31.

Perdue, C., Benazzo, S., & Giuliano, P. (2002). When finiteness gets marked: The relation between morphosyntactic development and use of scopal items in adult language acquisition. *Linguistics, 40*, 849–890.

Phelps, E., Furstenberg, F. F. J., & Colby, A. (Eds.). (2002). *Looking at lives: American longitudinal studies of the twentieth century.* New York: Russell Sage Foundation.

Robinson, P. (2001). Task complexity, cognition and second language syllabus design: A triadic framework for examining task influences on SLA. In P. Robinson (Ed.), *Cognition and second language instruction* (pp. 287–318). New York: Cambridge University Press.

Rogoff, B. (1995). Observing sociocultural activity on three planes: Participatory appropriation, guided participation, and apprenticeship. In J. V. Wertsch, P. D. Rio & A. Alvarez (Eds.), *Sociocultural studies of mind* (pp. 139–164). New York: Cambridge University Press.

Sato, C. (1990). *The syntax of conversation in interlanguage development*. Tübingen: Gunter Narr.

Schmidt, R. (1983). Interaction, acculturation, and the acquisition of communicative competence. In N. Wolfson & E. Judd (Eds.), *Sociolinguistics and language acquisition* (pp. 137–174). Rowley, MA: Newbury House.

Schumann, J. H. (1978). *The pidginization process: A model for second language acquisition*. Rowley, MA: Newbury House.

Scovel, T. (1988). *A time to speak: A psycholinguistic inquiry into the critical period for human speech*. Rowley, MA: Newbury House.

Singer, J. D., & Willett, J. B. (2003). *Applied longitudinal data analysis: Modeling change and event occurrence*. New York: Oxford University Press.

Skehan, P. (2002). Theorising and updating aptitude. In P. Robinson (Ed.), *Individual differences and instructed language learning* (pp. 69–93). Philadelphia, PA: John Benjamins.

Spada, N. (1997). Form-focussed instruction and second language acquisition: A review of classroom and laboratory research. *Language Teaching, 29*, 1–15.

Tashakkori, A., & Teddlie, C. (Eds.). (2002). *The handbook of mixed methods in social and behavioral research*. Thousand Oaks, CA: Sage.

Vavrus, J. (2002). Postcoloniality and English: Exploring language policy and the politics of development in Tanzania. *TESOL Quarterly, 36*, 373–398.

Watson-Gegeo, K. A. (2004). Mind, language, and epistemology: Toward a language socialization paradigm for SLA. *The Modern Language Journal, 88*, 331–350.

3. APTITUDE AND SECOND LANGUAGE ACQUISITION

Peter Robinson

Recent second language acquisition (SLA) research into the cognitive abilities implicated in implicit, incidental, and explicit learning, and in learning and performance on tasks differing in their information processing demands has prompted new theoretical frameworks for conceptualizing L2 aptitude. This research is reviewed and related to measures of abilities operationalized in existing aptitude tests, as well as to measures of abilities that are the focus of more recent research in cognitive psychology. Finally, prospects for developing aptitude tests to serve the purposes of predicting both early and advanced level language learning success are discussed in the light of the SLA findings and aptitude frameworks reviewed.

This review focuses on contemporary research into instructed second language acquisition (SLA), and the extent to which its constructs, procedures, and findings can inform theoretical models of aptitude and further development of measures of abilities administered during aptitude tests. Second language (L2) learning aptitude is characterized as strengths individual learners have—relative to their population—in the cognitive abilities information processing draws on during L2 learning and performance in various contexts and at different stages. Theoretical frameworks for aptitude research, characterized in this way, have been proposed recently (Robinson, 2001c; Skehan, 2002; Sternberg, 2002). It is also now possible to 'look down'(see Deary, 2000, p. 4) from cognitive abilities for information processing to the subcomputational, physical level at which neural differences underlying abilities (see e.g., Garlick, 2002) and SLA processes (see, e.g., Chee, Soon, Lee, & Pellier, 2004; Tokowitcz & MacWhinney, in press) can be described.[1] Correspondingly, it is possible to 'look up' from research into cognitive abilities and information processing during SLA and examine the joint contributions of these personality traits *and* conative factors to a more broadly defined 'aptitude' for achieving L2 learning success using techniques for multidimensional modeling (Ackerman, 1999, 2003; Shavelson & Roeser, 2002). Both of these prospects will be referred to but not treated in any substantial depth in this review.

Specifically the research reviewed in this chapter focuses on the effects of individual differences in cognitive abilities on learning prompted by intervention and manipulation at three levels of pedagogic context: (a) the level of *learning condition*, and the relative effectiveness of implicit, incidental and explicit processing of L2 input (see studies in Hulstijn & DeKeyser, 1997; Hulstijn & R. Ellis, 2005; and DeKeyser, 2003, N.Ellis, in press, for review); (b) the level of *focus on form* (FonF), and the effectiveness of a variety of techniques for inducing learner attention to language form during communicative activity (see Doughty & Williams, 1998, for review); and (c) the level of *pedagogic task*, and the effects of different dimensions of task demands on L2 learning and performance (see R. Ellis, 2004; Robinson, 2001b, 2003b, in press a; Skehan, 1998, 1999, for review).

Research into these areas has often sought to identify differences in the relative effectiveness of particular learning conditions, FonF techniques, or task manipulations, by using pre-posttest, whole group designs, and then comparing gain scores and effect sizes (Rosenthal, Rosnow, & Rubin, 2000) resulting from learning taking place under each. A smaller body of research has additionally measured individual differences in cognitive abilities hypothesized to facilitate, or inhibit, cognitive processes drawn on during L2 learning under these conditions, from these techniques, or on these tasks. An assumption underlying much of this, and other non-SLA 'interactionist' research (see Ceci, 1996; Clark, 1997; Corno et al., 2002; Kyllonen & Lajoie, 2003; Sternberg, 2002; Sternberg & Wagner, 1994; Snow, 1987, 1994) is that learning contexts (see, e.g., Collentine & Freed, 2004), the pedagogic interventions taking place within them (see e.g., DeKeyser, in press; R. Ellis, 1999; Long, in press; VanPatten, 2004), and the cognitive processes they implicate (see e.g., Doughty, 2001; N. Ellis, 2001; Robinson, 1995b, 2001d; 2003a; Schmidt, 2001; Segalowitz & Freed, 2004), all have the effects they do in *interaction* with the patterns of abilities learners bring to those contexts. Some learners, that is, may be especially suited to learning under one condition, from one technique, or on one task, versus others. Consequently, this research can not only contribute to the development of aptitude measures suitable for assessing the global ability to profit from contemporary approaches to L2 instruction—it can also be used to guide decisions about how to match learners to the learning contexts and options to which they are most suited.

Early Developed Measures of Aptitude

The last three decades have each seen the appearance of an edited collection evaluating, and reconceptualizing the theory, measurement, and use of L2 learning aptitude tests (Diller, 1981; Parry & Stansfield, 1990; Robinson, 2002a). Traditionally L2 learning aptitude tests have been developed to predict differences in the *rate* at which L2 learning takes places (Carroll, 1981, 1990; Skehan, 1998; Spolsky, 1995), when starting "from scratch" (Carroll, 1990), and during *instructed* exposure to the L2 in programs which initially shelter learners from complex naturalistic input, and the processing and other performance demands learning from, and responding to it entails. They were not developed to predict the very *high levels* of attainment some selected candidates can continue to make progress towards after exiting instructional programs, or to measure their ability to profit from incidental L2 *exposure*, as it occurs in either instructed or uninstructed settings. Contemporary aptitude research is therefore addressing the issues of whether traditional measures can predict very high levels of attainment, and also the ability to profit from incidental exposure to the L2, and if not, what additional measures are needed to help ensure this.

An important design constraint on traditional language aptitude tests has been convenience (of both the length and format) of test administration, to groups of test-takers at one sitting. Such tests were designed to meet the paper-and-pencil methods of test administration common in the 1950s through 1970s, when they were developed and first administered. Predominantly, aptitude test-developers adopted this purpose, and accommodated this constraint, so that their tests could provide a basis for *selection* of those candidates for L2 instruction with the potential for relatively optimum success, usually in the U.S. government-funded learning programs which invested in the original test development and research (see Reed & Stansfield, 2004; Spolsky, 1995). With this goal in mind, selection was made on the basis of total aptitude test scores, as they resulted from performance on the limited (and so administratively feasible—at one sitting) number of subtests each test involved.

Prediction of rate, and feasibility of administration, with the goal of selection into programs (and subsequent assignment to languages of different levels of difficulty), were therefore the main purpose, constraint, and objective which the Modern Language Aptitude Test (MLAT; Carroll & Sapon, 1959), the Defense Language Aptitude Battery (DLAB; Peterson & Al Haik, 1976), and also VORD (a test of an artificial language) (Parry & Child, 1990) were funded and developed to meet. Closely related to the MLAT, PLAB and VORD in format and measurement scope is Pimsleur's Language Aptitude Battery (PLAB; Pimlseur, 1966), which differs mainly in that it was developed to be administered to a younger population than the postpuberty, teenage, and young adult population for which the MLAT, DLAB, and VORD were developed. Additionally, a version of MLAT for elementary level school-learners (EMLAT) was also developed in the 1960s. The DLAB and VORD measures are protected tests, administered only to United States government personnel, but MLAT has been more widely distributed and has been extensively used (sometimes in various translated versions) in SLA research.

These tests have served both SLA research and SL pedagogy well: Scores on them have often correlated quite highly with instructed language learning success in a variety of institutional contexts (see Dörnyei & Skehan, 2003; Ehrman, Leaver, & Oxford, 2003; Sawyer & Ranta, 2001; Skehan, 1989, 1998, 2002, for review), and have been useful in predicting some areas of learning difficulty in the early stages of SLA (see Ehrman, 1996, 1998; Grigorenko, 2002; Sparks & Ganschow, 2001, for review). Additionally versions of MLAT (DeKeyser, 2000) and PLAB (Harley & Hart, 1997, 2002) have been used to show that learners with a postcritical period age of L2 learning onset are much more dependent on the analytic abilities measured by these tests than pre-critical period child L2 learners. As Spolsky has noted, in summarizing results of the early phase of aptitude test development, "in seeking to make further advances in the field, it is unwise not to build on the work of our predecessors" (1995, p. 338).

Four Issues for Research and Development of Traditional Aptitude Tests

Useful as these tests have been, it is not difficult to build on this early work. Carroll himself, the developer of the MLAT, made some proposals in 1990 about areas of further research that could inform the further development of existing aptitude tests. Four of these areas, together with Carroll's proposals for research into them, are summarized here:

1. <u>How do the cognitive abilities measured in aptitude tests facilitate learning under different conditions of instructional exposure</u>? In 1990 Carroll was well aware that in the thirty years that had passed since the MLAT was developed and piloted considerable research had taken place within an information processing framework in cognitive psychology (see, e.g., Baars, 1986; Pellegrino & Glaser, 1979; Sternberg, 1977), and that this research could inform a clearer understanding of how mental abilities interacted with conditions of learning to promote SLA. In urging aptitude researchers to examine the cognitive processes contributing to performance on aptitude tests Carroll had this to say:

> An ability describes a special relation between characteristics of individuals and the characteristics of the tasks they perform with varying degrees of success . . . [there should be] a closer focus on similarities and differences between the mental operations required in an aptitude test and those required in foreign language learning (Carroll, 1990, pp. 25–26).

Current SLA research, summarized below, has addressed this issue by examining the extent to which individual differences (IDs) in cognitive abilities—some measured by traditional aptitude tests—contribute to implicit, incidental, and explicit learning, as well as to learning from various techniques for focus on form.

2. <u>What are the aptitude components that predict the ability to learn, and perform successfully on different types of pedagogic tasks</u>? Current SLA research has also been concerned to identify the information processing demands of tasks contributing to their cognitive and performative complexity and to study the effects of these on L2 learning. Although this research was not available to Carroll in

1990, he observed the following about the componential analysis of task demands and their potential relationship to cognitive abilities: "Further research in foreign language aptitude would require a more refined analysis of foreign language learning tasks in terms of the different cognitive abilities they call upon. I am not aware that much has been done in this direction" (Carroll, 1990, p. 26). As had been argued in the 1970s and 1980s for other areas of the school curriculum (see, e.g., Fleishman, 1978; Fleishman & Quaintance, 1984; Snow, 1987, 1994), Carroll saw that different language learning tasks may require different sets, or combinations, of abilities to be successfully performed. Matching individual differences in abilities to the information processing demands of different L2 tasks is also an area that is also now beginning to be systematically researched.

3. How different are aptitudes for early and advanced language learning? By 1990, there was also concern that whereas traditional tests such as MLAT were effective in predicting initial progress in language learning, they were seen to be less effective at predicting success at more advanced stages. Carroll was aware of this:

> In most of my research on foreign language aptitude, the criterion has been, essentially, rate of learning a language "from scratch" . . . it is possible that . . . an individual might be an excellent translator or a facile simultaneous interpreter by virtue of special abilities that do not come into play in early language learning stages but that do come into play at later stages. This immediately suggests that research might focus on abilities that would possibly be relevant in the later stages of foreign language attainment (Carroll, 1990, pp. 24–25).

This issue is also the focus of current speculation and is prompting exploratory empirical research that raises interesting theoretical questions: For example, how continuous, and how discontinuous are the predictive influences of ability factors across early and later stages of SLA? Is it possible that there are distinct combinations of abilities that predict L2 learning success at different stages of development?

4. What are the aptitude components that predict acquisition of pragmatic abilities? Of course, by 1990 Carroll was aware that since the MLAT was initially developed a much heavier pedagogic emphasis was being placed on the development of communicative ability, and success in using language, than had

been the case in the audiolingual classrooms of the late 1950s and 1960s where the MLAT was first piloted and then used to predict achievement in language programs. With this in mind Carroll commented:

> One promising direction is to develop tests that would exemplify language learning tasks that are not covered in existing batteries (e.g., tasks requiring the learning of novel linguistic pragmatic rules, such as, the rules concerning forms of address that depend on social or family status) (Carroll, 1990, p. 26).

Once again, this issue—linked to the nature of aptitude for advanced level language learning—is beginning to be conceptualized and researched.

Aptitude and Current SLA Research

Current SLA research into the measurement of aptitude seeks to build on, but go beyond, traditional tests, both in conceptualization of the theoretical construct and in delivery of assessment measures. Much of the research into issues Carroll raise earlier has used traditional measures of aptitude, particularly the MLAT, but additionally it has investigated the influence of other individual difference variables not measured directly by MLAT, such as phonological working memory (WM) capacity (see Baddeley, 2000; Chee et al., 2004; N. Ellis, 2001; McLaughlin, 1995; Miyake & Friedman, 1998; Williams & Lovatt, 2003). There have also been proposals to integrate WM measures into a much broader battery of aptitude subtests than operationalized in MLAT and other traditional tests. One argument in support of this has been that abilities are not dissociated in their effects on SLA, but have their effects in combination or "complexes" (Robinson, 2001c, 2002b; cf. Snow, 1987) which jointly facilitate processing and learning in a specific instructional context.

Figure 1 identifies ten basic cognitive abilities (in the inner circle, e.g., PS, processing speed) and their contribution to higher order aptitude factors (in the second circle, e.g., NTG, noticing the gap) important to processing and learning from input during the early stages of SLA. An example of how these abilities, and the higher order factors they contribute to, combine to make a joint contribution to SLA is the "aptitude complex" drawn on during the processing of information available in recasts (Doughty, 2001). Processing speed (PS; Anderson, 1992) and pattern recognition (PR; Sasaki, 1996) combine to enable learners to "notice the gap" (NTG; Schmidt & Frota, 1986) between their own, and an interlocutor's utterance during L2 communication. But fast analytic abilities alone are not enough. In addition, phonological working memory capacity (PWMC) and speed (PWMS) contribute to individual differences in the factor memory for contingent speech (MCS) which enables the two utterances to be maintained in WM long enough for the analytic cognitive comparison (Nelson, 1987) to be made. Learning from recasts is jointly enabled by the abilities contributing to the notice the gap and memory for contingent speech factors. Other such complexes have been proposed (Robinson, in press c) and are beginning to be operationalized and researched.

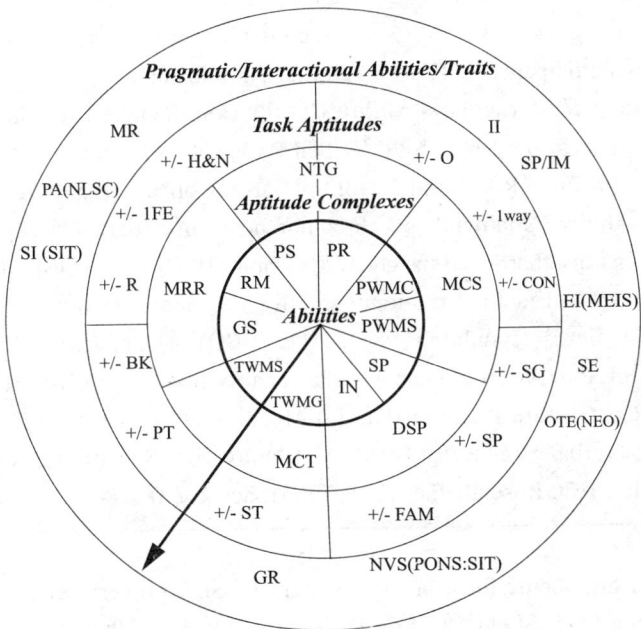

Figure 1: Aptitudes, development, and learning contexts: Changes in the relative contribution of aptitude factors to different aspects of L2 learning.
(Inner two circles: initial input-based learning; third circle: output practice and complex task performance; and outer circle: transfer of task performance to real-world interactive settings.)

> **Key to Figure 1:**
> **Abilities** (inner circle): PS = Processing Speed; PR = Pattern recognition; PWMC = Phonological Working Memory Capacity; PWMS = Phonological Working Memory Speed; SP = Semantic Priming; IN = Lexical Inferencing; TWMC = Text Working Memory Capacity; TWMS = Text Working Memory Speed; GS = Grammatical Sensitivity; RM = Rote Memory
> **Aptitude Complexes** (second circle): NTG = Noticing the Gap; MCS = Memory for Contingent Speech; DSP = Deep Semantic Processing; MCT = Memory for Contingent Text; MRR = Metalinguistic Rule Rehearsal
> **Task Aptitudes** (third circle): +/-ST = Single Task; +/-PT = Planning Time; +/-BK = Background Knowledge; +/-H&N = Here-and-Now; +/-FE = Few Elements; +/-R = Reasoning; +/-O = Open Task; +/-1way = 1-Way Task; +/-CON = Convergent Task; +/-SG = Same Gender Participants; +/-SP = Same Proficiency Participants; +/-FAM = Familiar Participants
> **Pragmatic/Interactional Abilities/Traits** (fourth circle): II = Interactional Intelligence (Levinson, 1995); SP/IM = Self Presentation/Impression Management (Goffman, 1967); MR = Mind Reading (Baron-Cohen, 1995); PA (NLSC) = Pragmatic Ability (Nonliteral speech comprehension; Langdon et al., 2002); SI (SIT) = Social Insight (Social Insight Test; Chapin, 1967); EI (MEIS) = Emotional Intelligence (Multifactor Emotional Intelligence Scale; Mayer et al., 2000); SE = Self-Efficacy (Bandura, 1986); OTE (NEO) = Openness to Experience (Neuroticism, Extroversion, Openness Personality Inventory; Costa & MacRae, 1985); GR = Gesture Reading (Goldin-Meadow et al., 1993); NVS (PONS; SIT) = Nonverbal Sensitivity (Profile of Nonverbal Sensitivity Test; Social Interpretation Test; Rosenthall et al., 1979; Archer, 1983)

Similar arguments for a broader battery of SLA process-sensitive aptitude subtests come from Skehan (2002; Dörnyei & Skehan, 2003) who argues that aptitude batteries should capture the abilities drawn on at different stages of L2 processing—broadly defined as the input, central processing, and output stages. These include the phonetic sensitivity, grammatical sensitivity (GS) and paired associates, rote memory (RM) abilities measured by MLAT, but also include abilities drawn on in effectively lexicalizing learned L2 grammatical patterns, and automatically accessing these during fluent L2 production (see also Segalowitz, 2003; Segalowitz & Freed, 2004). Innovations in online, computerized delivery and scoring of mental tests (e.g., Sands, Waters & McBride, 1997) have made the administration of larger test batteries (to individuals, over time, not whole groups at a single sitting) a very feasible prospect, with many advantages (to the test taker and test user) over traditional paper-and-pencil aptitude test administration procedures. Whether such larger batteries add any incremental validity to the predictive power of earlier, more parsimonious tests is an empirical issue. Certainly, if early and later stages of language learning draw on different abilities, or combinations of abilities, then larger batteries will be necessary to inform selection, and also diagnosis and pedagogic use of aptitude profiles. Similar issues are prompting renewed efforts to theorize and research the relationships between aptitude, achievement and pedagogy in other areas of instruction (see Kyllonen & Lajoie, 2003; Shavelson & Roeser, 2002; Sternberg & Grigorenko, 2003).

Finally, although some current aptitude studies still use intact classes to examine the influence of aptitude on learning, as assessed by tests of achievement following a variety of instructional programs over extended periods of time (see, e.g., Harley & Hart, 1997; Ranta, 2002)—a procedure Carroll and Sapon also followed in originally validating the MLAT—many studies now also adopt experimental designs and random selection and allocation of participants to learning conditions, with the aim of investigating the interaction of individual differences variables with specific learning processes in both the shorter (de Graaff, 1997; Robinson, 1997a, 1997b; Williams, 1999; Williams & Lovatt, 2003) and longer term (Robinson, 2002c, in press b). Both kinds of research strategy are, of course, necessary in clarifying the extent of the influence of individual differences in cognitive abilities on instructed SLA, and in further identifying the ability-structure of language learning aptitude.

Aptitude and Awareness: Implicit, Incidental, and Explicit Learning

The first area of SLA research and aptitude test development, described previously, concerns the relationship of cognitive abilities to learning under different conditions of instructional exposure. This research aims to identify relationships between the information processing demands of different "instructional sets" to the L2 learning targets (for example +/-awareness of targets, +/-intention to learn targets, and +/-explicit metalinguistic information about the "form" of targets), and the extent of the influence of these instructional sets on learning (de Graaff, 1997; de Jong, in press; DeKeyser, 1995, 1997; N. Ellis, 1993; Robinson, 1996a, 1997b, 2002c, in press b; Robinson & Ha, 1993; Williams, 1999). DeKeyser (1995), Robinson (1996a), and de Graaff (1997) all found that L2 learning in explicit conditions, involving some degree of metalinguistic awareness and instruction, was at least as effective as learning in implicit conditions where the stimulus domain was complex—and was, on the whole, much more effective where the L2 stimulus domain was simple. In addition, de Graaff (1997), Robinson (1997a), and Williams (1999) all found individual differences in aptitude (measured by subtests of traditional tests, such as the MLAT) and memory ability influenced learning across implicit and explicit conditions. This suggests that adult L2 learning under all conditions of exposure is fundamentally similar (Robinson, 1996b, 2001c) because differences in the extent of learning in these conditions are affected by individual differences in the conscious information processing abilities measured by the aptitude and memory tests. Further, where strengths in patterns of abilities, or aptitudes, match the processing demands of specific instructional sets, this research has suggested, such patterns of abilities additionally facilitate L2 learning. These findings stand in opposition to Krashen's (1982) claim that implicit learning, or "acquisition" is fundamentally different from explicit "learning" because (Krashen argued) the former (in contrast to the latter) draws on unconscious processes, outside of executive control, and is insensitive to individual differences in the abilities measured by traditional aptitude tests such as MLAT.

If "noticing" and awareness are necessary for SLA (as Schmidt, 2001, has claimed) then an issue for aptitude research is to identify individual differences in abilities that promote it—across a range of pedagogically relevant conditions of exposure to the L2. With this in mind Robinson (1996a, 1997a) studied the effects of four conditions (implicit, memorize examples only; incidental, process examples for meaning; rule-search, try to find rules; and instructed, apply a rule explanation to examples) on the acquisition of simple, versus complex L2 structures. Implicit learners in the study, in general, learned poorly. However, for implicit learners in particular, there was a strong link between one measure of L2 aptitude (the grammatical sensitivity subtest of the MLAT), posttest L2 learning success, and awareness (assessed by self-reports of looking for regularities in the input, and ability to verbalize partial rules about the structure of the input). Learners in the implicit learning condition with high aptitude were found to be those most likely to attest to having looked for rules, and also to be able to verbalize rules. This aptitude subtest, therefore, positively predicted awareness during implicit L2 exposure, and awareness led to more learning for implicit learners. Aptitude correlated significantly and positively with learning in all conditions, except, however, the incidental condition.

Krashen (1982) would take this latter finding as some support for his claim that incidental learning while processing for meaning ("acquisition") is insensitive to IDs in aptitude. However, the two MLAT subtests used (RM, rote memory and GS, grammatical sensitivity) were less likely to have matched the specific processing demands of this condition than other conditions (memorize examples, search for rules, or apply learned rules to examples). In a subsequent study (Robinson, 2002c) these measures of aptitude were similarly found to be poor predictors of incidental learning, but a measure of working memory for text, based on Daneman and Carpenter's (1980) reading span test, was significantly and positively correlated with incidental learning. This is understandable because processing input for meaning during incidental learning creates no opportunities for rote memorization or for the intentional application of explicit metalinguistic knowledge to input (see Hulstijn, 2001, 2003; Smith, Nobe, Robinson, Strong, Tani, & Yoshiba, 2004). However, it does draw on the ability to process for meaning while simultaneously switching attention to form during problems in semantic processing—an ability strongly related to working memory capacity (Arrington & Logan, 2004: Baddeley, 2000; Logan, 2004). One conclusion to be drawn from these studies, then, is that whereas conventional measures of aptitude are suitable for predicting successful learning during some conditions of exposure, they also need to be supplemented by other measures (such as working memory), especially where the instruction involves processing for meaning alone, with no intentional focus on form.

Aptitude, Attention, and Focus on Form (FonF) Techniques

Related to the laboratory research previously described is classroom research into the effects of different kinds of intervention that aim to direct learner attention to L2 form during activities which have a primary focus on meaning and the achievement of communicative goals (see, Doughty, 2004; Doughty & Williams, 1998). The degree of attention to, and awareness of, form during classroom L2 processing has been manipulated via use of various focus on form (FonF) techniques such as input flooding (a minimally intrusive technique for directing attention to form during input processing, see e.g., White, 1998); input enhancement (see Leeman, Arteagoita, Fridman, & Doughty, 1995; Robinson, 1997b); recasting (Doughty & Varela, 1998; Leeman, 2003; Lyster, 2004; Philp, 2003); and structured input processing with and without rule explanation (Benati, 2004; Farley, 2004; VanPatten & Cadierno, 1993)—the latter studies often adopting increasingly more communicatively intrusive, and attentionally demanding (and so message-content distracting) FonF techniques.

Findings for research into less communicatively intrusive FonF techniques have produced mixed results to date, with some studies showing input enhancement and recasting to have an effect on subsequent L2 learning, but not others. One reason for this may be that, in any studied population some L2 learners' aptitudes, or sets of abilities, are more suited to learning from one FonF technique versus another. Two studies to date indicate this may be so with regard to recasting. Mackey, Philp, Egi, Fujii, and Tatsumi (2002), using students at a range of levels in a foreign language EFL program, found significant positive relationships between measures of phonological working memory capacity and noticing of information targeted by recasts (features of wh-question formation) delivered on three consecutive days during communicative L2 interaction. However, learners at lower developmental levels showed this relationship more clearly than those at higher developmental levels. Similarly, Robinson and Yamaguchi (Robinson, 1999; Robinson & Yamaguchi, 1999) found high significant positive correlations of measures of phonetic sensitivity and also rote memory (using Sasaki's Language Aptitude Battery for the Japanese, LABJ, 1996), with learning from recasts by university-level, nonlanguage majors, during task-based interaction over a five-week period. Learning was measured by pre-and posttest gain scores on an elicited imitation measure of relative clause production, the form targeted in the study.

The findings for a positive relationship between phonetic sensitivity, memory ability and learning from recasts in Robinson and Yamaguchi's (1999) study, and phonological working memory capacity and noticing of recast information in Mackey et al. (2002) suggest that these abilities are positively implicated in aptitude for learning from the recasting FonF technique. However, as with the finding for incidental learning in Robinson (1997a), reported earlier, in Robinson and Yamaguchi (1999) there were nonsignificant correlations of learning of relative clauses during task-based interaction (supplemented by targeted recasts) and the grammatical sensitivity aptitude subtest. These findings therefore allow an inference across contexts (laboratory studies of incidental learning, and classroom studies of focus on form during task-based learning) about the noninfluence of individual differences in grammatical sensitivity on incidental learning during processing for meaning. As with the laboratory research described previously, then, these findings suggest that learners may differ in their aptitude(s) for learning from one FonF technique versus another.

Aptitude, Task-based Learning, and Task Design

The second issue for SLA-informed research into aptitude test development concerns the relationship of aptitude to the information processing demands of different task types. Design features of L2 tasks hypothesized to impose differential information processing demands (e.g., single versus dual task; +/-reasoning, +/-planning time for the task, or +/-prior knowledge of the task domain) have been studied in recent years for their effects on the accuracy, fluency, and complexity of L2 production, and also on the amount of interaction, and uptake from task relevant input (see e.g., Bygate, 2001; R. Ellis, 2004; Foster & Skehan, 1996; Hardy & Moore, 2004; Ortega, 1999; Rahimpour, 1999; Robinson, 1995a, 2001a, 2003b; Robinson, Ting & Urwin, 1995; Skehan, 1998, 1999). This research has begun to show that some features of L2 task design, such as the complexity of cognitive demands, do have effects on L2 performance. Broadly in line with the claims of the Cognition Hypothesis, that increasing the cognitive and functional demands of tasks has effects on production and learning (Robinson, 2001b, 2003b, in press a), on complex versions of tasks there is less fluency, but sometimes greater accuracy (Gilabert, 2004; Iwashita, Elder, & MacNamara, 2001; Rahimpour, 1997; Robinson, 1995a), as well as more interaction (Hardy & Moore, 2004; Robinson, 2001a), and more extensive uptake and incorporation of premodified input (Robinson, 2003b, in press a) compared to simpler versions. Task repetition (Bygate, 2001), and the provision of planning time (R. Ellis, in press; Foster & Skehan, 1996; Ortega, 1999) are two ways in which the demands of a task can be reduced, and these have been shown, in a number of cases, to positively affect the fluency of L2 production, with potentially important consequences for the effects of task practice, and task preparedness on automatizing access to known material.

Although there are few findings to date, as with the FonF research, task research is now beginning to theorize and research the influence of IDs on learning and performance as it takes place on specific tasks during task-based L2 learning. This includes individual differences in the use of learning styles and strategies (Cohen, 2003; Oxford, Cho, Leung, & Kim, 2004), and motivation (Dörnyei, 2002, in press), as well as aptitude (Robinson, 2001b, 2003b, in press a; Skehan, 1998). This is important for the same reasons given earlier. That is, individual differences in cognitive abilities (and other factors) may also interact with L2 task characteristics to systematically affect speech production, uptake and learning, such that one type of learner may be systematically more fluent, more accurate, or notice and use more new information provided in the task input, on one type of task versus another. These are important issues for the development of theoretically motivated and researched L2 task-aptitude profiles that can be used to maximize on-task practice, and learning opportunities for learners.

Related to this issue, Niwa, (2000) has shown that as L2 tasks increase in complexity so IDs in cognitive abilities increasingly differentiate performance. This relatively greater sensitivity of complex task performance and learning to individual differences in relevant abilities has been demonstrated in many previous studies of aptitude-treatment interactions outside the domain of SLA (see, e.g., Ackerman & Ciancolo, 2002; Fleishman & Quaintance, 1984; Lohman, 2000; Snow, Kyllonen, & Marshalek, 1984). In her study, Niwa (2000) assessed the influence of individual differences in working memory, aptitude, and intelligence on L2 production during narrative tasks performed at four different levels of reasoning complexity. The strongest pattern of significant correlations was found for individual differences in intelligence (using a short form of the Wechsler Adult Intelligence Scale) L2 learning aptitude (using Sasaki's LABJ) and working memory (using a measure of reading span) on the accuracy, and particularly fluency of speaker production on the most complex version of the narratives. This suggests that individual differences in cognitive abilities do lead to increasingly differentiated L2 speech production by learners on complex versions of tasks high in their reasoning demands.

A further study of the effects of increasing reasoning demands of L2 narrative tasks (Robinson, 2003b, in press a) has also found that, as tasks increase in complexity, so learners increasingly incorporate premodified L2 input available in the task materials into their own production. Related to this, Nagata, Aline, and Ellis (1999) found that learners higher in MLAT measures of aptitude benefit more from provision of premodified input during listening comprehension activities (as measured by the extent of pre-posttest gain in relevant vocabulary retention) than learners lower in MLAT aptitude. It remains to be seen whether findings for greater uptake and learning from premodified input on complex relative to simple versions of tasks found in Robinson (2003b, in press a) may also be related to individual differences in cognitive abilities, and thereby contribute to aptitude for task-based learning. It seems likely that they will be, but also that the ability variables predicting this will differ according to the cognitive dimension along which the information processing demands of the task are made complex; for example individual differences in reasoning ability (see Ayala, Shavelson, & Yin, 2002; Lohman, 2000; Stanovitch & West, 2000) in the case of the reasoning demands dimension, versus attention control and the ability to "switch" attention (see Arrington & Logan, 2004; Pashler, 2000; Segalowitz, 2003; Segalowitz & Freed, 2004) to simultaneously competing task demands in the case of the single to dual task dimension. The third circle in Figure 1 describes some of the dimensions along which task demands can be varied from simple to complex. Identifying individual differences in cognitive abilities that contribute to learning and performance of complex tasks along these dimensions will be important to predicting which learners have the capacity for optimal success in both the later stages of instructed language learning, as well as in transfer of learned L2 ability to the contexts of work related real-world language use.

Aptitude and the Development of Advanced Level Language Ability

Throughout this review I have assumed that what an aptitude test measures does not fall on one side of distinctions between competence and performance, implicit "acquisition" and explicit "learning," or knowledge of language and ability for use. An optimal L2 aptitude test should predict development of all of these. Whether it does is both a theoretical question SLA research of the kind I have reviewed can address and be informed by. At the same time, it is a question of great consequence to the decisions learners, teachers, and program administrators make on the basis of aptitude test scores, that is, whether to select one versus another area of career specialization, how to optimize instruction for learners, and how to select candidates for costly language training programs, respectively (see Sackett, Schmitt, Ellingson, & Kabin, 2001). Future SLA research into the issues raised in this review is essential to the development of aptitude tests that can be confidently used by each of these groups of consumer. Such confidence is particularly needed when learners, teachers and administrators have to make decisions about whether they, their students, or their clients can reach the highest levels of L2 ability—where the likelihood of success is lowest, and the costs of failure (personally, practically, and financially) are often considerable. It is also at this "high-end" of real-world L2 use to accomplish job goals, and life pursuits, that achievement and relative success are most starkly, and validly, defined.[2]

Will Cognitive Abilities Alone Predict Advanced Level Language Learning?

Advanced level fluency, comprehensibility, and appropriately organizing the discoursal delivery of, e.g., a sales pitch, are some hallmarks of the acquisition of high level L2 ability. These can, to a large extent, be learned and assessed before exit from language programs. Other hallmarks of high-level L2 ability (using the sales pitch example) are perceiving and responding appropriately to the intended illocutionary force of questions and statements about the product or service that is being described (Bardovi-Harlig, 2001; Baron-Cohen, 1995; Langdon, Coltheart, Ward & Catts, 2002; Levinson, 1995); use of appropriate discourse markers, address forms and register shifts (Archer, 1983; Kasper & Rose, 2002; Yoshimi, 2001); and the integration of these with accommodative behavior, and interactional routines specific to the foreign culture (Bandura, 1986; Chapin, 1967; Goffman, 1967; Goldin-Meadow, Alibali, & Church, 1993; Liddicoat & Crozet, 2001; Rosenthall, Hall, Rogers & Archer, 1979). Measures of abilities used in current aptitude tests were chosen to predict predominantly grammatical and lexical development, as it was assessed by achievement tests used to validate them in the 1960s and 1970s. It is not clear whether they could predict acquisition, or execution of these pragmatic aspects of L2 knowledge.

Research into the acquisition of L2 pragmatics, and its susceptibility to instruction (see Rose & Kasper, 2001) is beginning to address the role of noticing and awareness, and individual variation in the extent of this, in the way research reviewed earlier is exploring the influence of individual differences in abilities on learning under different conditions of exposure, from FonF techniques, and on different task types. But it is likely that the substantial variance in success in developing the pragmatic hallmarks of advanced L2 ability will not be reducible to variance on measures of individual differences in the cognitive abilities illustrated in the center of Figure 1 (or those assessed by traditional aptitude tests such as MLAT) alone. Figure 1 proposes that cognitive abilities are influential on the early input-based stages of language learning. Subsequently, as learners attempt and become proficient in complex L2 pedagogic task performance, individual differences in the abilities drawn on along the task dimensions illustrated in the third circle additionally become predictive. What these individual difference measures for predicting advanced task performance are is as yet unclear, and an important issue for future research. The outer circle of Figure 1 describes pragmatic and interactional abilities such as nonverbal sensitivity, and interactional intelligence that are drawn on to help ensure further learning and development outside L2 classrooms. Aptitude-personality trait complexes of the kind Ackerman (1999, 2003) has described need to be researched and—if identified—used to guide development of measures predicting individual differences in these areas, and which may add incremental validity to predictions based on measures of cognitive abilities (cf. Sternberg, 2004).

Conceivably, therefore, aptitude tests predicting success in early and later learning in language programs will look somewhat different. Carroll (1990) was well aware of this, stating (as cited previously) "an individual might be an excellent translator or a facile simultaneous interpreter by virtue of special abilities that do not come into play in early language learning stages but that do come into play at later stages" (Carroll, 1990, p. 24). This suggests that selection decisions for entry into advanced high level language training programs may need to be made both on initial entry, and at a subsequent later stage. The notion that aptitude(s) are dynamic, and that abilities contributing to them reconfigure as learners reach higher levels, and shift to different contexts of practice and exposure, is one which Snow (1994) and others (see Corno et al., 2002; Dai & Sternberg, 2004; Sternberg & Grigorenko, 2003) have also put forward. But aptitude tests for early and later attainment, if not the same, should be continuous. It is possible that some core abilities drawn on during the early stages of L2 learning (such as those contributing to noticing, and incidental learning) will continue to be robust predictors of the fast registration, analysis, and learning of pragmatic, collocational, and formal-informal register features of the L2 as they become available to advanced level users in the workplace, while they are using the L2 on the job. After exiting from instructional programs learners high in these core abilities should then continue to develop— perceiving, adapting to, and profiting from steady exposure to features of L2 form and function not available in classrooms. Time, and future research, will tell us if that is true, and if so, what those core abilities are.

Notes

1. The extent to which the computational, information processing level characterization of aptitude offered in this review "supervenes" on (see Kim, 1993) the physical level at which individual differences and SLA processes can be described is an issue "emergentist" explanations of SLA (N. Ellis, 2003; O'Grady, 2004) and neurolinguistic research are both addressing (Chee, Soon, Lee & Pallier, 2004; Schumann, Crowell, Jones, Lee, Schuchert, & Woods, 2004). Integrating computational and biological perspectives has been a recent concern of individual differences research (Plomin, 2002) and future explanations of individual differences in L2 aptitude will likely also integrate computational and biological accounts.

2. Changing a course grade from a C to a B because a student "tried hard" in class, or did a make-up assignment is something that may have happened more than once in the programs where the MLAT and other early L2 aptitude tests were piloted and validated by scores on achievement tests in the 1960s. These options won't keep you employed if you are working for a foreign company, and performing unsuccessfully in doing sales pitches in an L2—regardless of your reputation for, and ability in, doing sales pitches in your L1.

ANNOTATED BIBLIOGRAPHY

Corno, L., Cronbach, L., Kupermintz, H., Lohman, D., Mandinach, E., Porteus, A., & Talbert, J. (2002). *Remaking the concept of aptitude: Extending the legacy of Richard E. Snow*. Mahwah, NJ: Erlbaum.

This book describes Richard Snow's theoretical model of aptitude and its implications for instructional design and teaching practice. Snow was concerned throughout his career with aptitude for schooled instruction—not specifically with aptitude for language learning. There is little discussion of language learning aptitude, but the book is worth reading for those interested in the relationship between cognitive abilities, and affective and conative factors, and the contributions of all of these to success in various instructional contexts. Snow wrote extensively on how measures of abilities alone may underdetermine aptitude for school learning, and how aptitude may profitably be seen as a person-in-situation transaction. To this extent it is an interesting counterpoint to the work of Carroll who focused on the role of cognitive abilities, and their factor structure, in his own work. (see Carroll, 1993). Carroll's work is described, and work in mainstream educational psychology, and cognitive psychology, are also described. The chapters, differently authored, lack some cohesion, but it is worth considering how personality, and motivational factors might interact with abilities to promote instructed L2 learning, and also how this interaction may take place in real-world contexts of language use, outside language programs. The edited collections by Shavelson and Roeser (2002) and Kyllonen and Lajoie (2003) containing empirical studies, operationalizing many of Snow's ideas, can also be read as a supplement to this.

DeKeyser, R. M. (2000). The robustness of critical period effects in second language acquisition. *Studies in Second Language Acquisition, 22*, 499–533.

The issue of age-related changes in the abilities contributing to aptitude is of theoretical importance to our understanding of SLA, and also of great practical importance for the development of aptitude tests appropriate to child and adult learners. In this article, DeKeyser reports the results of a partial replication of an earlier study by Johnson and Newport. Consistent with the earlier study, he finds that very few adult Hungarian-speaking immigrants to the United States scored within the range of child arrivals on a grammaticality judgment test of English. Moreover, for adult (but not child) arrivals there are strong significant positive correlations of grammaticality judgment scores, and scores on a modified version of the words in sentences MLAT measure of grammatical sensitivity. This article complements the similar findings of Harley and Hart (1997, 2002) for differences in the extent to which language analytic abilities contribute to aptitude for post versus precritical period learners in Canadian immersion programs. Interestingly, Harley and Hart (1997) additionally found individual differences in memory abilities contributed more to aptitude for precritical, than postcritical period L2 learning in their program. Readers might want to consider whether similar measures might also have correlated significantly and positively with performance on the grammaticality judgment test by child arrivals in DeKeyser's study.

Mackey, A., Philp, J., Egi, T., Fujii, A., & Tatsumi, T. (2002). Individual differences in working memory, noticing of interactional feedback and L2 development. In P. Robinson (Ed.), *Individual differences and instructed language learning* (pp. 69–93). Amsterdam: Benjamins.

What are the measures of cognitive abilities that predict uptake and learning from the various FonF techniques that have been proposed? Is one consistently predictive across a range of techniques? Working memory capacity is a good candidate for such a basic, core ability that can contribute to language learning aptitude at early, and later stages. In this study Mackey et al. report some evidence that phonological working memory capacity (measured by nonword recall and listening span measures) is predictive of the ability to notice information about mismatches between their own L2 production and recasts of it provided during interaction. Aspects of <u>wh</u>-question formation were the targeted form, and learners were identified as being at one of two developmental stages prior to the treatment, based on their ability to produce these question forms. Learners at lower developmental levels were more likely to notice information available in recasts than learners at higher developmental levels. The small number of subjects, and the short length of treatment are limitations of this study, but it raises interesting issues for future research to consider and build on.

Robinson, P. (2001). Individual differences, cognitive abilities, aptitude complexes and learning conditions in second language acquisition. *Second Language Research*, *17*, 368–392.

This article describes a theory of the cognitive abilities contributing to aptitude for instructed SLA, which explains why learners profit from different kinds of instruction. It also explains why some learners learn well from *any* kind of instruction, and why some learn poorly from any kind of instruction. Four interlocking hypotheses underpin the theory. The Aptitude Complex Hypothesis claims abilities have their effects on learning in specific combinations, and that these complexes of abilities promote SLA under L2 learning conditions, and from focus on form techniques, that draw on them. Four such "complexes" of ability factors are illustrated. The Ability Differentiation Hypothesis claims some learners have very differentiated strengths in abilities contributing to aptitude complexes, and that instruction especially needs to match the ability profiles of these learners. The Fundamental Difference Hypothesis claims aptitudes prior to, and following the critical period draw on different abilities—as the findings of DeKeyser (2000) and Harley and Hart (1997) show. Finally, the Fundamental Similarity Hypothesis claims *adult* (not child) learning under any condition of exposure draws on abilities implicated in explicitly processing input, and 'noticing' features of it. *Most* learners need to be matched to the conditions of instructional exposure that match their abilities to explicitly process, and notice elements of the L2, as the first hypothesis claims. *Exceptional* learners are those with strengths in all abilities, who can learn from any kind of instructional exposure. *Disabled* learners are those with strengths in no abilities. This is an interactionist theory of aptitude (see Snow, 1994), motivated by findings from SLA research, as well as frameworks, and constructs in educational and cognitive psychology.

Skehan, P. (2002). Theorising and updating aptitude. In P. Robinson (Ed.), *Individual differences and instructed language learning* (pp. 69–93). Amsterdam: Benjamins.

One of the most consistently insightful commentators on the role of individual differences in SLA, Skehan proposes in this paper a framework for researching the abilities contributing to aptitude for SLA, which is motivated by findings from SLA research and by research into L2 comprehension and speech production. Skehan proposes that components of aptitude be conceptualized as contributing to different stages of L2 processing. These include the stage at which L2 input is initially "noticed"; the stage at which input is 'patterned' and elaborated into a plan at a higher level of abstraction; the stage at which the plan becomes "controlled" and automatically accessed in production; and the stage at which the plan becomes variably lexicalized, and the basis of a larger repertoire of linguistic expressions. Skehan relates his model to subtests of existing aptitude tests, such as MLAT, pointing out where additional measures of abilities need to be developed to assess potential for L2 processing and learning at each stage. What these measures are is not described in operational detail, but Skehan gives a functional account of what they should measure, and this can be used as a blueprint by those interested in developing psycholinguistically motivated tests of the abilities contributing to aptitude for SLA, at each of the processing stages Skehan describes.

Williams, J. N., & Lovatt, P. (2003). Phonological memory and rule learning. *Language Learning, 53*, 67–121.

As Carroll himself noted in 1990, the most likely way in which the predictive power of the MLAT could be improved is by adding additional memory measures to the paired associates measure of rote memory. The theory and operationalization of memory measures has changed considerably since the 1960s when traditional aptitude tests were developed and piloted. There is now an extensive literature on working memory and implicit memory not available then. Experimental studies of the extent to which measures of memory predict successful learning of L2 stimuli are important to deciding which candidate memory measures to choose to include in aptitude batteries. This is an example of such research. Two experiments examined the contribution of individual differences in phonological memory to the ability to learn rules for determiner-noun agreement in semiartificial microlanguages. Williams and Lovatt conclude from their study that both memory and nonmemory factors influenced learning and that explicit learning processes contributed to this: Rules do not emerge simply from phonological memory for input sequences. They limit the scope of their claim by noting that the rules to be learned depended on forming associations between phonological forms: they were not rules that depended on making form-meaning associations.

OTHER REFERENCES

Ackerman, P. L. (1999). Traits and knowledge as determinants of learning and individual differences: Putting it all together. In P.L. Ackerman, P. Kyllonen, & R. Roberts (Eds.),

Learning and individual differences: Process, trait and content determinants (pp. 437–462). Washington, DC: American Psychological Association.

Ackerman, P. L. (2003). Aptitude complexes and trait complexes. *Educational Psychologist, 38*, 85–93.

Ackerman, P. L., & Ciancolo, A. (2002). Ability and task constraint determinants of complex task performance. *Journal of Experimental Psychology: Applied, 8*, 194–208.

Anderson, M. (1992). *Intelligence and development: A cognitive theory.* Oxford: Blackwell.

Archer, D. (1983). The encoding of meaning: A test of three theories of social interaction. *Sociological Enquiry, 50*, 393–419.

Arrington, C. A., & Logan, G. D. (2004). The costs of a voluntary task switch. *Psychological Science, 15* (9), 610–616.

Ayala, C. C., Shavelson, R. J., Yin, Y., & Schultz, S. E. (2002). Reasoning dimensions underlying science achievement: The case of performance assessment. *Educational Assessment, 8*, 101–122.

Baars, B. (1986). *The cognitive revolution in psychology.* New York: Guilford.

Baddeley, A. (2000). Working memory and language processing. In B.E. Dimitrova & K. Hyltenstam (Eds.), *Language processing and simultaneous interpreting* (pp. 1–16). Amsterdam: Benjamins.

Bandura, A. (1986). *Social foundations of thought and action.* Englewood Cliffs, NJ: Prentice Hall.

Bardovi-Harlig, K. (2001). Evaluating the empirical evidence: Grounds for instruction? In K. Rose & G. Kasper (Eds.), *Pragmatics in language teaching* (pp. 13–32). New York: Cambridge University Press.

Baron-Cohen, S. (1995). *Mindblindness: An essay on autism and theory of mind.* Oxford: Oxford University Press.

Benati, A. (2004). The effects of structured input activities and explicit information on the acquisition of the Italian future tense. In B. Van Patten (Ed.), *Processing instruction: Theory, research and commentary* (pp. 207–226). Mahwah, NJ: Erlbaum.

Bygate, M. (2001). Effects of task repetition on the structure and control of oral language. In M. Bygate, P. Skehan, & M. Swain (Eds.), *Researching pedagogic tasks: Second language learning, teaching and testing* (pp. 23–48). Harlow: Longman.

Carroll, J. B. (1981). Twenty-five years of research on foreign language aptitude. In K. C. Diller (Ed.), *Individual differences and universals in language learning aptitude* (pp. 83–118). Rowley, MA: Newbury House.

Carroll, J. B. (1990). Cognitive abilities in foreign language aptitude: Then and now. In T. Parry & C. Stansfield (Eds.), *Language aptitude reconsidered* (pp. 11–29). Englewood Cliffs, NJ: Prentice Hall.

Carroll, J. B. (1993). *Human cognitive abilities: A survey of factor-analytic studies.* New York: Cambridge University Press.

Carroll, J. B., & Sapon, S. M. (1959). *The Modern Language Aptitude Test.* Washington, DC: Second Language Testing Incorporated.

Ceci, S. J. (1996). *On intelligence. . . more or less: A bio-ecological treatise on intellectual development.* Englewood Cliffs, NJ: Prentice Hall.

Chapin, F. S. (1967). *The social insight test.* Palo Alto, CA: Consulting Psychologists Press.

Chee, M. W., Hon, N., Lee, H. L., & Soon, C. S. (2001). Relative language proficiency modulates BOLD signal change when bilinguals perform semantic judgements. *Neuroimage, 13*, 1155–1163.

Chee, M. W., Soon, C. S., Lee, H. L. & Pallier, C. (2004). Left insula activation: A marker for language attainment in bilinguals. *Proceedings of the National Academy of Sciences, 101* (2), 15265–15276.

Clark, A. (1997). *Being there: Putting brain, body and world together again.* Cambridge, MA: MIT Press.

Cohen, A. D. (2003). The learner's side of foreign language learning: Where do styles, strategies and tasks meet? *International Review of Applied Linguistics in Language Teaching, 41*, 279–292.

Collentine, J., & Freed, B. F. (2004). (Eds.). Language context and its effects on second language acquisition [Special issue]. *Studies in Second Language Acquisition, 26,* 2.

Costa, P. T., & McCrae, R. R. (1985). *The NEO Personality Inventory Manual.* Odessa, FL: Psychological Assessment Resources, Inc.

Dai, D. Y., & Sternberg, R. J. (Eds.). (2004). *Motivation, emotion, and cognition: Integrative perspectives on intellectual functioning and development.* Mahwah, NJ: Erlbaum.

Daneman, M., & Carpenter, P. A. (1980). Individual differences in working memory and reading. *Journal of Verbal Learning and Verbal Behaviour, 19*, 450–466.

de Graaff, R. (1997). *Differential effects of explicit instruction on second language acquisition.* The Hague: Holland Institute of Generative Linguistics.

de Jong, N. (in press). Is listening enough for grammar acquisition? The effect of an aural training on reception and production in a second language. *Studies in Second Language Acquisition, 27,* 2.

Deary, I. J. (2000). *Looking down on human intelligence: From psychometrics to the brain.* Oxford: Oxford University Press.

DeKeyser, R. M. (1995). Learning second language grammar rules: An experiment with a miniature linguistic system. *Studies in Second Language Acquisition, 17*, 379–410.

DeKeyser, R. M. (1997). Beyond explicit rule learning: Automatizing second language syntax. *Studies in Second Language Acquisition, 19*, 195–221.

DeKeyser, R. M. (2003). Implicit and explicit learning. In C. Doughty & M. H. Long (Eds.), *Handbook of second language acquisition* (pp. 313–348). Oxford: Blackwell.

DeKeyser, R. M. (in press). (Ed.) *Practice in second language learning: Perspectives from applied linguistics and cognitive psychology*. New York: Cambridge University Press.

Diller, K. C. (1981). (Ed.) *Individual differences and universals in language learning aptitude*. Rowley, MA: Newbury House.

Dörnyei, Z. (2002). The motivational basis of language learning tasks. In P. Robinson (Ed.), *Individual differences and instructed language learning* (pp. 137–158). Amsterdam: Benjamins.

Dörnyei, Z. (in press). *Individual differences and second language learning*. Mahwah, NJ: Erlbaum.

Dörnyei, Z., & Skehan, P. (2003). Individual differences in second language learning. In C. Doughty & M. H. Long (Eds.), *Handbook of second language acquisition* (pp. 589–630). Oxford: Blackwell.

Doughty, C. (2001). Cognitive underpinnings of focus on form. In P. Robinson (Ed.), *Cognition and second language instruction* (pp. 206–257). Cambridge: Cambridge University Press.

Doughty, C. (2004). When PI is focus on form it is very, very good; but when it is focus on forms . . . . In B. VanPatten (Ed.), *Processing instruction: Theory, research and commentary* (pp. 121–132). Mahwah, NJ: Erlbaum.

Doughty, C. & Varela, E. (1998). Communicative focus on form. In C. Doughty & J. Williams (Eds.), *Focus on form in classroom second language acquisition* (pp. 114–138). New York: Cambridge University Press.

Doughty, C., & Williams, J. (1998). Pedagogical choices in focus on form. In C. Doughty & J. Williams (Eds.), *Focus on form in classroom second language acquisition* (pp. 197–262). New York: Cambridge University Press.

Ehrman, M. E. (1996). *Understanding second language learning difficulties*. Thousand Oaks, CA: Sage.

Ehrman, M. E. (1998). A Study of the Modern Language Aptitude Test for Predicting Learning Success and Advising Students. *Applied Language Learning, 9*, 31–70.

Ehrman, M. E., Leaver, B., & Oxford, R. (2003). A brief overview of individual differences in second language learning. *System, 31*, 313–330.

Ellis, N. C. (1993). Rules and instances in foreign language learning: Interactions of explicit and implicit knowledge. *European Journal of Cognitive Psychology, 5*, 289–318.

Ellis, N. C. (2001). Memory for language. In P. Robinson (Ed.), *Cognition and second language instruction* (pp. 34–68). Cambridge: Cambridge University Press.

Ellis, N. C. (2003). Constructions, chunking and connectionism: The emergence of second language structure. In C. Doughty & M. H. Long (Eds.), *Handbook of second language acquisition* (pp. 63–103). Oxford: Blackwell.

Ellis, N. C. (in press). At the interface: How explicit knowledge affects implicit language learning. *Studies in Second Language Acquisition, 27* (2).

Ellis, R. (1999). (Ed.) *Learning a second language through interaction.* Amsterdam: Benjamins.

Ellis, R. (2004). *Task-based teaching and learning.* Oxford: Oxford University Press.

Ellis, R. (in press). (Ed.) *Planning time and second language learning.* Amsterdam: Benjamins.

Farley, A. (2004). Processing instruction and the Spanish subjunctive: Is explicit information needed? In B. VanPatten (Ed.), *Processing instruction: Theory, research and commentary* (pp. 227–240). Mahwah, NJ: Erlbaum.

Fleishman, E. A. (1978). Relating individual differences to the dimensions of human tasks. *Ergonomics, 21,* 1007–1019.

Fleishman, E. A., & Quaintance, M. K. (1984). *Taxonomies of human performance: The description of human tasks.* New York: Academic Press.

Foster, P., & Skehan, P. (1996). The influence of planning and task type on second language performance. *Studies in Second Language Acquisition, 18,* 299–324.

Garlick, D. (2002). Understanding the nature of the general factor of intelligence: The role of individual differences in neural plasticity as an explanatory mechanism. *Psychological Review, 109,* 116–136.

Gilabert, R. (2004). *Task complexity, planning and L2 oral narrative production.* Unpublished Ph.D dissertation. Department of Applied Linguistics, University of Barcelona, Spain.

Goffman, E. (1967). *Interaction ritual: Essays in face-to-face behavior.* Chicago, IL: Aldine.

Goldin-Meadow, S., Alibali, M. W., & Church, C. (1993). Transitions in concept acquisition: Using the hand to read the mind. *Psychological Review, 100,* 279–297.

Grigorenko, E. L. (2002). Language-based learning disabilities. In P. Robinson (Ed.), *Individual differences and instructed language learning* (pp. 95–113). Amsterdam: Benjamins.

Hardy, I., & Moore, J. (2004). Foreign language student's conversational negotiations in different task environments. *Applied Linguistics, 25,* 340–370.

Harley, B., & Hart, D. (1997). Language aptitude and second language proficiency in classroom learners of different starting ages. *Studies in Second Language Acquisition, 19,* 379–400.

Harley, B., & Hart, D. (2002). Age, aptitude and second language learning on a bilingual exchange. In P. Robinson (Ed.), *Individual differences and instructed language learning* (pp. 301–330). Amsterdam: Benjamins.

Hulstijn, J. H. (2001). Intentional and incidental second language vocabulary learning: A reappraisal of elaboration, rehearsal and automaticity. In P. Robinson (Ed.), *Cognition and second language instruction* (pp. 258–286). Cambridge: Cambridge University Press.

Hulstijn, J. H. (2003). Incidental and intentional learning. In C. Doughty & M. H. Long (Eds.),

Handbook of second language acquisition (pp. 349–381). Oxford: Blackwell.

Hulstijn, J. H., & DeKeyser, R. M. (1997). (Eds.) Second language acquisition research in the laboratory: Special Issue. *Studies in Second Language Acquisition, 19*, 2.

Hulstijn, J. H., & Ellis, R. (2005). (Eds.) Implicit and explicit second language learning: Special issue. *Studies in Second Language Acquisition, 27*, 2.

Iwashita, N., McNamara, T., & Elder, C. (2001). Can we predict task difficulty in an oral proficiency test? Exploring the potential of an information processing approach to task design. *Language Learning, 51*, 401–436.

Kasper, G., & Rose, K. (2002). *Pragmatic development in a second language.* Malden, MA: Blackwell.

Kenyon, D. M., & MacGregor, D. (2004). (Eds.) *Final report of the Defense Language Aptitude Battery II project*. Washington, DC: Center for Applied Linguistics.

Krashen, S. D. (1982). *Principles and practice in second language acquisition*. Oxford: Pergamon.

Kim, J. (1993). *Supervenience and mind.* Cambridge: Cambridge University Press.

Kyllonen, P. C., & Lajoie, S. (2003). Reassessing aptitude: Introduction to a special issue in honor of Richard, E. Snow. *Educational Psychologist, 38*, 79–83.

Langdon, R., Coltheart, M., Ward, P., & Catts, S. (2002). Disturbed communication in schizophrenia: The role of pragmatics and poor theory-of-mind. *Psychological Medicine, 32*, 1273–1284.

Leeman, J. (2003). Recasts and second language development: Beyond negative evidence. *Studies in Second Language Acquisition, 25*, 37–64.

Leeman, J., Artegoitia, I., Fridman, B., & Doughty, C. (1995). Integrating attention to form with meaning: Focus on form in content-based Spanish instruction. In R. Schmidt (Ed.), *Attention and awareness in foreign language learning* (pp. 217–258). Honolulu, HI: University of Hawai'i Press.

Levinson, S. C. (1995). Interactional biases in human thinking. In E. Goody (Ed.), *Social intelligence and interaction* (pp.221–260). Cambridge: Cambridge University Press.

Liddicoat, A., & Crozet, C. (2001). Acquiring French interactional norms through instruction. In K. Rose & G. Kasper (Eds.), *Pragmatics in language teaching* (pp.125–144). New York: Cambridge University Press.

Logan, G. D. (2004). Working memory, task switching and executive control in the task span procedure. *Journal of Experimental Psychology: General, 133*, 218–236.

Lohman, D. F. (2000). Complex information processing and intelligence. In R. J. Sternberg (Ed.), *Handbook of intelligence* (pp. 285–340). New York: Cambridge University Press.

Long, M. H. (in press). Recasts: The story so far. *In Problems in SLA.* Mahwah, NJ: Erlbaum.

Lyster, R. (2004). Differential effects of prompts and recasts in form-focused instruction.

Studies in Second Language Acquisition, 26, 399–432.

Mayer, J. D., Salovey, P., & Caruso, D. (2000). Models of emotional intelligence. In R. J. Sternberg (Ed.), *Handbook of intelligence* (pp. 396–420). New York: Cambridge University Press.

McLaughlin, B. (1995). Aptitude from an information-processing perspective. *Language Testing, 12,* 370–387.

Miyake, A., & Friedman, N. (1998). Individual differences in second language proficiency: Working Memory as language aptitude. In A. Healy & L. Bourne Jr. (Eds.), *Foreign language learning: Psycholinguistic studies on training and retention* (pp. 339–364). Mahwah, NJ: Erlbaum.

Nagata, H., Aline, D., & Ellis, R. (1999). Modified input, language aptitude, and the acquisition of word meanings. In R. Ellis (Ed.), *Learning a second language through interaction* (pp. 133–150). Amsterdam: Benjamins.

Nelson, K. (1987). Some observations from the perspective of the rare event, cognitive comparison theory of language acquisition. In K. Nelson & A. vanKleek (Eds.), *Childrens' language* (pp. 289–331). Norwood, NJ: Erlbaum.

Niwa, Y. (2000). *Reasoning demands of L2 tasks and L2 narrative production: Effects of individual differences in working memory, intelligence and aptitude.* Unpublished master's dissertation, Department of English, Aoyama Gakuin University, Japan.

O'Grady, W. (2004). *Syntactic carpentry.* Mahwah, NJ: Erlbaum.

Ortega, L. (1999). Planning and focus on form in L2 oral discourse. *Studies in Second Language Acquisition, 20,* 103–135.

Oxford, R., Cho, Y., Leung, S., & Kim, H. (2004). Effect of the presence and difficulty of task on strategy use. *International Review of Applied Linguistics, 42,* 1–48.

Parry, T., & Child, J. (1990). Preliminary investigation of the relationship between VORD, MLAT and language proficiency. In T. Parry & C. Stansfield (Eds.), *Language aptitude reconsidered* (pp. 30–66). Englewood Cliffs, NJ: Prentice Hall.

Parry, T., & Stansfield, C. (1990). (Eds.) *Language aptitude reconsidered.* Englewood Cliffs, NJ: Prentice Hall.

Pashler, H. E. (2000). Task switching and multitask performance. In S. Monsell & J. Driver (Eds.), *Attention and performance XVIII: Control of cognitive processes* (pp. 277–308). Cambridge, MA: MIT Press.

Pellegrino, J., & Glaser, R. (1979). Cognitive correlates and components in the analysis of individual differences. In R. J. Sternberg & D. Detterman (Eds.), *Human intelligence: perspectives on its theory and measurement* (pp. 61–88). Noorwood, NJ: Ablex.

Peterson, C. R., & Al Haik, A. R. (1976). The development of the Defense Language Aptitude Battery (DLAB). *Educational and Psychological Measurement, 6,* 369–380.

Philp, J. (2003). Constraints on "Noticing the Gap:" Nonnative speakers' noticing of recasts in NS-NNS interaction. *Studies in Second Language Acquisition, 25*, 99–126.

Pimsleur, P. (1966). *Pimsleur Language Aptitude Battery* (PLAB). Washington, DC: Second Language Testing Incorporated.

Plomin, R. (2002). Individual differences research in the postgenomic era. *Personality and Individual Differences, 33*, 909–930.

Rahimpour, M. (1997). *Task complexity and variation in oral L2 narrative discourse.* Unpublished Ph.D. dissertation, CLTR, University of Queensland, Australia.

Rahimpour, M. (1999). Task complexity and variation in interlanguage. In N. O. Jungheim & P. Robinson (Eds.), *Pragmatics and pedagogy: Proceedings of the Third Pacific Second Language Research Forum, Vol. 2* (pp. 115–134). Tokyo: PacSLRF.

Ranta, L. (2002). The role of learners' analytic abilities in the communicative classroom. In P. Robinson (Ed.), *Individual differences and instructed language learning* (pp. 159–180). Amsterdam: Benjamins.

Reed, D., & Stansfield, C. (2004). An interview with John B. Carroll: The story behind the Modern Language Aptitude Test. *Language Assessment Quarterly, 1*, 21–38.

Robinson, P. (1995a). Task complexity and second language narrative discourse. *Language Learning, 45*, 99–140.

Robinson, P. (1995b). Attention, memory and the "noticing" hypothesis. *Language Learning, 45*, 283–331.

Robinson, P. (1996a). Learning simple and complex second language rules under implicit, incidental, rule-search and instructed conditions. *Studies in Second Language Acquisition, 18*, 27–67.

Robinson, P. (1996b). *Consciousness, rules and instructed second language acquisition.* New York: Lang.

Robinson, P. (1997a). Individual differences and the fundamental similarity of implicit and explicit adult second language learning. *Language Learning, 47*, 45–99.

Robinson, P. (1997b). Automaticity and generalizability of second language learning under implicit, incidental, enhanced and rule-search conditions. *Studies in Second Language Acquisition, 19*, 223–247.

Robinson, P. (1999). Second language classroom research in Japan: Issues, studies, and prospects. In T. Fujimura, Y. Kato & R. Smith (Eds.), *Proceedings of the 10th IUJ Conference on second language research* (pp. 93–116). Tokyo: International University of Japan.

Robinson, P. (2001a). Task complexity, task difficulty, and task production: Exploring interactions in a componential framework. *Applied Linguistics, 22*, 27–57.

Robinson, P. (2001b). Task complexity, cognitive resources, and syllabus design: A triadic framework for investigating task influences on SLA. In P. Robinson (Ed.), *Cognition and second language instruction* (pp. 287–318). Cambridge: Cambridge University Press.

Robinson, P. (2001c). Individual differences, cognitive abilities, aptitude complexes, and learning conditions in SLA. *Second Language Research, 17*, 368–392.

Robinson, P. (2001d). (Ed.) *Cognition and second language instruction.* Cambridge: Cambridge University Press.

Robinson, P. (2002a). (Ed.) *Individual differences and instructed language learning.* Amsterdam: Benjamins.

Robinson, P. (2002b). Learning conditions, aptitude complexes and SLA: A framework for research and pedagogy. In P. Robinson (Ed.), *Individual differences and instructed language learning* (pp. 113–133). Amsterdam: Benjamins.

Robinson, P. (2002c). Individual differences in intelligence, aptitude and working memory during adult incidental second language learning: A replication and extension of Reber, Walkenfeld, and Hernstadt (1991). In P. Robinson (Ed.), *Individual differences and instructed language learning* (pp. 211–266). Amsterdam: Benjamins.

Robinson, P. (2003a). Attention and memory during SLA. In C. Doughty & M. H. Long (Eds.), *Handbook of second language acquisition* (pp. 631–678). Oxford: Blackwell.

Robinson, P. (2003b). The Cognition Hypothesis, task design and adult task-based language learning. *Second Language Studies, 21*(2), 45–107.

Robinson, P. (in press a). Cognitive complexity and task sequencing: A review of studies in a Componential Framework for second language task design. *International Review of Applied Linguistics in Language Teaching, 43*(1).

Robinson, P. (in press b). Cognitive abilities, chunk-strength and frequency effects in implicit Artificial Grammar and incidental L2 learning: Replications of Reber, Walkenfeld, and Hernstadt (1991) and Knowlton and Squire (1996) and their relevance for SLA. *Studies in Second Language Acquisition, 27*(2).

Robinson, P. (in press c). Aptitude, abilities, contexts and practice. In R. M. DeKeyser (Ed.), *Practice in second language learning: Perspectives from applied linguistics and cognitive psychology.* New York: Cambridge University Press.

Robinson, P., & Ha, M. (1993). Instance theory and second language rule learning under explicit conditions. *Studies in Second Language Acquisition, 15*, 413–438.

Robinson, P., Ting, S.C-C., & Urwin, J. (1995). Investigating second language task complexity. *RELC Journal, 26*, 62–79.

Robinson, P., & Yamaguchi, Y. (1999). *Aptitude, task feedback and generalizability of focus on form: A classroom study.* Paper presented at the 12th AILA World Congress, Waseda University, Tokyo, August.

Rose, K., & Kasper, G. (2001). *Pragmatics in language teaching.* New York: Cambridge

University Press.

Rosenthal, R., Rosnow, R., & Rubin, D. (2000). *Contrasts and effect sizes in behavioral research: A correlational approach.* New York: Cambridge University Press.

Rosenthall, R., Hall, J., Rogers, P. L., & Archer, D. (1979). *Sensitivity to nonverbal communications: The PONS test.* Baltimore, MD: Johns Hopkins University Press.

Sackett, P., Schmitt, N., Ellingson, J., & Kabin, M. (2001). High-stakes testing in employment, credentialing, and higher education: Prospects in a post-affirmative action world. *American Psychologist, 56,* 302–318.

Sands, W., Waters, B., & McBride, J. (1997). (Eds.) *Computerized adaptive testing: From inquiry to operation.* Washington, DC: American Psychological Corporation.

Sasaki, M. (1996). *Second language proficiency, foreign language aptitude, and intelligence.* New York: Lang.

Sawyer, M., & Ranta, L. (2001). Aptitude, individual differences and instructional design. In P. Robinson (Ed.), *Cognition and second language instruction* (pp. 319–353). Cambridge: Cambridge University Press.

Schumann, J. H., Crowell, S., Jones, N., Lee, N., Schuchert, C., & Woods, L. (2004). *The neurobiology of learning: Perspectives from second language acquisition.* Mahwah, NJ: Erlbaum.

Schmidt, R. (2001). Attention. In P. Robinson (Ed.), *Cognition and second language instruction* (pp. 1–32). Cambridge: Cambridge University Press.

Schmidt, R., & Frota, S. (1986). Developing basic conversational ability in a second language: A case study of an adult learner of Portuguese. In R. Day (Ed.), *Talking to learn: Conversation in second language learning* (pp. 237–322). Rowley, MA: Newbury House.

Segalowitz, N. (2003). Automaticity and second language acquisition. In C. Doughty & M. H. Long (Eds.), *Handbook of second language acquisition* (pp. 382–408). Oxford: Blackwell.

Segalowitz, N., & Freed, B. F. (2004). Context, contact, and cognition in oral fluency acquisition: Learning Spanish in at home and study abroad contexts. *Studies in Second Language Acquisition, 26,* 201–226.

Shavelson, R. J., & Roeser, R. W. (2002). (Eds.) A multidimensional approach to achievement validation [Special Issue]. *Educational Assessment, 8,* 2.

Skehan, P. (1989). *Individual differences in second language learning.* London: Arnold.

Skehan, P. (1998). *A cognitive approach to language learning.* Oxford: Oxford University Press.

Skehan, P. (1999). Task-based language instruction. *Annual Review of Applied Linguistics, 18,* 268–286.

Smith, D. L., Nobe, S., Robinson, P., Strong, G., Tani, M., & Yoshiba, H. (2004). *Language and comprehension: Perspectives from linguistics and language education.* Tokyo: Kuroshio

Publishing.

Snow, R. E. (1987). Aptitude complexes. In R. E. Snow & M. J. Farr (Eds.), *Aptitude, learning and instruction, Vol. 3: Conative and affective process analysis* (pp. 11–34). Hillsdale, NJ: Erlbaum.

Snow, R. E. (1994). Abilities in academic tasks. In R. J. Sternberg & R. K. Wagner (Eds.), *Mind in context: Interactionist perspectives on human intelligence* (pp. 3–37). New York: Cambridge University Press.

Snow, R. E., Kyllonen, P. C., & Marshalek, B. (1984). The topography of ability and learning correlations. In R. J. Sternberg (Ed.), *Advances in the psychology of human intelligence* (pp. 47–103). Hillsdale, NJ: Erlbaum.

Sparks, R., & Ganschow, L. (2001). Aptitude for learning a foreign language. *Annual Review of Applied Linguistics, 21*, 90–111.

Spolsky, B. (1995). Prognostication and language aptitude testing, 1925–62. *Language Testing, 12*, 321–340.

Stanovitch, K., & West, R. (2000). Individual differences in reasoning: Implications for the rationality debate. *Behavioral and Brain Sciences, 23*, 645–665.

Sternberg, R. J. (1977). *Intelligence, information processing and analogical reasoning: The componential analysis of human abilities*. Hillsdale, NJ: Erlbaum.

Sternberg, R. J. (2002). The theory of successful intelligence and its implications for language aptitude testing. In P. Robinson (Ed.), *Individual differences and instructed language learning* (pp. 13–44). Amsterdam: Benjamins.

Sternberg, R. J. (2004). Comments on the 'Summary of the DLAB 2 project.' In D. M. Kenyon, & D. MacGregor (Eds.), *Final report of the Defense Language Aptitude Battery II project*, (Appendix I, pp.1–14). Washington, DC: Center for Applied Linguistics.

Sternberg, R. J., & Grigorenko, E. L. (2003). (Eds.) *The psychology of abilities, competencies and expertise*. New York: Cambridge University Press.

Sternberg, R. J., & Wagner, R. K. (Eds.) (1994). *Mind in context: Interactionist perspectives on human intelligence*. New York: Cambridge University Press.

Tokowitcz, N., & MacWhinney, B. (in press). Implicit and explicit measures of sensitivity to violations in second language grammar: An event-related potential investigation. *Studies in Second Language Acquisition, 27*, 2.

VanPatten, B. (2004). (Ed.) *Processing instruction: Theory, research and commentary*. Mahwah, NJ: Erlbaum.

VanPatten, B. & Cadierno, T. (1993). Explicit instruction and input processing. *Studies in Second Language Acquisition, 15*, 225–243.

White, J. (1998). Getting the learners' attention: A typographical input enhancement study. In C. Doughty & J. Williams (Eds.), *Focus on form in classroom second language acquisition* (pp.

85–113). Cambridge: Cambridge University Press.

Williams, J. N. (1999). Memory, attention, and inductive learning. *Studies in Second Language Acquisition*, *21*, 1–48.

Yoshimi, D. (2001). Explicit instruction and JFL learners' use of interactional discourse markers. In K. Rose & G. Kasper (Eds.), *Pragmatics in language teaching* (pp. 223–247). New York: Cambridge University Press.

RESEARCH ON LANGUAGE LEARNING PROCESSES

4. IMPACT OF LITERACY ON ORAL LANGUAGE PROCESSING: IMPLICATIONS FOR SECOND LANGUAGE ACQUISITION RESEARCH

Elaine Tarone and Martha Bigelow

In this chapter we describe a body of research on oral language processing that we believe has important implications for applied linguistics. This research documents the effects of literacy on human oral language processing. Studies in this area show that illiterate adults significantly differ from literate adults in their performance of oral processing tasks that require an awareness of linguistic segments. These studies provide evidence that the acquisition of the ability to decode an alphabetic script changes the way in which the individual processes oral language in certain kinds of cognitive tasks. At the same time, based on research establishing a clear reciprocal relationship between oral language processing skills and literacy, researchers on first language acquisition are extending the scope of their study to explore the way in which an individual's language competence is altered and extended by literacy itself. In this discussion, we describe the broad outlines of this new body of research and scholarship, and explore the implications for our understanding of second-language acquisition, and particularly for theories and research that explore the impact of "noticing" on SLA. We conclude by stressing the social and theoretical importance of including clearly-identified illiterate adults in our growing database on second language acquisition research.

Impact of Alphabetic Literacy on Oral Language Processing

In the past 10 years, immigrant and refugee English language learners with limited formal education have become a critical mass in many cities in North America and adult illiteracy is very high worldwide. Sadly, some 799 million people are still illiterate. Two-thirds of them are women, and more than 100 million children have no access to school (UNESCO, 2004). Interrupted or limited formal schooling is common among English language learners in U.S. public schools. In 1993, Fleischman and Hopstock found that 20% of English language learners at the high school level and 12% at the middle school level had missed two or more years of schooling since age six. Jamieson, Curry, and Martinez (2001) found that among newcomer Hispanic students ages 15 to 17, more than one-third are enrolled below grade level and are not literate in Spanish. However, despite low literacy, people around the world learn not only one, but often multiple languages. Multilingualism is the norm in many unschooled societies (Hill, 1970). Given the fact that illiteracy and multilingualism are common occurrences world wide, we believe that an adequate theory of SLA should account for the learning experiences of illiterate and low-literate multilinguals, and particularly, that much can be learned from the study of the L2 oral abilities of such learners. In this chapter, we review the work of first language acquisition (FLA) researchers and scholars who have examined the relationship between the acquisition of literacy in an alphabetic script and the ability to process oral language in terms of the formal linguistic segments encoded in that script. We consider the relevance of this research on first language for research on SLA and second language teaching. We focus specifically on a target audience of adult second language learners who are not literate in any alphabetic script, in any language.

The Construct of Literacy

Literacy is a complex construct. Ravid and Tolchinsky (2002) state that the mastery of written language involves two aspects: mastery of (1) written language as discourse style (that is, the recognition that the language used in writing is basically different from the language used in speech, and further, that there are many varieties of written language), and (2) written language as notational system (the recognition and ability to produce the representational system used in writing). Verhoeven (1994) also divides literate competence into components: grammatical, discourse, (de)coding, strategic, and sociolinguistic competence. Verhoeven's grammatical competence, "mastery of phonological rules, lexical items, morphosyntactic rules and rules of sentence formation" (p. 487), and his coding and decoding competence seem more or less equivalent to Ravid and Tolchinsky's "literacy as notational system." His discourse, strategic, and sociolinguistic competence seem equivalent to Ravid and Tolchinsky's notion of literacy as discourse style, which has also been the focus of such researchers as Biber (1988), Biber and Hared (1991), and Biber, Reppen, and Conrad (2002).

Similarly, Wiley (in press) states that research can be divided into two major orientations to the study of literacy: the "autonomous" orientation, which focuses on the formal properties of encoding and decoding text along with the individual cognitive consequences of this, and the "social practices" orientation, which views literacy not as an individual property, but as an activity deeply embedded in social relationships. Wiley includes as proponents of the first orientation Ong (1982), Olson and Torrance (1991), and Goody (1987), and as proponents of the second, Heath (1983), Street (1995) and Gee (1991, 2001). Although Wiley discusses these two orientations as somewhat antithetical, we follow Ravid and Tolchinsky (2002) in viewing them as more complementary, and relating to different components of literacy itself.

In this chapter, we focus on only a part of the large construct of literacy: the part that Ravid and Tolchinsky (2002) refer to as "notational system," and Verhoeven (1994) describes as the two literacy components of "(de)coding" and "grammatical competence." We are particularly interested in the relationship between mastery of the notational system and oral language processing skills. We further target the abilities of adult illiterates—and, ultimately, the oral skills those individuals bring to the process of second language acquisition.

Studies on the Oral Processing of Illiterate Individuals

Oral Processing and Child Literacy

A robust body of research and scholarship in several related disciplines has focused on the relationship between oral linguistic awareness and literacy in monolingual children. We refer the interested reader to the work of the "autonomous" and "social practices" scholars referenced earlier. In research on child language development, it has long been acknowledged that young children are not aware of, for example, words as phonological entities until about the age of six or seven, the age at which they also become literate; Kolinsky, Cary, and Morais (1987) cite here the work of such scholars as Piaget (1979), Vygotsky (1962), and Berthoud-Papandropoulou (1978). Olson (2002), for example, describes empirical evidence in his own and his students' work that supports the view that prereading children believe that words represent entities themselves, and not linguistic abstractions. His team has conducted studies showing that prereading children assume that written signs represent events and meanings rather than words or sentences about those events. For example, a prereading child asked to write "cat" writes one scribble; when asked to write two cats, he writes two scribbles; three cats is three scribbles. No cats is a wave of the pencil in the air and a statement such as, "There's no cats so I didn't write anything." The child is shown a card that says "three little pigs" and someone reads that phrase. Then one word is covered up and the child is asked to guess what it says now. The child says "'two little pigs'." The child assumes the text relates to objects and events, not language *about* objects and events. Olson concludes that the preliterate child does not have the concept of "word."

Although metalinguistic awareness of such entities as "words" and "phonemes" seems to be related to literacy in child language development, there has apparently not been a consensus as to the *directionality* of this relationship. Does the increasing linguistic awareness of the cognitively maturing child provide the foundation upon which literacy may be developed? Or does literacy produce children's linguistic awareness?

Ravid and Kolchinsky (2002), in proposing a model of "linguistic literacy" that we describe next, maintain neutrality on the question of directionality of causality, even as they stress the strong connection between children's oral language awareness and their acquisition of literacy. They summarize research on the relationship between children's phonological and morphological awareness and learning to read and write this way:

> We do not claim that there is a unidirectional, cause-and-effect relationship between oral language awareness of any dimension, on the one hand, and

linguistic literacy, on the other. Rather, specific aspects of language awareness, especially phonological and morphological awareness, both promote and are promoted by learning to read and write. They do so by establishing links between the internal representation of phonemes, syllables and morphemes and their written representations (Rubin, 1988; Fowler & Liberman, 1995; Goswami, 1999). Concomitantly, written representations modify these very same internal linguistic representations (Gillis & deSchutter, 1996; Levin et al., 2001; Tolchinsky & Teberosky, 1998); (Ravid & Tolchinsky, 2002, p. 432).

The assumption of most researchers on child language development and child reading development seems to have been that the development of reading depends on prior phonological awareness. Verhoeven (2002, p. 487), for example, seems to make this assumption: "readers activate speech codes during the decoding process-even in morphemic writing systems such as the Chinese. As such, literacy acquisition depends critically upon a child's speech processing skills" (Snowling, 1998).

Reading researchers such as Thompkins and Binder (2003) seem to make the same assumption, namely that successful development of reading skills depends upon prior phonological awareness. Noting that it is well-known that phonological awareness and reading level correlate strongly in studies of children, they propose to examine the same relationship among adults who are functionally illiterate, and compare this to that of children. They compare the phonological awareness and short-term memory skills of 60 functionally illiterate adults matched with a group of 99 children of similar reading abilities. Interestingly, they frame the results of the study in terms of identifying which phonological and memory skills account for the greatest amount of variance in reading level scores. In other words, implicit in their analysis is the assumption of directionality in the relationship: that it is reading level that is the dependent variable, and phonological awareness that is the independent variable.

However, there are other scholars in child language development who take the opposite position: that it is the development of literacy that causes increased phonological awareness. Berthoud-Papandropoulou (1978) stated that the development of children's awareness of words as phonological forms depended on their exposure to written words. Indeed, many of the scholars who Wiley (in press) lists as having an "autonomous" orientation to the study of literacy (e.g., Olson, 2002) argue quite strongly that it is the process of becoming literate that provides individuals with an awareness of the linguistic units encoded in the notational system of the written language.[1] Discussing the impact of literacy on their cognition, Olson (2002) states: "Children's important discovery is that their own and others' more or less continuous speech may be thought of as a sequence of lexical items or 'words' " (p. 158).

But perhaps it is not possible to establish directionality between phonological awareness and literacy development when working only with a population of children, where age/cognitive development and literacy level are typically confounded. Perhaps the directionality of this relationship is best explored in carefully designed studies of adult illiterates.

Oral Processing and Adult Illiteracy

As established earlier, there are a great many illiterate adults throughout the world, so it is quite feasible to study highly comparable groups of adults whose only distinction is their ability to encode/decode written language. When such groups differ in the linguistic awareness they display in processing oral language, then it seems much more likely that the causal factor is the mastery of the (en/de)coding skill itself. Importantly, such groups are often comparable in terms of the social practices of their local cultures; thus, it seems highly likely that it is decoding/encoding skill alone, and not their community of social practice, that is the differentiating variable that affects the way they process oral language.

Initially, research on the oral processing abilities of adult illiterates seems to have been carried out in Brazil by a team of researchers in the field of cognitive psychology and neuropsychology, with José Morais a frequent team member. These studies present evidence that the acquisition of the ability to decode an alphabetic script changes the way in which the individual processes oral language, as seen in their performance of certain kinds of cognitive tasks. Specifically, these researchers claim that literacy in an alphabetic script appears to significantly affect adults' performance of oral processing tasks that require an awareness of linguistic segments. These research studies in the 1970s and 1980s were published in such journals as *Cognition*, *Cognitive Neuropsychology*, and *Applied Psycholinguistics*. The primary goal of these researchers was to document the incidence of cognitive impairments of various kinds within a larger population of adults in Brazil and Portugal, many of whom were also illiterate; to do this, they needed to establish a baseline of performance by normally functioning illiterate adults. In such a study documenting the oral language processing abilities of normal illiterate adults, Morais, Cary, Alegría, and Bertelson (1979), and Morais, Bertelson, Cary, and Alegría (1986) found that whereas many of them performed oral tasks focusing on rhyme or on the analysis of speech into syllables just as well as literate adults did, illiterate adults performed far worse than literate adults on oral tasks requiring segmental analysis, particularly at the level of the phoneme. A typical oral task that was relatively easy for literate adults and almost impossible for illiterate adults asked them to add or delete an individual consonant at the beginning of a spoken word. Another task, assessing "phonological fluency," asked them to list all the words they could think of that started with a named phoneme (e.g. /t/); again, illiterate adults had trouble doing this task. The researchers argued that an individual's mastery of an alphabetic script, which requires the establishment of a grapheme-phoneme correspondence, establishes the ability of literates to process oral language in terms of the linguistic segment "phoneme." Illiterates, who lack the linguistic construct "phoneme," cannot perform oral tasks that require the awareness of that construct. In a similar study focusing on oral processing of words rather than phonemes, Kolinsky, Cary, and Morais (1987) examined the word awareness of adult illiterates and found that awareness of phonological length of words was related to degree of literacy, not age and its correlate, cognitive maturation.

A possible criticism of these Brazilian studies was that the two subject groups might have differed along dimensions other than their mastery of the grapheme-phoneme correspondence (e.g., local culture, school experience, knowledge of the world, and other analytical abilities promoted in general in school). In other words, the two groups may have been situated in different networks of social practice, and this itself could account for differences in their oral processing abilities. To address this possibility, and also to explore the influence of a nonalphabetic as opposed to an alphabetic script, Read, Xhang, Nie, and Ding (1986) focused on two comparable groups of adult Chinese participants, both educated and both living in a similar context of social practice. One group ($n = 18$) had become literate only in Chinese characters, having been educated in schools that had not yet adopted the Chinese alphabetic script (Hanyu Pinyin). The second group ($n = 12$), comparable to the first in level of education, age, and social group, had become literate in both Chinese characters and the alphabetic script. Their differential exposure to an alphabetic script was an accident of history and social change, and not to any differences in their cognitive ability or their social situation. Both groups were asked to perform oral tasks in Chinese; they were asked to add or delete a single consonant (*d*, *s*, *n*) at the beginning of a spoken syllable. All syllables and targets were possible words in Chinese (e.g., /an/, /san/); some targets were words and some were nonwords. The results showed that on this task the adults who had alphabetic literacy significantly outperformed those who did not. Where the targets were nonwords, the literate adults' accuracy was 93% compared to 37% for the illiterate group; for targets that were words, the literate adults' accuracy was 83% compared to 21% for the illiterates. The authors conclude that the ability to segment oral language develops *as a consequence* of the process of learning to read and write alphabetically. A similar study on Chinese readers by de Gelder, Vroomen, and Bertelson (1993) replicated Read et al.'s results.

Other studies were subsequently carried out in Spain, Portugal, and Brazil, to compare the performance of adults who were, or were not, literate. For example, Adrian, Alegría, and Morais (1995) administered an extensive battery of oral tasks to a group of 15 illiterate adults in Spain, comparing their performance to that of two other groups: one a group of "poor readers" and the other a group of "readers." The illiterate participants scored as well as the literate ones on a phonetic discrimination task asking participants whether pairs such as /me-me/ or /sa-ta/ were different. This showed that literacy did not affect phonological sensitivity. Half the illiterate participants did very well on rhyming tasks, so literacy had a negligible effect on this skill. However, the illiterate participants got very low scores on all tests that should require conscious awareness of phonemes (matching, monitoring, deletion, and reversal). They also were significantly worse than the literate adults on oral tasks requiring them to reverse words and syllables.

Perhaps the best-designed and most tightly-reasoned study in this area we found was Reis and Castro-Caldas (1997), who studied two groups of women in a fishing community in the south of Portugal, matched for intelligence and family/cultural environment, but differing solely in terms of their ability to know the phonemic value of a set of graphemes. Postulating that illiterate adults rely heavily on semantic strategies rather than phonological strategies to perform certain tasks, Reis and Castro-Caldas state: "Learning to match graphemes and phonemes is learning an operation in which units of auditory verbal information heard in temporal sequence are matched to units of visual verbal information which is spatially arranged" (p. 445). Reis and Castro-Caldas posit that literate individuals develop a strategy where visual-graphic meaning is given to units that are smaller than words, and so have no semantic meaning. These segments are introduced sequentially in a working memory system with a new content of visual experience. (To spell a word, we can evoke a visual image of the letters. Then we play with those written symbols, each coded to a sound, to form pseudowords with no semantic meaning.) This involves conscious phonological processing, visual formal lexical representations, and their associations—all of which are strategies available to literate and not illiterate individuals. To explore this general postulate, Reis and Castro-Caldas conducted three experiments: (a) an oral word/pseudoword repetition task, (b) an oral word-pair memory task in which some pairs were semantically-related and some were phonologically-related, and (c) verbal fluency tasks that were either semantically triggered (e.g., names of animals) or phonologically triggered (e.g., words that begin with /p/). Results showed that the illiterate group had significantly greater difficulty than the literate group with repetition of pseudowords but did equally well on repetition of frequent words. The illiterate group did significantly better on the semantic word pairs than the phonological ones, and on the semantic verbal fluency task than the phonological one. However, they did comparatively worse than the literate group on both semantic and phonological tasks in Experiment 2 and 3, suggesting to the experimenters that the illiterate subjects used strategies that were good for semantic processing, but not for phonological analysis, whereas literate individuals were able to use parallel semantic and phonological strategies at once, which greatly improved their accuracy. Reis and Castro-Caldas believe that semantic processing is implicit, and learning to read and write brings an explicit dimension to the process of phonological processing. They conclude that absence of the ability to associate grapheme and phoneme decreases the efficiency of explicit phonological processing of oral language in adult life: "The missing of a single skill (grapheme-phoneme association) interferes significantly in the higher development of the language system" (p. 449).

Olson (2002) cites an ongoing study by Alice Moro at the University of

Calgary showing that illiterate adults do the same thing children do when asked to count words on the page: shown a text that is simultaneously read to them that said "three wild horses," and then seeing one of the words covered up, 5 of 10 illiterate adults said it meant "two wild horses." Because the degree of illiteracy of these adults in Calgary is probably not absolute, but partial, given their social and physical environment, it is not surprising that half of these adults did not make this same mistake. But the fact they made it at all, and literate adults do not, provides support for the notion that the awareness of the linguistic construct "word" is a product of becoming literate.

Dellatolas, Willadino-Braga, Souza, Filho, Queiroz, and Deloche[2] (2003) explore the impact of degree of illiteracy on a wide range of phonological skills, verbal and visual memory, and visuospatial skills. The participants in the Dellatolas et al. study were 97 normally functioning self-described illiterate adults and 41 children (ages 7–8) in Brazil. The degree of literacy of all the participants was measured by asking them to read 16 short words and identify capital letters and numbers. Participants who could not read a single word were placed in a "nonreader" group, and those who could read at least one word were placed in a "reader" group. Twenty tests were administered individually to each participant in the study. These included measures of word and nonword repetition, semantic and phonological fluency, rhyme identification, initial phoneme deletion, and various memory span tests. Results replicated many of those described in the previous studies. Literacy significantly improved performance on phonological fluency and initial phoneme deletion tasks. A stepwise regression analysis showed that scores on four measures could classify 86.8% of the participants as readers or nonreaders; these were phonological fluency, initial phoneme deletion, visual recognition, and (with opposite sign) digit span. Illiterates' ability to name letters was significantly related to phonological fluency and initial phoneme deletion. Oral repetition was relatively easy overall for illiterate individuals, but they did have great difficulty with repetition of long nonwords, a finding that other studies have also replicated. The authors suggest that the ability to repeat long nonwords is an important language learning skill, because it means the individual can hold words they do not understand in short-term memory, giving them an opportunity to ask or search for a meaning.

These studies, growing out of research in the field of cognitive psychology and neuropsychology, and focusing on the impact of literacy on the oral language processing of adults, provide a growing body of evidence suggesting that the acquisition of grapheme-phoneme correspondence in learning to read an alphabetic script, and also the acquisition of the abstract concept of "word" acquired in the process of learning to read, both provide important cognitive tools for the processing of oral language. They seem to provide clear evidence that it is learning the skill of decoding an alphabetic script that produces these changes in cognitive processing.

A Broadening Agenda for First Language Acquisition Research

There is recent evidence that the fields of child language acquisition and child reading research are expanding their related agendas to include the study of the relationship between children's oral language processing and acquisition, and their acquisition of literacy skills. In 2002, Ravid and Tolchinsky published a position paper in the *Journal of Child Language*, proposing a new construct of "linguistic literacy." "Linguistic literacy" is defined as ". . . a constituent of language knowledge characterized by the availability of multiple linguistic resources and by the ability to consciously access one's own linguistic knowledge and to view language from various perspectives" (p. 419–420). The key property of linguistic literacy is rhetorical flexibility, or adaptability: being able to produce varied linguistic output attuned to different addressees and contexts and to create linguistic representations that can be manipulated for metalinguistic reflection. Linguistic literacy is late acquired, by school-age learners, as they add the major linguistic modality of writing to the earlier-acquired modality of speech. In the process, they become more aware of language itself.

Ravid and Tolchinsky (2002) are cited earlier in this chapter as stating that linguistic literacy has both a discourse dimension[3] and a notational code dimension. They discuss at some length the discourse dimension, which relates to the increasing variation in the discourse styles mastered by the learner[4]. Here however we focus on their discussion of the notational code, which for English is an alphabetic system. Alphabetic systems are said by these authors to have four types of knowledge systems to be mastered: phonology (grapho-phonemic link), orthography (fonts, upper/lower case), morpho-phonology (emic/etic distinctions like flap /t/), and morphology (past tense marker in English). Learning these systems entails constructing an internal model of the units of spoken language modeled by the features of the written script. For example, punctuation involves marking word boundaries and sentence boundaries. They state:

> Written text conventions promote metalinguistic thinking in various linguistic domains such as sound/letter correspondence, word and sentence boundaries, and appropriate grammatical constructions (e.g. past perfect in English, passé simple in French, or optional bound morphology in Hebrew).... the reciprocal character of speech and writing in a literate community makes it a synergistic system where certain features (e.g. basic syntax) originate in the spoken input, while others, such as complex syntax and advanced and domain-specific lexical items, originate in the written input. Together, however, they form a "virtual loop" where speech and writing constantly feed and modify each other. (p. 430)

Ravid and Tolchinsky suggest that before speakers of a language become literate, they focus out of necessity on the meaning of their utterances, and not on the linguistic form of language. But with literacy, those individuals begin to develop an explicit and analytical awareness of language itself. With that awareness comes increasing cognitive control. Links are established between the internal representation of phonemes, syllables, and morphemes and their written representations, and these newly articulated representations become the locus of increasing control.

The position paper of Ravid and Tolchinksky (2002) is followed in the same issue of the journal with 10 responses from a diverse group of leading scholars on child language development, among them Berman (2002); Verhoeven (2002), Biber, and Reppen, and Conrad (2002). Their responses suggest that the field of child language acquisition will be affected by Ravid and Tolchinsky's new construct. For example, Kail (2002) points out that the proposed model can help explain patterns of French L1 acquisition. In French, there is a particularly large gap between the oral and written code, for example, in verbal number agreement: *fille/filles, genous/ benous, il chante/ils chantent.* Children initially base their sentence interpretations on word order, and only later do they take morphology into account; a central puzzle has been what it is that causes children to change the way they interpret oral input. Kail (2002) states:

> The developmental change in French children's processing could be explained by their increasing mastery of morphological cues supplied by growing knowledge of the written code which is clearer and more regular than the oral one. It seems reasonable to assume that linguistic literacy makes French morphology more accessible and more consistent providing a stable representation for agreements. . . we have to predict that literacy may cause the child to notice conflict cases in the input (for example between word order and morphology) she has never noticed before. (p. 465)

Miller (2002) explores the implications of Ravid and Tolchinsky's construct for innatism itself, as the central approach to the study of child language. Considering the fact that complex syntactic structures such as the full relative clause system in English are acquired very late, he points out problems for nativist theories of language acquisition, which

> assume a large endowment of innate linguistic knowledge, without which it would (allegedly) be impossible for children to acquire the complex structures of any language. Once the complexities of written language are seen as learned over a longish period of schooling, once spontaneous spoken language is recognized as being relatively simple and once it is recognized that children do receive negative evidence (Sokolov & Snow 1994), nativist theories lose their *raison d'être*. This is the most important consequence of paying attention to literacy and the distinction between spoken and written language. (p. 473)

To summarize, then: researchers and scholars pursuing studies independently of one another in the different fields of child language acquisition and adult cognitive processing are at the same point in time reaching similar conclusions about the central interconnectedness of the acquisition of literacy in an alphabetic language and human beings' oral processing of language. We are particularly interested in the research that establishes a clear picture of what it is that illiterate adults can and cannot easily do in processing oral language. This gives us a much clearer idea of the abilities they bring to the acquisition of a second language. Those abilities appear to be qualitatively different in certain key areas from abilities commonly assumed by SLA researchers and theoreticians to be universally present in second-language learners.

So what are the implications of this new body of knowledge for current second-language acquisition research? What are the implications for the pedagogy of second-language learners who are not literate in any language?

Possible Implications for Research Agendas in Applied Linguistics

Much current research on second-language acquisition is guided by theories that assume that second-language learners are aware of linguistic segments. Indeed, Schmidt's Noticing Hypothesis (Schmidt, 1994, p. 17) claims that "noticing is a necessary and sufficient condition for converting input to intake" and that *conscious noticing* is necessary for learning to take place. The research reviewed in this article, although largely carried out in the participants' native languages, is intriguing with respect to the Noticing Hypothesis. If L2 learners who are not literate in any language do not consciously notice segmental linguistic units in oral input in the second language—(a reasonable assumption, given that the research shows they don't notice them in their native language)—then the Noticing Hypothesis would predict that they cannot acquire an L2 at all. And yet it is clear that many illiterate adults do acquire L2s through oral input. For example, illiterate Somali adults acquire very good fluency in oral English, their L2, apparently without possessing some key metalinguistic skills. One possibility, of course, is that the Noticing Hypothesis is just wrong—that humans don't need to notice L2 structures to acquire them. This might be Krashen's response (Krashen, 1982). But we can think of two other possibilities, either of which might reconcile these research results with the Noticing Hypothesis. One possibility is that the ability to consciously notice and analyze oral L2 input in terms of segmental linguistic units holds only for alphabetically literate L2 learners. Thus, illiterate adults retain the ability to unconsciously internalize the L2, in the same way they internalized their L1; once adults become literate, they must consciously notice an L2 structure to internalize it. Another possibility—one that is suggested by the Ravid and Tolchinsky article—is that the Noticing Hypothesis applies only or primarily to the acquisition of that set of more complex syntactic structures which characterize the written language—that is, it applies to the acquisition of linguistic literacy in the L2. In other words, a core set of simple syntactic structures may be acquired unconsciously and not require noticing; an illiterate L2 learner may become quite fluent in the use of these structures orally. However, the more complex set of syntactic structures characteristic of written English, and the full mastery of linguistic literacy in the L2, may require conscious attention and noticing if they are to be acquired. It would appear that the exploration of these alternative possibilities may generate some interesting SLA research and theory-building in the future.

A second implication for SLA research has to do with our interpretation of those recent studies that have focused on the influence of enhanced input or corrective feedback on the acquisition of core syntactic structures of an L2. Indeed, all SLA studies exploring Focus on Form (e.g., Doughty & Williams, 1998) should now be reconsidered. Such studies have typically targeted core syntactic structures such as simple verb tenses, question formation, and negation. The assumption of work in this area is that all L2 learners have the metalinguistic awareness to notice enhanced input or corrective feedback that is focused on such L2 forms. But if L2 learners do not have awareness or ability to consciously manipulate phonemes, morphemes, and words in the L2, then they cannot notice enhanced input or corrective feedback targeting those phonemes, morphemes, and words. For example, if corrective feedback adds a phoneme to a word they have just produced (e.g., /laik/, /laikt/, /bey/, /beyz/), they may not have the oral language processing tools to notice the difference between their own word and the corrected word, and then add the phoneme to the word in a subsequent utterance. Similarly, some studies we have reviewed in the section on oral language processing and adult illiteracy show that illiterate adults have a hard time reversing the order of syllables and words; if such individuals receive corrective feedback in L2 that inverts subject and auxiliary to form a question, will they be able to notice this reversal, and implement it in their own output? Such questions have led to emerging research on the SLA processes of relatively illiterate adults. Bigelow, Delmas, Hansen, and Tarone (under review) find that Somali adults who have low literacy levels are significantly less able to correctly recall oral recasts of their erroneous English L2 questions than similar learners with higher literacy levels.

There are surely also implications of the research on oral language processing and literacy for other areas of SLA research. For example, how do the oral processing constraints of illiterate adults interact with the cognitive processing strategies that Clahsen, Meisel, and Pienemann propose underlie the Multidimensional Model's stages of acquisition (see Clahsen, Meisel, & Pienemann, (1983); Meisel, Clahsen, & Pienemann (1981); Pienemann & Johnston, (1987)). Do illiterate adults follow the same stages of acquisition as the literate adults in their research? Space does not allow us to explore such implications in this chapter, but we hope that others will take up such considerations in future publications.

Finally, there may be important implications of this research for our understanding of the impact of literacy in an alphabetic script upon the acquisition of a lexicon in a second language. Reis and Castro-Caldas (1997) suggest that the ability to hold a pseudoword in the short term phonological store is directly related to the ability to acquire new lexical items in a language; they argue that the phonological short term memory of illiterate adults is negatively impacted and that this could affect lexical acquisition. Nation (2001) cites SLA research with literate L2 learners that shows that phonological memory and L2 lexical acquisition are related. But illiterate adults do acquire L2 words. We need research to determine whether illiteracy negatively affects adults' ability to acquire an L2 lexicon, and also research to identify their lexical acquisition processes.

Possible Implications for Research Agendas in Second Language Pedagogy

First, the research summarized in this chapter shows that illiterate adults have specific strengths (e.g., phonological sensitivity and rhyming) as well as specific weaknesses in their oral language processing (e.g., phonemic discrimination). Pedagogic strategies for illiterate adults should consider these findings both when teaching L2 oral skills and L2 literacy skills. For example, L2 teachers may wish to build on oral traditions in the cultures of their students that use rhyming (a strength) to build language awareness in the oral or written modes in the L2. Teachers might also wish to provide adult illiterate students in their classrooms who are just acquiring grapheme/phoneme awareness with training involving manipulation of linguistic segments to help them build connections between the oral and written media. Teachers can engage learners through whole-group, peer, and individual discussion and then make links to text. Teachers reading aloud to students from multiple genres may give meaning, purpose, context, and enjoyment to adult learners for whom text has always been a source of discomfort or simply avoided. Teachers will find engaging with adults, who bring mature cognitive abilities to the process of becoming literate, to be different from working with children, yet illiterate adults may still need to be explicitly taught the basics of grapheme-phoneme correspondence and word boundary, both in writing and orally, before moving on to more top-down literacy practices.

Conclusion

If SLA research is to account for human capacity for SLA, and if SLA research is to have implications for L2 pedagogy of learners who are not literate, then SLA studies must include illiterate adults. This research will be useful in further determining where such learners' strengths and weaknesses lie, and this in turn will have implications for teachers of adolescents and adults with limited formal schooling. If L2 pedagogy with illiterate older students is to be more effective, then we should explore the efficacy of teaching strategies that build oral and contextual support for development of grapheme/phoneme and other linguistic segmentation skills. Of course, this does not preclude strategies that give literacy instruction a meaningful context in which it unfolds in the classroom or take into account the uses students have for expanded literacy in their lives.

It will take more time and effort for SLA researchers to study illiterate adults. It may be challenging for some SLA researchers to focus their research efforts outside the walls of undergraduate world language programs or university intensive English centers. There are issues of access to illiterate adult learners, which must be hard earned through long-term trusting relationships, and there is difficulty obtaining informed consent from participants for whom verbal consent is the only option. Recruitment may be challenging when potential participants discover that the focus on the research deals with one of their weaknesses, not being able to read or write. (These concerns are outlined in Bigelow & Tarone, in press). However, given the results of the studies and scholarship reviewed here and their potential implications for second language learners, it is vital for our field to broaden its scope for both theoretical and practical reasons. We simply cannot claim that SLA theories apply widely to all second language learners unless we study a greater range of the circumstances in which L2 learning occurs and thereby expand our knowledge base.

Notes

1. We point out here that this is not the same thing as arguing, as Ong and Goody have done, that mastery of an alphabetic script is essential to logical thinking! Awareness of the boundaries of linguistic units in the stream of speech is one thing: Logical thinking is quite another.

2. The results of this study are also reported in Loureiro et al. (2004).

3. In the discourse dimension, linguistic literacy makes variability (both user-related, and context-dependent variation) both accessible and controllable. It enables the language user to increase their control over register (distinctions that express social dimensions like power, authority, distance, politeness), genre (text types defined by function, communicative purpose, and sociocultural practice), modality (oral vs. writing, with its lack of audience, stable language signal, more control over linguistic output).

4. Here Ravid and Tolchinsky rely heavily on the work of Biber and his colleagues (Biber 1988; Biber et al., 1991) who show that the registers of oral and written language are basically different, and that the syntactic constructions used in written registers are typically more complex, and the information structure of written registers more dense.

ANNOTATED BIBLIOGRAPHY

Adrian, J. A., Alegría, J., & Morais, J. (1995). Metaphonological abilities of Spanish illiterate adults. *International Journal of Psychology, 30*, 329–353.

This study, carried out in Spain, compares the metaphonological abilities of 15 illiterate adults with those of two groups: poorer readers and better readers. All were given a battery of tests, including a reading test, phonetic discrimination (e.g., *ta-sa*: same or different?), rhyme detection (e.g., *mepu/pepu*: rhyme or not?), syllable detection (e.g., is [pa] contained in [pati]? Or, if you delete [pa] from [pati], what do you have?), phoneme detection (e.g., do these words contain the same phoneme? '*kar/kus*'), syllable deletion (e.g., if we subtract [de] from the word [kade], we have ?), phoneme deletion (e.g., if we subtract [t] from the syllable [tal], we have ?), word reversal (e.g., say *zanahoria rota* backwards), syllable reversal (e.g., say [taro] backwards. Ans: [rota]), phoneme reversal (e.g., how would you say [los] backwards? Answer: [sol]).

All the participants did extremely well on the phonetic discrimination task. However, the illiterate participants got very low scores on all tests that should require conscious awareness of phonemes (matching, monitoring, deletion, and reversal of phonemes). The authors conclude that phonemic awareness (ability to segment speech on the basis of phonemes) is affected by the degree of literacy of these adults. Phonological sensitivity (ability to classify two utterances as same or different phonetically) is a different skill from phonemic awareness, one that literacy does not affect. Syllable tasks were easier for illiterates than phoneme tasks, though still more difficult for illiterate than for literate participants. The rhyming tasks were surprisingly difficult for both the illiterates and the poorer readers; this may have been because of rapid changing of tasks in the experimental design. (Authors cite other studies that show that illiterates can reach quite high levels of performance in rhyming sensitivity, cf. Bertelson, et al., 1989; Morais, et al., 1986).

Dellatolas, G., Willadino-Braga, L., Souza, L., Filho, G., Queiroz, E., & Deloche, G. (2003). Cognitive consequences of early phase of literacy. *Journal of the International Neuropsychological Society 9*, 771–782.

The article begins by citing research demonstrating that neuropsychological test performance depends on literacy, even for tasks that do not directly involve reading and writing. Adult illiterates scored lower than literates on such tasks as repetition of pseudowords, memory of pairs of phonologically related words, generation of words according to a phonological criterion, verbal abstraction, orientation, figure matching and recognition, naming line drawings, components of calculation and number processing. Literacy status did not affect verbal list delayed recall, nonverbal abstraction, category fluency, or counting elements of small sets.

The study reported herein addresses the question: Which specific cognitive processes are reading acquisition dependent, in adults and children? The study compared the performance of 97 adults and 41 children (ages: 7–8) living in Brasilia; those who could not read one of 16 common short words were classified illiterate, and those who could read at least one of these words were classified literate. Twenty tests were administered in individual intereviews: repetition of words and nonwords, semantic verbal fluency, phonological verbal fluency, visual recognition memory of nonsense figures, rhyme identification, minimal pairs phonetic discrimination, initial phoneme deletion, digit span, span for familiar monosyllabic words, span for monosyllabic nonwords, figure recall, embedded figures, counting dots, counting backwards, word list recall. A two-way ANOVA was run with adult/children and reader/nonreader as independent variables, and all the cognitive scores as dependent variables. Readers did better than nonreaders on all tasks except four (oral repetition of short and long words, short nonwords, digit span). The literacy effect for adults and children was not significantly different, except for counting backwards, which all nonreading children failed. Literacy significantly improved performance on phonological fluency and initial phoneme deletion tasks. The authors conclude that literacy does not affect the perceptual level, but the phonological fluency and initial phoneme deletion tasks both involve speech segmentation abilities, and these significantly relate to literacy level. Initial phoneme deletion with cluster onset (CCV) were particularly difficult for illiterates. The authors discuss the lower ability of illiterate adults to repeat nonwords, suggesting that the ability to hold a word one does not know (temporarily a 'nonword') in short term memory while one searches for its meaning is an important skill to have in acquiring new word meanings.

Olson, D. (2002). What writing does to the mind. In E. Amsel & J. P. Byrnes (Eds.), *Language, literacy, and cognitive development: The development and consequences of symbolic communication* (pp. 153–166). Mahwah, NJ: Erlbaum.

This paper begins with Olson's claim that "learning to read is to an important extent a matter of learning how to analyze one's speech in a new way, a way compatible with the properties of the writing system. Thus, the child has to learn to hear the sounds represented by letters in their own and others' speech, to hear the b represented by the letter /b/ in 'baby,' and 'bath'. . . . To segment words, the child has first to learn that an utterance can be segmented into words, and that knowledge too may be acquired in the process of becoming literate" (p. 156).

Olson cites research that supports this claim, beginning with a study by Ferreiro (1994) showing that prereading children interpret written words in the same way they interpret pictures. They do not know, until they learn to read, that representations of words require arbitrary signs that can be combined to make different words. He cites examples from Homer and Olson (1999). For example, a prereading child asked to write "*cat*" writes one scribble; when asked to write two cats, he writes two scribbles; three cats is three scribbles; no cats is a wave of the pencil in the air and the statement, 'there's no cats so I didn't write anything'. In another case, a prereading child is shown a card that says 'three little pigs' and someone reads that phrase. Then one word is covered up and the child is asked to guess what it says now. The child says 'two little pigs.' The child assumes the text relates to objects and events, not language *about* objects and events. They do not have the concept of 'word.' (He later cites an ongoing study by Alice Moro at the University of Calgary where illiterate adults did the same thing: Shown a text read to them that said 'three wild horses,' and then, seeing one of the words covered up, 5 of 10 of them said it meant 'two wild horses.') Olson also goes on to claim that thinking about words as they occur in writing leads to our notion of grammatical standards, which we use to correct ourselves and others.

Olson concludes:

Writing is what introduces our speech to us, revealing our speech as having a particular structure. Children do not know that they speak words, that is, that the flow of speech can be thought of as a string of lexical items. But children in an alphabetic society do come to think about language, mind, and world in terms of the category systems employed in writing. To paraphrase Whorf (1956), we dissect language along lines laid down by our scripts (p. 164).

Ravid, D., & Tolchinsky, L. (2002). Developing linguistic literacy: A comprehensive model. *Journal of Child Language, 29*, 417–447.

This position paper proposes a construct called *linguistic literacy*, which is the ability to produce different language varieties appropriate to different addressees and contexts, and to create linguistic representations that can be manipulated for metalinguistic reflection. Children become more aware of language itself when they add the major linguistic modality of writing to the earlier-acquired modality of speech. The authors distinguish different degrees of consciousness and explicitness in the process of acquisition; for example, recognition is implicit identification, and awareness is conscious access, which learners may not be able to verbalize. The authors stress that they do not view either spoken or written language as primary, but emphasize the reciprocal relationship between the two; in a literate society, language structures may predominate ("originate") in one or the other modality but be used in the other. Initially, in language development, language knowledge is implicit because the speaker focuses on meaning and not form; however, learners later develop an explicit and analytic awareness of language itself, an awareness that is necessary for cognitive control to be exercised. As awareness grows, the learner reorganizes linguistic representations into more coherent and accessible forms. The authors cite longstanding research showing that various types of oral language awareness correlate with both basic and advanced literacy skills, and take the position that phonological and morphological awareness both promote and are promoted by learning to read and write. Links are established between internal representation of phonemes, syllables, and morphemes and their written representations. They posit that alphabetic systems have four types of knowledge systems to be mastered: phonology (grapho-phonemic link), orthography (fonts, upper/lower case), morpho-phonology (emic/etic distinctions like flap 't'), and morphology (past tense marker in English). Learning these entails constructing an internal model of the units of spoken language modeled by the features of the written script. This article is followed in the same issue of the journal with 10 responses written by leading researchers and scholars.

Reis, A. & Castro-Caldas, A. (1997). Illiteracy: A cause for biased cognitive development. *Journal of the International Neuropsychological Society*, *3*, 444–450.

This study explores the proposition that learning to read and write affects the way in which some language processing operations are performed. The study participants were sisters aged 50–70 living in a remote fishing village in Portugal; in their youth the oldest daughter had been kept home from school to mind younger siblings while younger daughters had gone to school and learned to read and write.

After school, their social lives and social roles had been identical, and the need for reading and writing minimal.

These participants were studied in matched groups as they performed three experiments exploring three hypotheses: (1) repetition of pseudowords, which requires both explicit and implicit phonological processing, should be harder for illiterates than for literates; (2) in tasks that are solvable both by semantic content and knowledge of word form, illiterates will rely on knowledge of semantic content; (3) illiterates should have difficulty with tasks of verbal fluency based on language form (compared to literates) but not with tasks of verbal fluency based on semantic content. All three hypotheses were confirmed. In experiment 1: Repeating Words and Pseudowords, the participants were asked to repeat 24 highly frequent words and 24 pseudowords created by substituting consonants in words of the first group. An ANOVA showed no difference between the groups in ability to repeat meaningful words. Illiterate participants made significantly more errors repeating pseudowords than literates; 26% of their errors involved transforming pseudowords into meaningful words, something literates rarely did at all. For experiment 2: Word Pair Association, two sets of word pairs were developed. One set of word pairs was semantically related (e.g., *rose-carnation*) and the other set of pairs was words phonologically related (e.g., *mala-pala*). The tests were administered as directed on the Wechsler Memory Scale. The literate participants performed equally well on both types of word pairs, and overall significantly better than the illiterate participants. The illiterate participants performed significantly worse on the phonologically related word pairs than they did on the semantically related word pairs. In experiment 3: Verbal Fluency, participants performed two tasks. In the semantic fluency version, they had one minute to repeat the names of as many animals (subtask 1) and pieces of furniture (subtask 2) as they could think of. In the phonological fluency version, they had one minute to repeat as many words they could think of that began with /p/ (subtask 1) or /b/ (subtask 2).

All the participants did all the subtasks. The illiterate participants did significantly worse on the phonological fluency tasks than on the semantic fluency tasks. The literate participants did equally well on both types of task, and much better than the illiterate participants on all tasks. The authors conclude that in general, the illiterate participants used strategies that were good for semantic processing, but not for phonological analysis, whereas the literate individuals were able to use parallel phonological and semantic strategies at once. They also suggest that illiterate individuals cannot perform the mental operation of storing words in a short-term memory buffer that is phonologically structured.

OTHER REFERENCES

Berman, R. (2002). Peer commentary on 'Developing linguistic literacy: A comprehensive model'by Dorit Ravid and Liliana Tolchinsky. *Journal of Child Language*, 29, 453–457.

Bertelson, P., de Gelder, B., Tfouni, L. V., & Morais, J. (1989). Metaphonological abilities of adult illiterates: New evidence of heterogeneity. *European Journal of Cognitive Psychology*, 1, 239–250.

Berthoud-Papandropoulou, I. (1978). An experimental study of children's ideas about language. In W. J. M. Levelt, A. Sinclair & R. J. Jarvella (Eds.), *The child's conception of language* (pp. 55–64). Berlin: Springer-Verlag.

Biber, D. (1988). *Variation across spoken and written English*. Cambridge, UK: Cambridge University Press.

Biber, D., & Hared, M. (1991). Literacy in Somali: Linguistic consequences. *Annual Review of Applied Linguistics*, 12, 260–282.

Biber, D., Reppen, R., & Conrad, S. (2002). Developing linguistic literacy: Perspectives from corpus linguistics and multi-dimensional analysis. *Journal of Child Language*, 29, 458–462.

Bigelow, M., Delmas, R., Hansen, K., & Tarone, E. (under review). Literacy and the processing of oral recasts in SLA.

Bigelow, M., & Tarone, E. (in press). The role of literacy level in SLA: Doesn't *who* we study determine *what* we know? *TESOL Quarterly*, 38 (4).

Clahsen, H., Meisel, J. M., & Pienemann, M. (1983). *Deutsch als Zweitsprache. Der Spracherwerb auslandischer Arbeiter*. Tubingen: Narr.

De Gelder, B., Vroomen, J., & Bertelson, P. (1993). The effects of alphabetic-reading competence on language representation in bilingual Chinese subjects. *Psychological Research*, 55, 315–321.

Doughty, C. & Williams, J. (1998). *Focus on form in classroom second language acquisition*. Cambridge, UK: Cambridge University Press.

Ferreiro, E. (1994). Two literacy histories: A possible dialogue between children and their ancestors. In D. Keller-Cohen (Ed.), *Literacy: Interdisciplinary perspectives* (pp. 115–128). Cresskill, NJ: Hampton Press.

Fleischman, H. L., & Hopstick, P. (1993). *Descriptive study of services to limited English proficient students*. Arlington, VA: Development Associates.

Gee, J. P. (1991). Socio-cultural approaches to literacy (literacies). *Annual Review of Applied*

Linguistics, 12, 31–48.

Gee, J. P. (2001). Forward. In T. M. Kalmar, *Illegal alphabets: Latino migrants crossing the linguistic border* (pp. i–iv). Mahwah, NJ: Lawrence Erlbaum Associates.

Goody, J. (1987). *The interface between the written and the oral.* Cambridge, England: Cambridge University Press.

Heath, S. B. (1983). *Ways with words: Language, life and work in communities and classrooms.* Cambridge, England: Cambridge University Press.

Hill, J. (1970). Foreign accents, language acquisition and cerebral dominance revisited. *Language Learning, 20,* 237–248.

Homer, B. & Olson, D. (1999). Literacy and children's conception of words. *Written Language and Literacy, 2,* 113–137.

Jamieson, A., Curry, A., & Martinez, G. (2001). School enrollment in the United States: Social and economic characteristics of students. October, 1999. *In Current Population Reports* (pp. 520–533). Washington, DC: U.S. Census Bureau.

Kail, M. (2002). Sentence processing studies and linguistic literacy. *Journal of Child Language, 29,* 463–466.

Kolinsky, R., Cary, L., & Morais, J. (1987). Awareness of words as phonological entities: The role of literacy. *Applied Psycholinguistics, 8,* 223–232.

Krashen, S. (1982). *Principles and practice in second language acquisition.* Englewood Cliffs, NJ: Prentice Hall.

Loureiro, C., Willadino-Braga, L., Souza, L., Filho, G., Queiroz, E., & Dellatolas, G. (2004). Degree of illiteracy and phonological and metaphonological skills in unschooled adults. *Brain and Language, 89,* 499–502.

Meisel, J. M., Clahsen, H., & Pienemann, M. (1981). On determining developmental stages in natural second language acquisition. *Studies in Second Language Acquisition, 3,* 109–135.

Miller, J. (2002). Questions about constructions. *Journal of Child Language, 29,* 470–474.

Morais, J., Cary, L., Alegría, J., & Bertelson, P. (1979). Does awareness of speech as a sequence of phones arise spontaneously? *Cognition, 7,* 323–331.

Morais, J., Bertelson, P., Cary, L., & Alegría, J. (1986). Literacy training and speech segmentation. *Cognition, 24,* 45–64.

Nation, I. S. P. (2001). *Learning vocabulary in another language.* Cambridge, UK: Cambridge University Press.

Olson, D., & Torrance, N. (Eds.). (1991). *Literacy and orality.* Cambridge, UK: Cambridge University Press.

Ong, W. J. (1982). *Orality and literacy: The technologizing of the word.* London: Methuen & Co. Ltd.

Piaget, J. (1929). *The child's conception of the world.* New York: Harcourt Brace.

Pienemann, M., & Johnston, M. (1987). Factors influencing the development of language proficiency. In D. Nunan (Ed.), *Applying second language acquisition research* (pp. 45–141). Adelaide, Australia: National Curriculum Resource Centre.

Read, C., Zhang, Y., Nie, H., & Ding, B. (1986). The ability to manipulate speech sounds depends on knowing alphabetic spelling. *Cognition, 24*, 31–44.

Schmidt, R. W. (1994). Deconstructing consciousness in search of useful definitions for applied linguistics. *AILA Review: Consciousness and second language learning: Conceptual, methodological and practical issues in language learning and teaching, 11*, 11–26.

Snowling, M. J. (1998). Reading development and its difficulties. *Educational and Child Psychology, 15*, 44–58.

Street, B. V. (1995). *Social literacies: Critical approaches to literacy in development, ethnography, and education.* London: Longman.

Thompkins, A., & Binder, K. (2003). A comparison of factors affecting performance of functionally illiterate adults and children matched by reading level. *Reading Research Quarterly, 38*(2), 236–258.

UNESCO (2004). Literacy: UNESCO Institute for Statistics, 3.14. Retrieved September 26, 2004 from http://www.uis.unesco.org/ev.php?URL_ID=4926&URL_DO= DO_topic&URL_section=20

Verhoeven, L. (1994). *Functional literacy: Theoretical issues and educational implications.* Amsterdam: John Benjamins.

Verhoeven, L. (2002). Sociocultural and cognitive constraints on literacy development. *Journal of Child Language, 29*, 484–488.

Vygotsky, L.S. (1962). *Thought and language.* Cambridge, MA: MIT Press.

Wiley, T.G. (in press). Second language literacy and biliteracy. In E. Hinkel (Ed.), *Handbook of research in second language teaching and learning.* Mahwah, NJ: Erlbaum.

5. CURRENT APPROACHES TO RESEARCHING SECOND LANGUAGE LEARNER PROCESSES[1]

Gillian Wigglesworth

Language learning is a complex set of processes that largely take place in the learner's head. The extent to which learners consciously focus on specific aspects of language, the degree to which they notice particular features of language, and how this is done has been the object of considerable debate in different theoretical approaches to second language acquisition. For researchers in second language acquisition, one dilemma is how to find out what learners notice, and how, if at all, they incorporate this into their developing linguistic knowledge. Here, I discuss three approaches to researching learner cognitive processes that can be used to identify the knowledge that learners have about their second language, and obtain some insights into the cognitive processes of learners. These approaches have the potential to contribute to our understanding of how learners learn a second language, and, therefore, how this task may be facilitated. The first approach attempts to tap directly into the learner's thought through the use of think-aloud protocols, whereas the second involves having learners engage with activities that encourage them to talk aloud, thus providing insights into their thought processes. The third approach uses planning effects on task performance to investigate how learners monitor their language.

Learner Processes as Keys to Second Language Acquisition

The extent to which second language learners are conscious about the specifics of their language learning has been the subject of considerable debate. Krashen (1982, 1985) advocates that acquisition is an unconscious process, whereas others, such as Schmidt (1990, 1994, 2001) propose that it is a conscious process. The role of consciousness can be seen as an overarching concept which encompasses related questions about the role of explicit and implicit learning and knowledge, the roles of attention, awareness and noticing, and the extent to which learners monitor their language. Bearing these concepts in mind, this chapter investigates some of the ways in which learners process language, identify what they notice, and hypothesize about the ways in which they access and exploit their language knowledge. Three different methodological approaches are considered. The first is the use of verbal protocols, a procedure used to tap learner processes in reading and writing activities.

Verbal protocols involve considerable intervention on the part of the researcher in the sense that participants are instructed to perform an activity that is unrelated to the language learning task or activity in which they are participating. However, this type of data allows us probably the most direct insights into learner thought processes. The second methodological approach is less interventionist in that it investigates what learners do while they are performing language activities that involve dialogic discussion, including metalinguistic discussion, of the workings of the language. In a sense, the activity itself incorporates the learner's thinking aloud. The same can be said of the third type of methodology, which involves manipulating the planning conditions under which tasks are performed to explore learners' processes, in particular, their monitoring of their language output. In this case, however, the evidence of language processing is derived not directly from what learners say while performing the tasks, but from posthoc analyses of their language products, that is, the speaking or writing samples elicited under the different planning conditions. What all these approaches have in common is that they involve an analysis of learner output as discourse (verbal think-aloud, dialogic discussion, or monitored spoken or written output) and allow insights into learner processes from different perspectives.

Schmidt (1990) argued that it is essential for learners to actively notice features in their second language that will allow them to identify the gaps in their own linguistic knowledge of their second language. This in turn enables them to form hypotheses about their second language that they may then test in their language use. More recently, Schmidt (2001, pp. 3–4) has hypothesized that: "SLA [second language acquisition] is largely driven by what learners pay attention to and notice in the target language input and what they understand the significance of the noticed input to be." Noticing, therefore, is a crucial concept in understanding how learners process their second languages. Equally, it is well established that learners are limited both in terms of their processing capacity (Skehan, 1998), and in terms of their access to attentional resources (Schmidt, 2001). Because second language learners are exposed to more linguistic data than they can effectively process, they need to find some way to reduce the complexity of those data, which allows them to notice certain features of the data, and to make related hypotheses that they may subsequently test (Gass, Svetics, & Lemelin, 2003).

The ability of learners to process such complex data is related to the extent to which their language is automatized because the more automatized language comprehension and production is, the more processing and attentional resources can be deployed to other activities, which may include those of noticing gaps in their linguistic knowledge, or turning their attention to monitoring their output, or testing their hypotheses against data in the input. One way in which learners may identify these gaps, and improve their linguistic accuracy, is to tap into their explicit knowledge about the language they are learning, that is, "knowledge of language about which users are consciously aware" (Ellis, 2004, p. 229). Indeed, the difference between explicit and implicit knowledge of language rests precisely in the individuals' abilities to describe their knowledge of language (N. Ellis, 1994) and mirrors Krashen's (1985) distinction of learning versus acquisition. Children's linguistic knowledge of their first language is clearly implicit because children demonstrate knowledge of the rules of language in their speech, but cannot generally articulate them. Second language learners are likely to have both implicit knowledge of their second language acquired through interaction with the language either in or out of a classroom, as well as explicit knowledge of some aspects of the language that may be acquired through explicit learning. DeKeyser (2003) argues that although implicit knowledge tends to remain implicit, and explicit knowledge to remain explicit, it is possible that explicit knowledge may become implicit over time, contrary to Krashen's claim that learned and acquired knowledge remain separated; further, he points out that there is no evidence "that explicit learning and practice cannot lead to automatized procedural knowledge, only a dearth of evidence that it can" (DeKeyser, 2003, p. 329). The important question here rests with the definition of "acquired" knowledge:

If one takes lack of awareness to be as crucial for "acquired" knowledge as for implicit learning, then the end product of the learning process documented in DeKeyser cannot be called implicit, as students are still aware of the rules. If, however, the criterion for "acquired" knowledge is that it be available with the same degree of automaticity as implicitly acquired knowledge, then it is not clear why the end product of automatization processes as documented in DeKeyser (1997) could not be considered "acquired." Moreover, it is quite possible that, after large amounts of communicative use and complete automatization of the rules, learners eventually lose their awareness of the rules. At that point they not only have procedural knowledge that is functionally equivalent to implicitly acquired knowledge, but even implicit knowledge in the narrow sense of knowledge without awareness (DeKeyser, 2003, pp. 328–329).

Rod Ellis (2004) posits that explicit knowledge results from learning that involves attention to form as contrasted with implicit learning, where the focus is on meaning. Supporting the view that noticing is crucial to second language learning, recent reviews involving comparisons of the efficacy of implicit versus explicit instruction (see especially Norris & Ortega, 2000) and explicit learning (DeKeyser, 2003) indicate an advantage, at least in the short term, for explicit modes of learning over implicit modes of learning in both classroom and laboratory studies. The debates concerning the role of consciousness in language acquisition, the degree to which language is learned or acquired, and what explicit and implicit learning involves are complex. It is studies of language processing that will allow us to move beyond speculation and to gain greater insights through empirical evidence of the learning processes language learners use.

In focussing on the following methodologies, I would point out that my concern is not with the measurement of what learners know (i.e., the end product of learning), but rather with the process of identifying what it is that learners focus on as they move toward increasing their proficiency in their second language. The challenge for all these methodologies is to obtain observable, externalized data from unobservable, internalized processes to draw conclusions about the processes.

Introspection and Verbal Protocols

In his review of attention, awareness, and noticing, Al-Hejin (2004) points to the importance of collecting introspective data to identify what learners notice. Verbal protocols have been used widely in psychological research, and were originally grounded in information processing approaches to cognition (Ericsson & Simon, 1984/1993). There are three different types of verbal protocol: think-aloud protocols, introspective protocols, and retrospective protocols. The first two rely on working memory and are collected concurrent with the performance on the task under investigation, whereas retrospective protocols attempt to tap information available in the learners short term memory (Jourdenais, 2001). Leow and Morgan-Short (2003) point out that it is important to differentiate between metalinguistic verbalization where specific information is requested, and nonmetalinguistic verbalization where learners are focussed on a task and verbalize their thoughts as they proceed, thus providing self-revelational data (Cohen, 2000). In the following discussion, because our interest is in using this methodological tool to investigate learner processes, and particularly what they notice in the data, only concurrent, nonmetalinguistic protocols through which such phenomena are most likely to be revealed are discussed, because retrospective protocols are unlikely to reveal a great deal about unconscious processes. My concern here is not with a discussion of what these techniques reveal about what learners notice (but see Alanen, 1995; Leow, 2000; 2001; Rosa & O'Neill, 1999; Simard & Wong, 2001) but rather with a consideration of some of the issues related to the validity of the methodology as a tool for exploring cognitive processes.

Think-aloud techniques are applied concurrently with the learner performing a language-related task. The idea is that the learner is asked to think out loud while performing the task. The learner's speech is recorded for later analysis. Training, prior to the actual data collection itself, is a crucial aspect of think-aloud techniques because the idea underlying the think-aloud is that the flow of speech is uninterpreted, spontaneous, and elicited directly from working memory.

The ability to perform such think-aloud activity is probably not equal for all individuals with some individuals, tending to process their thoughts prior to articulating them, particularly if they are feeling self-conscious about the activity itself. As Jourdenais (2001) points out, encouraging learners to say everything that comes into their minds in some ways mitigates against the tendency to "edit" what is said, but there does probably remain an individual response to think-alouds which should not be overlooked. Some individuals may find the task much more difficult than others, and in analyzing the data it is important to find some way of recognizing where the speech is more edited. One approach to investigating the level of analysis with which learners may engage while participating in think-alouds may be, as R. Ellis (2004) argues, to analyze the resultant protocols for hesitation phenomena associated with the output as an indicator of when learners are editing their thoughts (although with second language learners, hesitation phenomena may be a marker of disfluency rather than editing).

The idea that cognition is a socially and culturally isolated phenomenon available for scrutiny, that underpins the information processing approach to think-alouds has been challenged recently with researchers considering how this type of retrospective or concurrent internal speech behavior may be affected by the different cultural and social perspectives of the participants (Sasaki, 2004; Smagorinsky, 2001). Smagorinsky (2001) suggests that protocol analysis may be used as a tool to investigate the ways in which speaking mediates thought. He questions whether concurrent and retrospective protocols, initially developed within an information processing framework and used to develop models of cognitive functioning, can be isolated from the cultural and social context in which they are taking place, and from the cultural and social backgrounds of the participants. The relationship between sociocultural factors and think-aloud protocols has been investigated empirically by Sasaki (2004) who asked eight Japanese native speakers to conduct think-aloud protocols while completing a pragmatic refusal task. In the analysis of the protocols, Sasaki identified social politeness markers, comments which addressed the researcher directly, metacomments made by the participants on their behavior, comments regrading the protocol process itself, and comments regarding the selectivity of the information they were providing. The instructions given to the participants were in line with those recommended by Ericsson and Simon (1984, 1993), and participants were expressly instructed not to monitor their speech. The researcher was not present during the data collection process. Sasaki argues that the verbal report data revealed both selectivity in the information provided, and the social orientations of the participants toward the researcher through the use of social politeness markers and other interactional phenomena (which would not have been available had the reports been conducted in English). As Smagorinsky (2001) also argues, taking account of the social nature of think-aloud protocols does not invalidate the data as an effective method for exploring the cognitive processing of individual learners; rather, Sasaki points out, not taking account of the ways learners socially orient to the researcher runs the risk of underrepresenting the complexity of the social and cognitive processes the protocols can be used to reveal.

Another major concern, particularly with concurrent verbal protocols, has been the potential for such protocols, (think-aloud and introspection) to change the nature of the activity itself. The potential for thinking aloud to change the cognitive processes under investigation when participants are required to both complete the task provided, and at the same time articulate their thought processes (known as *reactivity*), has been raised on numerous occasions (see for example Ericsson & Simon, 1984, 1993; Jourdenais, 2001; Smagorinsky, 2001; Stratman & Hamp-Lyons, 1994). Following a review of the (largely nonlinguistic) literature investigating reactivity and think-aloud protocols, which indicated that time-on-task was the factor most affected, Leow and Morgan-Short (2004) undertook an empirical investigation of reactivity in concurrent protocols motivated by the need to explore the validity of this research approach for studies of attention and awareness. Two equivalent groups of L2 Spanish learners were assigned to either a think-aloud group, or a non-think-aloud group, and half of each group was subsequently randomly assigned to either an enhanced reading condition, or a nonenhanced reading condition with a focus on the targeted form—the Spanish impersonal imperative. Three tasks were administered subsequent to the reading to evaluate the learners' comprehension, intake, and controlled production of the targeted form. The researchers found no significant effect for thinking aloud in any of the assessments tasks suggesting that, within the limitations of the study, reactivity was not at issue. However, further studies of reactivity, conducted with a variety of different tasks, are required to further support these findings.

In sum, verbal protocols are a useful tool with which to explore the cognitive processes of learners, and their use may be able to shed light on what, precisely, the features of language are that learners notice. However, the validity and usefulness of this approach may vary depending on who is thinking aloud, the interlocutor or audience of the think-alouds, and also according to task type. Because they involve a spoken response to the task, they are not appropriate for use with listening or speaking data because they necessarily conflict with the communicative nature of such activities. Therefore, to explore the kinds of features that learners notice in spoken language alternative methods need to be considered.

Analyzing Learners Talking Aloud About Language

In an approach pioneered by Swain and her colleagues, the effectiveness of different output-requiring tasks completed by pairs or small groups has been examined (e.g., Kowal & Swain, 1994; Swain & Lapkin, 1998, Swain, 2000). Research work in this paradigm has tended to adopt a sociocultural theoretical perspective (see, for example, Ohta, 2000; Swain, 2000). As Swain and Lapkin (1998) argue, this is complementary to the psycholinguistic perspectives of language learning but in addition provides new and significant insights into language learning processes. In this perspective, interaction is considered to be the site of cognitive development, including language development. In such interactions, language mediates cognitive development as well as reflects the processes taking place. The approach is based on the premise that interaction is critical to successful SLA and that classroom practice can be designed to maximize learners' opportunities to notice, test hypotheses, and receive and internalize feedback, processes which are hypothesized to occur within collaborative task-based interaction. The benefit of combining such tasks with group work is that these activities provide enhanced opportunities for noticing features of language in the output. In addition, it enables verbalization of the output, which then becomes an "objective product that can be explored further by the speaker or others" (Swain, 2000, p. 102), and enables dialogue about the language. Such activity has the added benefit of providing opportunities for learners to receive feedback on their hypotheses (Storch, 1997).

From a methodological point of view, learner talk provides a source of data for researchers to explore the ways in which language learning processes are realized and, ultimately, posttesting of the type conducted by Swain (1998), or post-task activities such as those used by Donato (1994) and Storch (2002) contribute directly to our ability to evaluate precisely what aspects of language learners may be noticing. In this approach, pair dialogues are analyzed, following Swain and Lapkin (1998), into "language related episodes," or metalanguage episodes. Language-related episodes are defined as "any part of the dialogue where learners talk about the language they are producing, question their language use, or other-or self-correct (Swain & Lapkin, 1998, p. 326). These episodes can then be examined for what is the focus of attention (e.g., a lexical item, a grammatical point, a semantic concept), how the learners resolve the discussion and any disagreements that may emerge (Storch, 1997). Loewen (2004), following Ellis (2001), used similar episodes, identified as focus-on-form episodes, to investigate the characteristics associated learners' uptake of incidental form focussed episodes in teacher/learner interactions that occurred in meaning-focussed lessons. Such episodes may also be a form of hypothesis testing in which learners also receive feedback from each other.

This type of methodological approach appears to provide a very fruitful line of inquiry for the investigation of noticing, hypothesis testing, and particularly feedback. Feedback from an interlocutor may allow the learners to notice specific gaps in their own linguistic knowledge of the second language. It may also provide them with information that assists them either in confirming, or disconfirming, their hypotheses. However, for the feedback to be useful, it must be noticed. As the findings of a number of studies (e.g., Qi & Lapkin, 2001; Sanaoui, 1984) have shown, it is not just the noticing *per se* which is important for second language learning, but the quality, or depth, of that noticing. Deeper noticing of linguistic information (i.e., not only noticing but actively engaging with the feedback information) is more likely to lead to language learning. Qi and Lapkin (2001) have also found that the quality of the noticing is different for learners with different levels of L2 proficiency.

A research study currently being conducted is using this research approach is examining which of two different types of feedback, editing or reformulation, promotes deeper noticing by the learners (Wigglesworth & Storch, 2004). Editing is a common form of feedback with written output, most commonly in the form of explicit error correction through annotations in the text or margins of the work. Surveys have shown that L2 students overwhelmingly welcome this form of feedback (e.g., Zhang, 1995) and indeed expect it from their language teachers (Leki, 1991). Reformulation, originally defined by Cohen (1983) as a technique which consists of native speaker rewriting the original text produced by the learner, preserves the learner's ideas, but makes the language sound as native-like as possible by having the text rewritten by a native speaker. Learners then compare the reformulated version with their own text. The purpose of this is for the learner to notice differences between their text and the native speaker's version of it. Theoretically, this should allow learners to notice gaps in their linguistic knowledge. Again, research findings (Lapkin, Swain, & Smith, 2002; Mantello, 1996) suggest that the effectiveness of reformulation may differ according to the learners' second language proficiency. The Wigglesworth study of how learners incorporate feedback into their writing is expected to shed light on what learners notice in the feedback, and how they integrate this into their second language knowledge. Thus this project is pursuing a new emphasis on the study of how learners process feedback; the design of the project allows empirical investigation of the notions of noticing the grammatical gap, hypothesis testing, and uptake of feedback through both an analysis of written scripts on which feedback (either editing or reformulation) is provided, which will provide insights into the extent to which feedback is noticed and integrated into the cognitive system. In addition, the design of the study enables us to investigate the processes learners are using in their language activity through examination of the dialogue of pairs as they respond to the different forms of feedback received.

Using Discourse Measures to Investigate Planning Effects

Over the last decade a number of studies (e.g. Ellis, 2005; Foster & Skehan, 1996; Mehnert, 1998; Ortega, 1999; Skehan & Foster, 1997; Yuan & Ellis, 2003) have examined planning effects on learner output, usually spoken (although Ellis & Yuan, 2004, the most recent study conducted within this paradigm, examined planning effects on learners' written output). Given the limited processing capacity available to learners, and the competition for attentional resources, studies of planning allow detailed investigation of how the learners apply their limited resources when adequate time is provided. Thus, analysis of the discourse produced by the learners under different planned and unplanned conditions may provide insights into the ways in which accuracy, fluency, and complexity improve (or do not) under planned conditions. These studies do not have as their focus the concept of "noticing" as conceptualized by Schmidt, but where accuracy is enhanced we may postulate that this is the result of the learner's ability to monitor his or her output, and apply explicit knowledge about rules to his or her output.

The various planning studies that have examined oral language conducted over the last decade (e.g. Foster & Skehan, 1996; Mehnert, 1998; Ortega, 1999; Skehan & Foster, 1997; Yuan & Ellis, 2003) have all found improvements in both fluency and complexity where planning time is provided, but the situation with respect to accuracy is less clear, which may in part result from the fact that the studies have used a variety of measures to investigate accuracy. The Foster/Skehan studies have used global measures of accuracy such as error free clauses, whereas others have used specific measures such as regular past tense endings (Ellis, 1987), articles, noun modifiers (Ortega, 1999), accuracy of verbal morphology, and plurals (Wigglesworth, 1997). However, these studies have all examined pretask planning, where participants are given (often varied) amounts of time to plan prior to completing the activity. Two recent studies, however, suggest that an examination of online planning (Ellis & Yuan 1994; Yuan & Ellis 1993) may provide valuable insights into learners monitoring of their linguistic output.

Yuan and Ellis (2003) and Ellis and Yuan (2004) investigated the effects of pretask planning, online planning, and no planning on oral and written narratives respectively elicited from a set of pictures. In the online planning (OLP) condition there was no time limit given for the task; in the planning (PTP) condition participants had 10 minutes of planning time, with the responses timed (5 minutes for the speaking task, 17 minutes for writing). In the no-planning (NP) condition responses were timed similarly. In the speaking task, four sentences for each of the six pictures were required; in the writing task a minimum of 200 words was required.

The OLP groups produced more accurate output in terms of both speaking and writing. In addition, the analyses of the spoken discourse revealed that the online planners spoke more slowly, and used more self-repairs suggesting a greater level of monitoring of their language. Yuan and Ellis (2003) suggest that the availability of online planning time allows learners to access their explicit knowledge about grammar, whereas in pretask planning learners tend to advantage content over form. Results from questionnaire and interview data for the writing study supported this view with participants reporting a greater focus on language (i.e., accuracy) with online planning (i.e., during the execution of the task) for both the PTP and OLP groups, but less for the NP group who presumably focus more on content planning during the limited time they have to write. Ellis and Yuan (2004) summarize:

It is likely that the on-line planners used the additional time at their disposal to attend carefully to linguistic accuracy by editing their internal and external output. Writing allows learners access to observable units of text and thereby induces attention to form. When on-line assembly is unpressured, this inherent tendency in writing may be accentuated. In support of this, it can be remarked that the on-line planners noted in their posttask interviews that they attempted to attend to everything, which suggests that they monitored the output of translation extensively before and after execution (2004, p. 80).

Studies of online planning, such as those briefly outlined previously, have the potential to provide us with greater insights into the ways in which learners use their limited processing and attentional resources, how they monitor their language, and the extent to which they are able to exploit their explicit knowledge of their language resources.

Taken together, these three research methodologies each provide us with different insights into the ways in which learners process language. Think-aloud protocols, although providing the most direct insights into learner processes are not always suitable, and may be particularly problematic with second language learners, particularly at lower levels of proficiency. In undertaking the think-aloud, should learners be required to report in their first language, which would be the most natural, or their second language, in which they are completing the task? In the former case, the interaction between the two languages must be taken into account, but in the latter, the proficiency of the learners may make it difficult for them to report and verbalize their thoughts. Dialogic interchanges are less direct than think-alouds, and cannot be entirely guaranteed to elicit the kinds of processes we are concerned with investigating, although the empirical evidence suggests they are likely to. However, Storch (1997) has argued that they may be a more suitable method of collecting data from second language learners than think-alouds because second language learners may find it difficult to fulfill the two competing and concurrent goals involved with think-aloud protocols—the verbalization of their thought processes as well as the task completion. The planning time studies are even less direct, and it is important to recognize that what learners do with planning time is likely to be very variable and reflect considerable individual differences. Elder and Iwashita (in press) discuss the importance of looking at what learners do in their planning time, an issue addressed by Ortega (1999) and Rutherford (2001). However, whereas think-alouds and dialogic language related episodes may help us to understand what learners do while on task, planning studies provide post hoc evidence of learner processes, which the former often do not attend to.

Useful directions for further inquiry are likely to include studies which combine attention to processes with evidence of the learning outcomes of the learners, studies combining different types of methodologies, and studies which explore the limitations of these different methodological approach in varied performance contexts.

Note

1. I am very grateful to Catherine Elder, Carsten Roever, and Neomy Storch for their very insightful and helpful comments, provided at very short notice, on earlier versions of this chapter.

ANNOTATED BIBLIOGRAPHY

Ellis, R. (Ed.) 2005. *Planning and task performance in a second language.* Amsterdam: John Benjamins.

This edited collection is introduced by a comprehensive discussion of the issues that bear on planning time and that have emerged from previous studies. In the following empirical studies, a broad range of topics are addressed, including the strategies learners use during pretask planning, how learners' attention to form can be manipulated through pretask planning, the effects of learners' proficiency level on their ability to use planning time, how unpressured planning affects oral and written production, and how learners use planning over extended periods of time.

Jourdenais, R. (2001). Cognition, instruction and protocol analysis. In P. Robinson (Ed.), *Cognition and second language instruction* (pp. 354–375). Cambridge, UK: Cambridge University Press.

This chapter provides a detailed discussion of the advantages of using protocol analysis for investigating cognitive processes relevant to second language acquisition. The chapter discusses the types of prompts which can be used, the importance of training, and approaches to the analysis of the protocols. Also included is a survey of previous research studies in language learning that have employed verbal protocols as a methodology. The chapter concludes with a discussion of concerns that have been raised about the use of protocols.

Swain, M. (2000). The output hypothesis and beyond: Mediating acquisition through collaborative dialogue. In J. Lantolf (Ed.), *Sociocultural theory and second language learning* (pp. 97–114). Oxford: Oxford University Press.

Swain's chapter focuses on the nature of collaborative dialogue and examines it within the context of contemporary views about the role of interaction in second language learning. The chapter situates the discussion within a sociocultural frame of mind and discusses the role of language as a mediational tool, and details a number of studies that have adopted this perspective. A range of examples of collaborative dialogue are used to illustrate the ways in which language is used for this purpose.

OTHER REFERENCES

Alanen, R. (1995). Input enhancement and rule presentation in second language acquisition. In R. W. Schmidt (Ed.), *Attention and awareness in foreign language learning* (pp. 259–302). (Tech Rep. No. 9). Honolulu: University of Hawai'i.

Al-Hejin, B. (2004). *Attention and awareness: Evidence from cognitive and second language acquisition research.* Working paper in TESOL & Applied Linguistics, 4(1), 1–19. Teachers College, Columbia University, New York.

Cohen, A. D. (1983). Reformulating compositions. *TESOL Newsletter, 17,* 1–5.

Cohen, A. D. (2000). Exploring strategies in test taking: Fine-tuning verbal reports from respondents. In G. Ekbatani & H. Pierson (Eds.), *Learner-directed assessment in ESL* (pp. 127–150). Mahwah, NJ: Erlbaum.

DeKeyser, R. (2003). Implicit and explicit learning. In C. Doughty & M. Long (Eds.), *The handbook of second language acquisition.* London: Blackwell.

Donato, R. (1994). Collective scaffolding in second language learning. In J. P. Lantolf & G. Appel (Eds), *Vygotskian approaches to second language research* (pp. 33–56). Norwood: Ablex.

Elder, C., & Iwashita, N. (2005). Planning for test performance: Does it make a difference? In R. Ellis (Ed.), *Planning and task performance in a second language* (pp. 219–237). Amsterdam: John Benjamins.

Ellis, N. (Ed.). (1994). *Implicit and explicit learning of languages.* San Diego, CA: Academic

Press.

Ellis, R. (1987). Interlanguage variability and narrative discourse: Style shifting in the use of the past tense. *Studies in Second Language Acquisition, 9,* 12–20.

Ellis, R. (2001). Investigating form-focused instruction. *Language Learning, 51* (Suppl. 1), 1–46.

Ellis, R. (2004). The definition and measurement of L2 explicit knowledge. *Language Learning, 54*(2) 227–275.

Ellis, R., & Yuan, F. (2004). The effects of planning on fluency, complexity, and accuracy in second language narrative writing. *Studies in Second Language Acquisition, 26,* 59–84.

Ericsson, K.A., & Simon, H. A. (1984/1993). *Protocol analysis: Verbal reports as data.* Cambridge, MA: The MIT Press.

Foster, P., & Skehan, P. (1996). The influence of planning and task type on second language performance. *Studies in Second Language Acquisition, 18,* 299–323.

Gass, S., Svetics I., & Lemelin, S. (2003). Differential effects of attention. *Language Learning, 53,*(3), 497–545.

Kowal, M., & Swain, M. (1994). Using collaborative language production tasks to promote students' language awareness. *Language Awareness, 3*(2) 73–93.

Krashen, S. (1982). *Principles and practice in second language acquisition.* Englewood Cliffs, NJ: PrenticeHall.

Krashen, S. (1985). *The input hypothesis: Issues and implications.* London: Longman.

Lapkin, S., Swain M., & Smith, M. (2002). Reformulation and the learning of French pronominal verbs in a Canadian French immersion context. *The Modern Language Journal, 86,* 485–498.

Leki, I. (1991). The preferences of ESL students for error correction in college-level writing classes. *Foreign Language Annals, 24,* 203–318.

Leow, R. P. (2000). A study of the role of awareness in foreign language behavior: Aware versus unaware learners. *Studies in Second Language Acquisition, 22,* 557–584.

Leow, R. P. (2001). Do learners notice enhanced forms while interacting with the L2? An online and offline study of the role of written input enhancement in L2 reading. *Hispania, 84,* 496–509.

Leow, R., & Morgan-Short, K. (2004). To think aloud or not to think aloud: The issue of reactivity in SLA research methodology. *Studies in Second Language Acquisition, 26,* 35–57.

Loewen, S. (2004). Uptake in incidental focus on form in meaning-focused ESL lessons. *Language Learning 54,*(1) 153–188.

Mantello, M. A. (1996). *Selective error correction in intermediate extended French writing programs: A comparative study of reformulation and coded feedback.* Unpublished master's thesis, Ontario Institute for Studies in Education, Toronto.

Mehnert, U. (1998). The effects of different lengths of time for planning on second language performance. *Studies in Second Language Acquisition, 20*, 52–83.

Norris, J., & Ortega L. (2000). Effectiveness of L2 instruction: A research synthesis and quantitative meta-analysis. *Language Learning, 50*, 417–528.

Ortega, L. (1999). Planning and focus on form in L2 oral performance. *Studies in Second Language Acquisition, 21*, 108–148.

Ohta, A. (2000). Rethinking interaction in SLA: Developmentally appropriate assistance in the zone of proximal development and the acquisition of L2 grammar. In J. P. Lantolf (Ed.), *Sociocultural theory and second language learning* (pp. 51–78). Oxford: Oxford University Press.

Qi, D. S., & Lapkin, S. (2001). Exploring the role of noticing in a three-stage second language writing task. *Journal of Second Language Writing, 10*, 277–303.

Rosa, E. & O'Neill, M. (1999). Explicitness, intake, and the issue of awareness: Another piece to the puzzle. *Studies in Second Language Acquisition, 21*, 511–556.

Rutherford, K. (2001). *An investigation into the effects of planning on oral production in a second language.* Unpublished dissertation. Department of Applied Language Studies and Linguistics, University of Auckland.

Sanaoui, R. (1984). The use of reformulation in teaching writing to ESL students. *Carleton Papers in Applied Language Studies, 1*, 139–146.

Sasaki, T. (2004). Recipient orientation in verbal report protocols: Methodological issues in concurrent think-aloud. *Hawaii Working Papers on Second Language Studies, 22*(1), 1–55.

Schmidt, R. (1990). The role of consciousness in second language learning. *Applied Linguistics, 11*(2), 192–196.

Schmidt, R. (1994). Consciousness and foreign language learning: A tutorial on the role of attention and awareness in learning. In R. Schmidt (Ed.), *Attention and awareness in foreign language learning* (pp. 1–64). [Technical report no. 9.] Honolulu: University of Hawai'i Press.

Schmidt, R. (2001). Attention. In P. Robinson (Ed.), *Cognition and second language instruction* (pp. 3–32). Cambridge, England: Cambridge University Press.

Simard, D., & Wong, W. (2001). Alertness, orientation, and detection: The conceptualization of attentional functions. *Studies in Second Language Acquisition, 23*, 103–124.

Skehan, P. (1998). *A cognitive approach to language learning.* Oxford: Oxford University Press.

Skehan, P., & Foster, P. (1997). Task type and task processing in second language performance. *Language Teaching Research, 1*, 185–211.

Smagorinsky, P. (2001). Rethinking protocol analysis from a cultural perspective. *Annual Review of Applied Linguistics, 21*, 233–245.

Storch, N. (1997). The editing talk of adult learners. *Language Awareness. 6*(4), 221–232.

Storch, N. (2002). Patterns of interaction in ESL pair work. *Language Learning, 52*(1), 119–158.

Stratman, J., & Hamp-Lyons, L. (1994). Reactivity in concurrent think-aloud protocols. In P. Smagorinsky (Ed.), *Speaking about writing: Reflections on research methodology* (pp. 89–112). London: Sage.

Swain, M. (1998). Focus on form through conscious reflection. In C. Doughty & J. Williams (Eds.), *Focus on form in classroom second language acquisition* (pp. 64–81). Cambridge: Cambridge University Press.

Swain, M., & Lapkin, S. (1998). Interaction and second language learning: Two adolescent French immersion students working together. *Modern Language Journal 82*(3), 320–337.

Wigglesworth, G. (1997). An investigation of planning time and proficiency level on oral test discourse. *Language Testing, 14*, 85–106.

Wigglesworth, G., & Storch, N. (2004). *Feedback in second language writing: Input and uptake.* Unpublished paper, University of Melbourne.

Yuan, F., & Ellis, R, (2003). The effects of pretask planning and on-line planning on fluency, complexity, and accuracy in L2 monologic oral production. *Applied Linguistics, 24*, 1–27.

Zhang, S. (1995). Reexamining the affective advantage of peer feedback in the ESL writing class. *Journal of Second Language Writing 4*, 209–222.

6. LANGUAGE LEARNING STRATEGY INSTRUCTION: CURRENT ISSUES AND RESEARCH

Anna Uhl Chamot

This chapter begins with definitions and an overview of methods used to identify learners' strategies, then summarizes what we have learned from the large number of descriptive studies of strategies reported by language learners. Research on language learning strategies has a history of only about thirty years, and much of this history has been sporadic. The 1980s and early 1990s were a period of substantial research on language learning strategies, much of it descriptive. This period was followed by an apparent loss of interest in language learning strategies, judging by limited reported research and few related conference presentations. Recently, however, a number of new investigations have reinvigorated the field. The focus of the chapter is on the evolution of research on language learning strategy intervention studies, the issues that have emerged from this research, and metacognitive models that can be useful in the language classroom. The discussion concludes by setting out directions for future research.

Definition and Importance of Strategies

Learning strategies are procedures that facilitate a learning task. Strategies are most often conscious and goal-driven, especially in the beginning stages of tackling an unfamiliar language task. Once a learning strategy becomes familiar through repeated use, it may be used with some automaticity, but most learners will, if required, be able to call the strategy to conscious awareness. Learning strategies are important in second language learning and teaching for two major reasons. First, by examining the strategies used by second language learners during the language learning process, we gain insights into the metacognitive, cognitive, social, and affective processes involved in language learning. The second reason supporting research into language learning strategies is that less successful language learners can be taught new strategies, thus helping them become better language learners (Grenfell & Harris, 1999). Numerous descriptive studies have addressed the goal of understanding the range and type of learning strategies used by good language learners and the differences in learning strategy use between more and less effective learners. However, until relatively recently there have been fewer studies focusing on the second goal of trying to teach language learning strategies in classroom settings.

Learning strategies are sensitive to the learning context and to the learner's internal processing preferences. If learners perceive, for example, that a task like vocabulary learning requires correct matching of a new word to its definition within a specified period of time (as in a test), they will likely decide to use a memorization strategy. Their choice of which memorization strategy to use will depend on their understanding of their own learning processes and on which strategies have been successful in the past (Hsiao, 2004). A different task, such as being able to discuss the theme of a short story will require strategies different from memorization—such as making inferences about the author's intended meaning and applying the learner's prior knowledge about the topic. The interpretation of a language learning task is closely related to the goals advocated within each learner's cultural context, for a learning strategy valued in one culture may be deemed inappropriate in another (Olivares-Cuhat, 2002; Wharton, 2000). A particular learning strategy can help a learner in a certain context achieve learning goals that the learner deems important, whereas other learning strategies may not be useful for that learning goal.

Methods for Identifying Learners' Strategies

Learning strategies are identified through various self-report procedures. Although self-report is always subject to error, no better way has yet been devised for identifying learners' mental processes and techniques for completing a learning task. Learning strategies are for the most part unobservable, though some may be associated with an observable behavior. For example, a student listening to new information may use *selective attention* (unobservable) to focus on the main ideas and might then decide to *take notes* (observable) on these main ideas. The only way to find out whether students are using *selective attention* during a listening comprehension task is to ask them. Mere observation has proven unsatisfactory in identifying learners' strategies (Cohen, 1998; O'Malley & Chamot, 1990; Rubin, 1975; Wenden, 1991).

Self-reports have been conducted through retrospective interviews, stimulated recall interviews, questionnaires, written diaries and journals, and think-aloud protocols concurrent with a learning task. Each of these methods has limitations, but at the present time they remain the only way to generate insights into the unobservable mental learning strategies of learners.

Interviews

In retrospective interviews, learners are prompted to recall a recently completed learning task and describe what they did to complete it (see Macaro, 2001). A stimulated recall interview is more likely to accurately reveal students' actual learning strategies because it is conducted immediately after a learning task. The actual task is videotaped, and the interviewer then plays back the videotape, pausing as necessary, asking the student to describe his or her thoughts at specific moments during the learning task.

Questionnaires

The most frequently used method for identifying students' learning strategies is through questionnaires. Some studies have developed questionnaires based on tasks that students have just completed (see Chamot & El-Dinary, 1999; Fan, 2003; Goh, 2002a; Kojic-Sabo & Lightbown, 1999; Ozeki, 2000; Rubin & Thompson, 1994; Weaver & Cohen, 1997). Most descriptive studies, however, have relied on a questionnaire developed by Oxford (1990), the *Strategy Inventory for Language Learning* (SILL). This instrument has been used extensively to collect data on large numbers of language learners (see Cohen, Weaver, & Li, 1998; Olivares-Cuhat, 2002; Oxford, 1990; 1996; Oxford & Burry-Stock, 1995; Wharton, 2000). The SILL is a standardized measure with versions for English as a second language

(ESL) students and students of a variety of other languages, and as such can be used to collect and analyze information about large numbers of students. It has also been used in studies to correlate strategy use with variables such as learning styles, gender, proficiency level, culture, and task (Bedell & Oxford, 1996; Bruen, 2001; Green & Oxford, 1995; Oxford, Cho, Leung, & Kim, 2004; Nyikos & Oxford, 1993; Oxford & Burry-Stock, 1995; Wharton, 2000). Oxford and her colleague are currently developing a task-based questionnaire to complement the SILL (Oxford et al., 2004).

Diaries and Journals

Written diaries and journals have also been used to identify language learners' strategies. In these, learners write personal observations about their own learning experiences and the ways in which they attempted to solve language problems (see, for example, Carson & Longhini, 2002). Rubin (2003) suggests using diaries for instructional purposes to help students develop metacognitive awareness of their own learning processes and strategies. An interesting variant on the diary study was recently conducted by Takeuchi (2003), who examined published books and essays by Japanese good language learners of various languages and analyzed each author for evidence of learning strategy use included in their descriptions of their foreign language learning histories.

Think-Aloud Protocols

A think-aloud protocol can be used for individual interviews in which the learner is given a target language task and asked to describe his or her thoughts while working on it. The interviewer may prompt with open-ended questions such as, "What are you thinking right now? Why did you stop and start over?" Recordings of think-aloud interviews are then analyzed for evidence of learning strategies. The rich insights into language-learning strategies provided through think-aloud protocols tend to reveal online processing, rather than metacognitive aspects of planning or evaluating (see Chamot & Keatley, 2003; Cohen et al., 1998; O'Malley & Chamot, 1990).

Although self-report may be inaccurate if learners do not report truthfully or cannot remember their thinking, it is still the only way available to us to develop some understanding of learners' mental processing. As Grenfell and Harris have pointed out: "It is not easy to get inside the 'black box' of the human brain and find out what is going on there. We work with what we can get, which, despite the limitations, provides food for thought" (1999, p. 54).

Identification of Language Learning Strategies

The language learning strategies identified through these self-report methods have identified characteristics of good language learners and compared the strategies of more- and less-effective language learners. Such studies have been important in identifying and classifying strategies used by language learners and understanding how strategies are actually used in the learning process. This information has in turn guided instructional investigations that have sought to teach learning strategies to language learners and to measure relationships between strategy use and language proficiency, metacognition, motivation, and self-efficacy.

Language learning strategies research began in the 1970s with the seminal work of Joan Rubin, who, like Stern (1975), suggested that a model of "the good language learner" could be constructed by looking at special strategies used by successful L2 students (Rubin, 1975). Other researchers followed with descriptions of learner characteristics and strategic techniques associated with effective second and foreign language learning (Naiman, Fröhlich, Stern, & Todesco, 1978/1996; O'Malley, & Chamot, 1990). More recently, Takeuchi (2003) identified the characteristics of Japanese good language learners through their biographies. Taken together, these studies identified the good language learner as one who is a mentally active learner, monitors language comprehension and production, practices communicating in the language, makes use of prior linguistic and general knowledge, uses various memorization techniques, and asks questions for clarification.

Later studies comparing more and less effective language students have revealed a recurring finding that less successful learners do use learning strategies, sometimes even as frequently as more successful peers, but that their strategies are used differently (Chamot & El-Dinary, 1999; Khaldieh, 2000; Vandergrift, 1997a, 1997b). A recent study by Vandergrift (2003a) compared the listening comprehension strategies of more- and less-skilled Canadian seventh-grade students of French. Students listened to several French texts and were prompted to think aloud during the process. The more skilled listeners used more metacognitive strategies, especially comprehension monitoring, than did their less skilled peers. In addition, more skilled listeners engaged in questioning for clarification, whereas the less skilled used more translation. Graham (2004) investigated the attitudes toward learning French of upper secondary English students and found that the less successful students did not seem to be aware of the potential role of learning strategies in improving their language performance.

These studies have confirmed that good language learners are skilled at matching strategies to the task they were working on, whereas less successful language learners apparently do not have the metacognitive knowledge about task requirements needed to select appropriate strategies. This trend is apparent with children in foreign language immersion classrooms, secondary school ESL and foreign language students, and adult language learners (Chamot & El-Dinary, 1999; Chamot & Keatley, 2003). In addition, more proficient L2 learners use sequences of strategies to complete a task effectively (Chamot, Barnhardt, El-Dinary, & Robbins, 1999; Goh, 2002b; Oxford et al., 2004).

The large number of descriptive studies of language learning strategies reveals suggestive differences between more and less successful learners. Can less successful language learners be taught to use the learning strategies that contribute to the achievements of their more successful peers? Proponents of language learning strategy instruction point to the substantial body of research in first language contexts that supports the explicit teaching of learning strategies for academic achievement in other content areas (De La Paz & Graham, 2002; Graham & Harris, 2000; National Reading Panel, 2000; Pressley, 2000). Because learning strategy instruction has been shown to improve performance on first language tasks such as vocabulary learning, reading comprehension, and writing, it is likely that it could prove equally helpful for language learners in these and other L2 tasks such as listening and speaking, modalities not investigated in the first language literature.

Classroom Research on Language Learning Strategy Instruction

Although the majority of language learning strategy investigations have been simply descriptive, a number of researchers have conducted studies in which language learning strategies have been taught to students. This section briefly reviews representative studies carried out in language classroom settings in which teachers and/or researchers have provided more or less explicit instruction on learning strategies.

The relatively small number of instructional language learning strategy studies may be due, in part, to the inherent difficulties in conducting classroom research. Ideally, an intervention study should have randomly assigned participants to either a control or an experimental/treatment group. Instruction in each group should be identical except for the presence or absence of the innovation being studied. Participants should be pre-and posttested on valid and reliable instruments that identify not only knowledge about and use of the innovation (e.g., learning strategies), but also measure other factors deemed important in learning, such as achievement/proficiency, motivation, attitude, and/or self-efficacy. It is rarely possible to adequately control for all of these possible variables in any natural classroom setting.

In one of the first experimental studies of language learning strategies instruction, high school ESL students were taught how to apply learning strategies to three different types of tasks, and their performance was compared to that of students in a nonstrategies control group (O'Malley & Chamot, 1990). This study was conducted with 75 high school ESL students randomly assigned to experimental or control groups. Students were pretested on three types of language tasks—vocabulary, listening comprehension, and speaking from prepared notes—but not on their use of learning strategies. The experimental group students were taught various strategies for the same types of tasks over a two week period. The instruction was provided by the researchers, all of whom had ESL teaching experience. Students were posttested on the same types of tasks, but did not report on their use of learning strategies. The main conclusions of this first language learning strategies experimental study were as follows:

- Vocabulary learning strategies were effective only for students who had not already developed alternative effective strategies.
- Listening comprehension improved for students instructed in learning strategies on texts that were accessible, not on those that were too difficult and/or for which students lacked relevant prior knowledge.

- Oral reports (presented from written notes) given by strategy-instructed students were judged to be significantly more comprehensible and organized than those of control group students.
- Explicit learning strategy instruction embedded within the language syllabus appeared to be effective.

These conclusions support some of the major tenets proposed in current language learning strategy instructional models, including the importance of not overlooking students' current learning strategies, careful choice of tasks for practicing learning strategies, and providing explicit and embedded learning strategy instruction. Although this study of L2 learning strategies was successful in showing that second language learners could improve their language performance by using instructed learning strategies, limitations of the study are clear. These interrelated limitations include the study's short duration (only two weeks) and absence of follow-up; the lack of a measure of students' use of learning strategies prior and subsequent to instruction; and the fact that researchers rather than the normal classroom teachers provided the instruction. Many of these limitations have been addressed in subsequent intervention studies regarding the effects of language learning strategy instruction for listening comprehension, speaking and oral communication, reading comprehension, vocabulary learning, and writing strategies.

Listening Comprehension Strategies Studies

Several studies have sought to help language learners use strategies to increase their comprehension of oral texts. For example, Ross and Rost (1991) first identified the listening comprehension strategies used by higher proficiency students and then successfully taught these to lower proficiency students. Another study of listening comprehension was conducted over an entire academic year (Thompson & Rubin, 1996). Students receiving strategy instruction showed significant improvement on a video comprehension posttest compared to the students in the control group. In addition, students in the strategies group demonstrated metacognitive awareness through their ability to select and manage the strategies that would help them comprehend the videos.

More recently, Ozeki (2000) followed the example of Ross and Rost (1991) by first identifying the listening strategies students already used as a basis for selecting strategies to be taught. In this case, however, the strategies to be taught were those students had reported that they used least frequently. Although intact classes of students of English in a Japanese women's college were used for the treatment and control groups, randomization was achieved by the assignment of students to class sections alphabetically by surname. Strategy instruction was provided in the treatment class during 12 ninety-minute classes focusing on listening comprehension distributed over a 20-week semester. The sequence of instruction was as follows: a preparation stage in which students were explicitly taught a new strategy and earlier strategies were reviewed; and a lesson stage in which students practiced the strategies with listening comprehension tasks. Pretest and posttest scores were compared to evaluate the effects of learning strategy instruction. Improvement in the treatment group was noted in the following dimensions: development of listening comprehension ability; increased use of learning strategies (including some not explicitly taught); positive attitudes towards strategy instruction; transfer of strategies to new tasks; and durability of strategy use after the completion of strategy instruction.

Carrier (2003) taught listening comprehension strategies to a small group of high school ESL students. This exploratory study focused on academic listening tasks during six weeks of instruction. The strategies included both bottom-up and top-down approaches to listening. The teacher modeled and defined the strategies, then provided practice opportunities for the students. Actual strategies taught included *selective attention* to various aspects of the text and *note-taking*. Pre- and posttests on both discrete and overall listening comprehension showed that students had significantly improved both aspects of listening comprehension.

In another recent study of listening comprehension strategies, Vandergrift (2003b) undertook a study of French as a second language university students in which he sought to raise awareness of the listening process through tasks designed to develop effective listening strategies. After being told the topic of the listening task, students completed a column on a worksheet in which they listed (in French and/or in English) their predictions about information they might hear. Then they listened to the text, checking off predictions and vocabulary they had anticipated and adding new information. Next, they worked in pairs to compare and discuss what they had understood. A second listening to the text allowed students to fill in additional information comprehended, and this was followed by a class discussion in which students shared the strategies they had used to comprehend the text. After a third listening, students wrote a personal reflection on what they had learned about their own listening processes and what strategies they might use in future to improve listening comprehension. Similar procedures were followed for an additional listening task. Students' written reflections revealed positive reactions to the strategies, increased motivation, and understanding of their own thinking processes during listening tasks.

Oral Communication Strategies Studies

Perhaps the most challenging language modality for learning strategy instruction is oral communication, for deliberate use of a strategy could restrict the flow of natural speech. Presentational speaking, rather than interactive speaking, has been the focus of several studies (see Cohen, 1998; O'Malley & Chamot, 1990). In interactive speaking, researchers have looked at communication strategies with some reservations because of doubts that using a communication strategy (such as using a gesture when the needed word or phrase is not known) actually can lead to learning (Cohen, 1998; Macaro, 2001, Nakatani, in press).

A comprehensive study of speaking strategies investigated the impact of strategies-based instruction on college foreign language students taught by their regular instructors over during 10 weeks of instruction (Cohen, et al., 1998; Cohen, 1998). The intervention groups received instruction in learning strategies for speaking tasks. Students were pre-and post-tested on speaking tasks and on the Strategy Inventory for Language Learning (SILL) (Oxford, 1990). In addition, a sample of students provided think-aloud data as they were completing task checklists. The results indicated that integrating strategies instruction into the language course was beneficial to students, although the relationship of reported strategy use to performance was complex.

In a recent study of oral communication strategies, Nakatani (in press) compared pre- and posttest oral communication test results of students receiving metacognitive awareness-raising and a control group. The subjects were students at a women's college in Japan who had completed six years of prior English study. The strategy training group was taught communication strategies that could help students learn more of the language such as asking for clarification, checking for comprehension, and paraphrasing, rather than communication strategies without a direct influence on learning, such as abandoning a message or reverting to the L1. Results showed that students taught to use strategies showed significant improvement on oral proficiency tests.

Reading Comprehension Strategies Studies

Although reading strategy interventions in first language contexts have been plentiful (see, for example, Pressley, 2000), this modality has attracted less attention among language learning instruction researchers. A recent study investigating different approaches to literacy development in high school ESL students with low literacy in their native language included a learning strategies instructional component (Chamot & Keatley, 2003). A curriculum of scripted literacy lessons included explicit language learning strategy instruction for reading comprehension, including *sounding out, selective attention, summarizing, cooperation, predicting, brainstorming of prior knowledge, visualization, and making inferences.* Six of the teachers provided initial strategy instruction in the students'L1, then asked students to use the same strategies when reading in English. The remaining eight teachers attempted to teach the strategies only in English. Data from classroom observations and from end-of-year individual think-aloud interviews in which students described (in L1) the strategies they were using to read an unfamiliar text in English showed the following:

- Teachers found it easier to teach strategies in the native language.
- Some students reported using the instructed strategies during the think-aloud interviews.
- Students who were more able to verbalize their thinking processes (in L1) displayed greater comprehension of the L2 text than those unable to describe their thoughts.

Another recent study of reading comprehension investigated the effects of strategy instruction on lower and higher proficiency levels and also assessed students'continuing use of strategies after the conclusion of instruction (Ikeda & Takeuchi, 2003). Participants were 210 students of English at a Japanese university. Students were divided into two groups according to their English language proficiency; each group was then further divided into an experimental and a control group. The experimental groups received explicit reading strategy instruction integrated into their regular class over an eight-week period. Instructed strategies included *making inferences, using selective attention, using imagery*, and *summarizing*. Pre- and post-tests (carried out at different intervals) consisted of reading English texts, then completing a survey in Japanese of strategies used during the reading task. The results indicated that the strategy instruction affected the frequency of students' use of the strategies only for the high proficiency level group. The authors' interpretation was that most of the strategies taught involved top-down processing, but that what the low proficiency group probably needed was a focus on bottom-up processing strategies. Students were tested after instruction and then again three months and five months later to see if they continued to use the instructed strategies. An encouraging finding was that students retained their use of learning strategies for reading five months after the conclusion of instruction.

A recently completed study built on Ikeda and Takeuchi's (2003) work to further explore the effects of task difficulty in reading comprehension and use of strategies (Oxford et al., 2004). ESL college students completed two reading tasks (one easy, one difficult); these scores were used to determine whether students were either more-or less-proficient readers, and also completed questionnaires about their strategy use for the two readings. For the easy reading, there was little difference in strategy use between more and less proficient readers. However, for the more difficult reading, less proficient students actually used more strategies than their more proficient peers. The authors attributed this finding to the fact that the "difficult" reading was actually not much of a challenge for the higher proficiency students, and thus they did not need to use many learning strategies.

Vocabulary Strategies Studies

Learning new vocabulary in a second language is a continuing process rather than a single event. Beginning level students often believe that vocabulary learning is all that is involved in second language acquisition and may focus their efforts and strategies on this single component. Deep processing strategies such as association have been found more effective in vocabulary retention than rote repetition strategies (see Cohen & Aphek, 1981; Hulstijn, 1997; O'Malley & Chamot, 1990; Schmitt, 2000).

In a recent descriptive vocabulary study of Hong Kong university students learning English, Fan (2003) identified important implications for strategy instruction. For example, when students perceived that a strategy was useful, they used it more often than strategies they did not perceive as useful. Even so, students with higher vocabulary proficiency used strategies significantly more often even when they did not perceive them as useful. This finding suggests that students might use more learning strategies if teachers were to first convince students of their usefulness.

This approach was taken in a series of case studies in England in which researchers worked closely with five secondary teachers of modern languages as teachers experimented with learning strategy instruction for a variety of tasks (Grenfell & Harris, 1999). Three of the teachers focused on teaching memorization strategies for vocabulary. The strategy instruction was generally explicit and students' metacognition was developed through a variety of consciousness-raising activities. Most students were willing to adopt the new strategies, though they rarely used them in combination. Performance on tests indicated that the memorization strategies had been helpful for many in learning new vocabulary.

Writing Strategies Studies

Writing in a second language is arguably the most difficult of the modalities in which to achieve communicative competence. Beginning level students struggle with finding the words they need and remembering grammatical conventions, whereas more advanced students find it difficult to link their ideas with coherence and to produce appropriate target language discourse. Given these difficulties, instruction in writing strategies could be beneficial for second language learners.

A study of writing strategies instruction was recently conducted in England with six classes of secondary students of French (Macaro, 2001). In this Oxford Writing Project, classes were randomly assigned to control or experimental groups. Pre-and posttests included questionnaires, writing tasks, and think-aloud interviews during a French writing task. Students in the experimental groups received about five months of instruction on a variety of writing strategies that included the metacognitive strategies of *advance preparation*, *monitoring*, and *evaluating*. At posttest, experimental groups had made significant gains in the grammatical accuracy of their writing. In addition, they reported a change in their approach to writing, becoming less reliant on the teacher, more selective in their use of the dictionary, and more careful about their written work.

Another recent writing strategies study explored the effects of translation (a learning strategy) from the L1 on the quality of essays written in French by university students of French (Cohen & Brooks-Carson, 2001). Students were given prompts in the target language, then instructed to either write directly in French or to write the essay first in their L1, then translate it to French. Strategy checklists completed after students wrote the essays showed that students writing directly in French reported less thinking in English during the composing process and their essays were also rated higher than those who had gone through the translation process.

Methodological and Practical Issues in Learning Strategy Instruction

Although we can be cautiously optimistic about the effectiveness of learning strategy instruction, given that it has been well established in first language contexts and shows promise in second language learning, a number of issues still remain concerning specific teaching approaches. These include the language of strategy instruction, the practicality of integrating strategy instruction into the regular language class, and the use of metacognitive models to classify learning strategies for instructional purposes. Although these issues are far from resolved, some recent studies that have addressed them are briefly described in this section.

Language of Strategy Instruction

This issue is particular to teaching learning strategies to language learners. In first language contexts, strategies are taught through a language medium in which students are proficient, but in second or foreign language contexts, this is not necessarily so. Beginning level students, in particular, do not have the L2 proficiency to understand explanations of why and how to use learning strategies, yet postponing learning strategy instruction until intermediate or advanced level courses deprives beginners of tools that could enhance language learning and increase motivation for further study. It is probably not possible to avoid using the first language during strategy instruction for beginning to low intermediate level students (Macaro, 2001). Suggestions have been made to initially teach the learning strategies in the students' native language, assuming it is the same for all students and that the teacher knows the language; alternatively, teachers have been urged to give the strategy a target language name, explain how to use it in simple language, and model the strategy repeatedly (Chamot et al., 1999).

Some recent studies have used a combination of the native and target languages for strategy instruction. In an investigation of strategy instruction by secondary French and German teachers in London, some materials were in English (especially those used by students for planning and evaluating their own work), whereas checklists, descriptions of strategies, and strategy activities were written in the target language, simplified as needed (Grenfell & Harris, 1999). In a study of Japanese college students learning English as a foreign language, questionnaires, journal prompts, and self-evaluation checklists were written in "simple" English, but students could respond in Japanese; actual strategy instruction and review was conducted in English (Ozeki, 2000). In Chamot and Keatley's (2003) ESL literacy study, bilingual teachers were able to first teach the learning strategies in students' native language, then had them use the same strategies in English for similar reading tasks in English. Teachers providing instruction in English alone encountered difficulties in teaching learning strategies because of the low level of students' English proficiency, and most then abandoned the attempt to teach strategies. From these few studies, it seems clear that the issue of language of instruction in teaching language learning strategies is far from resolved, and may need to be addressed as a context-specific factor.

Explicit and Integrated Learning Strategy Instruction

Explicit instruction includes the development of students' awareness of their strategies, teacher modeling of strategic thinking, identifying the strategies by name, providing opportunities for practice and self-evaluation. Researchers in both L1 and L2 contexts agree that explicit instruction is far more effective than simply asking students to use one or more strategies and also fosters metacognition, students' ability to understand their own thinking and learning processes (Anderson, 2002, in press; Carrier, 2003; Chamot, 2004, 2005; Chamot et al., 1999; Cohen, 1998, 2003; Goh, 2002b; Graham & Harris, 2000; National Reading Panel, 2000;

O'Malley & Chamot, 1990; Oxford & Leaver, 1996; Pressley, 2000; Shen, 2003).

Less agreement is found on whether strategy instruction should be integrated into and taught concurrently with the language course, or whether to provide a separate "how to learn" course independent of the language course. Although all of the studies reviewed here have included strategy instruction as part of the regular language class, it has been argued that strategies taught in a language class are less likely to transfer to other tasks and that it may not be practical to prepare all language teachers to teach strategies (Gu, 1996). Clearly, expertise in teaching language learning strategies must be integrated into pre-and in-service preparation if teachers are to provide it to their L2 students.

Impact of Task and Learner Context

As noted earlier, learning strategies are directed toward particular tasks that can vary in both obvious and subtle ways. Tasks differ depending on whether the context is a second language or foreign language setting and whether the learner's goal is to acquire social or academic language or both (Chamot, 2004; Cohen, 2003; Cummins, 2000; Oxford et al.; 2004). Differences in strategy use also vary according to proficiency level. Takeuchi's (2003) multiple case studies of learner journals found that learners reported shifting their use of strategies as they advanced to higher proficiency levels. Similarly, a recent reading study found that perceived difficulty of the task affected use of learning strategies, which were used on more challenging tasks (Oxford et al., 2004).

The learner's goals, the context of the learning situation, and the cultural values of the learner's society will also influence choice and acceptability of language learning strategies. For example, in a culture that prizes individual competition and has organized its educational system around competitive tasks, successful language learners may prefer strategies that allow them to work alone rather than social strategies that call for collaboration with others.

Two SILL studies illustrate the learning strategy preferences reported by students in different cultural contexts. A study of ethnically Chinese, bilingual Singaporean university students studying a foreign language (French or Japanese) found that students reported a preference for social strategies as well as a disinclination to use affective strategies (Wharton, 2000). Another study examined the language learning strategies of students in a university advanced

Spanish writing class and compared achievement on a writing sample between those students speaking Spanish as a first or heritage language and those learning Spanish as a foreign language (Olivares-Cuhat, 2002). As expected, students with a Spanish language background were graded higher on their writing samples than the other students, but they also showed a greater preference for affective and memory strategies, and these latter were highly correlated with writing achievement. Preliminary findings of a current study of learning strategies used by university students of less commonly taught languages indicate that both heritage speakers of Arabic and students of Arabic as a foreign language share many of the same challenges and consequent learning strategies for learning Modern Standard Arabic (MSA), but also demonstrate differences (Keatley, Chamot, Spokane, & Greenstreet, 2004). For instance, heritage speakers reported using metacognitive strategies to overcome interference from their Arabic dialects when they attempted to speak MSA, but, unlike the foreign language students, had no difficulty in discriminating Arabic sounds and hence did not report any learning strategies for listening comprehension.

The implications for teaching are that language teachers need to find out what learning strategies students already use for different tasks. An open discussion of reasons why students use the strategies they identify can help teachers understand cultural and contextual factors that may be influencing their students. This can lead to clarification of task demands where there is a mismatch with students' current learning strategies. By understanding the task more clearly, students will likely be more motivated to try new strategies to complete it.

Metacognitive Models

The development of students' metacognition, or their ability to understand and regulate their own thinking and learning, has been urged by a number of learning strategy researchers (Anderson, 2002; Chamot et al., 1999; National Capital Language Resource Center, 2003; Rubin, 2001; Wenden, 2000). Metacognition is believed to involve both declarative (self-knowledge, world knowledge, task knowledge, strategy knowledge) and procedural knowledge (planning for learning, monitoring a learning task while it is in progress, and evaluating learning once a task has been completed; Chamot, 1994). Evidence that language learners actually engage in metacognitive knowledge and processes is reported in most of the research on language learning strategies, both descriptive and instructional. Even young children in language immersion classrooms can often describe their thinking processes, demonstrating metacognitive awareness in their ability to describe their own thinking (Chamot, 1999).

There are several current models for strategy identification, development, and instruction that emphasize metacognition. My colleagues and I have proposed a metacognitive model for learning strategy instruction that includes four recursive (rather than sequential) processes: planning, monitoring, problem-solving, and evaluating (Chamot, 1994; Chamot et al., 1999). In this model, teachers select learning strategies to teach depending on the point in a learning task where students need the most help. For example, students who do not seem to realize that a learning task is not progressing well can be taught to *monitor* their comprehension, production, or recall so that they can identify difficulties and select *problem-solving* strategies to address the difficulties. Rubin (2001) equates self-management with self-regulation as defined in the first language learning strategies literature (see, for example, Pressley, 1995). Her learner self-management model includes five metacognitive strategies: plan, monitor, evaluate, problem-solve, and implement. The model is partly linear and partly recursive, and interacts with learners' knowledge and beliefs. Anderson (2002) proposes a five-stage interactive process that includes planning, selecting and using learning strategies, monitoring strategy use, orchestrating various strategies, and evaluating the strategies used. In addition to describing this metacognitive model, he also suggests how teachers can use it to teach students how to become better language learners.

Similarly, the National Capital Language Resource Center (NCLRC; 2003) has proposed a metacognitive model in which the learner's problem-solving goals are at the center of the circular model. Surrounding these learner goals are the metacognitive strategies of planning, monitoring, managing learning, and evaluating language learning and learning strategy effectiveness. Task-based learning strategies comprise the outer circle of the model and are grouped into four categories: use what you know, use your imagination, use your organizational skills, and use a variety of resources. Teacher resource guides developed for elementary immersion classrooms (NCLRC, 2003), high school foreign language classrooms (NCLRC, 2004a), and higher education foreign language classrooms (NCLRC, 2004b) apply this model to classroom instruction.

Developing Teacher Expertise

These metacognitive models of language learning strategies can serve an important instructional goal for learning strategy instruction in second and foreign language classrooms by offering a way to think about language learning strategies from the perspective of the learner and the teacher, rather than from that of the researcher (as has characterized the claims of different strategy classification systems, for example, Hsiao & Oxford, 2002). Comprehensive classification schemes of learner strategies are needed to describe the information derived from descriptive studies that seek to chart the subtle permutations and often slippery definitions of learners' self-reported strategies. However, these extended and complex definitions may be less useful in the language classroom where the teacher is trying to help students become more strategic as they cope with actual learning tasks rather than the hypothesized learning tasks proposed in the many questionnaires and interviews designed to identify strategies that language learners claim to use.

Directions for Future Research

The study of language learning strategies will continue to develop as second language acquisition researchers seek to understand different learner characteristics and the complex cognitive, social, and affective processes involved in processing language input and using the language for a variety of purposes. Likewise, language educators and methodologists will continue their quest for more effective instructional approaches, and, with the increasing emphasis on learner-centered instruction and learner empowerment in all areas of education, instruction in learning strategies will assume a greater role in teacher preparation and curriculum design.

First, rigorous intervention studies would provide information about the effects of learning strategy instruction on achievement and language proficiency. Such studies need to be conducted with a variety of language students, including children in foreign language immersion and nonimmersion programs, school-aged students in bilingual and second language programs, older students with differing educational levels in their native language, and students in different learning contexts around the world.

A second area for future research is in the development of language teacher expertise for integrating learning strategies into classroom instruction. The evaluation of different models for teacher preparation in learning strategies instruction could lead to refining and improving current models. In addition, studies need to be undertaken to identify the relationship of effective learning strategy instruction to teacher characteristics such as teaching approach, attitude and teacher beliefs, amount and type of preservice and/or in-service preparation in learning strategy instruction, and years of teaching experience and length of time teaching learning strategies—it might be that effective learning strategy instruction is closely tied to specific individual teacher characteristics and experiences.

It is important that learning strategies research continue, both in these and other directions, for only through a better understanding of the learning and teaching process can more language learners achieve the level of success that currently characterizes only a small proportion of all students studying a foreign or second language around the world. Strategy instruction can contribute to development of learner mastery and autonomy and increased teacher expertise, but additional research in specific language learning contexts is essential to realizing its potential to enhance second language acquisition and instruction.

REFERENCES

Anderson, N. J. (2002). The role of metacognition in second language teaching and learning. *ERIC Digest*, April 2002. Washington, DC: Center for Applied Linguistics.

Anderson, N. J. (in press). L2 learning strategies. In E. Hinkel (Ed.), *Handbook of research in second language teaching and learning*. Mahwah, NJ: Erlbaum.

Bedell, D. A., & Oxford, R. L. (1996). Cross-cultural comparisons of language learning strategies in the People's Republic of China and other countries. In R. L. Oxford (Ed.), *Language learning strategies around the world: Cross-cultural perspectives* (pp. 47–60). Honolulu, HI: University of Hawaii Press.

Bruen, J. (2001). Strategies for success: Profiling the effective learner of German. *Foreign Language Annals, 34*(3), 216–225.

Carrier, K. A. (2003). Improving high school English language learners' second language listening through strategy instruction. *Bilingual Research Journal, 27*, 383–408.

Carson, J. G., & Longhini, A. (2002). Focusing on learning styles and strategies: A diary study in an immersion setting. *Language Learning, 52*(2), 401–438.

Chamot, A. U. (1994). A model for learning strategy instruction in the foreign language classroom. In J. E. Alatis (Ed.), *Georgetown University Round Table on Languages and Linguistics 1994* (pp. 323–336). Washington, DC: Georgetown University Press.

Chamot, A. U. (1999). How children in language immersion programs use learning strategies. In M. A. Kassen (Ed.), *Language learners of tomorrow: Process and promise!* (pp. 29–59). Lincolnwood, IL: National Textbook Company.

Chamot, A. U. (2004). Issues in language learning strategy research and teaching. *Electronic Journal of Foreign language Teaching, 1*(1), 12–25.

Chamot, A. U. (2005). The Cognitive Academic Language Learning Approach (CALLA): An update. In P. A. Richard-Amato & M. A. Snow (Eds.), *Academic success for English language learners: Strategies for K–12 mainstream teachers* (pp. 87–101). White Plains, NY: Longman.

Chamot, A. U., Barnhardt, S., El-Dinary, P. B., & Robbins, J. (1999). *The learning strategies handbook.* White Plains, NY: Addison Wesley Longman.

Chamot, A. U., & El-Dinary, P. B. (1999). Children's learning strategies in immersion classrooms. *The Modern Language Journal, 83*, 3, 319–341.

Chamot, A. U., & Keatley, C. W. (2003). Learning strategies of adolescent low-literacy Hispanic ESL students. Paper presented at the 2003 Annual Meeting of the American Educational Research Association, Chicago, IL.

Cohen, A. D. (1998). *Strategies in learning and using a second language.* London: Longman.

Cohen, A. D. (2003). The learner's side of foreign language learning: Where do style, strategies, and tasks meet? *International Review of Applied Linguistics, 41*, 279–291.

Cohen, A. D., & Aphek, E. (1981). Easifying second language learning. *Studies in Second Language Learning, 3*, 221–236.

Cohen, A. D., & Brooks-Carson, A. (2001). Research on direct versus translated writing: Students' strategies and their results. *Modern Language Journal, 85*(2), 169–188.

Cohen, A. D., Weaver, S., & Li, T.-Y. (1998). The impact of strategies-based instruction on speaking a foreign language. In A. D. Cohen, *Strategies in learning and using a second language* (pp. 107–156). London: Longman.

Cummins, J. (2000). *Language, power, and pedagogy: Bilingual children in the crossfire.* Clevedon, England: Multilingual Matters.

De La Paz, S., & Graham, S. (2002). Explicitly teaching strategies, skills, and knowledge: Writing instruction in middle school classrooms. *Journal of Educational Psychology, 94*(4), 687–698.

Fan, M. Y. (2003). Frequency of use, perceived usefulness, and actual usefulness of second language vocabulary strategies: A study of Hong Kong learners. *Modern Language Journal, 87*(2), 222–241.

Goh, C. C. M. (2002a). Learner's self-reports on comprehension and learning strategies for listening. *Asian Journal of English Language Teaching, 12*, 46–68 [Special issue on learning and teaching English in the Chinese context].

Goh, C. C. M. (2002b). Exploring listening comprehension tactics and their interaction patterns. *System, 30*, 185–206.

Graham, S. J. (2004). Giving up on modern foreign languages? Students' perceptions of learning French. *Modern Language Journal, 33*(2), 171–191.

Graham, S., & Harris, K. R. (2000). The role of self-regulation and transcription skills in writing and writing development. *Educational Psychologist, 35*, 3–12.

Green, J. M., & Oxford, R. (1995). A closer look at learning strategies, L2 proficiency, and gender. *TESOL Quarterly, 29*(2), 261–297.

Grenfell, M., & Harris, V. (1999). *Modern languages and learning strategies: In theory and practice.* London: Routledge.

Gu, P. Y. (1996). Robin Hood in SLA: What has the learning strategy researcher taught us? *Asian Journal of English Language Teaching, 6*, 1–29.

Hsiao, T.-Y. (2004). Testing a social psychological model of strategy use with students of English as a foreign language. *Psychological Reports, 95*, 1059–1071.

Hsiao, T.-Y., & Oxford, R. L. (2002). Comparing theories of language learning strategies: A confirmatory factor analysis. *Modern Language Journal, 86*(3), 368–383.

Hulstijn, J. H. (1997). Mnemonic methods in foreign language vocabulary learning. In J. Coady & T. Huckin (Eds.), *Second language vocabulary acquisition* (pp. 203–224). Cambridge: Cambridge University Press.

Ikeda, M., & Takeuchi, O. (2003). Can strategy instruction help EFL learners to improve their reading ability?: An empirical study. *JACET Bulletin, 37*, 49–60.

Keatley, C., Chamot, A. U., Spokane, A., & Greenstreet, S. (2004). Learning strategies of students of Arabic. *The Language Resource, 8* (4). Retrieved from http://www.nclrc.org/nectfl04ls.pdf

Khaldieh, S. A. (2000). Learning strategies and writing processes of proficient vs. less-proficient learners of Arabic. *Foreign Language Annals, 33*(5), 522–533.

Kojic-Sabo, I., & Lightbown, P. M. (1999). Students' approaches to vocabulary learning and their relationship to success. *Modern Language Journal, 83*(2), 176–192.

Macaro, E. (2001). *Learning strategies in foreign and second language classrooms.* London: Continuum.

Naiman, N., Fröhlich, M., Stern, H. H., & Todesco, A. (1978/1996). *The good language learner.* Clevedon, England: Multilingual Matters. (Original work published 1978.)

Nakatani, Y. (in press). The effects of awareness-raising training on oral communication strategy use. *Modern Language Journal, 89*(1).

National Capital Language Resource Center (NCLRC). (2003). *Elementary immersion learning strategies resource guide*. Washington, DC: National Capital Language Resource Center.

National Capital Language Resource Center (NCLRC). (2004a). *The secondary education learning strategies resource guide*. Washington, DC: National Capital Language Resource Center.

National Capital Language Resource Center (NCLRC). (2004b). *The post-secondary education learning strategies resource guide*. Washington, DC: National Capital Language Resource Center.

National Reading Panel (2000). *Report of the National Reading Panel: Teaching children to read*. Retrieved from http://www.nichd.nih.gov/publications/nrp/smallbook.htm

Nyikos, M., & Oxford, R. L. (1993). A factor analytic study of language learning strategy use: Interpretations from information-processing theory and social psychology. *Modern Language Journal, 77*, 11–22.

O'Malley, J. M., & Chamot, A. U. (1990). *Learning strategies in second language acquisition*. Cambridge, UK: Cambridge University Press.

Olivares-Cuhat, G. (2002). Learning strategies and achievement in the Spanish writing classroom: A case study. *Foreign Language Annals, 35*(5), 561–570.

Oxford, R. L. (1990). *Language learning strategies: What every teacher should know*. New York: Newbury House.

Oxford, R. L. (1996). (Ed.) *Language learning strategies around the world: Cross-cultural perspectives*. Honolulu, HI: University of Hawaii Press.

Oxford, R. L., & Burry-Stock, J. A. (1995). Assessing the use of language learning strategies worldwide with the ESL/EFL version of the *Strategy Inventory for Language Learning*. *System, 23*(2) 153–175.

Oxford, R. L., & Leaver, B. L. (1996). A synthesis of strategy instruction for foreign language learners. In R. L. Oxford (Ed.), *Language learning strategies around the world: Cross-cultural perspectives* (pp. 227–246). Honolulu, HI: University of Hawaii Press.

Oxford, R., Cho, Y., Leung, S., & Kim, H-J. (2004). Effect of the presence and difficulty of task on strategy use: An exploratory study. *International Review of Applied Linguistics, 42*, 1–47.

Ozeki, N. (2000). *Listening strategy instruction for female EFL college students in Japan*. Tokyo: Macmillan Language House.

Pressley, M. (1995). More about the development of self-regulation: Complex, long-term, and thoroughly social. *Educational Psychologist, 30*(4), 207–212.

Pressley, M. (2000). What should comprehension instruction be the instruction of? In M. L. Kamil, P. B. Mosenthal, P. D. Pearson, & R. Barr (Eds.), *Handbook of reading research: Volume III*, (pp. 545–561). Mahwah, NJ: Erlbaum.

Ross, S., & Rost, M. (1991). Learner use of strategies in interaction: Typology and teachability.

Language Learning, 41(2), 235–273.

Rubin, J. (1975). What the "good language learner" can teach us. *TESOL Quarterly, 9*, 41–51.

Rubin, J. (2001). Language learner self-management. *Journal of Asian Pacific Communication, 11*(1), 25–37.

Rubin, J. (2003). Diary writing as a process: Simple, useful, powerful. *Guidelines, 25*(2), 10–14.

Rubin, J., & Thompson, I. (1994). *How to be a more successful language learner.* Second edition. Boston: Heinle & Heinle.

Schmitt, N. (2000). *Vocabulary in language teaching.* Cambridge: Cambridge University Press.

Shen, H-J. (2003). The role of explicit instruction in ESL/EFL reading. *Foreign Language Annals, 36*(3), 424–433.

Stern, H. H. (1975). What can we learn from the good language learner? *Canadian Modern Language Review, 31*, 304–318.

Takeuchi, O. (2003). What can we learn from good language learners: A qualitative study in the Japanese foreign language context. *System, 31*, 385–392.

Thompson, I., & Rubin, J. (1996). Can strategy instruction improve listening comprehension? *Foreign Language Annals, 29*(3), 331–342.

Vandergrift, L. (1997a). The comprehension strategies of second language (French) Listeners: A descriptive study. *Foreign Language Annals, 30*(3), 387–409.

Vandergrift, L. (1997b). The Cinderella of communication strategies: Reception strategies in interactive listening. *Modern Language Journal, 81*(4), 494–505.

Vandergrift, L. (2003a). Orchestrating strategy use: Towards a model of the skilled L2 listener. *Language Learning, 53*, 461–494.

Vandergrift, L. (2003b). From prediction to reflection: Guiding students through the process of L2 listening. *Canadian Modern Language Review, 59*, 425–440.

Weaver, S. J., & Cohen, A. D. (1997). *Strategies-based instruction: A teacher-training manual.* Minneapolis: Center for Advanced Research on Language Acquisition, University of Minnesota.

Wenden, A. L. (1991). *Learner strategies for learner autonomy.* London: Prentice-Hall International.

Wenden, A. L. (2000). Learner development in language learning. *Applied Linguistics, 23*(1), 32–55.

Wharton, G. (2000). Language learning strategy use of bilingual foreign language learners in Singapore. *Language Learning, 50*(2), 203–243.

LITERACY STUDIES

7. PROGRESS AND PROCRASTINATION IN SECOND LANGUAGE READING

Elizabeth Bernhardt

This chapter presents a model of second language reading that illustrates the evolution of research and thought from the 1970s and 1980s, characterized as being influenced extensively by schema theory and psycholinguistics, and from 1990s thought and research that investigated the interdependence of language and literacy hypothesis versus the threshold hypothesis. The chapter then synthesizes the perspectives by acknowledging the necessary components of a contemporary L2 reading model, including L1 literacy level, L2 knowledge level, recognizing the interactions of background knowledge, processing strategies, vocabulary level, relationships between and among various cognate and non-cognate L1s and L2s, as well as the need to examine emerging L1/L2 readers in addition to adult L2 readers. The review argues for a compensatory processing conceptualization: one that recognizes that knowledge sources act in an interactive, synergistic fashion, not an additive one. Finally, the chapter notes a set of impediments to conducting research in the field: assessing subjects in languages unknown to researchers and the assessment of L1 literacy in an array of languages, and concludes with the recognition that second language reading is a critical area for research and scholarship well beyond the borders of applied linguistics.

Groundbreaking Work: The 1970s and 1980s

The field of second language reading has suffered historically from accusations of being derivative and nonoriginal (Weber, 1991). Certainly much of the research of the 1980s could be in part characterized as the slavish replication of studies conducted in first language. Studies such as Carrell (1983) and Lee (1986)— obvious, but by no means exclusive examples—seem at first glance to merit such criticism. Carrell (1983), for example, replicated the famous "washing clothes passage" and "balloon serenade" used in Bransford and Johnson (1973) with English as a second language subjects. And Lee (1986) translated the famous passages and replicated Carrell with Spanish as a second language subjects. Similarly, second language scholars routinely adopted first language conceptual frameworks for conducting research with second language learners. Their studies were considered to be psycholinguistic in nature and used either miscue or cloze as analytic tools (Barnett, 1986, Bhatia, 1984; Clarke, 1979, 1980; Connor, 1981; Cziko, 1978; Dank & McEachern, 1979; Devine, 1981, 1987; Elley, 1984; Groebel, 1980; Hodes, 1981; MacClean & d'Anglejan, 1986; McLeod & McLaughlin, 1986; Rigg, 1978; Tatlonghari, 1984; and others). The variables investigated within this framework are consolidated in Coady's (1979) perspective.

This imitative trend is also evidenced in the overadoption of schema theory—researchers making assumptions about the second language reading process based on first language literacy research without fully exploring the underlying dimensions of either the first or second language process. Most of this research can be characterized as the search for a smoking gun, a Holy Grail, that would conveniently and efficiently explain the process. The classic Steffensen, Joag-Dev, and Anderson study (1979) was often taken as the model and second language investigations examining background knowledge followed (Carrell, 1983, 1984a, 1987; Carrell & Wallace, 1983; Cohen, Glasman, Rosenbaum-Cohen, Ferrar, & Fine, 1979; Connor, 1981, 1984; Johnson, 1981, 1982; Mohammed & Swales, 1984; Steffensen, 1988; Zuck & Zuck, 1984; among others). The interpretation of the findings from these and other studies like them led the field to believe that the second language issue was either a "grammar issue" (if one looks at the result of the cloze studies) or a "prior knowledge issue" as in the case of the latter investigations. There were, of course, individuals who investigated word-level and phonological issues (Bernhardt, 1983; Favreau, Komoda, & Segalowitz, 1980; Favreau & Segalowitz, 1982; Hatch, Polin, & Part, 1974; Hayes, 1988; Haynes, 1981; Koda, 1987; Muchisky, 1983; Reeds, Winitz, & Garcia, 1977; among others). The variables were examined using classic quantitative research techniques and dependent measures such as time of voice onset and reading aloud.

Yet, seen as elements in the scientific process, whereby researchers must do broad and overreaching work to conduct their individual observations, these and studies like them must be seen as critical developmental steps in trying to unpack and then to understand the process whereby a reader who already has a first oral language attempts to cope with material written in a second. Continuing investigation into the 1990s called for holistic examinations of second language reading. How prior knowledge was being used by readers—whether that knowledge was text-based or extra-text based—seemed to be overrated and overemphasized. Research indicated it was highly possible that a reader who had all appropriate and relevant knowledge could fail to use it; other times, no apparent relevant or appropriate prior knowledge and didn't need it. And if one looked more closely at reader performances—well beneath the superficiality of whether readers "got" a text or did not—the interaction of word recognition, syntax, vocabulary, between and among each other and with prior knowledge also affected performance. Based on a synthesis of these studies and the addition of data from English-speaking readers of French, German, and Spanish, Bernhardt (1991) posited a model that tried capturing a holistic depiction of the interaction of variables in the second language reading process. The model is a developmental plot of sets of variable curves set against error rates using qualitative data. The examination of several hundred recall protocols made it appear at the time that processes such as word recognition and phonological issues involved in recognizing and understanding words became fairly rapid and accurate over a relatively short period of time in L2 reading development. The other classic bottom-up feature that appeared in the literature, syntax, was not as predictable. In fact, syntax appeared to function at an instance of low error rate at the early levels of proficiency and then appeared to become a complicating factor causing an increased error rate before leveling off. The function of syntax in second language reading (the more you learn the worse you get) is not intuitively obvious yet it is consistent with other observed "U-shaped" patterns in the second language acquisition literature (Ellis, 1986).

Within the data set, conceptual processes did not react throughout the development of proficiency in a consistent fashion. The development of understanding within particular texts followed no predictable pattern other than the fact that once readers made a decision about text content they did not go back to question that decision. In other words, readers did not seem to psycholinguistically guess their way through a text, testing hypotheses. Once second language readers made an initial decision, they guessed their way through that decision—not through the text. A parallel phenomenon occurred with background knowledge. Readers sometimes used the knowledge they had, and sometimes they did not. In some cases, it appeared that readers had no appropriate background knowledge and, nevertheless, achieved a high level of comprehension. These two features— essentially strategic features—did not appear to be part of the development process of reading; they were either at play or they were not; they emerged at times; they do not emerge at other times throughout the second language reading process.

The 1990s: Starting Over Again

The research in the 1970s and 1980s laid out many of the variables associated with the second language reading process. After 20 years of study, it was clear that the variables involved are significantly more complicated than the set involved in the general L1 reading, the general L1 literacy research literature. To summarize: the grammatical nature of a language, the orthographic nature of a language, sociocultural reader variables, sociocultural text variables, and additional influences were involved in second language reading. Yet, even though these variables were laid out and specified, there was still no satisfactory integrated model of these traits. Indeed, theory and studies still were rather unidimensional in nature. Text-based features such as *text structure* (Riley, 1993; Tang, 1992; Yano, Long, & Ross, 1994;); *syntax* (Berkemeyer, 1994; Takahashi & Roitblatt, 1994), and *word knowledge* (Chun & Plass, 1996; DeBot, Paribakht, & Wesche, 1997; Hulstijn, 1993; Kim, 1995; Knight, 1994; Leffa, 1992: Laufer & Hadar, 1997; Luppescu & Day, 1993; Parry, 1991; Zimmerman, 1997) remained areas of investigation as did conceptual features such as *affect* (Chi, 1995; Davis, 1992; Davis, Caron-Gorell, Kline, & Hsieh, 1992; Kramsch & Nolden, 1994). The interest in phonological aspects of reading examined the linking of reading to other language modalities, most specifically writing (Carrell & Connor, 1991; Hedgcock & Atkinson, 1993; Lund, 1991). Yet all of these investigations evolved as univariate studies without contributing to theory development.

The field owes much to Alderson (1984; Alderson & Urquhart, 1984) who consistently highlighted the need to examine the question of whether the field of second language reading should focus principally on the *reading* part of the proposition or on the *language* part of the proposition. Holding firm on this particular issue has brought the field to much of the progress it has experienced even though it confuses the procedures of reading and meaning construction with the social uses of literacy. The field remains conflicted about the relationship of literacy and language, often conflating issues of oral language, oral vocabulary, the ability to participate orally in school settings, with abilities in understanding written materials at social and academic levels. Somehow Cummins's (1984) view of Cognitive Academic Language Proficiency and Basic Interpersonal and Communicative Skills (CALP/ BICS), an important conceptualization that distinguishes language use in the broadest sense in different social settings has often been taken as a model of literacy development. Cummins's work, which vivifies these distinctions in language use (academic or personal) with the metaphor of two mountain peaks that share a common foundation, does not stand as a model with explanatory or predictive power.

Ironically, the variable missing at the beginning of the 1990s was also the most obvious: the role of first language literacy in the second language process. Of course, there had been some substantial discussion of the social variables surrounding first language literacy—most of which was couched as cultural or background knowledge related. And certainly, in the bottom-up/top-down/ interactive period, there had been a discussion of transfer and interference of one language to another (Clarke, 1979, 1980; Dank & McEachern, 1979; de Suarez, 1985; Devine, 1981, 1987; Douglas, 1981; Elley, 1984; Groebel, 1980; Irujo, 1986; MacLean & d'Anglejan, 1986; Roller, 1988; Sarig, 1987; Wagner, Spratt & Ezzaki, 1989; among others). The 1990s witnessed a continued discussion of transfer and interference processes (Block, 1992; Chikamatsu, 1996; Everson, 1998; Everson & Ke, 1997; Harrington & Sawyer, 1992; Horiba, 1996; Kern, 1994; Koda, 1993; Royer & Carlo, 1991; Tang, 1997, among others). These interference/transfer studies investigated relationships or correlations and asked questions such as *How do readers read in one language and then in the other?*

Yet, the actual act or ability in using a first literacy was never really included in the array of research variables surrounding second language text processing until the mid-1990s. The late 1990s saw a revisiting of the "is it a reading problem or a second language problem?" (Alderson, 1984) from a different perspective. Late 1990s' discussions of second language reading focused on the impact of first language literacy knowledge on the learning and the use of the second. In other words, the question was no longer one of difference and influence, but rather of accountability—how much did first language literacy *account for* literacy in a second? These studies also probed the language knowledge question. How much was raw grammatical knowledge in a language able to *account for* a given second language performance? To probe these questions, significantly different kinds of research tasks and designs were required. Readers whose first language literacy level was known or measured had to be observed and measured reading the same text type in two languages. Further, the level of language knowledge in the second language also had to be established. Finally, there was an acknowledgement of continuous, developmentally constituted variables rather than of discrete variables, implying a need for a more sophisticated statistical design than ones used in previous contexts; i.e., a move from analysis of variance designs into multivariate designs such as regression. Reformulating the second language reading problem within new configurations and analytic designs enabled an analysis of the contribution of first language literacy and second language knowledge to second language reading performance. Two Turkish/Dutch studies (Bossers, 1991; Hacquebord, 1989), one French/English (Brisbois, 1995), and two Spanish/English studies (Bernhardt & Kamil, 1995; Carrell, 1991) constitute the group that approached second language reading in this reformulated manner. Considering that cognate and noncognate languages were studied; both children and adults were considered; and different measurement schemas employed, the studies produced remarkably consistent findings: They all estimated the contribution of first language reading to second language reading to be between 14% and 21% and the contribution of language knowledge to second language reading performance to be around 30%.

Yet, even the acknowledgement of those two critical variables, surely significant ones—for it appears that L1 literacy accounts for 20% of the variance in a second language performance and grammatical knowledge accounts for another 30% (according to Brisbois, 27% vocabulary and 3% syntax)—was insufficient. Including these two variables, too, falls short of providing satisfying explanations of the second language process or of second language reading instruction for in the end they only account for around half of the variance in any given second language performance. These quantitative studies were modeled in Bernhardt (2000).

This model tried to capture the development of second language reading over time and at different proficiency levels and underlines the vastness of the territory to be investigated. The role of affect and interest in second language text processing is yet to be understood. The role of alternative conceptions of literacy (i.e., non-Western) and the impact such conceptions have on cognitive processes is critical toward understanding how persons read and learn to read when one oral language already exists in cognition. Clearly, a theoretical distribution of factors should not be perceived in a generic fashion. There are issues of level of first language literacy in relation to actual language knowledge. At the same time, however, the relationship of factor to factor was acknowledged to be also a function of the linguistic overlap between two languages (Spanish-German, for example, sharing an overlapping orthographic system; Spanish-Thai, in contrast, having virtually nothing in common linguistically).

These recognitions mandate the formulation of a view based on the interrelationships of languages, on the impact of linguistic and literacy knowledge, and on principles of learning. This model also falls short of a satisfying model of second language reading particularly because it does not effectively capture interactivity and simultaneity. It still appears to reflect a sequential and additive process. The question is not *if* language and literacy skills transfer. The question is *how much transfers*, under *what conditions*, and in *which contexts*. The question is not one of identifying a linguistic threshold. It *is* one of clarifying the relationship of linguistic knowledge to literacy knowledge to individual/idiosyncratic knowledge.

Requirements of a Contemporary Model of Second Language Reading

Part of the failure to provide a satisfying model thus far is actually the limitation of conceptualizing a multidimensional process within two dimensions. A contemporary model of second language reading must, in the first place, acknowledge the significant contribution of first language reading ability to second language comprehension. The 20% estimate appears to hold over age groups and languages fairly distinct from each other, but there are no such data from nonsyllabic languages. The field must come to understand whether this generalization holds. In addition, a contemporary model must enable a conceptualization of comprehension as consisting of different elements and influences (not just raw grammar and vocabulary). Different languages realize their meanings with different surface structures (such as restrictive word order in English versus relatively free word order in German) and models have to acknowledge that to move toward higher levels of proficiency, readers must acquire processing strategies specific to the language at hand. Further, a viable model of second language reading must also concede that in the reading of cognate languages there is no such thing as "no knowledge" if the reader is already literate and, at the same time, admit that when switching to noncognate languages, the threshold is set at a very different point. In Figure 1, the X axis refers to time (in learning, instruction, or development of proficiency); the Y axis denotes percentage of comprehension. Scores 1, 2, and 3 refer to three points in time, either scores from one person over time or from three people at different stages of development.

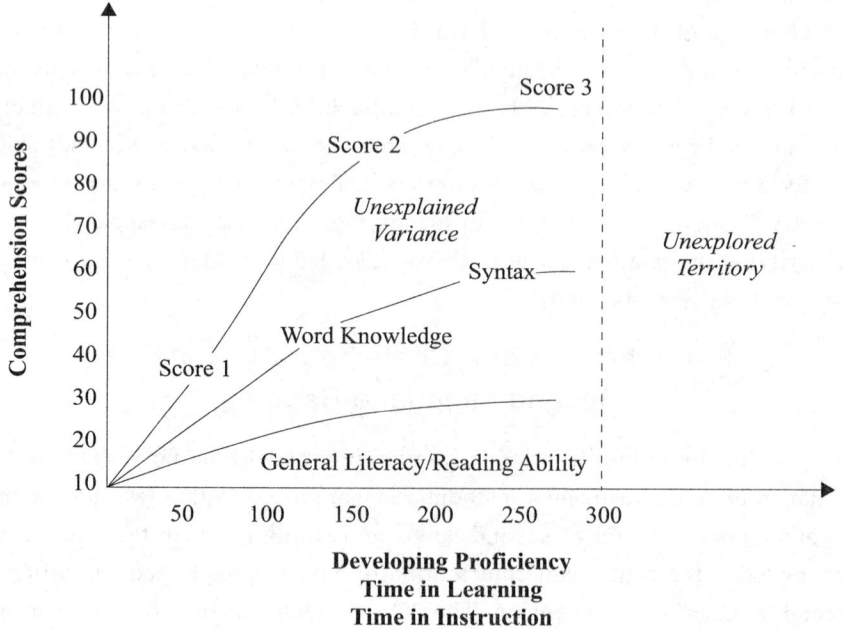

Figure 1: A statement of theoretical distribution of reading factors (from Bernhardt, 2000, p. 803).
(©Lawrence Erlbaum Associates. Permission to reproduce gratefully acknowledged.)

In the 2000 model (Figure 1), the origin is not 0, but rather 10, acknowledging that there is already some literacy knowledge on the part of all readers especially from cognate languages. But perhaps for literate L1 readers from noncognate languages, there is an origin of "10-x". This same concern reveals itself in considering and reconciling the performance of children and adults in second language reading for surely cognitive capacity has a role to play as well as how much and whether L1 literacy has developed if at all. Finally, a second language model must also encompass a consideration of unexplained variance in individual performance *and* after considerable time in learning (both formal and informal).

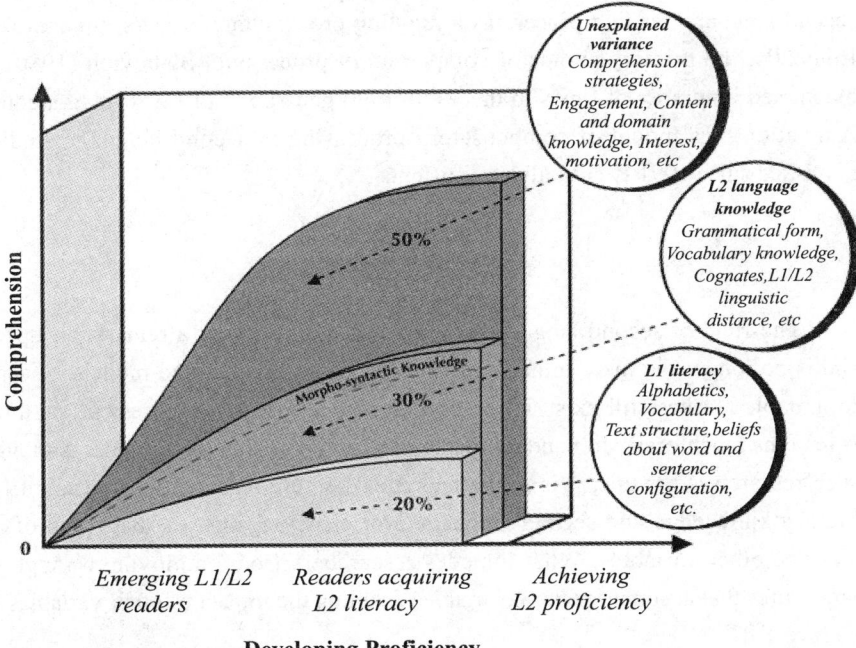

Figure 2: **A compensatory model of second language reading.**

Perhaps a more satisfying conceptualization of the second language reading process lies in the concept of compensatory processing. A compensatory model tries to model how knowledge sources assist or take over for other knowledge sources that are inadequate or nonexistent—i.e., what they use to compensate for deficiencies. This view is modeled in Figure 2. The model is three dimensional in nature and captures the current knowledge base regarding literacy knowledge, language knowledge with a particular emphasis on vocabulary, and dimensions under investigation, but not yet explained. It illustrates that knowledge sources are not additive, but rather operate synchronically, interactively, and synergistically. The model in Figure 2 attempts to conceptualize how familiarity with orthographic patterns can facilitate the word recognition process without actual language knowledge; or how the higher the L1 literacy level, the more it is available to buttress impoverished second language processes or how the more word knowledge is developed, the more it frees up resources to operate on more complex syntactic patterns and so forth. The model intends to revitalize the conceptualizations of the second language reading process as a juggling or switching process in cognition. Ironically, the primary author of compensatory processing, Stanovich (1980) is mentioned a number of times in the 1970–1990 generation of L2 reading studies. A mention of a model of compensatory processing in second language studies published since 1991 is virtually nonexistent.

Procrastination

The field of second language reading has progressed at a remarkable speed and is no longer the mere imitator of first language research and models. Several formidable hurdles still exist, however, that stymie research progress in the area. It remains much easier to conduct literacy research variable by variable. Although such research is pristine, it is also atheoretical. Future research must account for literacy knowledge and second language proficiency against the backdrop of an array of other variables. What impedes researchers from employing a range of procedures that account for these variables enabling the impact of other variables to be revealed?

First, the issue of language is a sensitive one and is of concern in first language and most certainly in second language research. There are not many reading researchers who can function in a language other than English. The result is that research is conducted principally in English. Models of reading such as Carpenter and Just (1977), Goodman (1968), Gough (1972), LaBerge and Samuels (1974), and Rumelhart (1977) have always been based on English. This means that they are inherently biased toward a particular surface structure (all published models are right-branching, for example) and a particular view of literacy (all take the view that there are no class and gender differences in the use of or access to literacy). How can one take an alternative view when one has no alternative view?

This is not an exclusive criticism to first language research. There is a notorious monolinguality within second language research. A review of the data base reveals this narrowness. There are many studies that have subject groups from across multiple language backgrounds. Of the 121 research studies reviewed in Bernhardt (1991), 56 provide no indication of the number and variety of subjects from different language backgrounds. "105 ESL learners at three proficiency levels" is the typical information given. In other words, in a huge portion of the second language reading data base, the variables introduced by these multiple languages have never been acknowledged. The field will not know truly rich research and have confident knowledge until the data base acknowledges and reveals crosslingual information. An added dimension to the concerns over monolinguality involves assessment. It is clear that the language of assessment with L2 populations is critical (Shohamy, 1982, 1984, for example). If readers are assessed in comprehension tasks in their stronger language (almost always L1 until the highest proficiency/fluency levels), their comprehension seems to be much more significant than when it is measured within the context of their impoverished second language skills. When called on this point, researchers often lament that because *they* do not know the language of the subjects with whom they are working, they are forced to assess *them* (the subjects) in the researchers' language. The field will not progress until researcher deficiencies no longer interfere with the ability to provide solid and trustworthy data. Alderson's book (2000) provides a helpful start in resolving these dilemmas as does *Methods of Literacy Research* (Kamil, Mosenthal, Pearson, & Barr, 2002).

The second dimension that encumbers research development is the measurement of literacy level. On the one hand, this, too, is an old-fashioned concept and a sensitive one. Measurement of literacy level somehow smacks of large-scale testing and the concomitant political agenda. But, politics aside, developing and validating a measure of literacy in an array of languages other than English is a formidable task—and the thought of doing it even before beginning a study of second language issues is even more formidable. But not measuring or accounting for L1 literacy has profound implications. *If* L1 literacy is truly the significant variable that it appears to be, *then* in most of the available studies, first language literacy level has merely been remeasured rather than revealing any credible information about second language reading. To be more concrete—it is a rare L2 study that appears to have an effect size large enough to overcome a 20% (or even a 10%) variance attributable to first language literacy.

Lingering Dilemmas and a Bright Future

A legitimate question is whether the field needs models. In truth, each scientific endeavor has a model whether that model is explicitly stated or not. Samuels and Kamil (1984) remind the field of the value of a good model: Such theory building consolidates information from the past, synthesizes present information, and predicts the future. In other words, good models and theory building are economical. They allow the field to move forward rather than reliving a past; they permit a conceptualization of the current state of affairs; and perhaps most importantly they aid in the direction of research development, revealing important variables and processes for fruitful investigation.

The model in Figure 2 highlights the need to examine critical literacy variables *in light of variables that already exist.* It calls, for example, for basic research in the interplay of syntax and vocabulary in text processing, posing questions such as, *Can strategic knowledge compensate for weaknesses in syntax and can these elements be overwhelmed by vocabulary knowledge and so forth?* The model also calls for true experiments involving presently unexplained variance. *Can more variance be accounted for by using reading tasks that simulate different levels of interest and motivation against the backdrop of language and literacy knowledge?* Samuels and Kamil (1984) contend that "an absolutely critical characteristic of a good model is that it be precise enough to lead to testable hypotheses. It is only through the process of testing a model that we are able to determine its validity" (p. 192).

The specter of effective instruction remains a lingering dilemma (Grabe, 2004; Grabe & Stoller, 2002). A theory is only as good as its practical application. If the variables outlined in Figure 2 effectively conceptualize the second language reading process, then the field needs to gather data regarding effective instruction that reflects this process. The model points toward nonadditive integrative instruction: instruction that accommodates literacy variables, language variables, and affective, social, and strategic variables. Key questions are what this accommodation looks like, which accommodations bring about the highest levels of comprehension among learners, and how to work with teachers who wish to learn new integrative methodologies. Another lingering dilemma is how to understand the use of electronic aids in independent reading. Readers with no instructional support, forced to fend for themselves, often rely on the internet in conjunction with electronic dictionaries for a significant portion of critical information. Yet these readers are haunted by the fact that they have no real way of knowing whether they have understood highly technical material. How the field can meet its ethical demand to support such readers is a critical yet open question.

Several bright spots also characterize the field. Every recent major synthesis on scientifically based reading research has acknowledged the importance of research in second language reading. These include *The Handbook of Reading Research, Volume II* (Barr, Kamil, Mosenthal, & Pearson, 1991) and *Volume III* (Kamil, Mosenthal, Pearson, & Barr, 2000); the National Reading Panel Report (National Institute of Child Health and Human Development, 2000); the RAND Study Group (2002); the U.S. Institute for Education Sciences commission, the National Literacy Panel for Language Minority Youth (forthcoming, 2005); and the International Reading Association, which has commissioned a special panel to work on second language literacy. These are critical indicators that the findings on second language reading development are much more broadly acknowledged than most work in applied linguistics. A new collection of essays (Brantmeier, forthcoming, 2005) also contributes crucial information to the data base as does important work in the journal *Reading in a Foreign Language*. All of these endeavors point to the vibrancy and urgency that surround the field of reading in a second language.

ANNOTATED BIBLIOGRAPHY

Alderson, J. C. (2000). *Assessing reading.* New York: Cambridge University Press.

This volume reviews and critques the most frequently used methods for assessing comprehension of written text. It clearly lays out the opportunity costs encountered in the use of each methodology both for research and for testing purposes.

Brantmeier, C. (2005, forthcoming). (Ed.). Adult foreign language reading: Theory, research, and implications.

This special issue published by *The Southern Journal of Linguistics, 27*(1), consists of reports that either offer new empirical evidence or examine existing investigations to support a comprehensive theory of second language reading research by researching both micro-and macrolevel features of the reading process with learners of several different languages at different levels of language instruction.

Grabe, W., & Stoller, F. L. (2002). *Teaching and researching reading.* New York: Longman.

This volume on reading is directed specifically at practitioners who wish an understanding of current research and theory perspectives and who wish to come to their own conclusions about the second language reading process. The volume urges teachers to investigate the reading behaviors of their students.

Kamil, L., Mosenthal, P. B., Pearson, P. D., & Barr, R. (2000). (Eds.) *Handbook of reading research, Volume III.* Mahwah, NJ: Erlbaum.

This is the most comprehensive volume to date on literacy research. With almost 1000 pages and 47 chapters, this volume focuses specifically on literacy policy, practices, and processes. The volume includes two chapters on second language reading.

Kamil, L., Mosenthal, P. B., Pearson, P. D., & Barr, R. (2002). (Eds.) Methods of literacy research; The methodology chapter from the *Handbook of Reading Research, Volume III.* Mahwah, NJ: Erlbaum.

This individually published excerpt from the third *Handbook of Reading Research* focuses specifically on research methodology and is extremely helpful for researchers designing studies in literacy. It emphasizes qualitative research methodologies in particular: narrative approaches, critical approaches, and think alouds as examples.

OTHER REFERENCES

Alderson, J. C. (1984). Reading in a foreign language: A reading problem or a language problem? In J. C. Alderson & A. H. Urquhart (Eds.), *Reading in a foreign language* (pp. 1–24). London: Longman.

Alderson, J. C., & Urquhart, A. (Eds.). (1984). *Reading in a foreign language.* London:

Longman.

Barnett, M. (1986). Syntactic and lexical/semantic skill in foreign language reading: Importance and interaction. *Modern Language Journal, 70,* 343–349.

Barr, R., Kamil, M. L., Mosenthal, P., Pearson, P. D. (Eds.). (1991). *Handbook of reading research, Volume II.* Mahwah, NJ: Erlbaum.

Berkemeyer, V. (1994). Anaphoric resolution and text comprehension for readers of German. *Die Unterrichtspraxis 27,* (2), 15–22.

Bernhardt, E. B. (1983). Three approaches to reading comprehension in intermediate German. *Modern Language Journal, 67,* 111–115.

Bernhardt, E. B. (1991). *Reading development in a second language: Theoretical, research, and classroom perspectives.* Norwood, NJ: Ablex.

Bernhardt, E. B. (2000). Second language reading as a case study of reading scholarship in the twentieth century. In M. Kamil, P. Mosenthal, P. D. Pearson., & R. Barr, (Eds.), *Handbook of reading research, Volume III* (pp. 793–811). Hillsdale, NJ: Erlbaum.

Bernhardt, E. B., & Kamil, M. L. (1995). Interpreting relationships between L1 and L2 reading: Consolidating the linguistic threshold and the linguistic interdependence hypotheses. *Applied Linguistics, 16,* 15–34.

Bhatia, V.K. (1984). Syntactic discontinuity in legislative writing for academic legal purposes. In A. K. Pugh & J. M. Ulijn (Eds.), *Reading for professional purposes: Studies and practices in native and foreign languages* (pp. 90–96). London: Heinemann Educational Books.

Block, E. (1992). See how they read: Comprehension monitoring of L1 and L2 readers. *TESOL Quarterly, 26,* (2), 319–343.

Bossers, B. (1991). On thresholds, ceiling, and short circuits: The relation between L1 reading, L2 reading, and L1 knowledge. *AILA Review, 8,* 45–60.

Bransford, J. D., & Johnson, M. (1973). Consideration of some problems of comprehension. In W. Chase (Ed.), *Visual information processing* (pp. 383–438). New York: Academic Press.

Brisbois, J. (1995). Connections between first-and second language reading. *Journal of Reading Behavior, 24,* 565–584.

Carpenter, P. A., & Just, M. A. (1977). Reading comprehension as eyes see it. In M. A. Just & P. A. Carpenter (Eds.), *Cognitive processes in comprehension* (pp. 109–139). Hillsdale, NJ: Erlbaum.

Carrell, P. L. (1983). Three components of background knowledge in reading comprehension. *Language Learning, 33,* 183–207.

Carrell, P. L. (1984a). Evidence of a formal schema in second language comprehension. *Language Learning, 34,* 87–112.

Carrell, P. L. (1987). Content and formal schemata in ESL reading. *TESOL Quarterly, 21*(3), 461–481.

Carrell, P. (1991). Second language reading: Reading ability or language proficiency? *Applied Linguistics*, *12*, 159–179.

Carrell, P., & Connor, U. (1991). Reading and writing persuasive texts. *Modern Language Journal*, *75*, 314–324.

Carrell, P., & Wallace, B. (1983). Background knowledge: Context and familiarity in reading comprehension. In M. A. Clarke & J. Handscombe (Eds.), *On TESOL'82* (pp. 245–308). Washington, DC: TESOL.

Chi, F.-M. (1995). EFL readers and a focus on intertextuality. *Journal of Reading 38*(8), 638–644.

Chikamatsu, N. (1996). The effects of L1 or thography on L2 word recognition: A study of American and Chinese learners of Japanese. *Studies in Second Language Acquisition*, *18*(4), 403–432.

Chun, D., & Plass, J. (1996). Facilitating reading comprehension with multimedia. *System*, *24*(4), 503–519.

Clarke, M. A. (1979). Reading in Spanish and English: Evidence from adult ESL students. *Language Learning*, *29*, 121–150.

Clarke, M. A. (1980). The short circuit hypothesis of ESL reading: Or when language competence interferes with reading performance. *Modern Language Journal*, *64*, 203–209.

Coady, J. (1979). A psycholinguistic model of the ESL reader. In R. Mackay, B. Barkman, & R. R. Jordan (Eds.), *Reading in a second language* (pp. 5–12). Rowley, MA; Newbury House.

Cohen, A., Glasman, H., Rosenbaum-Cohen, P., Ferrar, J., & Fine, J. (1979). Reading English for specialized purposes: Discourse analysis and the use of student informants. *TESOL Quarterly*, *3*, 551–564.

Connor, U. (1981). The application of reading miscue analysis to diagnosis of English as a second language learners' reading skills. In C. W. Twyford, W. Diehl, & K. Feathers (Eds.), *Reading English as a second language: Moving from theory* (pp. 47–55). Bloomington: Indiana University School of Education.

Connor, U. (1984). Recall of text: Differences between first and second language readers. *TESOL Quarterly*, *18*, 239–255.

Cummins, J. (1984). *Bilingualism and special education: Issues in assessment and pedagogy.* Clevedon, UK: Multilingual Matters.

Cziko, G. A. (1978). Differences in first-and second language reading: The use of syntactic, semantic, and discourse constraints. *Canadian Modern Language Review/ La revue canadienne des langues vivantes*, *34*, 473–489.

Dank, M., & McEachern, W. (1979). A psycholinguistic description comparing the native language oral reading behavior of French immersion students with traditional English language students. *Canadian Modern Language Review/La revue canadienne des langues vivantes, 35*, 366–371.

Davis, J. (1992). Reading literature in the foreign language: The comprehension/response connection. *The French Review 65*(3), 359–370.

Davis, J., Gorell, L., Kline, R., & Hsieh, G. (1992). Readers and foreign languages: A survey of undergraduate attitudes toward the study of literature. *Modern Language Journal, 73*, 320–332.

DeBot, K., Paribakht, S., & Wesche, M. B. (1997). Toward a lexical processing model for the study of second language vocabulary acquisition: Evidence from ESL reading. *Studies in Second Language Acquisition, 19*(3), 309–329.

Devine, J. (1981). Developmental patterns in native and non-native reading acquisition. In S. Hudelson (Ed.), *Learning to read in different languages* (pp. 110–114). Washington, DC: Center for Applied Linguistics.

Devine, J. (1987). General language competence and adult second language reading. In J. Devine, P. L. Carrell, & D. E. Eskey (Eds.), *Research in reading in English as a second language* (pp. 73–86). Washington, DC: Teachers of English to Speakers of Other Languages.

Douglas, D. (1981). An exploratory study of bilingual reading proficiency. In S. Hudelson (Ed.), *Learning to read in different languages* (pp. 93–102). Washington, DC: Center for Applied Linguistics.

Elley, W. B. (1984). Exploring the reading difficulties of second language readers and second languages in Fiji. In J. C. Alderson & A. H. Urquhart (Eds.), *Reading in a foreign language* (pp. 281–297). London: Longman.

Ellis, R. (1986). *Understanding second language acquisition*. Oxford: Oxford University Press.

Everson, M. E. (1998). Word recognition among learners of Chinese as a foreign language: Investigating the relationship between naming and knowing. *Modern Language Journal, 82*, 194–204.

Everson, M. E., & Ke, C. (1997). An inquiry into the reading strategies of intermediate and advanced learners of Chinese as a foreign language. *Journal of the Chinese Language Teachers Association, 32*, 1–20.

Favreau, M., & Segalowitz, N. S. (1982). Second language reading in fluent bilinguals. *Applied Psycholinguistics, 3*, 329–341.

Favreau, M., Komoda, M. K., & Segalowitz, N. S. (1980). Second language reading: Implications of the word superiority effect in skilled bilinguals. *Canadian Journal of Psychology/Revue canadienne de psychologie, 34*, 370–380.

Goodman, K. (Ed.). (1968). *The psycholinguistic nature of the reading process*. Detroit, MI: Wayne State University Press.

Gough, P. B. (1972). One second of reading. In J. F. Kavanagh & I. G. Mattingly (Eds.),

Language by eye and ear (pp. 331–358). Cambridge: MIT Press.

Grabe, W. (2004). Research on teaching reading. *Annual Review of Applied Linguistics, 24*, 44–69.

Groebel, L. (1980). A comparison of students' reading comprehension in the native language with their reading comprehension in the target language. *English Language Teaching Journal, 35*, 54–59.

Hacquebord, H. (1989). *Reading comprehension of Turkish and Dutch students attending secondary schools*. Groningen: RUG.

Harrington, M., & Sawyer, M. (1992). L2 working memory capacity and L2 reading skill. *Studies in Second Language Acquisition, 14*, 25–38.

Hatch, E., Polin, P., & Part, S. (1974). Acoustic scanning and syntactic processing: Three reading experiments: First and second language learners. *Journal of Reading Behavior, 6*, 275–285.

Hayes, E. B. (1988). Encoding strategies used by native and non-native readers of Chinese Mandarin. *Modern Language Journal, 72*, 188–195.

Haynes, M. (1981). Patterns and perils of guessing in second language reading. In J. Handscombe, R. Oren, & B. Taylor (Eds.), *On TESOL'83* (pp. 163–176). Washington, DC: TESOL.

Hedgcock, J., & Atkinson, D. (1993). Differing reading-writing relationships in L1 and L2 literacy development? *TESOL Quarterly 27*, 329–333.

Hodes, P. (1981). Reading: A universal process. In S. Hudelson (Ed.), *Learning to read in different languages* (pp. 27–31). Washington, DC: Center for Applied Linguistics.

Horiba, Y. (1996). Comprehension processes in L2 reading: Language competence, textual coherence, and inferences. *Studies in Second Language Acquisition 18*, 433–473.

Hulstijn, J. (1993). When do foreign-language readers look up the meaning of unfamiliar words? The influence of task and learner variables. *Modern Language Journal 77*, 139–147.

Irujo, S. (1986). Don't put your leg in your mouth: Transfer in the acquisition of idioms in a second language. *TESOL Quarterly, 20*, 287–304.

Johnson, P. (1981). Effects on reading comprehension of language complexity and cultural background of a text. *TESOL Quarterly, 15*, 169–181.

Johnson, P. (1982). Effects on comprehension of building background knowledge. *TESOL Quarterly, 16*, 503–516.

Kern, R. G. (1994). The role of mental translation in second language reading. *Studies in Second Language Acquisition, 16*, 441–461.

Kim, S.-A. (1995). Types and sources of problems in L2 reading: A qualitative analysis of the recall protocols of Korean high school EFL students. *Foreign Language Annals, 28*, 49–70.

Knight, S. (1994). Dictionary: The tool of last resort in foreign language reading? A new perspective. *Modern Language Journal, 78,* 285–299.

Koda, K. (1987). Cognitive strategy transfer in second language reading. In J. Devine, P. L. Carrell, & D. E. Eskey (Eds.), *Research in reading in English as a second language.* Washington, DC: TESOL, 125–144.

Koda, K. (1993). Transferred L1 strategies and L2 syntactic structures in L2 sentence comprehension. *The Modern Language Journal, 77,* 490–499.

Kramsch, C., & Nolden, T. (1994). Redefining literacy in a foreign language. *Die Unterrichtspraxis, 27,* 28–35.

LaBerge, D., & Samuels, S.J. (1974). Toward a theory of automatic information processing in reading. *Cognitive Psychology, 6,* 293–323.

Laufer, B., & Hadar, L. (1997). Assessing the effectiveness of monolingual, bilingual, and "bilingualized" dictionaries in the comprehension and production of new words. *The Modern Language Journal, 81,* 189–196.

Lee, J. F. (1986). Background knowledge and L2 reading. *Modern Language Journal, 70,* 350–354.

Leffa, V. (1992). Making foreign language texts comprehensible for beginners: An experiment with an electronic glossary. *System, 20,* 63–73.

Lund, R. (1991). A comparison of second language listening and reading comprehension. *The Modern Language Journal, 75,* 196–204.

Luppescu, S., & Day, R. (1993). Reading, dictionaries, and vocabulary learning. *Language Learning, 42,*(2) 263–287.

MacLean, M., & d'Anglejan, A. (1986). Rational cloze and retrospection: Insights into first and second language reading comprehension. *Canadian Modern Language Review/La revue canadienne des langues vivantes, 42,* 814–826.

McLeod, B., & McLaughlin, B. (1986). Restructuring or automaticity? Reading in a second language. *Language Learning, 36,* 109–123.

Mohammed, M. A. H., & Swales, J. M. (1984). Factors affecting the successful reading of technical instructions. *Reading in a Foreign Language, 2,* 206–217.

Muchisky, D. M. (1983). Relationships between speech and reading among second language learners. *Language Learning, 33,* 77–102.

National Institute of Child Health and Human Development (NICHD). (2000). *Report of the National Reading Panel: Teaching children to read: An evidence-based assessment of the scientific research literature on reading and its implications for reading instruction: Reports of the subgroups.* Washington, DC: Author.

National Literacy Panel for Language Minority Youth. (Forthcoming, 2005). Washington, DC: US Department of Education.

Parry, K. (1991). Building a vocabulary through academic reading. *TESOL Quarterly, 25,* 629–

653.

RAND Reading Study Group. (2002). *Reading for understanding: Toward an R&D program in reading comprehension*. Santa Monica, CA: RAND.

Reeds, J. A., Winitz, H., & Garcia, P. A. (1977). A test of reading following comprehension training. *International Review of Applied Linguistics (IRAL)*, *15*, 307–319.

Rigg, P. (1978). The miscue-ESL project. In H. D. Brown, C. Yorio, & R. Crymes (Eds.), *On TESOL 77* (pp. 109–117). Washington, DC: TESOL.

Riley, G. (1993). A story structure approach to narrative text comprehension. *Modern Language Journal*, *77*, 417–430.

Roller, C. M. (1988). Transfer of cognitive academic competence and L2 reading in a rural Zimbabwean primary school. *TESOL Quarterly*, *22*(2), 303–328.

Royer, J., & Carlo, M. (1991). Transfer of comprehension skills from native to second language. *Journal of Reading*, *34*, 450–455.

Rumelhart, D. (1977). Toward an interactive model of reading. In S. Dornic (Ed.), *Attention and performance V* (pp. 573–603). Hillsdale, NJ: Erlbaum.

Samuels, S. J., & Kamil, M. L. (1984). Models of the reading process. In P. D. Pearson (Ed.), *Handbook of reading research* (pp. 185–224). New York: Longman.

Sarig, G. (1987). High-level reading in the first and in the foreign language: Some comparative process data. In J. Devine, P. L. Carrell, & D. E. Eskey (Eds.), *Research in reading in English as a second language* (pp. 105–120). Washington, DC: TESOL.

Shohamy, E. (1982). Affective considerations in language testing. *Modern Language Journal*, *66*, 13–17.

Shohamy, E. (1984). Does the testing method make a difference? The case of reading comprehension. *Language Testing*, *1*, 147–170.

Stanovich, K. E. (1980). Toward an interactive-compensatory model of individual differences in the acquisition of literacy. *Reading Research Quarterly*, *16*, 32–71.

Steffensen, M. S. (1988). Changes in cohesion in the recall of native and foreign texts. In P. L. Carrell, J. Devine, & D. E. Eskey (Eds.), *Interactive approaches to second language reading* (pp. 140–151). Cambridge: Cambridge University Press.

Steffensen, M. S., Joag-Dev, C., & Anderson, R. C. (1979). A cross-cultural perspective on reading comprehension. *Reading Research Quarterly*, *15*, 10–29.

Suarez, J. de. (1985). Using translation communicatively in ESP courses for science studies. In J. M. Ulijn & A. K. Pugh (Eds.), *Reading for professional purposes: Methods and materials in teaching languages* (pp. 56–68). Leuven, Belgium: Acco.

Takahashi, S., & Roitblatt, H. (1994). Comprehension processes of second language indirect requests. *Applied Psycholinguistics*, *15*, 475–506.

Tang, G. (1992). The effect of graphic representation of knowledge structures on ESL reading comprehension. *Studies in Second Language Acquisition, 14*, 177–195.

Tang, G. (1997). The relationship between reading comprehension processes in L1 and L2. *Reading Psychology, 18*, 249–301.

Tatlonghari, M. (1984). Miscue analysis in an ESL context. *RELC Journal, 15*, 75–84.

Wagner, D. A., Spratt, J. E., & Ezzaki, A. (1989). Does learning to read in a second language always put the child at a disadvantage? Some counter evidence from Morocco. *Applied Psycholinguistics, 10*, 31–48.

Weber, R. (1991). Linguistic diversity and reading in American society. In R. Barr, (Ed.) *Handbook of reading research, Volume III* (pp. 97–119). New York: Longman.

Yano, Y., Long, M., & Ross, S. (1994). The effects of simplified and elaborated texts on foreign language reading comprehension. *Language Learning, 44*, 189–219.

Zimmerman, C. (1997). Do reading and interactive vocabulary instruction make a difference? An empirical study. *TESOL Quarterly, 31*, 121–140.

Zuck, L. V., & Zuck, I. G. (1984). The main idea: Specialist and nonspecialist judgments. In A. K. Pugh & I. M. Ulijn (Eds.), *Reading for professional purposes: Studies and practices in native and foreign languages* (pp. 130–135). London: Heinemann Educational Books.

8. CRITICAL LITERACIES AND LANGUAGE EDUCATION: GLOBAL AND LOCAL PERSPECTIVES

Brian Morgan and Vaidehi Ramanathan

Increasingly aware of the "critical" turn in our disciplines, we offer a partial survey of scholarship in two key realms—English for academic purposes (EAP) and globalization—where the term "critical literacy" has particular relevance. We begin by addressing some key concepts and ideological tensions latent beneath the term "critical." We then address the pedagogical priorities that arise from this conceptualization, in particular, the use of texts to distance individual and group identities from powerful discourses. Next, we review studies that demonstrate how different teachers and researchers have engaged in unraveling and cross-questioning the rhetorical influences of various texts types, including multimodal ones. In the final section, we discuss the intertwined processes of homogenization and diversification arising from the economic, cultural, and political strains of globalization with particular emphasis on their implications for critical literacies and language education.

It is prudent practice to begin a review of this type by forewarning readers of the plurality and complexity of the field in question. The notion of critical literacy certainly fits this seemingly unmanageable profile. Still, for researchers, teachers, teacher educators, or policy makers, key unifying themes emerge around our topic. Although a meeting place of many disciplines (e.g., cultural anthropology, cognitive psychology, applied linguistics, literary studies, to name a few), literacy is increasingly conceptualized as a *social practice*. This sociality does not ignore the cognitive and semiotic processes involved in the production and reception of texts. Instead, it is recognition that literacy practices deemed basic, functional, or of a higher-order—or that stand as emblematic of nation or ethnicity—are at root social arrangements, embedded in and constitutive of issues relating to unequal distributions of power within communities and institutions (e.g., Carr, 2003; Gee, 2002; Lewis, 2001; Luke & Elkins, 2002; Nieto, 2002; Rassool, 1999; Reder & Davila, this volume). In this respect, literacy can be seen as doing the work of discourse and power/knowledge (cf. Foucault, cited in Pennycook, 2001). Through schooling, a prominent site we address, literacy practices provide the textual means by which dominant values and identities (e.g., avid consumers, obedient workers, patriotic citizens) are normalized and, at times, resisted. Because this topic is vast with several intertwining strands, this chapter will selectively focus on (1) delineating some key aspects and conceptual underpinnings latent beneath the term "critical," and (2) offer a partial survey of research in two key sites—EAP and globalization—where critical literacy has particular resonance.

Laying the Groundwork: Critical Literacy and Its Conceptual Underpinnings

By underscoring the power-related aspects of literacy, critical educators seek to understand meaning making within wider contextual domains: the ideological antecedents and disjunctures of the existing order and transformations in representational technologies that have facilitated histories, imagined and real. As we begin the 21st century, the threats posed and opportunities created by way of political, economic, and cultural globalization present a world context of intense debate, parts of which we will summarize. It is also a contextual domain in which the future of schools, work, and public life—or traditional definitions of literacy and orality—are reconceptualized in light of new digital capacities (e.g., image manipulation, multimedia, and hypermedia) and global information systems (i.e., the Internet) that challenge our perceptions of reality, locality, and community (Darley, 2000; Kramsch, 2000; Kramsch & Thorne, 2002; Warnick, 2002; Warschauer, 2004). Critical educators, in response, advocate a pluralized notion of *literacies* and *multiliteracies* to help students negotiate a broader range of text-types and modes of persuasion, not only via print, but also sound, images, gestures, spaces, and their multimodal integration (e.g., Cope & Kalantzis, 2000; Hunter &

Morgan, 2001; Jewitt & Kress, 2003; Kress, 2003; Lotherington, 2001, 2003; Norton & Vanderheyden, 2004; Quinlisk, 2003; Stein, 2004).

Arguably, such skills are not just options but necessities, if not forms of self-defense against the intrusiveness of corporate advertising, the growing sameness of cultural products and information from global media empires, and the expansion of sophisticated forms of surveillance and data sharing employed in the name of security (e.g., McChesney, 1999; Rutherford, 2000). Although one could make the argument that such concerns are irrelevant for applied linguists and language teacher education because they have little to do with actual reading and writing, critical literacy practitioners are likely to maintain that multiple texts, modalities, and technologies are crucial to the literacy setting because our job as educators partially entails cultivating a citizenry that is able to negotiate and critically engage with the numerous texts, modalities, and technologies coming at learners, and because we now collectively occupy globalized, interconnected spaces that insist on such critical engagement. Latent beneath such debates, of course, is how we understand the notion of "critical" and how this understanding circumscribes our engagement with the local and global power relations in which texts circulate and acquire their rhetorical potency. The following excerpt from Luke (2004) succinctly sums up some of what the term entails:

> To be critical is to call up for scrutiny, whether through embodied action or discourse practice, the rules of exchange within a social field. To do so requires an analytic move to self-position oneself as Other even in a market or field that might not necessarily construe or structurally position one as Other . . . .This doubling and positioning of the self from dominant text and discourse can be cognate, analytic, expository, and hypothetical, and it can, indeed, be already lived, narrated, embodied, and experienced (Luke, 2004, p. 26).

Critical literacies, informed by the previous passage, presuppose fluid and emergent notions of identity that bridge Cartesian dichotomies of mind/body, reason/emotion, and subject/object. Neither the thought processes of the mind nor the self-contained properties of page or screen provide independent foci for an adequate understanding of meaning making. The primary unit of analysis—

and the pedagogical interventions it supports—is the "subject-in-discourse," a conceptual unity illuminated through the lens of various postmodern theories (e.g., feminist poststructuralism, social constructivism, performativity, queer theory, and community of practice models). Individual and collective understandings, in this perspective, do not preexist their linguistic expression but are, instead, created and contested through dominant and subversive language practices (Canagarajah, 2004a; Norton, 2000). Similarly, the possibilities for human *agency*, following Luke, do not preexist discourse, but arise from within and as an effect of its particularities.

By extension, we may think of texts (i.e., oral, written, imaged, or embodied) as multidimensional—not only informational or genre-specific, but also *person-formative*. In understanding how subjects are discursively formed or positioned, we need to conceive of texts as conveying a dual *materiality*. On the one hand, texts both carry and address the "rules of exchange" of the social milieu in which they circulate (cf. intertextuality, Bazerman, 2004). Through implicit and explicit reference, and elements of style and genre, texts give voice to the tensions of their times—the antagonistic, class-based materiality conceived by Marx and running through the *heteroglossia* of Bakhtin, the *multiaccentual, ideological sign* of Volosinov, the *cultural* and *symbolic capital* of Bourdieu, and the *dialogism* of Freire. On the other hand, materiality also refers to the specific textual modality used. Whether we speak or write, take a photograph, produce a play, or create a website, each communicative vehicle will offer specialized compositional choices whose particular carrying capacities or *affordances* (Kress, 2003) shape what we can mean and how the experience of those meanings will be understood and retained over time (e.g., Goldstein, 2003; Kramsch, 2000). When addressing "subjects-in-discourse," then, critical practitioners attend to both shifts in meaning potential *across* semiotic modes but also to their fundamental integration. As sites of practice, literacies, texts, even grammars, are conceived *holistically*, in the post-Cartesian sense of integrating a full range of emotive, sensorial, and experiential meanings and not just as discrete, rational systems (e.g., Kress, 2000, 2003; Kress & van Leeuwen, 1996; Lemke, 2002; Morgan 2004a, 2004b; Stein, 2004).

In sum, Luke's passage invokes a longstanding critical tradition whereby *self*-awareness precedes and facilitates effective social action; that is, to "read the word and the world" (cf. Freire, 1997) we must begin to "read" ourselves and uncover our complicity in the commonsensical maintenance of social inequalities (cf. hegemony, Gramsci). Toward this end, and through the strategic deployment of texts, pedagogy becomes a process of *unlearning* internalized and habitual ways of seeing and being, naming the world and imagining social futures. Yet the achievement of "uncommon" sense through *dialogue* and *critical consciousness* (Freire, 1997), *meta-awareness* (Ramanathan, 2002), *reflexivity* (Canagarajah, 1999; Morgan, in press) or *problematizing practices* (Benesch, 2001; Pennycook, 2001) is no straightforward matter in classrooms, and key tensions arise in offering guidelines for critical literacies.

As "subjects-in-discourse," for example, both students and teachers are differentially positioned—gendered, racialized, marked as immigrants or nonnative speakers—in multiple and often contradictory ways that belie simple binaries of oppressor and oppressed. Further complexity arises in the textual forging of schooled voices, the merging—to various degrees of success—of cultural memories and prior forms of language socialization with conscious and unconscious strategies of imitation, accommodation, or opposition to the dominant norms of the academic discourse community (Canagarajah, 2002, 2004b; Casanave, 2002; Bayley & Schecter, 2003). Then there is the unmistakable diversity of English language teaching (ELT) sites and contexts of practice. Across the privileged confines of universities, English in the workplace programs (Goldstein, 2001; Katz, 2000) or in rural village literacy programs (Egbo, 2004; Purcell-Gates & Waterman, 2000; Sahni, 2001), universal methods and conceptions of power may certainly be inappropriate, as widely acknowledged (Kumaravadivelu, 2003a), but local specificities indiscernible or of marginal relevance to the diversity of life stories unfolding across the globe. Indeed, as Janks (2001) observed in a racially mixed, South African classroom, the pedagogical distancing of self from dominant text may be resented when such texts serve to unify fragile and threatened solidarities.

Other key tensions, paradigmatic in nature, concern assumptions about the world we are empowered to read. Is it a world whose ontological "truths" can be represented or revealed scientifically (cf. emancipatory modernism, Pennycook, 2001), or, is "reality" a textualized illusion (cf., nihilistic deconstructive postmodernism, Shea, 1998) always open to new discursive readings and always dangerous in terms of the new subjectivities and forms of power/knowledge that result? Or, is it something metaphorically in between—a recursive world both real and mediated? Paradigmatic assumptions of these sorts shape how critical literacies unfold. They can influence what teachers accept or reject as valid, emancipatory outcomes of dialogue, for example, or they can contribute to forms of epistemic skepticism in which teachers, newly conscious of the partiality of their knowledge, fear to act. As "subjects-in-discourse" we are each (students, teachers, researchers, scholars in ELT) in positions where we can turn the critical lens on ourselves to where we hold everything about our professional lives to the light: our teaching, choice of pedagogic materials, discipline's orientations, valued genres, socialization practices. A justification of such self-critical analyses is partially this: By taking deliberate steps to create contexts for ourselves and our learners whereby we begin to critically distance ourselves and analytically reflect on our numerous participations (in hallways, in student conferences, in writing proposals and papers, in conference presentations) we will eventually be in a better position to change aspects of our social and disciplinary worlds that we deem necessary.

Negotiating Critical Literacies in Classrooms: Pedagogical Priorities

In a world imagined through postmodernism, where new orthodoxies of contingency, indeterminacy, and hybridity command our attention, there is strong consensus against prescribed, transmission-oriented methods of critique as well as strong concern for the ideological complacency and paternalism that can arise from such assumptions (e.g., Clarke, 2003, Ch. 6; Johnston, 2003, Ch. 3). Reflecting the interpretive and experiential dynamics that mediate knowledge, transformative practitioners focus on creating possibilities rather than certainties. Critical distancing is not guaranteed through any one specific form of literacy, but arises from articulated practices (Lin & Luk, 2002), when critical moments and memories briefly align in novel ways, and when even seemingly mundane or compulsory reading/writing tasks can be recontextualized and invigorated with an empowering potential, opening up new identity options and new opportunities to subvert or transform institutional power relations (cf. *rights analyses*, Benesch, 2001; the *praxicum*, Pennycook, 2004a). In this respect, the preferred goal of critical literacies is to create space for the agency of others and not to determine if or how that agency will be realized. The space that a teacher might create will vary across educational domains, subject to the application of standardized curricula and high-stakes testing and the relative autonomy afforded local administrators and educators.

The metaphor of *bricolage* might aptly describe the context-sensitive, improvisational strategies suggested here, but there is also recognition that critical literacies need explicit support through the provision of text-analytic tools—a *metalanguage*—for print, visual, and multimedia (e.g., Bazerman & Prior, 2004; Cooke, 2004; Cope & Kalantsis, 2000; Corbett, 2003, Ch. 6; Cummins, 2001, Ch. 5; Kress & van Leeuwen, 1996; New London Group, 1996; Rutherford, 2000, Ch. 1) as well as the thick description of case studies from which practitioners might adapt their own critical pedagogies (e.g., Comber & Simpson, 2001; Edelsky & Johnson, 2004; Toohey, 2000).

Still, as Wallace (2001) notes, "there is little consensus about what *kind* of metalinguistic knowledge is facilitative of enhanced critical awareness" (p. 213, italics in original). A "politics of access" (cf. Pennycook, 2001)—the modeling of powerful genres and texts—on its own, may presume a degree of disciplinary stability and textual uniformity at variance with the co-constructed dynamics observed in discourse communities (e.g., Ramanathan, 2002; Casanave, 2002). Furthermore, as Toohey and Waterstone (2004) observe, power does not inhere to text types, alone, but obtains, as well, from the social and institutional status of text users. On the other hand, a "politics of voice" (cf. Pennycook, 2001)—the affirmation of minority literacies and vernaculars in schools—on its own, may be irresponsible preparation for a world in which textual chauvinism often provides a defensible justification for racial and ethnic discrimination. Many researchers suggest that we combine elements of access and voice by encouraging critical negotiation of identities and literacies within institutional hierarchies and by providing analytic tools that link the micro features of texts with powerful, local and global discourses (Canagarajah, 2002, 2004a; Carr, 2003; Cooke, 2004; Lin & Luk, 2002). In support, researchers also recommend that we openly discuss systemic forms of discrimination and validate students' experiences and forms of resistance within syllabus design (e.g., Benesch, 2001; Canagarajah, 2004b; Kubota, 2004; Goldstein, 2003).

Such discussions are themselves, distancing or Othering, following Luke, in that they illuminate how we *language* our realities into existence—how discourses and power/knowledge operate on and through our micro-interactions with students, and how the labels we assign them (e.g., nonnative speaker, low achiever) are also systemic and discriminatory, functioning, in effect, to *produce* the social and educational margins that they name (e.g., Harklau, 2003).

Critical Literacies in English for Academic Purposes: A "Tool-Kit" in Action

The rules of a social field both limit and create their possible transgressions. In the field of EAP, one of the central rules of instruction is to help students manage unfamiliar disciplinary content and text types. Situated within these cognitive demands, critical EAP develops as an embedded, co-occurring literacy strategy— to raise students' awareness of how academic content "manages" them, in the person-formative sense stated earlier, shaping their desires, world views, and life chances beyond the school. So conceived, critical EAP literacies invigorate, rather than replace, conventional academic skill sets, as convincingly argued by many researchers (Benesch, 2001; Cummins, 2001; Schleppegrell & Colombi, 2002; Starfield, 2004). Through distancing strategies that denaturalize and demystify disciplinary content, "subjects-in-discourse" become aware of the partiality—hence contestability—of the dominant knowledge claims in their chosen fields of study. Moreover, through literacy acts of reading, writing, interpreting, and debating concepts, subjects/students become aware of their integral role in the practices that (re)constitute the academic discourse communities to which they seek membership (Canagarajah, 2002; Ramanathan, 2002; Varghese, 2004).

The following set of points capture both some distancing practices in EAP and some general purposes they are intended to serve, as well as an abbreviated sense of a critical literacy "tool-kit" in action:

1. The use of narratives/autobiographies to link personal experiences with sociohistorical and institutional power relations.

    In community of practice and feminist poststructural thought, self-writing evokes an experiential authenticity that has rhetorical potency for counter-discourse (e.g., Granger, 2004; Kanno, 2003; Pavlenko, 2004). Vandrick (1999), for example, explores the common threads of cultural and linguistic superiority and paternalism running through her missionary past to her current role as an ESL scholar and teacher, indicating "the possibility of a 'colonial shadow' over our profession" (p. 63). Wihak's (2004) personal narrative, a reflection on her teaching experiences with the Inuit in Nunavut, becomes a vehicle to examine white privilege and systemic racism in Canadian society. In Pavlenko's (2003) language teacher education course, autobiographical assignments provide the means for reimagined life chances, whereby nonnative speaking students come to reflect on and recognize the intercultural and bilingual expertise they bring to their future profession. In Casanave and Vandrick's (2003) edited collection, contributors reveal the often-perilous road toward scholarly publishing through personalized accounts that encourage new scholars to persevere.

2. The juxtaposition of texts in ways that question and subvert received disciplinary knowledge.

As conceptualized by Benesch (1998, 2001), EAP classes are not subservient to the functional language needs of more prestigious disciplines in the university. In a linked, undergraduate EAP-psychology course she taught, Benesch used readings and essay assignments in ways that problematize the topic of anorexia, presenting its source as gendered and socialized—linked to impossible images of feminine beauty—and not simply as an individualized pathology as often foregrounded in psychological discourse.

Teacher talk, itself, is a text and an immediate resource for juxtaposing classroom materials in ways that encourage multiple meanings or oppositional readings. As Wallace (2001) both argues and demonstrates, strategic interventions by teachers bring about the kinds of revisions and recontextualizations that are essential to the reading process and a key component to critical literacies. Even at the primary school level, as Dyson (2001) observed, teacher talk can have a crucial, mediating effect on the reception (or rejection) of dominant gender norms as conveyed through children's stories and popular culture.

3. The pluralization and denaturalization of dominant cultural codes and historical representations.

In an EAP workshop, Thompson (2002) introduced visiting students to one of Australia's most contentious issues: aboriginal land claims. Four short texts on the origins of aboriginals—of distinctive historical genres, and two by indigenous authors—were closely analyzed in ways that support critical evaluation of academic research materials. Yet through this analysis, and as a cumulative effect of the workshop structure, participants were encouraged to reflect on their own cultural biases and the politics of representation—how textual choices shape our judgment of historical truth and, consequently, our willingness to rectify past injustices.

Toward comparable objectives, Kubota (2001) introduced a unit on World Englishes to a group of U.S. high school students, native speakers of English, with several related goals: to raise students awareness of the global spread of English, the linguistic features and varieties of English, and of their shared responsibility in negotiating cross-cultural communication with speakers of limited English proficiency and nonstandard varieties. As Kubota argues, prejudice against nonstandard varieties is challenged, and the status and confidence of their users enhanced, when these varieties become the focus of classroom instruction, a crucial point that similarly underscores a participatory curriculum on Cape Verdean language, culture and history for U.S. immigrants from the former Portuguese colony (Brito, Lima, & Auerbach, 2004). In the Cape Verdean program, as in the critical approaches used by Thompson and Kubota, the foregrounding of linguistic differences is only a starting point from which colonial histories, attitudes, and their persistence are examined and from which power relations within and between communities are potentially transformed.

4. Use of multimodal, semiotic strategies.

The use of visual, digital, and embodied texts for distancing and repositioning "subjects-in-discourse:" Multimodal, semiotic theories invigorate critical literacies and multiliteracies in fundamental ways. The conceptualization of "reading" as an active process of sign-making, and not just information retrieval, supports both creative and oppositional meaning making. Semiotic analyses expand our metalinguistic tool-kit in that they apply across spoken, written, visual, and spatial modalities, also drawing attention to the unique capacities of modes in isolation and on the shifts in meaning potential that occur across modes or in their combination (cf. *synaesthesia*, Kress, 2000, 2003). Thus, when critical practitioners choose or combine materials from among books, audiotapes, photographs, a play, or a website, they do so not just for variety purposes, but also in the expectation that each text type will engage identities and the imagination in provocative ways unmet through other textual resources.

Innovative analyses and practices integrating film (Mackie, 2003), advertising (Corbett, 2003; Quinlisk, 2003), video games (Gee, 2001), rap and hip hop music (Ibrahim, 2003), teen magazines (Young, 2002), and comic books (Norton & Vanderheyden, 2004) seek to develop critical engagement with these multimedia while building on the cognitive skills that arise from students' investments in popular cultural forms. Dramaturgical texts have also been innovatively adapted. In a multilingual, English medium high school, where racial tensions over Chinese students' use of L1 was prevalent, Goldstein's (2003) play, *Hong Kong, Canada*, became a pedagogical resource for "represent[ing] everyday dilemmas and tensions in ways that allow performers and spectators to participate more fully in the emotional process of resolving conflicts" (p. 39). Through Goldstein's encouragement, students wrote and performed their own plays, these "performed ethnographies" giving public voice to the experiences of otherwise marginalized students at the school. Nelson (2002a) similarly used the theatrical medium as a forum to express subjugated identities in ESL. Inspired by queer theory, Nelson's script goes beyond issues of inclusion for gay and lesbian students, engaging both actors and audience in collaborative reflection on the social construction of *all* sexualities, and on heteronormativity as a powerful discourse in our lives.

Conceived by Nelson and Goldstein, a play serves as both public spectacle and as a vehicle for identity negotiation, in the *performative* sense theorized by Judith Butler (e.g., Nelson, 2002b; Pennycook, 2004b). As communicative medium, the dual effectiveness of a play can be attributed, in part, to its multimodal, embodied, and interactive affordances—the interanimation of sounds, spaces, movements, and spontaneous reactions that contingently shape the force of words and their reception. This holistic and dynamic conceptualization of performance aptly describes Stein's (2004) examination of storytelling and Morgan's (2004b) discussion of teacher identity as pedagogy, both studies exploring the notion of the body as text, as an effect of discourse, but also as a multimodal source of agency.

Embodied experiences of intimacy, community, and reality are displaced and reconfigured by way of digital texts and information systems, a point that makes computer-mediated communication (CMC) a promising tool for distancing practices in second and foreign language education. Linked CMC classes facilitate global conversations or virtual "contact zones" that create the appropriate conditions for seeing oneself in "strange" ways. Still, this technological achievement does not ensure intercultural understanding, as Kramsch and Thorne's (2002) study clearly shows. The ease of global communication, in fact, may inadvertently create conditions by which presumed commonalities (i.e., a global youth culture) are ruptured, exposing and exacerbating nationalistic ideologies that prevent dialogue from progressing.

A critical literacies tool-kit is enhanced by way of digital technologies (Warnick, 2002; Warschauer, 2004). Through the Internet, subjects-in-discourse have access to an expanded range of oppositional texts not available through mass media. Through various synchronous and asynchronous environments, students/ citizens also gain access to virtual discourse communities mobilized in service of global environmental and social justice initiatives (Rassool, 1999). Kramsch and Thorne's study, however, offers a countervailing microperspective on the tensions that pervade globalization processes and the technoscapes and mediascapes (cf. Appadurai, 1996; Warschauer, 2004) that seem both unifying and divisive in ways unforeseen. The appearance or promise of commonality—a linked CMC class, for example—can, in effect, be polarizing. Conversely, the appearance of diversity can, in effect, be superficial and assimilative. The thousand-channel, digital universe, for example, is meaningless if the majority of programming reflects the same cultural formulae. We examine these types of tensions and their implications for critical literacies in the following section on globalization.

Globalization, Critical Literacy, and Language Education

The multiplicity and breadth of textual practices in the previous section reflect, in part, a pervasive assumption characteristic of postmodern inclinations. Specifically, because our realities are so very different, if not incommensurable, by default critical literacies must always be provisional, emerging from new contexts of struggle. Globalization, and the preeminence of English flowing through it, however, complicates such assumptions. Our divergent realities are in fact closely intertwined in ways that elude categorical explanation. Indeed, ELT debates on whether the globalization-English nexus encourages heterogeneity or casts a homogenizing blanket over divergent realities are themselves literacy acts, "semiotic struggle[s] to control the definition of reality" (Hassan, 2003, p. 437). These definitions, when reified in policy, reflect the performative work (cf. Butler) we do as applied linguistics. Languaged into existence, such debates invite the same critical examination as other semiotic signs, not only for their veracity but also for the self-interests they serve, particularly in a profession prone toward lingua-centric remedies.

One recurrent theme that seems to resonate through the literature relates the learning of languages—English in particular—to market-oriented concerns, with education viewed as being constructed within and by capitalist social relations (Atkinson, 2002; Corson, 2002). The capitalistic push toward viewing our world as a "shrinking global village" given the numerous ways in which landscapes (Appadurai, 1996) are being connected through global forms of communication and mass media seems to highlight the homogenizing and diffusing tendencies of globalization, where borders and boundaries between realities collapse. When the scene is languaged in this way, schools run the risk of being rendered as powerless agents in effecting change, relegated to the provision of human "capital" for a global marketplace, where the quality of something is decided according to the price it can fetch" (Corson, 2002, pp. 5–6), and where notions of *equality* and *freedom* are narrowly equated with "equality of opportunity" and "freedom to consume" (Spring 2001, p. 12).

Threaded through this subnarrative (of the capitalistic tendencies around the globalization and English nexus) are the implications for what this means for literacy. Atkinson (2002), for instance, suggests that market-based practices are latent beneath L2 compositional practices, where our collective emphasis on "clear writing" might be seen "as part of a functional system in which efficiency and speed of delivery are central—in which knowledge is defined as a movable, transposable, commercial phenomenon—literacy as commodity" (p. 52). If "effective, clear" communication is the new norm for literacy, then we as language educators have to consider not only the extent to which stressing particular ways of speaking, teaching, and interacting with texts are a part of capitalistic tendencies (Block & Cameron, 2002; Cameron, 2002) that we can and need to critically address and pull back from, but also ways in which we are collectively contributing to this focus by our writing and speaking of it in particular ways. This self-conscious examination of how we are simultaneously both subjects and agents, of how these "realities" are both perceived by us and construct us in turn is crucial, especially if we wish to keep from both perpetuating the profession's "McCommunication" tendencies, a term Block (2002) uses for the instrumental, utilitarian approaches typically advocated in "negotiation of meaning" research, whose primary focus has been the enhancement of speaking skills.

These globalizing/capitalizing tendencies also seem to have wrought a change in how literacy, especially English language literacy (because narratives about globalization assume English as their undertow) is perceived with a decided shift away from a generally "universalist" position that tended to stress the norms of grammatical and phonological accuracy to a "differentialist" one where English is viewed as plural ("Englishes") with diverse and local ways in which it is entrenched, learned, and appropriated (Kramsch, 2000; Kumaravadivelu, 2002, 2003b; Pennycook, 2003; Toohey, 2000). Such a view of English literacies not only opens up the possibility of viewing English as a language that is simultaneously a syncretic language that makes room for vernacular codes in local varieties, but also as a language that binds "diverse periphery and centre communities together" getting remolded for a variety of purposes (Wallace, 2002, p. 112). In the realm of language teaching, this has meant forays into ways in which ELT can be decolonized: that we go beyond "teaching methods" to "decentering the authority Western interests have over the ELT industry" by partially "restoring agency to professionals in the periphery communities" (Kumaravadivelu, 2003b, p. 540), to recognizing and valuing local vernacular modes of learning and teaching (Canagarajah, 1999, 2004a), of the continuing vernacularization of English in postcolonial contexts (Ramanathan, 2004, 2005), and of uncovering the politics beneath the ELT textbook industry (Gray, 2002). In each of these cases, the authors are arguing for a self-conscious, critical examination of the Western-based ELT practices by turning the critical lens on the profession itself, even its historical propensity toward wholesale change in the name of progress, a point that is picked up by Morgan (2004b, p. 540) who speaks of the need to "expand the knowledge base and interdisciplinary scope of our profession—but in an *intra*disciplinary way, grounded in familiar contexts of language research and practice" (p. 174).

Language and literacy practices around the globalization-English nexus, then, are key contested sites with anxieties being articulated not just about its homogenizing or heterogenizing tendencies—whether to stress processes of assimilation and monoculturalization (e.g., Mondiano, 2004; Heller, 2003) or to emphasize diffusion and hybridization (as partially evident in phenomena like rap/hip-hop music; Pennycook, 2003)—but about how all of it is being languaged, as well, simultaneously constructing and reifying our realities even as we are in the midst of them. If the globalization currents are, indeed, making us "commodify" language (Harris, Leung, & Rampton, 2002; Heller, 2003), or overstress its communicative "efficiency" (Cameron, 2002), then it is imperative that we language teachers find small ways of countering these discursive processes in our literacy practices.

Conclusion

Given the thick strains of uncertainty that flow through all critical work—where all "givens" and "default" positions in the field are held up to cross-examination—we end this piece by raising some fundamental concerns about critical literacies *per se*. In an interconnected, transnational world, where theories and their consequences have expanded reach, critical educators rightfully scrutinize their actions and responsibilities through a discursive lens. Under this close scrutiny, advocates of critical literacies have often written about the need to divest them of their Eurocentric assumptions—to decolonize them in ways more relevant to postcolonial settings.

Although we certainly support the need for locally relevant pedagogies, we also wish to draw attention to the paradox that arises in the decolonizing impulse. That is, the appropriation of critical literacies carries a latent assumption that critical literacies do not and have not existed in non-Western realities and as such have to be imported into local contexts. We feel that it would be more pedagogically productive to suppose that all realities, Western and non-Western, have versions of oppositional readings, cross-examinations, and self-conscious, self-analytic orientations in them. While these may not transpire in the same ways as they do in the West—in classrooms, or in English—or may not get extensively reported in the West—for a range of socioeconomic and political reasons—they do occur, and we applied linguists, Western and non-Western alike, need to not only be open to recognizing and interpreting them as such, but to reflecting on and revising our own assumptions and practices. By distancing ourselves from "dominant text and discourse," and by opening ourselves to new sites and possibilities, we engage in the simultaneous learning and unraveling that is so central to critical literacy.

ANNOTATED BIBLIOGRAPHY

Comber, B., & Simpson, A. (Eds.). (2001). *Negotiating critical literacy in language classrooms.* Mahwah, NJ: Erlbaum.

Assuming the classroom as its primary site, this volume offers a diverse array of readings on various aspects around critical literacies: how they are fostered through classroom interactions, problems and tensions around them, and the local forms they take in different cultural contexts.

Gee, J. (2001). *What video games have to teach us about learning and literacy.* New York: Palgrave.

This volume offers an in depth argument and justification for why critical visual literacy is so crucial today, and why it is imperative that we teach children to critically navigate the videogames they play. The book stresses the fluidity inherent in all literacies and ways in which divergent images/videogames position us to "read" these "texts" in different ways.

Jewitt, C., & Kress, G. (Eds.). (2003). *Multimodal literacy.* New York: Peter Lang.

This anthology presents readings that complicate our takes on literacy by closely examining how meanings are made, distributed, and reinterpreted through a variety of signs and modes. Assuming a generally social semiotic approach, the authors wrestle with issues related to how readers/viewers make sense of images/texts/signs coming at them, and how meaning making occurs in the dynamics between viewer-reader and text/sign/image.

Norton, B., & Toohey, K. (Eds.). (2004). *Critical pedagogies and language learning.* Cambridge: Cambridge University Press.

This volume offers a wide range of readings on the ways in which power is embedded in various nooks and crannies of all aspects of education: in pedagogic practices, in entrenched notions and bodies of knowledge in the field, in feedback offered by teacher-educators to student-teachers. The negotiation of identities within and through various textual practices is a prominent theme in many chapters. Several chapters, as well, take up a multimodal/multiliteracies framework. A common, underlying theme across these readings is the pluralistic and transformative powers of critical literacies.

OTHER REFERENCES

Appadurai, A. (1996). *Modernity at large: Cultural dimensions of globalization.* Minneapolis, MI: University of Minnesota Press.

Atkinson, D. (2002). Writing and culture in the post-process era. *Journal of Second Language Writing, 12*, 49–63.

Bayley, R., & Schecter, S. R. (Eds.). (2003). *Language socialization in bilingual and multilingual societies.* Clevedon, UK: Multilingual Matters.

Bazerman, C. (2004). Intertextuality: How texts rely on other texts. In C. Bazerman & P. Prior (Eds.), *What writing does and how it does it: An introduction to analyzing texts and textual practices.* Mahwah, NJ: Erlbaum.

Bazerman, C., & Prior, P. (Eds.). (2004). *What writing does and how it does it: An introduction to analyzing texts and textual practices.* Mahwah, NJ: Erlbaum.

Benesch, S. (1998). Anorexia: A feminist EAP curriculum. In T. Smoke (Ed.), *Adult ESL: Politics, pedagogy, and participation in classroom and community programs* (pp.101–114). Mahwah, NJ: Erlbaum.

Benesch, S. (2001). *Critical English for academic purposes.* Mahwah, NJ: Erlbaum.

Block, D. (2002). 'McCommunication': A problem in the frame for SLA. In D. Block & D. Cameron (Eds.), *Globalization and language teaching* (pp. 117–133). London: Routledge.

Block, D., & Cameron, D. (Eds.). (2002). *Globalization and language teaching.* London: Routledge.

Brito, I., Lima, A., & Auerbach, E. (2004). The logic of nonstandard teaching: A course in Cape Verdean language, culture and history. In B. Norton & K. Toohey (Eds.), *Critical pedagogies and language learning* (pp. 181–200). Cambridge: Cambridge University Press.

Cameron, D. (2002). Globalization and the teaching of 'communication skills.' In D. Block & D. Cameron (Eds.), *Globalization and language teaching* (pp. 67–82). London: Routledge.

Canagarajah, S. (1999). *Resisting linguistic imperialism in language teaching.* Oxford: Oxford University Press.

Canagarajah, S. (2002). Multilingual writers and the academic community: Towards a critical relationship. *Journal of English for Academic Purposes, 1*, 29–44.

Canagarajah, S. (2004a). Subversive identities, pedagogical safehouses, and critical learning. In B. Norton & K. Toohey (Eds.), *Critical pedagogies and language learning* (pp. 116–137). Cambridge: Cambridge University Press.

Canagarajah, S. (2004b). Multilingual writers and the struggle for voice in academic discourse. In A. Pavlenko & A. Blackledge (Eds.), *Negotiation of identities in multilingual contexts* (pp. 266–289). Clevedon, UK: Multilingual Matters.

Carr, J. (2003). Culture through the looking glass: An intercultural experiment in sociolinguistics. In A. J. Liddicoat, S. Eisenchlas, & S. Trevaskes (Eds.), *Australian perspectives on internationalizing education* (pp. 75–86). Melbourne: Language Australia.

Casanave, C. P. (2002). *Multicultural case studies of academic literacy practices in higher education.* Mahwah, NJ: Erlbaum.

Casanave, C. P., & Vandrick, S. (Eds.). (2003). Writing for scholarly publication. Mahwah, NJ: Erlbaum.

Clarke, M. A. (2003). *Essays for educators in troubled times: Surviving innovation (Vol. 1).* Ann Arbor, MI: University of Michigan Press.

Cooke, D. (2004). What can a text mean? *New Zealand Journal of Adult Learning, 32,* 52–64.

Cope, B., & Kalantzis, M. (Eds.). (2000). *Multiliteracies: Literacy learning and the design of social futures.* London: Routledge.

Corbett, J. (2003). *An intercultural approach to English language teaching.* Clevedon, UK: Multilingual Matters.

Corson, D. (2002). Teaching and learning for market-place utility. *International Journal of Leadership in Education, 1,* 1–13.

Cummins, J. (2001). *Negotiating identities: Education for empowerment in a diverse Society* (2nd ed.). Ontario, CA: California Association of Bilingual Education.

Darley, A. (2000). *Visual digital culture: Surface play and spectacle in new media genres.* London: Routledge.

Dyson, A. H. (2001). Children appropriating literacy: Empowerment pedagogy from young children's perspective. In B. Comber & A. Simpson (Eds.), *Negotiating critical literacies in classrooms* (pp. 3–18). Mahwah, NJ: Erlbaum.

Edelsky, C., & Johnson, K. (2004). Critical whole language practice in time and place. *Critical Inquiry in Language Studies, 1,* 121–141.

Egbo, B. (2004). Intersections of literacy and construction of social identities. In A. Pavlenko & A. Blackledge (Eds.), *Negotiation of identities in multilingual contexts* (pp. 243–265). Clevedon, UK: Multilingual Matters.

Freire, P. (1997). *Pedagogy of the oppressed.* New York: Continuum.

Gee, J. P. (2002). Literacies, identities, and discourses. In M. J. Schleppegrell & M. C. Colombi (Eds.), *Developing advanced literacy in first and second languages: Meaning with power* (pp. 159–175). Mahwah, NJ: Erlbaum.

Goldstein, T. (2001). Researching women's language in multilingual workplaces. In A. Pavlenko, A. Blackledge, I. Piller, & M. Teutsch-Dwyer (Eds.), *Multilingualism, second language learning, and gender* (pp. 77–101). Berlin: Mouton de Gruyter.

Goldstein, T. (2003). *Teaching and learning in a multilingual school.* Mahwah, NJ: Erlbaum.

Granger, C. A. (2004). *Silence in second language learning: A psychoanalytic reading.* Clevedon, UK: Multilingual Matters.

Gray, J. (2002). The global coursebook in English language teaching. In D. Block & D. Cameron (Eds.), *Globalization and language teaching* (pp. 151–167). London: Routledge.

Harklau, L. (2003). Representational practices and multi-modal communication in U.S. high schools: Implications for adolescent immigrants. In R. Bayley & S. R. Schecter (Eds.), *Language socialization in bilingual and multilingual societies* (pp. 83–97). Clevedon, UK: Multilingual Matters.

Harris, R., Leung, C., & Rampton, B. (2002). Globalization and the commodification of bilingualism in Canada. In D. Block & D. Cameron (Eds.), *Globalization and language teaching* (pp. 29–64). London: Routledge.

Hassan, R. (2003). Globalization, literacy, and ideology. *World Englishes, 22,* 433–488.

Heller, M. (2003). Globalization, the new economy, and the commodification of language and identity. *Journal of Sociolinguistics, 7,* 473–492.

Hunter, J., & Morgan, B. (2001). Language and public life: Teaching multiliteracies in ESL. In I. Leki (Ed.), *Academic writing programs* (pp. 99–109). Alexandria, VA: TESOL.

Ibrahim, A. (2003). "Whassup, homeboy?" Joining the African diaspora: Black English as a symbolic site of identification and language learning. In S. Makoni, G. Smitherman, A. Ball, & A. Spears (Eds.), *Black linguistics: Language, society and politics in Africa and the Americas* (pp. 169–185). London: Routledge.

Janks, H. (2001). Identity and conflict in critical literacy. In B. Comber & A. Simpson (Eds.), *Negotiating critical literacy in classrooms* (pp. 137–150). Mahwah, NJ: Erlbaum.

Johnston, B. (2003). *Values in English language teaching.* Mahwah, NJ: Erlbaum.

Kanno, Y. (2003). *Negotiating bilingual and bicultural identities: Japanese returnees betwixt two worlds.* Mahwah, NJ: Erlbaum.

Katz, M. (2000). Workplace language teaching and the intercultural construction of ideologies of competence. *Canadian Modern Language Review, 57,* 144–172.

Kramsch, C. (2000). Global and local identities in the contact zone. In C. Gnutzmann (Ed.), *Teaching and learning English as a global language* (pp. 131–143). Tübingen, Germany: Stauffenberg Verlag.

Kramsch, C., & Thorne, S. (2002). Foreign language learning as global communicative practice. In D. Block & D. Cameron (Eds.), *Globalization and language teaching* (pp. 83–100). London: Routledge.

Kress, G. (2000). Multimodality. In B. Cope & M. Kalantzis (Eds.), *Multiliteracies: Literacy learning and the design of social futures* (pp. 182–202). London: Routledge.

Kress, G. (2003). *Literacy in the new media age.* London: Routledge.

Kress, G., & van Leeuwen, T. (1996). *Reading images: The grammar of visual design.* New

York: Routledge.

Kubota, R. (2001). Teaching world Englishes to native speakers of English in the USA. *World Englishes, 20,* 47–64.

Kubota, R. (2004). Critical multiculturalism and second language education. In B. Norton & K. Toohey (Eds.), *Critical pedagogies and language learning* (pp. 30–52). Cambridge: Cambridge University Press.

Kumaravadivelu, B. (2002). From coloniality to globality: (Re)visioning English language education in India. *Indian Journal of Applied Linguistics, 28*(2), 45–61.

Kumaravadivelu, B. (2003a). *Beyond methods: Macrostrategies for language teaching.* New Haven, CT: Yale University Press.

Kumaravadivelu, B. (2003b). Critical language pedagogy: A postmethod perspective on English language teaching. *World Englishes, 22,* 539–550.

Lemke, J. L. (2002). Multimedia semiotics: Genres for science education and scientific literacy. In M. J. Schleppegrell & M. C. Colombi (Eds.), *Developing advanced literacy in first and second languages: Meaning with power* (pp. 21–44). Mahwah, NJ: Erlbaum.

Lewis, C. (2001). *Literary practices as social acts: Power, status, and cultural norms in the classroom.* Mahwah, NJ: Erlbaum.

Lin, A., & Luk, J. (2002). Beyond progressive liberalism and cultural relativism: Towards critical postmodernist, socio-historically situated perspectives in classroom studies. *Canadian Modern Language Review, 59,* 97–124.

Lotherington, H. (2001). Reshaping literacies in the age of information. *Contact, 27*(2), 4–11.

Lotherington, H. (2003). Multiliteracies in Springvale: Negotiating language, culture and identity in suburban Melbourne In R. Bayley & S. R. Schecter (Eds.), *Language socialization in bilingual and multilingual societies* (pp. 200–217). Clevedon, UK: Multilingual Matters.

Luke, A. (2004). Two takes on the critical. In B. Norton & K. Toohey (Eds.), *Critical pedagogies and language learning* (pp. 21–29). Cambridge: Cambridge University Press.

Luke, A., & Elkins, J. (2002). Towards a critical, worldly literacy. *Journal of Adolescent and Adult Literacy, 45,* 668–673.

Mackie, A. (2003). Race and desire: Toward critical literacies for ESL. *TESL Canada Journal, 20*(2), 23–37.

McChesney, R. W. (1999). *Rich media, poor democracy: Communication politics in dubious times.* Urbana, IL: University of Illinois Press.

Mondiano, M. (2004). Monoculturalization and language dissemination. *Journal of Language, Identity, and Education, 3,* 215–227.

Morgan, B. (2004a). Modals and memories: A grammar lesson on the Quebec referendum on sovereignty. In B. Norton & K. Toohey (Eds.), *Critical pedagogies and language learning* (pp. 158–178). Cambridge: Cambridge University Press.

Morgan, B. (2004b). Teacher identity as pedagogy: Towards a field-internal conceptualization in bilingual and second language education. *International Journal of Bilingual Education and Bilingualism, 7*, 172–188.

Morgan, B. (in press). Poststructuralism and applied linguistics: Complementary approaches to identity and culture in ELT. In J. Cummins & C. Davison (Eds.), *Kluwer handbook of English language teaching*. Dordrecht: Kluwer Academic Publishers.

Nelson, C. (2002a). Queer as a second language: Classroom theatre for everyone (Featured presentation), TESOL Convention, Salt Lake City, Utah.

Nelson, C. (2002b). Why queer theory is useful in teaching: A perspective from English as a second language teaching. In K. H. Robinson, J. Irwin, & T. Ferfolja (Eds.), *From here to diversity: The social impact of lesbian and gay issues in education in Australia and New Zealand* (pp. 43–53). Binghamton, NY: Harrington Park Press.

Nieto, S. (2002). *Language, culture, and teaching: Critical perspectives for a new century*. Mahwah, NJ: Erlbaum.

New London Group. (1996). A pedagogy of multiliteracies: Designing social futures. *Harvard Educational Review, 66*, 60–92.

Norton, B. (2000). *Identity and language learning: Gender, ethnicity and educational change*. London: Longman.

Norton, B., & Vanderheyden, K. (2004). Comic book culture and second language learners. In B. Norton & K. Toohey (Eds.), *Critical pedagogies and language learning* (pp. 201–222). New York: Cambridge University Press.

Pavlenko, A. (2003). "I never knew I was bilingual": Reimagining teacher identities in TESOL. *Journal of Language, Identity, and Education, 2*, 251–268.

Pavlenko, A. (2004). 'The making of an American:' Negotiation of identities at the turn of the twentieth century. In A. Pavlenko & A. Blackledge (Eds.), *Negotiation of identities in multilingual contexts* (pp. 34–67). Clevedon, UK: Multilingual Matters.

Pennycook, A. (2001). *Critical applied linguistics: A critical introduction*. Mahwah, NJ: Erlbaum.

Pennycook, A. (2003). Global Englishes, Rip Slyme, and performativity. *Journal of Sociolinguistics, 7*, 513–533.

Pennycook, A. (2004a). Critical moments in a TESOL praxicum. In B. Norton & K. Toohey (Eds.), *Critical pedagogies and language learning* (pp. 327–345). Cambridge: Cambridge University Press.

Pennycook, A. (2004b). Performativity and language studies. *Critical Inquiry in Language Studies, 1*, 1–20.

Purcell-Gates, V., & Waterman, R. A. (2000). *Now we read, we see, we speak: Portrait of literacy development in an adult Freirean-based class*. Mahwah, NJ: Erlbaum.

Quinlisk, C. C. (2003). Media literacy in the ESL/EFL classroom: Reading images and cultural stories. *TESOL Journal, 12*(3), 35–40.

Ramanathan, V. (2002). *The politics of TESOL education: Writing, knowledge, critical pedagogy.* New York: Routledge Falmer.

Ramanathan, V. (2004) (In production). *The English-vernacular divide: Postcolonial language politics and practice.* Clevedon, UK: Multilingual Matters.

Ramanathan, V. (2005) Seepage, contact zones, and amalgam: Internationalizing TESOL. *TESOL Quarterly, 39*(1), 119–123.

Rassool, N. (1999). *Literacy for sustainable development in the age of information.* Clevedon, UK: Multilingual Matters.

Rutherford, P. (2000). *Endless propaganda.* Toronto: University of Toronto Press.

Sahni, U. (2001). Children appropriating literacy: Empowerment pedagogy from young children's perspective. In B. Comber & A. Simpson (Eds.), *Negotiating critical literacy in classrooms* (pp. 19–35). Mahwah, NJ: Erlbaum.

Schleppegrell, M., & Colombi. M. C. (Eds.). (2002). *Developing advanced literacy in first and second languages: Meaning with power.* Mahwah, NJ: Erlbaum.

Shea, C. M. (1998). Critical and constructive postmodernism: The transformative power of holistic education. In H. S. Shapiro & D. E. Purpel (Eds.), *Critical social issues in American education: Transformation in a postmodern world* (2nd ed.) (pp. 337–354). Mahwah, NJ: Erlbaum.

Spring, J. (2001). *Globalization and educational rights: An intercivilizational analysis.* Mahwah, NJ: Erlbaum.

Starfield, S. (2004). "Why does this feel empowering"? Thesis writing, concordancing, and the corporatizing university. In B. Norton & K. Toohey (Eds.), *Critical pedagogies and language learning* (pp. 138–157). Cambridge: Cambridge University Press.

Stein, P. (2004). Representation, rights, and resources: Multimodal pedagogies in language and literacy. In B. Norton & K. Toohey (Eds.), *Critical pedagogies and language learning* (pp. 95–115). Cambridge: Cambridge University Press.

Thompson, C. (2002). Teaching critical thinking in EAP courses in Australia. *TESOL Journal, 11*(4), 15–20.

Toohey, K. (2000). *Learning English at school: Identity, social relations and classroom practice.* Clevedon: Multilingual Matters.

Toohey, K., & Waterstone, B. (2004). Negotiating expertise in an action research community. In B. Norton & K. Toohey (Eds.), *Critical pedagogies and language learning* (pp. 291–310). Cambridge: Cambridge University Press.

Vandrick, S. (1999). ESL and the colonial legacy: A teacher faces her 'missionary kid'past. In G. Haroian-Guerin (Ed.), *The personal narrative: Writing ourselves as teachers and scholars* (pp. 63–74). Portland, ME: Calendar Islands Publishers.

Varghese, M. (2004). Professional development for bilingual teachers in the United States: A site for articulating and contesting professional roles. In J. Brutt-Griffler & M. Varghese (Eds.), *Bilingualism and language pedagogy* (pp. 130–145). Clevedon, UK: Multilingual Matters.

Wallace, C. (2001). Critical literacy in the second language classroom: Power and control. In B. Comber & A. Simpson (Eds.), *Negotiating critical literacies in classrooms* (pp. 209–228). Mahwah, NJ: Erlbaum.

Wallace, C. (2002). Local literacies and global literacy. In D. Block & D. Cameron (Eds.), *Globalization and language teaching* (pp. 101–114). London: Routledge.

Warnick, B. (2002). *Critical literacy in a digital era: Technology, rhetoric and the public interest.* Mahwah, NJ: Erlbaum.

Warschauer, M. (2004). *Technology and social inclusion: Rethinking the digital divide.* Cambridge, MA: MIT Press.

Wihak, C. (2004). The meaning of being white in Canada: A personal narrative. *TESL Canada Journal, 21*(2), 110–115.

Young, J. P. (2002). Displaying practices of masculinity: Critical literacy and social contexts. *Journal of Adolescent and Adult Literacy, 45,* 4–14.

9. CONTEXT AND LITERACY PRACTICES

Stephen Reder and Erica Davila

This chapter reviews recent progress in resolving tensions between conceptions of literacy as a system of locally situated cultural practices and conceptions of literacy as a broader system of written language that transcends specific individuals and local contexts. Such theoretical tensions have arisen out of earlier, long-standing literacy debates—the Great Divide, the Literacy Thesis, and even debates about situated cognition itself. Recent reviews and critiques of the "New Literacy Studies" examined here—Brandt and Clinton, 2002; Collins and Blot, 2003; Street, 2003a, 2003b—are reaching toward new theoretical ground to address emerging concerns about the adequacy of current literacy theories framed in terms of locally situated social practices. This new work should be of interest not only to those working in the field of literacy but also to applied linguists in general, because the core issues have to do with the nature and role of context in language use, whether in oral or written form.

The current debate regarding the nature of literacy has intellectual roots that can be traced back to earlier contrasts Street (1984) drew between "autonomous" and "ideological" models of literacy. This important contrast was itself a reaction to influential debates at the time about the consequences of literacy for individuals and societies. We focus here on a related but quite distinct contrast evident in the more recent work, that between the *local* and *remote* (sometimes termed "global" or "distant") contexts for literacy events and practices. There is not space here to review in detail the well-known and important controversies about the "consequences of literacy." Nevertheless a brief overview of these earlier developments will set the stage for the ongoing debate about context that we will examine more closely.

The Great Divide, the Literacy Thesis, and Other Binaries

The so-called "Great Divide" theories of literacy (Finnegan, 1988; Scribner & Cole, 1981) hold that there are fundamental and far-reaching cognitive differences between literate and nonliterate societies and individuals. Various Great Divide theories, once very popular in the social sciences from the 1960s through the early 1980s, focused on cognitive difference (including broad differences in language use) at the societal or the individual level. Anthropologists and historians constructing Great Divide theories were primarily concerned with broad differences between literate and nonliterate societies, whereas psychologists and other social scientists constructing Great Divide theories were concerned primarily with cognitive differences among individuals of varying literacy statuses within literate societies (e.g., Olson, 1988, 1994; Olson & Torrance, 1991).

Societal-level Great Divide theories grew out of seminal articles and books such as Levi-Strauss'(1962) *The Savage Mind*, Goody and Watt's (1963) article "The Consequences of Literacy," Havelock's (1963) *Preface to Plato*, and McLuhan's (1962) *The Gutenberg Galaxy*. Individually-focused Great Divide theories were developed through influential articles by cross-cultural and cognitive psychologists such as Greenfield's (1972) "Oral or Written Language: The Consequences for Cognitive Development in Africa, the United States and England," Olson's (1977) "From Utterance to Text: The Bias of Language in Speech and Writing," and Scribner and Cole's (1978) "Literacy without Schooling: Testing for Intellectual Effects."

Whether focused primarily on differences at the individual or societal level, the Great Divide theories asserted categorical differences in cognition and language as consequences of literacy, a notion some have termed the "Literacy Thesis." Literacy was presumed to have broad and ubiquitous consequences in such areas as: abstract versus context-dependent uses and genres of language; logical, critical, and scientific versus irrational modes of thought; analytical history versus myth; and so forth. The influence of structuralism in the social sciences of this period can be seen in the strong dualities used to describe the deep differences posited between literate and nonliterate societies (e.g., "primitive" vs. "civilized," "simple" vs. "advanced"), modes of thought (e.g., "prelogical" versus "analytic," "concrete" vs. "abstract"), and ways of using language (e.g., "utterance" vs. "text," "context-dependent" vs. "abstract").

By the early 1980s, these Great Divide theories came under attack for being too simplistic and for exaggerating differences to create false dichotomies between types of societies, modes of thought, and uses of language. Poststructuralists such as Derrida, Barthes, and Foucault provided powerful critiques of the structuralist positions underlying the work of Havelock (1963), Ong (1982), and Goody (1986). New empirical evidence further challenged the sweeping assumptions and interpretations of Great Divide theorists. At the societal level, for example, in-depth historical studies questioned the simple unidirectional causality of literacy in social and economic development as described by Great Divide theorists. Historically rising national literacy levels, once believed to drive economic development, turned out, on closer analysis, to be more complexly intertwined in the development cycle, sometimes being as much the result as the cause of economic growth (Graff, 1979, 1987).

New studies also challenged the idea that literacy necessarily has a direct effect on individual cognition as well. The landmark study by Scribner and Cole (1981) among the Vai of Liberia was extremely influential in breaking down the Great Divide theory at the individual level, failing to find broad differences in cognition that could uniquely and categorically be attributed to literacy. Linguistic research was also contributing to the demise of the Great Divide theories, providing empirical data that challenged the very assumptions of categorical differences between oral and written language underpinning the Literacy Thesis (e.g., Biber, 1986; Feldman, 1991; Halverson, 1991, 1992; Tannen, 1982).

Scribner and Cole's (1981) work also persuasively introduced the concept of *literacy practices.* Rather than seeing literacy as a set of portable, decontextualized information processing *skills* which individuals *applied*, Scribner and Cole reframed literacy as a set of socially organized *practices* (conceptually parallel to religious practices, childrearing practices, etc.) in which individuals *engaged.* This conception of literacy as social practice spread rapidly among social scientists and educators in the early 1980s, helped considerably in its advance by the simultaneous dissolve of the Great Divide theories separating oral and written language. The emerging theory of literacy-as-social-practice drew on the well-developed theories and methodologies of sociolinguistics and the ethnography of communication as it moved forward. The application of social practices theory to literacy was also advanced by authors who critiqued literacy as one more exclusionary device used by powerful groups to further their social and economic interests. Education scholars such as Street (1984) and Gee (1988) argued persuasively that literacy often functions restrictively and hegemonically in societies to implement social controls and maintain social hierarchies.

As ethnographic studies of literacy practices in a variety of contexts accumulated during the 1980s, theorists began to systematize new ways of understanding the development, acquisition, and use of literacy. The approach termed the "New Literacy Studies" (Gee, 1991; Street, 1995) was based on two key principles: seeing *context* as fundamental to understanding literacy, and eradicating any clear distinction between orality and literacy.[1] Operating with these core principles, ethnographic studies explored how text and speech are intertwined in daily use and how local contexts inevitably determine the shapes and uses of literacy. As a counterpoint to the many problems of the Literacy Thesis, the New Literacy Studies (NLS) research turned away from a general examination of broad sociopolitical and economic forces and began a careful consideration of concrete, local uses of literacy (e.g., Barton, 2001; Barton & Hamilton, 1998; Barton, Hamilton, & Ivanič, 2000; Heath, 1983; Street, 1993).

Brandt and Clinton: Limits of the Local

In their 2002 article, *Limits of the Local: Expanding Perspectives on Literacy as a Social Practice*, Deborah Brandt and Katie Clinton consider how the NLS framework has shaped literacy research, especially the growing collection of ethnographies of literacy. As the title of their article suggests, Brandt and Clinton are not satisfied that literacy can be fully understood by looking only through the lens of the local context in which a literacy event takes place. They ask: "Can we not see the ways that literacy arises out of local, particular, situated human interactions while also seeing how it also regularly arrives from other places— infiltrating, disjointing, and displacing local life?" (2002, p. 343). They contend that by privileging the local context as the *only* relevant context, NLS creates a "great divide" between local and global contexts that is not only unnecessary, but also hinders our understanding of the forces at play in everyday literacy events.

Brandt and Clinton describe the reach and depth of the NLS theoretical perspective as they discuss Besnier's (1995) ethnography of literacy in a Polynesian community:

> So absorbed into local context does literacy appear in this study, in fact, that Besnier suggests that we can treat literacy practices as windows into a group's social and political structure—that is, not only can one look to local contexts to understand local literacy, but one can also look to local literacy practices to understand the key forces that organize local life. This is the radical analytical accomplishment of the social-practice perspective (Brandt & Clinton, 2002, p. 343).

Though they acknowledge the fundamental importance of local context, Brandt and Clinton disagree with Besnier's formulation of literacy practices as simply a reflection of the local context. They argue that local context alone is insufficient to explain the uses and forms of literacy. They find an example of the limits of the local context in Besnier's own work: Local residents commonly ignore the content of English slogans on the t-shirts they wear. Besnier uses this example to point to the power of the local context—these slogans have no meaning for local t-shirt wearers and so they are ignored and do not enter into local literacy practices in any way. Brandt and Clinton argue on the contrary that the presence of these slogans demonstrates the connections between the local context of this Polynesian island and more remote contexts.

Brandt and Clinton readily admit that literacy research must be rooted in people's intimate everyday experiences with text. However, their critique of NLS rests on the idea that the local and global contexts are not two discrete realms. Rather than restrict their analytical framework to consider only how literacy is shaped by *local* social and cultural phenomena, the authors suggest that literacy practices can include transcontextualizing components. To this end, they propose the constructs of *localizing moves* and *globalizing connects*. The concept of *localizing moves* describes the work people do when they shape literacy practices to meet personal needs and to match local social structures. *Localizing moves* have been abundantly described in NLS ethnographies of literacy.

A *globalizing connect* describes a local literacy practice that has far-reaching implications and uses outside of the local context. Brandt and Clinton provide an example in the shape of a local representative of a national agricultural company. This representative reads the local weather forecast and talks to local farmers in order to gauge crop outputs. In other words, he is a participant in the same types of literacy practices as the local farmers themselves. However, he uses this local literacy event in a different context when he relays local information to headquarters and thus plays a role in a literacy event that unfolds on a much larger scale. This example shows how local literacy events can serve multiple interests and play a part in remote literacy events and large-scale processes of knowledge creation.

Brandt and Clinton also use the concept of *literacy sponsors* to highlight the ways that multiple forces can be at play in local literacy practices. The idea of literacy sponsors (Brandt, 1995) refers to the institutions, policies, and people that make the acquisition and practice of literacy possible: the government, corporate scholarship foundations, religious groups, and so on. Literacy sponsors often wield power over uses of literacy and they can provide and control access to literacy materials (textbooks, the Internet, etc.) Using literacy sponsors as an analytical tool highlights the tension among different immediate and remote forces at play in a given literacy practice. Brandt and Clinton explain this concept:

> When we use literacy, we also get used. Things typically mediate this relationship. Attention to sponsors can yield a fuller insight into how literate practices can be shaped out of the struggle of competing interests and agents, how multiple interests can be satisfied during a single performance of reading or writing, how literate practices can relate to immediate social relationships while still answering to distant demands (2002, p. 350–351).

Thus, when looking at literacy events, the local context is only part of the picture. The written materials at the center of a literacy event are often not locally produced. Their presence allows for remote actors to play a role (more or less consequential) in local practice. Brandt and Clinton highlight the material aspects of literacy as the key factor that allows multiple remote actors to influence a given literacy event and to shape local literacy practices.

It is important to note that Brandt and Clinton do not advocate a wholesale disavowal of the importance of the local context, nor do they contend "that the technology of literacy carries its own imperatives no matter where it goes" (2002,

p. 344). Rather, their formulation of context allows for distant influences on local practices to be clearly identified not as disinterested "autonomous" forces, but as ideological players in their own right. They deny the existence of some remote, "autonomous" literacy and they view distant influences on local practices as integral, subjective participants in local literacy events. They contend that "local literacy events cannot exhaust the meanings or actions of literacy" (2002, p. 344). Brandt and Clinton continue:

> Social practices are not necessarily the shapers of literacy's meaning; indeed, they may be the weary shock absorbers of its impositions. That people manage to absorb or mollify these demands in different ways may be evidence of local ingenuity, diversity, agency, as much recent research emphasizes, but it is just as much evidence of how powerfully literacy as a technology can insinuate itself into social relations anywhere (2002, p. 354).

Brandt and Clinton repeatedly note that literacy as a technology has the ability to travel, integrate, and endure. It is these unique properties that contribute to literacy's transcontextualizing capabilities. Brandt and Clinton contend that there is no divide between local and global contexts: People's everyday intimate experiences of literacy are in conversation with remote forces at play in the larger sociocultural context.

Street: Yes, but Not *Autonomous* Remote Influences

In responding to recent critiques of NLS, Brian Street (2003a, 2003b) vigorously defends NLS as a solid theoretical foundation for investigations into the nature of literacy. First, he reiterates that literacy, as a social practice embedded in existing social structures, cannot be separated from the ideological baggage which participants bring to any literacy event. Street emphasizes that even literacy acquisition is not a neutral process—it is a social practice involving students and teachers. Likewise, literacy practices that are taught in school are not neutral or autonomous, but serve certain ideological interests.

In specifically discussing the *Limits of the Local*, Street agrees with Brandt and Clinton's focus on the *relationship* between the local and the "distant" as a more fruitful focus for research than either realm in isolation. However, he cautions that Brandt and Clinton not confuse "distant" forces at play in literacy events with "autonomous" literacy. Street emphasizes that "distant" influences are indeed ideological. Brandt and Clinton seem to answer this concern in their discussion of literacy sponsors and the subjective control they can wield over the shape of local literacy practices.

Street acknowledges that "we need a framework and conceptual tools that can characterize the relation between local and 'distant'" (2003b, p. 4). However, he contends that NLS provides ample theoretical space for this type of analysis in its conceptualization of literacy events and literacy practices. Street quotes Heath's definition of literacy events, "any occasion in which a piece of writing is integral to the nature of the participants' interactions and their interpretative processes" (Heath, 1982, p. 93). Literacy practices, on the other hand, are more complex social phenomena which include the larger social and cultural meanings that participants ascribe to a given literacy event. In this way—through reference to the larger sociocultural background that participants bring to a literacy event—Street contends that the concept of the literacy practice functions as a framework that accommodates "distant" influences on local literacy events.

The paired concepts of literacy events and literacy practices effectively highlight the difference between a local event and the larger forces that shape the participants in that event. However, it seems that these concepts provide an analytical *space* for understanding the relationship between the local and the distant, but without further development these concepts do not yet constitute a coherent framework for understanding this relationship. What exactly are these "distant" forces? If we concede that literacy is not an autonomous entity, then what is the nature of literacy within the broader sociocultural context? Likewise, how do these "distant" forces impact individual literacy events? The concepts of literacy events and literacy practices provide an answer as to *where* the local and the distant collide (in many everyday literacy events), but they fail to provide an answer as to *how* this interaction occurs.

Street offers insight into these questions in his discussion of literacy practices as *hybrids*:

> The result of local-global encounters around literacy is always a new hybrid

rather than a single essentialized version of either. It is these hybrid literacy practices that NLS focuses upon rather than either romanticizing the local or conceding the dominant privileging of the supposed "global." As we shall see when we discuss practical applications of NLS across educational contexts, it is the recognition of this hybridity that lies at the heart of an NLS approach to literacy acquisition regarding the relationship between local literacy practices and those of the school (2003b, p. 4).

If we acknowledge that local literacies do not exist autonomously, but commonly draw on perspectives that participants have developed through participation in other literacy practices—school literacies, work literacies, religious literacies, bureaucratic literacies—then we see that a "single essentialized version" of local literacy practices ignores much of the context that participants use to create the practice in the first place. Likewise, "global" literacy does not exist in an essentialized, pure form, but only emerges as one piece of hybrid literacy practices that are always, necessarily locally constituted. We come to see that "local" and "global" (or distant, remote) contexts do not exist in contrast to one another, but as constituents of a larger whole. This conceptualization of all literacy practices as hybrid constructions echoes Brandt and Clinton's analysis of local literacy practices as "weary shock absorbers" of the impositions of distant participants.

Collins and Blot: A Proposed Resolution with Power and Identity

In his foreword to Collins and Blot's *Literacy and Literacies: Text, Power and Identity*, Street (2003a) addresses critics of situated, ethnographic studies of literacy who claim that NLS promotes a "relativistic" definition of literacy. These critics contend that even thousands of individual ethnographies of literacy would not form a coherent composite picture of the impacts of literacy on society at large. Street concedes that some NLS research "runs the danger of romanticizing such local [literacy] practice against that of the dominant culture. It is here, perhaps, that NLS has hit an impasse: how to account for the local whilst recognizing also the general— or the global" (2003a, p. xii). Though NLS was founded on the idea that local context must be the focus of research on literacy as a situated social practice, advocates have recently emerged for a shift in focus to include the broader ways in which literacies pattern in society.

In the first chapter of their book, Collins and Blot identify what they term a universalist/particularist impasse in current debates about literacy research and theory. Like Brandt and Clinton, Collins and Blot identify the origins of NLS as a response to the Literacy Thesis. The "universalist" view is aligned with autonomous views of literacy that deal with the broad social and cognitive impacts that ensue from the widespread introduction of alphabetic literacy into a society. Adherents of the autonomous theory of literacy contend that a written document contains an independent meaning that is wholly recoverable and transferable regardless of the contexts in which the text is created and used. Though many of the more strident initial claims of the Literacy Thesis have been refuted by in-depth historical analysis, the view of literacy as having the ability to transform both individual people and society at large remains a powerful current in modern Western thought.

The "particularist" view includes the many detailed ethnographies of literacy that have demonstrated how the immediate social context determines the use and nature of texts. Situated approaches to literacy have shown that literacy and orality are not discrete categories, but rather written and spoken language commingle and inhabit the same communicative space. Ethnographic accounts of literacy offer fascinating details into how people bring life to texts in everyday literacy practices. According to the NLS view, literacy practices simply cannot be understood without reference to the local context in which they exist.

Collins and Blot note the need for an explanation that adequately addresses the quotidian reality of literacy as a locally-determined social practice while at the same time accounting for the unique place that literacy inhabits in modern Western society and thought. Such an analysis would shed light on the continuing patterns of access to, and use of, literacy among various groups in society. To achieve this end, Collins and Blot draw on post-structural theorists—primarily Bourdieu, de Certeau, Derrida, and Foucault—as they bring language, education, texts, and identity into the core of an argument about literacy and power in modern Western society. In their work, Collins and Blot agree with many NLS researchers, and they find much that is useful in their work. However, what Collins and Blot find missing in ethnographic accounts of literacy is an "account of why literacy matters in the way that it does in the modern West." (2003, p. 65). This question arises from the many long-standing and recurring connections between literacy practices and the exercise of power in society. Because an investigation of this issue would necessarily involve a scope of study larger than the immediate ethnographic context, this sort of analysis has not been a primary concern in many NLS accounts of literacy.

Collins and Blot contend that considerations of *power* have largely been absent from most ethnographies of literacy. They cite Heath's (1983) seminal work as an example. Though this work provides an extraordinarily detailed view of how the different literacy practices of various groups in society impact (help or hinder) children as they encounter school literacy and discourse practices, Heath does not include an overt discussion of the ways that power in society has shaped what we know as "school literacy." She does not address the ways in which forces outside of the immediate context have contributed to the significance of "school literacy" and guaranteed its preeminent place in education and in society.

This argument about the partisan nature of "school literacy" is strongly reminiscent of Street's (1984) core contention that all literacy events carry ideological meanings. Literacy education in schools does not simply teach a set of decontextualized, discrete cognitive skills. Rather, the types of literacies that are taught—for example, sustained silent reading, comprehension questions, fill-in-the-blank forms—contribute to an organization of society according to the vision of those who have captured the power to create, endorse, promote, and institute particular brands of literacy in society.

As they discuss Heath's (1983) work in terms of ideological literacy and power, Collins and Blot praise the work for its eloquent and detailed description of the differences in literacy practices among communities, and for its implicit acknowledgment that "school literacy" is only one type of literacy among equals. But Collins and Blot claim that the book comes with a surprise ending. Throughout the book, Heath discusses locally-developed projects and strategies designed to incorporate the skills students acquire at home and in the community into their developing "school literacy" practices. The surprise comes in an epilogue which details changes in federal education policies that blocked and reversed many of these local efforts and replaced them with programs based on a more autonomous view of literacy that emphasized decontextualized, skill-based training and standardized testing. Collins and Blot contend that the body of Heath's analysis is missing a key point that ties her micro-analysis of language and literacy in local contexts to decidedly nonlocal federal policy decisions that nevertheless impact local life.

For Collins and Blot, the key point is that "writing is usually associated with power, and particularly with specifically modern forms of power" (2003, p. 5). This leads them into a detailed consideration of the nature and consequences of power in society. Drawing on the work of the French poststructuralists, they see power not only as a macro-level force imposed in the form of institutions, bureaucracies and overt violence, but also as an intimate presence in all facets of everyday life. Power relations on a societal level create the shape of everyday life that in turn determines how individuals are educated, how each of us fits into society, and how we are able to define our identities. Thus, macro-level power translates into intimate and personal decisions about micro-level identity and conceptions of self. This analysis includes "school" or dominant literacy as a mode of delivery of macro-level power, whereas identity includes conceptions of a literate self built through years of education, bureaucratic involvement, and employment. Thus Collins and Blot see literacy and power going hand in hand. Collins and Blot attempt to bridge the local/global divide with careful consideration of power and identity at the micro-and macro levels.

Discussion: Connecting Local and Remote Contexts

These authors present different conceptions of *context* in their understandings of literacy. Although they agree that theories of literacy as social practices need to represent nonlocal contextual influences more explicitly, they differ in how they suggest we understand such distant influences. A key difference among their theories is in how they propose to connect the local and global contexts of literacy.

Street argues that the NLS already has the requisite theoretical framework in place, in which local contextual features interact in as yet unspecified ways with more global *literacy practices* to generate locally constructed *literacy events*. Brandt and Clinton propose a framework in which literacy events are understood in terms of both *localizing moves* and *globalizing connects*. Collins and Blot attempt to integrate local and distant influences through the dynamic interplay between micro-and macro-levels of *identity* and *power* in discourse and interaction.

In accepting Brandt and Clinton's argument that "remote" influences need to be accounted for, Street cautions against formulating these as "autonomous" influences. But without further development, it is not clear how the NLS framework of literacy practices offers a less "autonomous" formulation of remote influences than that proposed in the Brandt and Clinton framework. Why should the social and cultural forces included in NLS conceptions of literacy practices be considered less "autonomous" and somehow integrally linked to the local context, whereas the concept of global connects proposed by Brandt and Clinton is labeled "autonomous"? Street seems more comfortable with Collins and Blot's power-based formulation, although again it is not theoretically clear why "power" should wield a less "autonomous" type of global influence than "sponsorship" or other *remote* influences considered by Brandt and Clinton. Although power as formulated by Collins and Blot is certainly "ideological" in NLS terms, it is not clear why *remote* sources of power that influence *local* interactions are operating in a more "ideological" framework than other types of remote influence. How are we to tell? How do we avoid replacing an autonomous theory of literacy with an autonomous theory of power? Further theoretical elaboration and clarification are needed here.

Part of the difficulty may be that Street's (1984) contrast between "autonomous" and "ideological" models of literacy does not serve well as a dichotomous classification of contextual influences on social interactions. The original distinction, rooted in the debate about the Literacy Thesis, was intended to contrast ways of understanding the apparent "consequences" of literacy. When conceptualizing the manner in which distant influences are involved in the construction of local literacy events, "autonomous" and "ideological" may not be suitable contraries. *From the perspective of local interactants*, might some distant influences be perceived as having relatively more "autonomous" influence than others? How are we to tell? At the very least, we need here a better formulation of the ways in which remote influences on locally constructed literacy practices may or may not be "autonomous."

Although many theorists adhere to the distinction between "ideological" and "autonomous" models of literacy, others focus more on a related distinction between conceptions of literacy as "situated" versus "decontextualized." From our perspective, it is less productive to ask *whether* (or which aspects of) literacy practices are *situated* than to ask about what contexts those literacy practices are situated *in*. In building theories based on close examination and analysis of local practices, NLS has not dealt systematically with identifying what makes a context "local." The context in which literacy practices are said to be situated is usually taken as a given for both the participants and the observer. But how do we locate the boundaries of the contexts in which literacy practices are situated? Where are the spatial and temporal margins? Although such questions about context boundaries have long been asked in microethnographic investigations (e.g., Shultz, Florio & Erickson, 1982), they also come to the fore again in discussing "local" versus "remote" influences on literacy.

There are several promising theoretical directions that can build on and extend the ideas developed in the three pieces reviewed here toward connecting local and global contexts of literacy practices. We will sketch two possibilities here. One way to connect the local and the distant is by conceiving of literacy as being situated in *multiple* contexts, each of which has its own time and space margins. One context is the "immediate" one, locally bounded in time, space, and interaction in much the way that studies of locally situated practices have described. That is the *local context*. There is another type of context in which the literacy event is also situated, a context usually having much broader space and time boundaries, expanded by the durable and portable material properties of writing as used in culturally and historically shaped literacy practices. A typical (but, we emphasize, *not* an inevitable or "autonomous") realization of the use of writing in social practices is the mediation of distant or remote social interactions, resulting in the expansion of context for specific literacy practices. That is a *mediated context*.

There are some parallels between this dual-context framework and the localizing moves and global connects suggested in Brandt and Clinton's framework. However, there are some important conceptual differences here that could be usefully explored in future research. The dual-context formulation, framed within the *polycontextuality* and *heterochronicity* of communicative activity (Engeström, Engeström, & Kärkkäinen, 1995; Reder, 1993) posits multiple distinct contexts, whereas Brandt and Clinton propose a unitary context comprised of two different kinds of interactional components.

Key to developing theory in this area would be studies that carefully trace the historical development of *specific* communicative practices as they come into contact with writing (and other information technologies). Such research needs to describe carefully and analyze how writing both reshapes local literacy events and how it mediates distant social relationships and interactions and, in so doing, expands the mediated context. Reder's (1992) description of the impact of the introduction of Vai script into existing oral message-sending practices provides an interesting example, although much of the interpretation was retrospective and limited by sparse data. A more recent example based on the individual experience of a Burundese asylum seeker in Belgium appears in Blommaert (2004). Richer and more systematic studies will likely need to be prospective, closely following over time and space the impact of the introduction of writing (or other information and communication technologies) on the historical development of specific social practices *and* their contexts. Recent work by Hull (in press), Hayes (in press), and others provides rich data about the impact of new technologies on the formation of social worlds and communities among children and adults. Such work can provide important new data about the ways in which contexts and identities expand through the mediation of new literacies.

A second direction for future research is the application of theories originating in the sociology of science and technology to the analysis of literacy. Actant-network theory (also frequently termed actor-network theory), initiated by Callon (1986) and Latour (1987) in their seminal studies of the development of scientific knowledge, has been extended broadly to the sociology of knowledge by Law (1994) and others. Actant-network theory (ANT) conceives of *agency* as operating within heterogeneous networks comprised of *both* human beings and material objects. In attributing agency to networks of juxtaposed human and nonhuman "actants," ANT does *not* assume that the agencies enacted by people and by inanimate objects are necessarily the same. A key distinction is that only human actors are able to create or put non-human actants into circulation in the networked system.

Originally ANT was used to characterize the dynamic processes in heterogeneous networks through which new scientific knowledge and ideas gradually become accepted, new methods and tools become adopted, and through which decisions are effectively made about what is known and valued. Key concepts for understanding the operation of such heterogeneous networks are *translation*, (the creation of a network through stages of *problematization, interessment,* and *enrollment* of actants into *alliance* with definitions and identities created by focal actors), *inscription* (a process of creating material artifacts that protect actors' interests), and *irreversibility* (the extent to which it is subsequently impossible to return to an earlier point in the system's development where alternative possibilities exist).

Although the early developers of ANT were directly concerned with the role that texts (and other inscriptions) played in the development of science and technology, literacy theorists did not seriously engage this theoretical framework until Brandt and Clinton (2002). Brandt and Clinton began to work with some of these ideas, adopting in particular Latour's notion that written documents may have agency within human interactions. They saw such textual agency as enabling the "transcontextualizing" potential of literacy.

Barton and Hamilton (in press) have developed the application of ANT to literacy studies much further. Like Collins and Blot (2003), Barton and Hamilton are concerned with the theoretical representation of power within literacy research. They suggest that the concept of *reification* (Wenger, 1998) can serve as a useful conceptual bridge between communities of practice research and literacy studies. They offer many examples of how literacy serves to reify knowledge and understandings within communities of practice, a construct reminiscent of inscription in ANT. Building on the concept of reification, Barton and Hamilton develop the notion of *textually-mediated social worlds*. They argue that the model of a textually-mediated social world adds something vital to the community of practice theory that has been missing until now, the recognition and theoretical representation of the key roles played by language, literacy, and power within the dynamics of communities and social networks.

The insights of Barton and Hamilton may offer an important theoretical path forward. Future research may be able to extend these ideas by borrowing yet another construct from ANT, that of irreversibility. As noted previously, irreversibility in ANT is the extent to which an actant-network, at a given point in its development, is able to return to an earlier state in which alternative possibilities for future network development exist. An important feature of irreversibility to consider is its variable and continuous quality. This may provide some important new theoretical machinery for representing the remote influences of literacy (i.e., of inscriptions) within social networks. We suggest that the contexts inscribed by written materials in relatively irreversible states of actant networks will endow literacy with the appearance of having a relatively fixed ("autonomous") influence on social practices, whereas in more reversible network states, the inscriptions will endow literacy with influence that appears less "autonomous." In other words, when social groupings are in a state of flux (i.e., power players still forming alliances and meanings still have loose definitions) there is more focus on the players and their not-disinterested involvement is more readily apparent. When stable states of networks become institutionalized, the static (irreversible) relations of power seem "natural" and the influence of the tools of the powerful (e.g., literacy) *seem* to be inherent in the tools themselves. In this way, the powerful influence of the people who control literacy is misassigned to literacy itself, thereby endowing literacy with an *apparently* "autonomous influence." This may provide a step towards resolving the issues noted earlier about characterizing the nature of distant literacy influences on local interactions.

Implications for Educational Policy and Practice

As such theories of context and literacy continue to develop, it is important that they connect with issues of educational policy and practice. Ethnographically-based literacy studies have inspired many teachers and literacy practitioners with their accounts of the diversity of learners, literacy practices, and contexts and with their insights about the ideological content of school-based literacy. But such literacy studies are open to criticism that they have not developed a practical alternative pedagogy for literacy:

> Understandably, those working within this ethnographic framework seem to prefer description and analysis to prescription . . . Teachers may be convinced by the insights of NLS, but they must work within the increasingly narrow constraints of the school system . . .while sociolinguists argue that varieties of literacy are structurally equal and practice theorists decry the arbitrary dominance of one form of literacy over another, practitioners must decide whether and how to teach dominant literacies without becoming complicit in the reproduction of power. (Kim, 2003)

This is a major challenge for literacy educators, whether teaching in K-12 schools or adult education programs. Better theories about how contexts shape literacy practices should help teachers to see the literacy events in their classrooms and programs in relation to the multiple contexts in which they are situated, including the local classroom context and the broader and more distant contexts of home, community, and beyond. Good theory may provide educators with increased opportunities to perceive, understand, and create literacies that can appropriately inscribe and mediate these polycontextual and heterochronic spaces. Two simple examples illustrate the ways in which theoretical developments described in this chapter may be useful in improving educational practice.

First, studies which carefully follow the introduction of the use of writing into existing social practices (e.g., introducing the use of recipes into food preparation in the home) may provide educators with valuable insights about bridging classroom and home contexts, that is, about situating literacy practices in these dual contexts. A second example is systematic research on the Latour-like agency of both human teachers and written materials in students' acquisition of a second language (e.g., Ohta, 2004). Insights derived from such research and the theory-building it would drive could help educators to develop new models of language and literacy education with applications to improved curricula and programs.

Note

1. Later scholars extended the leveling of differences between orality and literacy to the leveling of such categorical differences among other modalities as well, within frameworks of both *multimodal* literacy (Kress & van Leeuwen, 2001) and *metamedia* literacy (Lemke, 1998).

ANNOTATED BIBLIOGRAPHY

Barton, D., & Hamilton, M. (in press). Literacy, reification and the dynamics of social interaction. In D. Barton & K. Tusting (Eds.), *Beyond communities of practice: Language, power and social context.* Cambridge, UK: Cambridge University Press.

In this chapter, Barton and Hamilton bring together theories of communities of practice, theories of literacy as situated social practices, and macro-level theories of social structure. They contend that because so many social interactions involve literacy in some way, a communities of practice perspective needs to include an account of the various ways that literacy is used to mediate interactions between people. The authors propose the concept of textually mediated social worlds. They discuss a variety of recent research that looks at how people create and use things as semiotic tools. Alternatively called reification, stable mobiles, or cultural artifacts, these things are often literacy materials. A theoretical focus on the properties of literacy as an object allows for connections to be made between macro-and micro-level perspectives of human interaction and the construction of knowledge in society.

Brandt, D., & Clinton, K. (2002). Limits of the local: Expanding perspectives on literacy as a social practice. *Journal of Literacy Research 34*(3), 337–356.

Brandt and Clinton argue that New Literacy Studies has insufficiently theorized key aspects of literacy, thereby creating unnecessary fissures between local and global contexts, and between social actors and the objects (often texts) that play a role in their interactions. The authors draw on the work of Latour to argue for a greater focus on the material aspects of literacy. Looking at the properties of literacy as a material object reveals how the meanings and uses of literacies are not created solely by local actors, but are influenced by interested remote actors as well (e.g., government, boss, publisher). Brandt and Clinton provide a set of analytical terms to guide further research.

Collins, J., & Blot, R. (2003). *Literacy and literacies: Texts, power, and identity.* New York: Cambridge University Press.

This book traces the roots of New Literacy Studies (NLS) through an in-depth analysis of key works from both the "autonomous" model of literacy (Goody, 1986; Olson, 1994) as well as foundational works of NLS (Heath, 1983; Finnegan, 1988; Street, 1984). Collins and Blot identify a "particularist/universalist" impasse in current NLS work, which focuses on describing local literacies while giving only secondary consideration to the ways that local literacy events coalesce into broader patterns of literacy in society. Drawing on the Tolowa language revitalization program as a concrete example, the authors propose to move forward by situating literacy studies within the French poststructuralist tradition (Derrida, de Certeau, Bourdieu and Foucault) in order to draw out (1) the nature of text, (2) how literacy is entangled with issues of power in society, and (3) the intimate impact of literacy on individual identity.

Street, B. V. (2003a). Foreword. In J. Collins & R. Blot, *Literacy and literacies: Texts, power and identity* (pp. xi–xv). New York: Cambridge University Press.

In this essay, Street provides a succinct framework for recent debates in the field of literacy studies. Situated approaches to literacy have been accused of "relativism" and of "romanticizing" the local context. New Literacy Studies has struggled to account for the ways in which distant influences impact local literacy practices. Street suggests that this impasse can be dealt with through a consideration of broader theories of social structure and power. He introduces the Collins and Blot volume as an example of such conceptual developments.

Street, B. V. (2003b). What's "new" in New Literacy Studies? Critical approaches to literacy in theory and practice. *Current Issues in Comparative Education* [Online], 5(2). Retrieved November 4, 2004, from http://www.tc.columbia. edu/cice/articles/ bs152.htm.

In this article, Street responds to critiques of New Literacy Studies (NLS). He argues that the NLS view of literacy as a situated social practice provides ample theoretical support for literacy research through the concepts of literacy events and literacy practices. Ethnographies of literacy document observable literacy events while also providing insight into the construction of literacy practices. Although agreeing that the focus on the *relationship* between local literacy and distant (global or school) literacy is key, he warns against returning to an "autonomous" view of literacy. Street concludes with a discussion of the pedagogical implications of the literacy debate.

OTHER REFERENCES

Barton, D. (2001). Directions for literacy research: Analysing language and social practices in a textually mediated world. *Language and Education, 15*(2 & 3), 92–104.

Barton, D., & Hamilton, M. (1998). *Local literacies: Reading and writing in one community.* London: Routledge.

Barton, D., Hamilton, M., & Ivanič, R. (Eds.) (2000). *Situated literacies: Reading and writing in context.* London: Routledge.

Besnier, N. (1995). *Literacy, emotion, and authority: Reading and writing on a Polynesian atoll.* New York: Cambridge University Press.

Biber, D. (1986). Spoken and written textual dimensions in English: Resolving the contradictory findings. *Language, 62,* 384–414.

Blommaert, J. (2004) Writing as a problem: African grassroots writing, economics of literacy, and globalization. *Language in Society, 33*(5), 643–671.

Brandt, D. (1995). Sponsors of literacy. *College Composition and Communication, 49*, 165–185.

Callon, M. (1986). Some elements of a sociology of translation: Domestication of the scallops and the fishermen of St. Brieuc Bay. In J. Law (Ed.), *Power, action and belief: A new sociology knowledge* (pp. 196–233). London: Routledge & Kegan Paul.

Engeström, Y., Engeström, R., & Kärkkäinen, M. (1995). Polycontextuality and boundary crossing in expert cognition: Learning and problem solving in complex work activities. *Learning and Instruction, 5*, 319–336.

Feldman, C. F. (1991). Oral metalanguage. In D. R. Olson & N. Torrance (Eds.), *Literacy and orality* (pp. 47–65). Cambridge: Cambridge University Press.

Finnegan, R. (1988). *Literacy and orality*. Oxford: Basil Blackwell.

Gee, J. P. (1988). The legacies of literacy: From Plato to Freire through Harvey Graff. *Harvard Educational Review, 58*, 195–212.

Gee, J. (1991). *Social linguistics: Ideology in discourses*. London: Falmer Press.

Goody, J. (1986). *The logic of writing and the organization of society*. Cambridge: Cambridge University Press.

Goody, J., & Watt, I. (1963). The consequences of literacy. *Comparative Studies in Society and History, 5*(3), 304–345.

Graff, H. J. (1979). *The literacy myth*. New York: Academic Press.

Graff, H. J. (1987). *The labyrinths of literacy*. London: Falmer.

Greenfield, P. (1972). Oral or written language: The consequences for cognitive development in Africa, the United States, and England. *Language and Speech, 15*, 169–178.

Halverson, J. (1991). Olson on literacy. *Language in Society, 20*, 619–640.

Halverson, J. (1992). Goody and the implosion of the literacy thesis. *Man, 27*, 301–317.

Havelock, E. (1963). *Preface to Plato*. Cambridge, MA: Harvard University Press.

Hayes, E. (in press). Reconceptualizing adult literacy education and the digitial divide. In A. Belzer & H. Beder (Eds.), *Defining and improving quality in adult education: Issues and challenges*. Mahwah, NJ: Erlbaum.

Heath, S. B. (1982). Protean shapes in literacy events: Ever shifting oral and literate traditions. In D. Tannen (Ed.), *Spoken and written language: Exploring literacy and orality* (pp. 91–118). Norwood, NJ: Ablex.

Heath, S. B. (1983). *Ways with words: Language, life and work in communities and classrooms*. Cambridge, UK: Cambridge University Press.

Hull, G. (in press). Shaping future selves in workplaces and vocational education: An identity framework for exploring adult development. In A. Belzer & H. Beder (Eds.), *Defining and improving quality in adult education: Issues and challenges.* Mahwah, NJ: Erlbaum.

Kim, J. (2003). Challenges to NLS: Response to "What's 'new' in New Literacy Studies". *Current Issues in Comparative Education* [Online], 5(2). Retrieved November 4, 2004, from http://www.tc.columbia.edu/cice/articles/jk152.htm.

Kress, G. & van Leeuwen, T. (2001). *Multimodal discourse: The modes and media of contemporary communication.* Oxford: Oxford University Press.

Latour, B. (1987). *Science in action.* Cambridge, MA: Harvard University Press.

Law, J. (1994). *Organizing modernity.* Oxford: Blackwell.

Lemke, J. L. (1998). Metamedia literacy: Transforming meanings and media. In D. Reinking, M. C. McKenna, L. D. Labbo, & R. D. Kieffer (Eds.), *Handbook of literacy and technology: Transformations in a post-typographic world* (pp. 283–302). Mahwah, NJ: Erlbaum.

Levi-Strauss, C. (1962). *The savage mind.* London: Trafalgar Square.

McLuhan, M. (1962) *The Gutenberg galaxy.* New York: Signet.

Ohta, A. S. (2004). *The ZPD and adult L2 development: Beyond social interaction.* Paper presented at the annual meeting of the American Association of Applied Linguistics, Portland OR, May 1–4.

Olson, D. R. (1977). From utterance to text: The bias of language in speech and writing. *Harvard Educational Review, 47,* 257–281.

Olson, D. R. (1988). Mind and media: The epistemic functions of literacy. *Journal of Communication, 38*(3), 27–36.

Olson, D. R. (1994). *The world on paper.* New York: Cambridge University Press.

Olson, D. R., & Torrance, N. (Eds.). (1991). *Literacy and orality.* Cambridge: Cambridge University Press.

Ong, W. J. (1982). *Orality and literacy.* London: Methuen.

Reder, S. (1992). Getting the message across: Cultural factors in the intergenerational transfer of cognitive skills. In T. Sticht, B. McDonald, & M. Beeler (Eds.) *The intergenerational transfer of cognitive skills. Volume II: Theory and research in cognitive science* (pp. 202–228). Newark, DE: Ablex.

Reder, S. (1993). Watching flowers grow: Polycontextuality and heterochronicity at work. *Quarterly Newsletter of the Laboratory of Comparative Human Cognition, 15*(4), 116–125.

Scribner, S., & Cole, M. (1978). Literacy without schooling: Testing for intellectual effects. *Harvard Educational Review, 29*(2), 96–106.

Scribner, S., & Cole, M. (1981). *The psychology of literacy.* Cambridge, MA: Harvard University Press.

Shultz, J. J., Florio, S., & Erickson, F. (1982). Where's the floor? Aspects of the cultural organization of social relationships in communication at home and in school. In P. Gilmore & A. A. Glatthorn (Eds.), *Children in and out of school* (pp. 91–123). Norwood, NJ: Ablex.

Street, B. V. (1984). *Literacy in theory and practice.* Cambridge, UK: Cambridge University Press.

Street, B. V. (Ed.) (1993). *Cross-cultural approaches to literacy.* Cambridge, UK: Cambridge University Press.

Street, B. V. (1995). *Social literacies.* London: Longman.

Tannen, D. (1982). The myth of orality and literacy. In W. Frawley (Ed.), *Linguistics and literacy* (pp. 37–50). New York: Plenum Press.

Wenger, E. (1998). *Communities of practice: Learning, meaning and identity.* Cambridge, UK: Cambridge University Press.

10. TECHNOLOGIES FOR SECOND LANGUAGE LITERACY

Denise E. Murray

Information and communication technology (ICT) has been used in language classrooms for more than two decades. Over this time, classroom use has moved from drill, text manipulation, and word processing to more interactive and communicative applications such as e-mail, chat, and web-based programs, requiring learners to acquire computer literacies. This chapter will begin by discussing both the parameters of ICT and the scope of literacies. It is then organized around discussion of the two types of literacies at the intersection of ICT and L2 learning: how new technologies facilitate acquisition of L2 literacies and what L2 literacies are needed for learners to participate in an increasingly digital world. Although research has mostly been limited to small-scale context-dependent case studies of individual classrooms, it has identified a number of issues that need to be considered as teachers (and learners) use ICT for language learning. Although ICT provides a natural context for learner autonomy, that autonomy needs to be developed systematically. In addition, ICT provides a context for learner identity formation through hybrid uses of language(s), in ways unexpected by teachers and learners. These new ways of using language may empower and motivate learners. Similarly, whereas ICT provides opportunities for collaboration and interaction, they are not automatic, and instruction needs to be skillfully scaffolded for learners to benefit from such opportunities.

Both concepts in this title are contested in the literature on language education. In the 21st century, technologies almost always refer to computer-based technologies, rather than earlier (and still existing) technologies such as overhead projectors, language labs, videos, or even print or pen. That some of these older technologies are now also digital and computer-based is usually ignored. In this chapter, I will refer only to computer-based technologies where the computer is obvious to the user. Even so, advances in digital technology are leading us to an era where the computer as we know it may not be transparent to the user (Murray, 2004). For the purposes of this chapter, I refer to these technologies as ICT, information and communication technology, rather than CALL (computer-assisted language learning). ICT captures the two primary uses of these technologies— they provide a context for human-human and human-machine communication, and they provide a context for information production, delivery, and sharing. I will not use CALL, except for packaged language learning materials, because CALL is the earliest term used in language teaching and is therefore often associated with the metaphor of computer as a tool for language learning and language lesson delivery, even though Warschauer argued eloquently for the reintroduction of CALL to replace cyber (see Murray, 2004; Warschauer, 2001 for discussions of nomenclature) even though some of his readers have tried to use NBLT (network-based language teaching) for those ICTs available only with networked computers. ICT is more commonly used in Europe, despite EUROCALL having defined CALL as the "academic field that explores the role of information and communication technologies in language learning and teaching" (Davies, 2001, p. 13).

Literacy is also a contested concept, with definitions and use ranging from the ability to read and write, that is, to code and decode, to the ability to function in reading and writing in everyday events to understanding how language and ideology function through written texts and being able to appropriate written language for one's own creative and personal needs (see, for example, Gee, 1996; Street, 1995). These differing perspectives are often summarized as opposing views—literacy as individual skill and literacy as social practice. For the purposes of this chapter, I will take the view that literacies are socioculturally constructed and inherently ideological, but, like Freebody and Luke (1990), acknowledge that mastery of the other roles in literacy behavior (such as code breaker or text participant) are also essential underpinnings of a more critical approach.

The title is also ambiguous in that, on first glance, it seems to refer only to how technologies can support L2 literacy development; however, there is the additional reading of what L2 literacies are needed to use the technologies, an equally important focus for L2 education because knowing the literacies required to use the new technologies is often critical for learners to meet their social, personal, and educational needs (Goodwin-Jones, 2000). This chapter will therefore discuss both how new technologies facilitate acquisition of L2 literacies and what L2 literacies are needed for learners to participate in an increasingly digital world.

Literacies for Using New Technologies

Scholars have identified a variety of ways of referring to reading and using the new technologies, whether in one's first or other languages—digital literacies (Snyder, 1999), silicon literacies (Snyder, 2002), electronic literacies (Warschauer, 1999), web literacy (Sorapure, Inglesby, & Yatchisin, 1998), information literacy (American Library Association, 2000), and computer literacy (Corbel & Gruba, 2004). It is interesting to note that all these terms focus on the means of production of these new worlds and are usually juxtaposed to print literacy. Because computer literacy is often narrowly defined as how to manipulate a mouse or use specific software (such as a word processor), scholars and researchers have suggested these other, more encompassing terms that include how to communicate online and how to access, evaluate, and use information presented in an electronic medium. They have also identified the increasing need for visual literacy (Kress, 1997) in the new digital media. However, computer literacy narrowly defined is essential for competence in the other literacies. As Corbel and Gruba (2004) note, many CALL programs and ESL teachers assume their learners are computer literate. However, research with adult second language learners in Australia (McPherson & Murray, 2003; Murray & McPherson, 2002) has shown that this assumption is flawed. It is likely that this assumption is also not accurate in many settings where English is being taught to adult refugees or to children in countries or areas of nations with low technology uptake (see, for example, Murray, 1999). Even in nations with high technology uptake, access may be limited for a variety of reasons such as socioeconomic class or cultural usage patterns. If we take a broader definition of digital literacies, we find that access to not only the computer and the Internet but also to their various functions is limited for many learners (Hargittai, 2002). For example, in a study of U.S. German learners interacting with German English learners (Savignon & Roithmeier, 2004), German learners posted less to the discussion board than did the U.S. learners. The researchers note that the

German students were less familiar with and had less access to CMC than did their American counterparts.

For language learners, such reading and using includes learning digital literacy in another language, learning how to navigate the new technologies (Murray & McPherson, 2004b) and also learning how to read new digital texts such as web pages (Thurstun, 2004). "While the Web contains texts that follow the conventions of print-based texts (for example, narratives, information texts), the Web also contains new configurations of texts, where more than one genre might appear on one webpage, for example" (Murray & McPherson, 2004a, p. 3). Little research has been conducted on how language learners navigate the web in their target language, whereas a number of studies have been conducted on how such learners read on the web. Ganderton (1999), in a study of French L2 learners observing both navigation and reading, found that his groups of learners were able to navigate one site reasonably successfully, but had difficulty with a second site, when links outside the main site came up as a second browser window. He also found that learners tried to extrapolate from experiences on English web sites, when they didn't understand the L2 vocabulary for a specific navigation action such as *"Validez"* in French (i.e., "confirm"). One experimental study conducted with low-literate adults (who were not necessarily second language learners), however, provides some insights on what may be the navigation difficulties of adults using another language in which they are not very proficient. This research confirmed much of the research on readability—that scrolling is difficult, links are not always clearly identified, graphics do not always clarify, redundancy needs to be built in, the path history needs to be displayed, and guidelines in simple language need to be provided (Zarcadoolas, Blanco, Boyer, & Pleasant, 2002).

Research into web page reading for native speakers has identified characteristics that facilitate reading and those that hinder, as compared to print reading (e.g., Thurstun, 2004). In general, they conclude that screen reading is more difficult than print reading. They have identified features such as color, font size, scrolling, nominalization, graphics, and white space as contributing to the readability of online texts. However, in addition to reading the Web, learners also need to learn how to construct knowledge from a nonlinear, hypertext navigation. Second language learners, even if quite fluent readers of print text, have difficulties reading texts specific to the Web, such as home pages (Murray & McPherson,

2004b); have difficulty determining which online texts have reliable information or information in a genre they need (Murray & McPherson, 2004a; Walz, 2001); lack skills for evaluating nontext features such as visuals (Sutherland-Smith, 2002) or pop-ups and advertisements (Murray, 2003); or of how to skillfully modify, rather than copy online texts (Bloch, 2001; Sutherland-Smith, 2002). Research with fluent English native speaker readers also indicates that Web reading, especially the hypertext environment of the Web, is more cognitively demanding (for example, Calisir & Gurel, 2003). However, the skills of literacy to navigate the Web are essential for life, whether social, personal, or educational, in an increasingly digital world; for many learners, these skills will need to be in an L2, especially English because it still dominates information on the Web.

Using New Technologies to Learn Language

These new technologies provide the potential "... to engage native speakers at a distance, to utilize authentic materials and to enable learners to interact with rich, multi-dimensional learning environments" (Levy & Debski, 1999 p. 7), all of which are contexts that facilitate language acquisition. However, much of the literature on ICT in language teaching and learning has been anecdotal, written by the innovators and early adopters (Rogers, 1995), intended to persuade and help the uncommitted or resistant to use the new technologies. Studies on ICT in language education have primarily been case studies of particular learners in particular contexts, focusing on the process of using ICT in language learning, with little attention being paid to learning outcomes. This has lead researchers such as Chappelle (2001) to advocate for a closer link between interactionist SLA research methodologies and research in CALL. In contrast, other researchers (Warschauer & Kern, 2000) claim that the advantages of ICT are best researched in "particular practices of use in particular contexts" (p. 2).

Although this focus on the particularities of contexts and use has produced many studies, generalizing from the extant literature is somewhat difficult, although some trends can be identified. Over the 1980s and 1990s, many studies focused on second language learners composing using new technologies, including comparing peer review online with face-to-face, the amount of revision after online feedback compared with face-to-face feedback. Other studies of online discussion compared online dialogue journals with pen-and-ink dialogue journals. More recently, research has moved away from comparing online and face-to-face interactions and have focused more on examining literacy uses using computer-mediated communication (CMC) or students' use of the Web for information gathering. This chapter will therefore focus on these recent trends.

Computer-Mediated Communication (CMC)

Because CMC provides language learners with opportunities for interaction, often with native speakers, it has been more widely researched than other aspects of ICT use in language learning. CMC can be used as a means in learning tasks and projects or can be used instructionally as a goal in itself. In the former, the product of instruction also needs to be investigated, whereas in the latter, the captured online interactions are both process and product. However, much of the research has focused only on the process. Because these are written forms of interaction, in the language learning setting, they have been seen as a bridge to oral interaction; yet, as indicated above, acquiring the skills of CMC in the target language can be a goal in itself. However, a recent study found that although there was an increase in quantity of language produced in asynchronous CMC compared with synchronous CMC and face-to-face discussion, there were no significant differences among the three groups in quality on lexical and syntactic measures (Abrams, 2003).

Interaction

The new technologies provide opportunities for learners to interact with native speakers at a distance through a variety of different online tools such as e-mail, chat, and discussion boards. The literature overall supports the use of CMC with language learners, an exception being a survey conducted by Corbel and Taylor (2003), in which a majority (56%) of teachers of adult immigrants felt that e-mail had low educational cost effectiveness. However, in a nondirected self-access situation, adult immigrants themselves chose e-mail in preference to all other applications, but their choice of language was primarily their home language (Lever, 2004), including accessing news from their home country. Left to their own devices, these students did not choose educational packages to increase their

English language learning. Their choice mirrors computer use in noneducational settings, where e-mail has become the "killer app" (application).

Most commentators and researchers have noted the advantage of asynchronous CMC modes such as e-mail and discussion lists because they allow learners to interact in their own time and place. Savignon and Roithmeier (2004), for example, demonstrated how two classes, one a U.S. class learning German, the other a German class learning English, collaborated to produce a jointly-constructed CMC conversation on a bulletin board. These learners used "the potential of CMC to engage . . . in the interpretation, expression, and negotiation of meaning essential for the development of communicative competence" (p. 284). Similarly, Schwienhorst (2004) found that in NS/NNS interactions in MOO (text-based synchronous interaction), there was no significant difference in topic initiation between the two groups. However, as in much of the extant literature, studies in different contexts have produced differing results, as is often the case when research is context-dependent and not large scale. In an interchange via e-mail between students of Japanese in Australia and students of intercultural communication in Japan, students seldom tried to deal with breakdowns in communication (Stockwell, 2004).

However, synchronous CMC such as chat and teleconferencing have also been found to be effective in language teaching and learning, although because of the synchronous nature of this medium, there are overlapping turns, with little time to compose messages reflectively (see for example, Sengupta, 2001). Asynchronous CMC such as e-mail, because of its time delay, gives learners the opportunity to produce more syntactically complex language (Sotillo, 2000). Although, as Biesenbach-Lucas and Weasonforth (2001) have found, whereas e-mail and word processed texts shared similar cohesive features, e-mail texts were shorter and provided less initial orientation for the reader.

Because negotiation of meaning has been found to be necessary for language acquisition (see for example, Pica, 1994), several studies have examined whether in fact negotiation of meaning occurs in CMC and whether learner output increases. Most of this research has examined various forms of chat—either restricted chat, available only to the learners and their instructors, or chat in public chat rooms where learners can interact with native speakers. Sotillo (2000) found similar discourse features occurring in internet relay chat as in face-to-face interactions, with rapid interactions and negotiations among their ESL students; however, learners were often unfocussed, discussing issues not pertinent to the task. Learners of Japanese, interacting with native speakers via chat in a virtual world, on encountering difficulties in understanding each other, negotiated meaning (Toyoda & Harrison, 2002), as did learners of English (Smith, 2003). Similarly, learners of Italian, participating in public chat rooms "negotiate[d] for meaning and modif[ied] their interlanguage when engaged in open ended conversational tasks with unfamiliar interlocutors" (Tudini, 2003 p. 141). Most negotiations were the result of lexical or syntactic problems. In general then, the research on synchronous CMC has found it provides learners with opportunities for informal conversational practice and facilitates fluency, rather than accuracy. However, Smith (2003) also found that task type affected the extent of learner negotiations and that this effect was different from what has been identified as used in face-to-face interactions, prompting him to develop a new model for describing negotiated interaction via CMC.

Although most CMC research has examined written versions, recent developments in the technology have made voice CMC possible for language learning. Researching a distance education context, Wang (2004) found that using NetMeeting (a proprietary desktop videoconferencing system) supported learners' oral and visual interaction. With increasing availability of broadband in some areas and of the convergence of visual, audio, and text, research into technology use and L2 learning will need to investigate these new channels of communication.

Identity formation

"In the presentation of self online, one is not recognized by one's physical appearance, but through one's textual behaviors" (Wood & Smith, 2001, p. 55). In the online context, identity is formed through interaction, by how people create identities through CMC in their home language and the target language. As Turkle (1995) has noted, the Internet provides opportunities for multiple subjective identity, opportunities that Warschauer (2000) identified in his study of a Hawaiian language class. He demonstrated how several of the learners, through synchronous discussions, e-mail and the writing of projects on web pages, found symbolic value in Hawaiian language use on the Internet, "allowing them to say to themselves and to the world that they are Hawaiian and proud of it" (p. 11). For one of these learners, the online activities allowed her to express her Hawaiianness, which had been difficult in face-to-face encounters, not only because of her shyness, but also because of her fair coloring. Examining a Usenet forum popular with Chinese students in the United States, Bloch (2004) found them liberated in using English as they adopted a traditional Chinese rhetorical style, finding their collective argumentative voice in English. In contrast, Warschauer, El Said, and Zohry (2002) express concern that the use of English among a group of Egyptian professionals was encroaching on the more traditional use of classical Arabic for formal written communication. They found that a diglossic situation developed: the Egyptian professionals used English for formal CMC, but Egyptian Arabic for more informal uses, thus creating both a global and local identity. In a recent groundbreaking study of informal, noninstructed chat use, Lam (2004) found that the two teenage Chinese immigrants she studied developed new identities as bilingual speakers of English and Cantonese. In this chat room, participants used both languages, code-switching between them, using a variety of English constructed by the group that differed from standard American English. Her focal learners were more comfortable using English in the chat room than in face-to-face situations.

What these studies have in common is how the interaction of global and local identities give rise to hybridized language varieties in these increasingly glocal discourse contexts (Koutsogiannis & Mitsikopoulou, 2004). Just as these language learners choose among their available languages to communicate and indeed, develop hybridized forms, so too might learners want to choose among the available technology modes to interact. Almost two decades ago, with the much more primitive CMC tools then available, Murray (1988) found that highly technologically savvy workers chose among the available modes depending on the context. Recent research (Thorne, 2003b) on American students learning French and being required to use e-mail with a French keypal found that for some learners, e-mail was not a mode of choice for developing interpersonal relations with age-peers, which had been the purpose for the teacher assigning the keypal interactions. Some learners did not participate in e-mail, even though the e-mail part of the course was graded. For these learners, identity with age-peers is established through immediate, synchronous modes such as instant messaging (IM) or short message service (SMS), the latter of which has yet to be exploited in instructed language learning.

Collaboration

Second language acquisition research has shown that collaboration among learners facilitates language acquisition. Such advantages of collaboration have also been noted in online collaborative activities, such as project-based learning (Debski, 2000) or other task-based activities that require collaboration (Shield, Weininger, & Davies, 1999). Most supporting research has been of case studies in natural, not experimental, settings. Recently, however, a quasi-empirical study (Beatty & Nunan, 2004) of two groups of students, one working with an interface that was based on constructivist principles, the other on one that followed a behaviorist model, found that the constructivist interface did not lead to more collaboration, as hypothesized. The researchers note that, although hypertext provides learners with more choices and is said to lead to greater learner autonomy, in fact, learners may not have the necessary skills to navigate the choices productively, a finding similar to that of Toyoda (2001) for project-oriented CALL. Schwienhorst's analysis (2003) suggests that in keypal activities, in addition to computer literacy skills, activities need to be set up so that they are embedded in coursework, teachers need to explicitly teach learners to reflect, learners need to participate in the design of the activities, and time needs to be provided for reflection. In other words, collaboration is not a necessary consequence of CMC, but may need to be contextualized and scaffolded for learners.

Telecollaboration has been identified as "the application of global computer networks to foreign (and second) language learning and teaching in institutionalized settings" (Belz, 2003a, p. 2) and involves learners using CMC for a variety of interactions (for example, debate) with other learners distributed around the world. Within this broader theme, a focus on the sociocultural dimensions of such interactions has arisen, in addition to the more descriptive linguistic analyses of the language of interaction, the argument being that, not only does the distributed communication network of CMC facilitate access to native speaker language models and interaction, but to native culture. These studies (Belz, 2003b; Thorne, 2003a) have examined intercultural competence and found, among other things, that the medium provides an opportunity for cultures-of-use to co-evolve, just as other researchers have identified the evolution of hybrid discourses (see, for example, Lam, 2004).

CALL Programs

In a three-dimensional simulation program, learners doing the tasks required engaged in L2 (Spanish in this case) negotiation of meaning (Gonzalez-Lloret, 2003). In a broad survey of learners' perceptions of and attitudes to language learning activities delivered on the Web, Felix (2001) found that learners perceived the Web "as a viable environment for language learning in tertiary settings, especially as an add-on to face-to-face teaching" (p. 314). She does note, however, that another group that had been included in the study pulled out because of their frustrations with the technical difficulties they encountered, with two mature-age learners claiming to have lost all interest in learning the language. As in other studies (Toyoda, 2001), the limited computer literacy skills of the learners had a significant impact on student perceptions, perseverance, and success with online learning.

Using the Web to Support Learning

The World Wide Web provides the opportunity for language learners to access authentic materials in the target language. However, this very authenticity can be problematic for learners, in terms of the level of the language they access, the genres with which they are unfamiliar, and their ability to determine the reliability of the source (see, for example, Murray, 2003).

Research has identified a number of strategies teachers can use to prevent students from being lost in cyberspace, strategies that include teacher selection of web sites for students to visit (Corbel & Taylor, 2003; Murray, 2003), teacher-designed web pages (Murray & McPherson, 2004a), or careful scaffolding of web site reading (Murray & McPherson, 2004b). Such teacher-direction may seem antithetical to one of the purported advantages of using technology, that is, learner autonomy or self-direction (Healey, 1999; Jones, 2001). Yet another strategy is to design language learning activities that are essentially CALL, but delivered on the web rather than through CDs, a strategy has been discussed under CALL previously.

<u>Motivation</u>. Research has indicated that learners are highly motivated by the use of technology. For adult immigrants, this motivation is tied very closely to specific uses, ones that meet their needs to settle in their new country, but maintain links

with their country of origin. Therefore, sites with information they desperately need, such as the driver knowledge test, or news sites of their own countries or e-mail to friends and family are a focus when left to their own devices (Lever, 2004). Learners do not always make the same choices of useful sites as their teachers do. Murray and McPherson report a teacher action research project in which the teacher chose music as the theme for his adult immigrant learners, but students soon dissuaded him, choosing Australian animals as a topic of more interest to them (2004a).

Conclusion

Although much of the literature on technology in language teaching and learning claims it promotes learner autonomy, several studies have now emerged indicating that, far from the technology automatically causing autonomy, just as in other instruction, the teacher needs to support learners' progress toward autonomy; that is, teachers need to scaffold instruction using technology. In general school education, Lankshear, Snyder, and Green (2000) propose a three-dimensional model that includes literacy education with digital technologies. Their operational dimension includes how the language system operates and how to operate the technology, from computer literacy to online searches; their cultural dimension refers to the fact that the operation of both language and technological systems takes place "in authentic forms of social practice and meaning" (p. 45); their critical dimension refers to critically evaluating texts, software, and online information. For learners to be digitally literate in the 21st century, they need to master all three dimensions, often in more than one language. To achieve this requires teachers to carefully scaffold L2 literacy learning. In research, we need systematic investigations that examine both process and product (learning outcomes) of both the linguistic and cultural dimensions of online language learning and that account for the factors in addition to the technology that influence language learning.

ANNOTATED BIBLIOGRAPHY

Belz, J. A. (2003b). Linguistic perspectives on the development of intercultural competence in telecollaboration. *Language Learning and Technology*, *7*(2), 68–117.

Belz examines intercultural competence in the e-mail discourse of two

German university students of English and a U.S. university student of German. However, her analysis of intercultural competence is based on linguistic analyses, rather than the more usual content analysis or interviews of participants. To do this, she usees appraisal theory from systemic functional linguistics, a theory that describes and explains evaluative language, how interlocutors manage interpersonal relationships in interaction. She also analyses modality. Their telecollaboration was not sustained, largely because of an inability on the part of the three participants to understand the culturally appropriate linguistic norms of the other's culture.

Lam, W. S. E. (2004). Second language socialization in a bilingual chat room: Global and local considerations. *Language, Learning and Technology, 8*(3), 44–65.

Lam describes a study of two teenage Chinese immigrants to the United States, who engaged in chat room interactions with other bilingual Chinese and Cantonese teenagers around the world. The participants moved between both languages and co-constructed a mixed-code variety of English with features from Chinese. These two young people carved out identities for themselves in this hybrid English that they were not able to do in standard American English in face-to-face contexts, a blending of the local and global.

Murray, D. E., & McPherson, P. (Eds.). (2004b). *Navigating to read; reading to navigate.* Sydney, Australia: National Centre for English Language Teaching and Research.

This edited volume discusses research conducted with five teachers of adult ESL learners in Australia using a collaborative action research model. The chapters include a discussion of the research findings, discussion of reading on-and off-line, scaffolding and chapters by each of the teachers describing their educational context and the activities they used with learners. Samples of teacher-developed activities are included.

OTHER REFERENCES

Abrams, Z. I. (2003). The effect of synchronous and asynchronous CMC on oral performance in German. *The Modern Language Journal, 87*(2), 157–167.

American Library Association. (2000). *Information literacy competency standards for higher education.* Retrieved October 7, 2004, from http://www.ala.org/ ala/acrl/acrlstandards/informationliteracycompetency.htm

Beatty, K., & Nunan, D. (2004). Computer-mediated collaborative learning. *System, 32,* 165–183.

Belz, J. A. (2003a). From the special issue editor. *Language Learning and Technology, 7*(2), 2–5.

Biesenbach-Lucas, S., & Weasonforth, D. (2001). E-mail and word processing in the ESL classroom: How the medium affects the message. *Language Learning and Technology, 5*(1), 135–165.

Bloch, J. (2001). Plagiarism and the ESL student: From printed to electronic texts. In D. Belcher & A. Hirvela (Eds.), *Linking literacies: Perspectives on L2 reading-writing connections* (pp. 209–228). Ann Arbor: University of Michigan Press.

Bloch, J. (2004). Second language cyberrhetoric: A study of Chinese L2 writers in an online Usenet group. *Language Learning and Technology, 8*(3), 66–82.

Calisir, F., & Gurel, Z. (2003). Influence of text structure and prior knowledge of the learner on reading comprehension, browsing and perceived control. *Computers in Human Behaviour, 19,* 135–145.

Chappelle, C. (2001). CALL in the 21st century: Looking back on research to look forward for practice. In P. Brett (Ed.), *CALL in the 21st century* (CD-ROM). Whitstable, Kent: IATEFL.

Corbel, C., & Gruba, P. (2004). *Teaching computer literacy.* Sydney, Australia: NCELTR.

Corbel, C., & Taylor, T. (2003). *Online for all? Evaluating current and potential use of Internet-based activities for AMEP students.* Sydney, Australia: NCELTR.

Davies, G. (2001). New technologies and language learning: A suitable subject for research? In A. Chambers & G. Davies (Eds.), *ICT and language learning: A European perspective* (pp. 13–24). Lisse, The Netherlands: Swets & Zeitlinger.

Debski, R. (2000). Project-oriented CALL: Implementation and evaluation. *Computer Assisted Language Learning, 13*(4/5).

Felix, U. (2001). *Beyond Babel: Language learning online.* Melbourne: Language Australia.

Freebody, P., & Luke, A. (1990). "Literacies" programs: Debates and demands in cultural context. *Prospect, 5*(7), 7–16.

Ganderton, R. (1999). Interactivity in L2 web-based reading. In R. Debski & M. Levy (Eds.), *World CALL: Global perspectives on computer-assisted language learning* (pp. 49–66). Lisse, The Netherlands: Swets & Zeitlinger.

Gee, J. P. (1996). *Social linguistics and literacies: Ideology in discourses.* London: Taylor & Francis.

Gonzalez-Lloret, M. (2003). Designing task-based CALL to promote interaction: En busca de esmeraldas. *Linguistics and Education, 7*(1), 86–104.

Goodwin-Jones, B. (2000). Emerging technologies: Literacies and technology tools/trends. *Language Learning and Technology*, *4*(2), 11–18.

Hargittai, E. (2002). *Second-level digital divide: Differences in people's online skills.* Retrieved July 9, 2002, from http://firstmonday.org/issues/issue7_4/hargittai

Healey, D. (1999). Theory and research: Autonomy and language learning. In J. Egbert & E. Hanson-Smith (Eds.), *CALL environments: Research, practice, and critical issues* (pp. 116–136). Alexandria, VA: TESOL.

Jones, J. (2001). *CALL and the teacher's role in promoting learner autonomy. CALL-EJ Online 3*(1). *Retrieved October 7,* 2004, from http://www.clec.ritsumei.ac.jp/english/callejonline/6–1/jones.html

Koutsogiannis, D., & Mitsikopoulou, B. (2004). *The Internet as glocal discourse environment.* Retrieved September 30, 2004, from http://llt.msu.edu/vol8num3/koutsogiannis/default.html

Kress, G. (1997). Visual and verbal modes of representation in electronically mediated communication: The potentials of new forms of text. In I. Snyder (Ed.), *Page to screen: Taking literacy into the electronic era* (pp. 53–79). Sydney: Allen and Unwin.

Lankshear, C., Snyder, I., & Green, B. (2000). *Teachers and technology literacy: Managing literacy, technology and learning in schools.* Sydney: Allen and Unwin.

Lever, T. (2004). AMEP students online: The view from morning self-access. *Prospect*, *19*(2), 39–55.

Levy, M., & Debski, R. (1999). Introduction. In R. Debski & M. Levy (Eds.), *World CALL: Global perspectives on computer-assisted language learning* (pp. 7–10). Lisse, The Netherlands: Swets & Zettlinger.

McPherson, P., & Murray, D. E. (2003). *Communicating on the Net.* Sydney, Australia: NCELTR.

Murray, D. E. (1988). The context of oral and written language. *Language in Society*, *17*, 351–373.

Murray, D. E. (1999). Access to information technology: Considerations for language educators. *Prospect*, *14*(3), 4–12.

Murray, D. E. (2003). Materials for new technologies: learning from research and practice. In W. A. Renandya (Ed.), *Methodology and materials design in language teaching: Current perspectives and practices and their implications* (pp. 30–43). Singapore: SEAMEO Regional Language Centre.

Murray, D. E. (2004). New frontiers in technology and teaching. In C. Davison (Ed.), *Information technology and innovation in language education* (pp. 25–44). Hong Kong: University of Hong Kong Press.

Murray, D. E., & McPherson, P. (2002). *Using Planet English with AMEP learners.* Sydney, Australia: NCELTR.

Murray, D. E., & McPherson, P. (2004a). *Using the Web to support language learning.* Sydney, Australia: NCELTR.

Pica, T. (1994). Research on negotiation: What does it reveal about second-language learning conditions, processes, and outcomes? *Language Learning, 44,* 493–527.

Rogers, E. M. (1995). *Diffusion of innovations.* New York: The Free Press.

Savignon, S. J., & Roithmeier, W. (2004). Computer-mediated communication: Texts and contexts. *CALICO Journal, 21*(2), 265–289.

Schwienhorst, K. (2003). Learner autonomy and tandem learning: Putting principles into practice in synchronous and asynchronous telecommunications environments. *Computer Assisted Language Learning, 16*(5), 427–443.

Schwienhorst, K. (2004). Native-speaker/non-native-speaker discourse in the MOO: Topic negotiation and initiation in a synchronous text-based environment. *Computer Assisted Language Learning, 17*(1), 35–50.

Sengupta, S. (2001). Exchanging ideas with peers in network-based classrooms: An aid or a pain? *Language, Learning and Technology, 5*(1), 103–134.

Shield, L., Weininger, M. J., & Davies, L. B. (1999). A task-based approach to using MOO for collaborative language learning. In K. Cameron (Ed.), *CALL and the learning community* (pp. 391–401). Exeter: Elm Bank Publications.

Smith, B. (2003). Computer-mediated negotiated interaction: An expanded model. *The Modern Language Journal, 87*(1), 38–57.

Snyder, I. (1999). Digital literacies: Renegotiating the visual and the verbal in communication. *Prospect, 14*(3), 13–23.

Snyder, I. (2002). *Silicon literacies.* London: Routledge.

Sorapure, M., Inglesby, P., & Yatchisin, G. (1998). Web literacy: Challenges and opportunities for research in a new medium. *Computers and Composition, 15,* 409–424.

Sotillo, S. (2000). Discourse functions and syntactic complexity in synchronous and asynchronous communication. *Language Learning and Technology, 4*(1), 82–119.

Stockwell, G. (2004). Communication breakdown in asynchronous computer-mediated communication (CMC). *Australian Language and Literacy Matters, 1*(3), 7–10, 31.

Street, B. (1995). *Social literacies: Critical approaches to literacy in development, ethnography and education.* London: Longman.

Sutherland-Smith, W. (2002). Web-text: Perceptions of digital reading skills in the ESL classroom. *Prospect, 17*(1), 55–70.

Thorne, S. L. (2003a). Artifacts and cultures-in-use in intercultural communication. *Language Learning and Technology, 7*(2), 38–67.

Thorne, S. L. (2003b, April 21). *The Internet as artifact: Immediacy, evolution, and educational contingencies, or "The wrong tool for the right job?"* Paper presented at the American

Educational Research Association Annual Meeting, Chicago.

Thurstun, J. (2004). Teaching and learning the reading of homepages. *Prospect, 19*(2), 56–71.

Toyoda, E. (2001). *Exercise of learner autonomy in project-oriented CALL.* Retrieved October 8, 2004, from http://www.clec.ritsumei.ac.jp/ english/callejonline/5–2/contents2–2.html

Toyoda, E., & Harrison, R. (2002). Categorization of text chat communication between learners and native speakers of Japanese. *Language Learning and Technology, 6*(1), 82–99.

Tudini, V. (2003). Using native speakers in chat. *Language Learning and Technology, 7*(3), 141–159.

Turkle, S. (1995). *Life on the screen: Identity in the age of the Internet.* New York: Simon & Shuster.

Walz, J. (2001). Reading hypertext: Lower level processes. *Canadian Modern Language Review, 57*(3), 475–494.

Wang, Y. (2004). Supporting synchronous distance learning with desktop videoconferencing. *Language Learning and Technology, 8*(3) 90–121.

Warschauer, M. (1999). *Electronic literacies: Language, culture and power in online education.* Mahwah, NJ: Erlbaum.

Warschauer, M. (2000). Language, identity, and the Internet. In B. Kolko, L. Nakamura, & G. Rodman (Eds.), *Race in cyberspace* (pp. 151–170). New York: Routledge.

Warschauer, M. (2001). The death of cyberspace and the rebirth of CALL. In P. Brett (Ed.), *CALL in the 21st century* (CD-ROM). Whitstable, Kent: IATEFL.

Warschauer, M., El Said, G. R., & Zohry, A. (2002). *Language choice online: Globalization and identity in Egypt.* Retrieved October 10, 2004, from http://www.ascusc.org/jcmc/vol7/issue4/warschauer.html

Warschauer, M., & Kern, R. (2000). *Network-based language teaching: Concepts and practice.* Cambridge: Cambridge University Press.

Wood, A. F., & Smith, M. J. (2001). *Online communication: Technology, identity and culture.* Mahwah, NJ: Erlbaum.

Zarcadoolas, C., Blanco, M., Boyer, J. F., & Pleasant, A. (2002). Unweaving the Web: An exploratory study of low-literate adults' navigation skills on the World Wide Web. *Journal of Health Communication, 7*, 309–324.

RESEARCH IN LANGUAGE ASSESSMENT

11. TRENDS IN ASSESSMENT SCALES AND CRITERION-REFERENCED LANGUAGE ASSESSMENT

Thom Hudson

Two current developments reflecting a common concern in second/foreign language assessment are the development of: (1) scales for describing language proficiency/ability/performance; and (2) criterion-referenced performance assessments. Both developments are motivated by a perceived need to achieve communicatively transparent test results anchored in observable behaviors. Each of these developments in one way or another is an attempt to recognize the complexity of language in use, the complexity of assessing language ability, and the difficulty in interpreting potential interactions of scale task, trait, text, and ability. They reflect a current appetite for language assessment anchored in the world of functions and events, but also must address how the worlds of functions and events contain non skill-specific and discretely hierarchical variability. As examples of current tests that attempt to use performance criteria, the chapter reviews the Canadian Language Benchmark, the Common European Framework, and the Assessment of Language Performance projects.

Two complementary developments in second and foreign language testing relate to issues surrounding characteristics of proficiency or ability scales and how these scales are conceptualized in criterion-referenced performance assessment. These developments have been motivated by a perceived need to produce test results that are more transparent than has traditionally been the case. They are alternative views to those reflected by traditional testing enterprises that provide a single numerical score with an associated indication of the percentile position of the examinee's standing relative to other examinees who took the test. In many ways, each of these developments attempts to address the complexity of language in the assessment of language use. They reflect a current appetite for language assessment anchored in the world of functions and events. These developments interact to promote language assessment that recognizes the need to expand beyond a tradition that has focused on language primarily as a decontextualized cognitive skill or ability. Language takes place in a social context as a social act, and this frequently needs to be recognized in language assessment. This chapter examines three language testing projects that have attempted to reflect these concerns: the Canadian Language Benchmarks project (Pawlikowska-Smith, 2000, 2002); the Common European Framework (Council of Europe, 2001; North, 2000); and the Assessment of Language Performance project (Norris, Brown, Hudson & Yoshioka, 1998; Brown, Hudson, Norris, & Bonk, 2002).

The focus here is on criterion-referenced testing projects that employ behaviorally oriented scales. As such, the three projects discussed here are not meant to provide a representative sample of all criterion-referenced testing endeavors currently being undertaken. There are many current test projects that are criterion-referenced in their construction process; indeed, *Education Week* (2002) indicates that all but three states in the United States use criterion-referenced tests in their English/language arts assessments. However, their reporting scales often tend to provide more general proficiency or skill descriptors than contextualized performance indicators. Hence, they are not directly addressed here. Their absence should not be taken as an indication that there are not a large number of other criterion-referenced testing projects in the United States or elsewhere.

It must be admitted openly that here are criticisms of, and drawbacks with, both performance assessment and many currently available language ability scales. There are differing views as to the utility and effectiveness of anchoring scale scores directly to performance tasks. However, there are areas of language use where assessment focuses on tasks that cannot be deconstructed into primary traits or skills and still capture the richness of the language performance. For example, tasks such as composing a synthesis from sources or writing a summary of a text inherently involve both reading and writing (Carson, 1993). Rating a synthesis such that the focus is solely on evaluating the characteristics of the composition itself ignores much that is of interest in the task. It may be the case that we need now to explore ways to report language as more complex literacy acts rather than simply reducing performance to one of the traditional four language skills. An analogy for the results of such reduction can be seen in how weather forecasters report the heat index along with measured temperature. If we say that it is 85 degrees because that is what the thermometer reads, when in fact there is 80% humidity with no breeze and the resulting heat index means that it feels like 92 degrees, then by only reporting 85 degrees we have not accounted for the actual effect of the weather on those who are living in it. Similarly, certain performances in Olympic sports such as diving and gymnastics are accorded a "degree of difficulty" rating considered inherent to the particular type of performance. Not all dive routines are considered to be about just whether the athlete moves from the diving board into the water. John Tukey notes that the most important maxim for data analysis to heed is: "Far better an approximate answer to the *right* question, which is often vague, than an *exact* answer to the wrong question, which can always be made precise" (1962, pp. 13–14). There may be times when it will be most productive to look only at what the thermometer reads, while at other times it is most informative to look at the temperature in context and evaluate it as such.

Criterion-referenced tests are designed to assess the learners' knowledge of a well-defined domain of knowledge. As noted in the previous introduction to performance testing concerns, specifying that domain and operationalizing it are often difficult endeavors. How to approach such direct measures of performance is one current focus of criterion-referenced language testing. The general notion of criterion-referenced educational testing is usually traced back to Glaser and Klaus (1962) or to Glaser (1963). Although this is relatively recent given the long history of educational and psychological measurement, criterion-referenced testing has emerged as an important tool in educational testing circles over the past few decades. Although only about 40 years old in educational measurement, the central tenets of criterion-referenced testing have been around through history and pervade the ways humans deal with the world (Brown & Hudson, 2002). Conway Twitty, an American country and western singer, sings, "Don't call him a cowboy till you've seen him ride." The basic principles of directly referencing ability to a particular domain of behavior run deep in human interactions, and this anchoring of test results to a domain is the essence of criterion-referenced testing. How to put this criterion referencing in place relates directly to the ability scales that report score results.

Scales

Scales are implicit in measurement, and are central to the validity of test score interpretation (Alderson, 1991). There are *nominal* scales, such as teacher, student, husband, wife; *ordinal* scales, such as first, second, or third; and *interval* scales, such as test scores of 22 points, 75 points, and so on. There have also been scales that are not so clearly interpreted, such as freshman, sophomore, junior, where the scale is sometimes treated as nominal, sometimes ordinal, or sometimes interval in nature. Scales commonly include *size, amount, frequency, intensity, importance,* or *rank* related to the depth or breadth of a demonstrated ability. The two terms, scales and rubrics, are often used in interchangeably. Rubrics are defined in the *Standards for Educational and Psychological Measurement* as: The established criteria, including rules, principles, and illustrations, used in scoring responses to individual items and clusters of items (AERA/APA/ NCME, 1999, p. 182).

Scales are sometimes used to indicate the numerical characteristics of the measurement. Generally, a rubric may be seen as a set of rules used in scoring performance assessment items, and is generally viewed as most useful for the assessment of tasks requiring responses that are other than selected response tasks. However, scales are frequently used to encompass the range of complex tasks along with the associated numerical scores. The terms scales and rubrics are used interchangeably here because of the way the terms are used in the literature, where sometimes there is a clear distinction and at others the two terms are conflated.

Typically, a rubric or scale
1. Is based on a continuum of performance quality, with a scale of varying potential score points to be assigned
2. Identifies the significant traits or dimensions to be examined and assessed (e.g., *reading, vocabulary, or listening comprehension*)
3. Provides key criteria of performance for each level of scoring, in "descriptors," which reflect whether and to what extent the key requirements of the performance have been demonstrated

There are several fundamental issues with scales in general that arise as we examine different scales and their contexts. First, there is a basic question of what the underlying nature of the scale is considered to be. Is the scale being used to indicate progression along a trait continuum or the actual achievement of defined and meaningful steps? Second, what kinds of comparisons are to be made with the scale, norm-referenced types of comparisons or criterion-referenced type comparisons? Third, does the scale really represent a set of discrete criteria that are themselves then rated on a numerical scale, as with analytic scoring of compositions or other performances? Fourth, what do the endpoints of the scale represent? Fifth, was the scale developed and evaluated empirically? These are areas that will come up throughout the discussion of scales, and they do not always have clear and satisfactory answers.

Language scales and rubrics can be created for many different functions, from large-scale high stakes tests that function to make decisions regarding university admission or immigration status all the way to self-assessment for purely personal interest. It is well to keep the different functions of scales in mind. Alderson (1991) has indicated that scales have the three different functions of: (1) describing levels of performance; (2) providing guidance for assessors who are rating the performances; and, (3) for guiding test constructors with a set of specifications. Additionally, Mislevy, Steinberg, Breyer, Almond, and Johnson (2002a) point out that the complexity of the variables to be included in the scale depends upon the purposes to which the assessment will be put. They note that, "[a] single variable characterizing overall proficiency might suffice in an assessment meant to support only a summary pass-fail decision" whereas "a coached practice system that helps students develop the same proficiency would require a finer grained student model for monitoring how a student is doing on particular aspects of skill and knowledge for which we can provide feedback" (Mislevy, Steinberg, & Almond, 2002b, p. 367). So, some scales may simply function to provide univariate information while others are designed to communicate more richly contextualized description.

However, not all scales are equally helpful in describing language ability. There is a trade-off in terms of generalizability versus deeper description. This, in part, is because of the complexity of the construct. The attempt to develop a comprehensive scale for language ability that is succinct enough to be easily comprehensible yet is transparent and functional presents us with complications of some depth. Language is perhaps the most complex of human abilities, and consequently we can expect that its assessment will be equally complex. We are, after all, assessing an individual's performance interacting within a very social context.

As Brindley (1998) has pointed out, language scales of achievement or proficiency tend to fall into one of two types. The first type of rating scale is one that is defined independently of content and context. It is derived from a theoretical model of language, and attempts to define a decontextualized ability or proficiency. The following example after Wilds (1975), shows one example of a scale that does not explicitly indicate context, content, or performance conditions.[1] The scale does not anchor either end of the continuum for the different evaluation dimensions.

1. Accent   foreign   ___: ___: ___: ___: ___ native
2. Grammar inaccurate ___: ___: ___: ___: ___ accurate

The scale proposed by Bachman (1990) and Bachman and Palmer (1983, 1996) in Table 1 is also of this decontextualized scale type, but provides more explicit discussion of the intermediate stages between the two end points of 0 or 4. It matches performance against vocabulary and cohesion in pragmatic competence.

Table 1 Sample of Bachman and Palmer decontextualized scale (1983, 1996)

Rating	Pragmatic competence	
	Vocabulary	**Cohesion**
0	*Extremely limited vocabulary* (A few words and formulaic phrases. Not possible to discuss any topic, because of limited vocabulary)	*No cohesion* (Utterances completely disjointed, or discourse too short to judge.)
1	*Small vocabulary* (Difficulty in talking with examinee because of vocabulary limitations.)	*Very little cohesion* (Relationships between utterances not adequately marked; frequent confusing relationships among ideas.)
2	*Vocabulary of moderate size* (Frequently misses or searches for words.)	*Moderate cohesion* (Relationships between utterances generally marked; sometimes confusing relationships among ideas.)
3	*Large vocabulary* (Seldom misses or searches for words.)	*Good cohesion* (Relationships between utterances well-marked.)
4	*Extensive vocabulary* (Rarely, if ever, misses or searches for words. Almost always uses appropriate word.)	*Excellent cohesion* (Uses a variety of appropriate devices; hardly ever confusing relationships among ideas.)

Adapted from Bachman (1990)

Scales of this type are terse, efficient, and seemingly straightforward in their application. Their primary advantage is that they specify the language components that are of importance and provide specific reference to them. A potential disadvantage is that operationalizing terms like "small vocabulary" and "vocabulary of moderate size" clearly becomes normative in nature. Finally, scales of this type consciously exclude mention of context and content. The scale criteria are structured to represent broad learning targets rather than specific tasks.

This perspective follows from Bachman's long held position that in language assessment it is of paramount importance to "clearly distinguish the ability to be measured from the methods or procedures used to elicit evidence of this ability" (Bachman, 1988, p. 150). Such a scale attempts to provide a decontextualized indication of a person's language ability according to different trait competencies that are intended to represent the construct of language ability. Bachman further notes that the "interpretation of test scores is problematic, since traits are frequently difficult to distinguish from methods. This is particularly true with performance tests, such as oral interviews, in which the modality (productive) and channel (oral/aural) of the ability (speaking) match the modality and channel of the elicitation procedure, or test method, thereby making it difficult to clearly distinguish ability from test method" (p. 153). Bachman and Palmer indicate that the "construct definitions from which rating scales can be developed may be based on either a theoretical model of language ability... or on the content of a language learning syllabus. Both of these theoretical construct definitions refer only to areas of language ability, independent of any considerations of the characteristics of the specific testing situation and prompt with which they might be used." (1996, p. 213). More recently, however, Bachman has indicated that performance assessments need to be both construct-based and task-based (2002).

The second type of scale noted by Brindley (1998), the type of primary interest here, is behaviorally based and attempts to describe proficiency according to "real-world" performance in specific contexts. Borman (1986) indicated several different types of behavior-based rating scales. The first type represents the Behaviorally Anchored Rating Scales (BARS). These scales list descriptions of very specific behaviors, and examinees are rated as to whether they reflect these specific behaviors. This type of scale has the potential drawback that some of the description might fit the examinee whereas some components do not. For instance, the descriptor might say "Can carry out an effective fluent interview, departing spontaneously from prepared questions, following up and probing interesting replies." However, this description might be only partially true, in that the examinee might not decide to follow up and probe interesting replies. Thus, another type of scale Borman introduces is the Behavior Summary Scale (BSS). These scales anchor the performance to less specific behaviors that represent a more generalized level of ability by representing a wider range of behavior representative of several specific incidents considered to be at a common level. The third approach that Borman introduces is the Behavior Observations Scale (BOS). This approach takes a different strategy in that observable behavioral statements are presented, and the rater is asked to determine if this is true about the candidate on a scale of frequency, such as *almost never* to *almost always*. Regardless of the particular approach, each is an attempt to link performance to behaviors that represent important behavioral criterial factors of assessment.

The functionality and apparent transparency of behavioral performance scales is the reason that they have generally had the most influence, although this does not absolve them of their problems. The descriptions of the levels often specify the particular tasks associated with each of the levels in the scale. The examinee's performance on the tasks is taken as an indicator that can generalize to a universe of similar tasks. It is this interpretation that is so troubling to many critics of behavioral scales. There are basically two approaches to developing such scales. The first is to assert intuitive orders of language performance, whereas the second approach is to elicit task orders from experts, such as teachers, and then to test them to see which ones order in an empirical manner.

Three Criterion-Referenced Projects

Three current orientations to behavioral scales as represented in the Canadian Language Benchmarks (Pawlikowska-Smith (2000, 2002), the Council of Europe Common European Framework (Council of Europe, 2001; North, 2000), and the Assessment of Language Performance task-based assessment project (Brown et al., 2002; Norris et al., 1998), attempt to address descriptions of language ability in differing ways. All these scales are steeped in notions of communicative competence as it has emerged since Canale and Swain's (1980) seminal article in *Applied Linguistics*. They take into account notions of language competence, strategic competence, sociocultural competence, textual competence, and so on. Additionally, they do not assume that an idealized native speaker is the goal.[2]

The Canadian Language Benchmarks

The Canadian Language Benchmarks Assessment (CLBA; Norton & Stewart, 1999; Pawlikowska-Smith, 2002) represents an example of scales following an intuitive developmental approach. The CLBA is a task-based assessment for adult immigrants to Canada intended to help place adult language learners across Canada in instructional programs appropriate for their level of proficiency in English (Norton & Stewart, 1999). The benchmarks are based on a functional view of language, language use, and language proficiency, explicitly following this behavioral orientation. The developers note that "[s]uch a view relates language to the contexts in which it is used and the communicative functions it performs" (Pawlikowska-Smith, 2002, p. 6). Here, "communicative proficiency is not an abstract concept of absolute language ability. Rather, it depends on situations of language use" (p. 6). The CLBA instruments address several functions, and in this they may be too broadly conceived. These functions are: (1) a descriptive scale of communicative proficiency; (2) a set of descriptive standards; (3) statements of communicative competencies and performance tasks in which the learner demonstrates application of knowledge competence and skill; (4) a framework of reference for learning, teaching, programming and assessing adult English as a second language in Canada; and (5) a national standard for planning second language curricula for a variety of contexts and a common "yardstick" for assessing the outcomes (Pawlikowska-Smith, 2000, p. viii). As such, the benchmarks are intended to be one-size-fits all scales for multiple uses.

The competencies are "directly observable and measurable performance or measurable outcomes of instruction in a curriculum framework" (Pawlikowska-Smith, 2000, p. 25). The competencies and tasks are seen to be only samples indicative of the range of a person's language ability at a particular benchmark level. "Similar competencies require increasing complexity of performance across the three stages of proficiency because of the progressively demanding tasks, contexts and performance expectations" (p. 25). There are three general levels with four benchmark divisions within each of those levels (see Table 2). The structure of Table 2 indicates that there are benchmarks for each of the four skill competencies. One aspect that is somewhat confusing is that in the CLBA descriptors in Table 2, listening and speaking are listed together, but in actuality each does receive a separate benchmark score. The three general levels move from nondemanding contexts and simple texts, through moderately demanding and complex texts, to demanding contexts and complex texts.

Table 2 Organization of Canadian Language Benchmark components

Benchmark	Proficiency Level	Speaking and Listening Competencies	Reading Competencies	Writing Competencies
AN OVERVIEW				
STAGE I: BASIC PROFICIENCY				
1	Initial	Creating/interpreting oral discourse in routine non-demanding contexts of language use in: • Social interaction • Instructions • Suasion (getting things done) • Information	Interpreting simple texts: • Social interaction texts • Instructions • Business/service texts • Information texts	Creating simple texts: • Social interaction • Recording information • Business/service messages • Presenting information
2	Developing			
3	Adequate			
4	Fluent			
STAGE II: INTERMEDIATE PROFICIENCY				
5	Initial	Creating/interpreting oral discourse in moderately demanding contexts of language use in: • Social interaction • Instructions • Suasion (getting things done) • Information	Interpreting moderately complex texts: • Social interaction texts • Instructions • Business/service texts • Information texts	Creating moderately complex texts: • Social interaction • Recording information • Business/service messages Presenting information/ideas
6	Developing			
7	Adequate			
8	Fluent			
STAGE III: ADVANCED PROFICIENCY				
9	Initial	Creating/interpreting oral discourse in very demanding contexts of language use in: • Social interaction • Instructions • Suasion (getting things done) Information	Interpreting complex and very complex texts • Social interaction texts • Instructions • Business/service texts • Information texts	Creating complex and very complex texts: • Social interaction • Recording information • Business/service messages Presenting information/ideas
10	Developing			
11	Adequate			
12	Fluent			

Note how this approach to scale development explicitly incorporates performance conditions. For example, Table 3 shows the performance conditions associated with Benchmark 6. These explicitly situate the speech sample to be evaluated by noting such conditions as "Interactions are face to face or on the phone."

Table 3   Performance conditions from Canadian Language Benchmarks (adapted, Pawlikowska-Smith, 2002)

Speaking: Stage II Benchmark 6

Performance Conditions:
- Interaction is face to face, or on the phone, with familiar and unfamiliar individuals and small informal groups.
- Rate of speech is slow to normal.
- Context is familiar, or clear and predictable.
- Context is moderately demanding (e.g., real-world environment, limited support from speaker).
- Circumstances range from informal to more formal.
- Setting or content is familiar, clear and predictable.
- Topic is concrete and familiar.
- Presentation is informal or formal.
- Use of pictures or other visuals.
- Presentation is five to seven minutes long

Interactions one-on-one
- Interactions are face to face or on the phone.
- Interaction is formal or semiformal
- Learner can partially prepare the exchange.

Interactions in a group
- Interaction occurs in a familiar group of three to five people.
- Topic or issue is familiar, nonpersonal, concrete.
- Interaction is informal or semi-formal.

Also, see how the benchmarks progress as shown through the global performance descriptors in Table 4.

Table 4 An overview of Speaking Benchmarks-Global performance descriptors. First Benchmark for each stage, and final Benchmark example (Source: Pawlikowska-Smith, 2000)

B.1 Learner can speak very little, mostly responding to basic questions about personal information and immediate needs in familiar situations. Speaks in isolated words or strings of 2 to 3 words. Demonstrates almost no control of basic grammar structures and verb tenses. Demonstrates very limited vocabulary. No evidence of connected discourse. Makes long pauses, often repeats the other person's words. Depends on gestures in expressing meaning and may also switch to first language at times. Pronunciation difficulties may significantly impede communication. Needs considerable assistance.

Sample Tasks: Hello, how are you? My name is X. Please come in, wait. Please sit down. Excuse me, Bob. Help me please. Answer questions about basic personal information in short interviews with teachers, other learners, and counselors.

B.5 Learner can participate with some effort in routine social conversations and can talk about needs and familiar topics of personal relevance. Can use a variety of simple structures and some complex ones, with occasional reductions. Grammar and pronunciation errors are frequent and sometimes impede communications. Demonstrates a range of common everyday vocabulary and a limited number of idioms. May avoid topics with unfamiliar vocabulary. Demonstrates discourse that is connected (and, but, first, next, then, because) and reasonably fluent, but hesitations and pauses are frequent. Can use the phone to communicate simple personal information; communication without visual support is still very difficult.

Sample Tasks: Respond to small talk comments. Express and respond to compliments and congratulations. Extend an invitation for a coffee, dinner, party. Direct a person to a place with or without maps, diagrams, sketches. Request permission to leave work early or take a day off.

B.9 Learner can independently, through oral discourse, obtain, provide, and exchange key information for important tasks (work, academic, personal) and complex routine and a few nonroutine situations in some demanding contexts of language use. Can actively and effectively participate in 30-minute formal exchanges about complex, abstract, conceptual, and detailed information and ideas to analyse, to problem-solve, and to make decisions. Can make 15-to 30-minute prepared formal presentations. Can interact to coordinate tasks with others, to advise or persuade (e.g., to sell or recommend a product or service), to reassure others, and to deal with complaints in one-on-one situations Grammar, vocabulary, or pronunciation errors very rarely impede communication.

Prepared discourse is mostly accurate in form, but may often be rigid in its structure/ organization and delivery style.

> *Sample Tasks: Convey appropriately respect, friendliness, distance and indifference in a variety of conversations in a variety of contexts. Give complex instructions on familiar first aid and emergency procedures in the work place. Discuss concerns about your child's progress in school with the child's teacher and school principle.*

B.12: Learner can create and co-create oral discourse, formal and informal, general or technical, in own field of study or work, in a broad range of complex situations . . . Discourse is fluent and "natural" (native-like in phrasing). Language is complex . . .

The tasks associated with each of these levels are then assessed against a checklist for Effectiveness, Organization, Appropriateness, Grammar, Vocabulary, Legibility /Mechanics, Cohesion, and Relevance. Thus, a profile of scales can be presented as an alternative to the type of scale intended to present only a single numeric score. These CLBA scales are broad and do not use a native speaker as the norm, although they do use such terms as "native-like." Further, they have not yet been empirically validated. However, also note that in this approach, the scales indicate at times what the learner cannot do. For example, B1 says "No evidence of connected discourse" or "Almost no control of basic grammar structures." This differs from the approach taken in the next scale, the Common European Framework.

Common European Framework

Scales such as the *Common European Framework of Reference for Languages* (CEF) developed by the Council of Europe, and the related scales of the Association of Language Testers in Europe, and the Dialang project, provide a framework that allows for more restricted descriptions of language where only partial language knowledge is required (Council of Europe, 2001; North, 2000). This view of scales provides a "can do" approach that recognizes lower levels in the scale as having a place of functional importance. It is the Council of Europe's position that giving formal recognition to these partial and functional abilities will promote plurilingualism through the learning of a wider variety of European languages (p. 1–2). In the CEF, the "ideal native speaker" is not the ultimate model. This is reflected in the form and scope of the scales as shown in Table 5. There are six scales divided into three larger bands. To the degree that they have the three overall levels divided into sublevels, they are similar to the Canadian benchmarks. However, these descriptors do not have negative directionality as with the other scales. That is, there are no statements of the form "has a speaking vocabulary sufficient to respond simply with some circumlocutions; accent, although often quite faulty, is intelligible," or "no evidence of connected discourse."

Table 5 Common European Framework—global scale

Proficient	C2	Can understand with ease virtually everything heard or read. Can summarize information from different spoken and written sources, reconstructing arguments and accounts in a coherent presentation. Can express him/herself spontaneously, very fluently and precisely, differentiating finer shades of meaning even in more complex situations.
User	C1	Can understand a wide range of demanding, longer texts, and recognize implicit meaning. Can express him/herself fluently and spontaneously without much obvious searching for expressions. Can use language flexibly and effectively for social, academic, and professional purposes. Can produce clear, well-structured, detailed text on complex subjects, showing controlled use of organizational patterns, connectors, and cohesive devices.
Independent	B2	Can understand the main ideas of complex text on both concrete and abstract topics, including technical discussions in his/her field of specialization. Can interact with a degree of fluency and spontaneity that makes regular interaction with native speakers quite possible without strain for either party. Can produce clear, detailed text on a wide range of subjects and explain a viewpoint on a topical issue giving the advantages and disadvantages of various options.
User	B1	Can understand the main points of clear standard input on familiar matters regularly encountered in work, school, leisure, etc. Can deal with most situations likely to arise whilst travelling in an area where the language is spoken. Can produce simple connected text on topics which are familiar or of personal interest. Can describe experiences and events, dreams, hopes, and ambitions and briefly give reasons and explanations for opinions and plans.

Basic	A2	Can understand sentences and frequently used expressions related to areas of most immediate relevance (e.g., very basic personal and family information, shopping, local geography, employment). Can communicate in simple and routine tasks requiring a simple and direct exchange of information on familiar and routine matters. Can describe in simple terms aspects of his/her background, immediate environment and matters in areas of immediate need.
User	A1	Can understand and use familiar everyday expressions and very basic phrases aimed at the satisfaction of needs of a concrete type. Can introduce him/herself and others and can ask and answer questions about personal details such as where he/she lives, people he/she knows and things he/she has. Can interact in a simple way provided the other person talks slowly and clearly and is prepared to help.

Source: Council of Europe (http://culture2.coe.int/portfolio//documents/0521803136txt.pdf)

The CEF aims to provide a comprehensive, transparent, and coherent framework of reference for language learning, teaching, and assessment. It is designed to be useable across the many different languages of Europe. The purpose of the CEF is to: (1) promote and facilitate cooperation among educational institutions in different countries; (2) provide a basis for mutual recognition of language specifications; and, (3) assist learners, teachers, course designers, examining bodies, and educational administrators to situate and coordinate their efforts.

In constructing these scales, a comprehensive survey of over 30 existing language scales was carried out. The contents of each of the reviewed scales were broken up into sentences. Each sentence in these scales was analyzed to determine what category it seemed to be describing. In looking at the various scales, six levels emerged and were adopted. The over 2,000 potential descriptors that emerged were converted into statements that could be answered *yes* or *no*. Duplicated descriptors from across the scales were eliminated. In a series of workshops, teachers evaluated the descriptors and indicated which were desirable and which were not.

Finally, the descriptors were evaluated against examinee videotaped performances. Teachers observed the tapes and scored a form of the observation questionnaire (North, 2000). This process yielded scores for each of the descriptors in terms of the examinee's language ability level. Items that did not scale or that did not fit the model were eliminated. The descriptors were then calibrated using Multifaceted Rasch (MR) model analysis (Linacre, 1992). From this analysis, the scale level descriptors were created. That is, the sentences in each level of the scale were ordered hierarchically. Thus, here is an empirically evaluated scale of language ability. This is a primary difference from the CLBA, which is not empirically based. Some of the descriptors can be seen in Table 6. Note again, that the statements are all "can do" statements designed to indicate the positive aspects of the learner's language. This places a focus on the functional abilities that the examinee has as opposed to focusing on the examinee's linguistic shortcomings.

Table 6 Example descriptors for the CEF (Adapted from North, 2000)

C1:
Can communicate spontaneously, often showing remarkable fluency and ease of expression in even longer complex stretches of speech.
Can relate own contribution skillfully to those of other speakers.
Can use circumlocution and paraphrase to cover gaps in vocabulary and structure.
Can carry out an effective fluent interview, departing spontaneously from prepared questions, following up and probing interesting replies.
Can follow the essentials of lectures, talks, and reports and other forms of academic/professional presentation that are propositionally and linguistically complex.
Can develop an argument systematically with appropriate highlighting of significant points, and relevant supporting detail.

A2:
Can write simple notes to friends.
Can ask and answer questions about personal details, such as here they live, people they know, and things they have.
Can reply in an interview to simple direct questions spoken very slowly and clearly in direct nonidiomatic speech about personal details.
Can indicate time by such phrases as next week, last Friday, in November, three o'clock.

> Can understand instructions addressed carefully and slowly to him/her and follow short, simple directions.

However, as a result of the MR analysis, the Council of Europe test developers were unable to include certain aspects of language use, areas such as literary appreciation and several pragmatic and strategic aspects of language. These areas appeared to represent different factors or aspects of language use than language proficiency. Consequently, there are questions about the comprehensiveness of the scale as a full description of language user abilities. A second potential problem with interpreting the initial CEF is that whereas the descriptors were empirically scaled based on performance ratings, the particular descriptors were not subsequently cast as actual test prompts and then calibrated again to determine if they still scale hierarchically.

Assessment of Language Performance

Central to performance assessment throughout the CLBA and CEF scalar models is the concept of the language task. *Real-world* tasks play a central role in the design of various types of performance assessments. The Assessment of Language Performance (ALP) project at the University of Hawai'i focused on how real-world tasks can function to reveal an examinee's language ability in use for pedagogical goals (Brown, Hudson, Norris, & Bonk, 2002). The project recognized that ultimately task accomplishment is a focus for evaluating much of human performance. It follows that L2 general performance assessment and task-based approaches to language assessment will likely share a great deal of theoretical and practical common ground. After all, task-based language teaching has received increasing recognition in the second language acquisition and second language pedagogy literature over the past two decades. By employing the communicative task as the basic unit of analysis for motivating syllabus design and L2 classroom activities, advocates claim that contemporary theories of language learning and acquisition that are supported by empirical findings can be effectively implemented. Here, task-based tests are held to be assessments that require students to engage in some sort of behavior which simulates, with as much fidelity as possible, goal-oriented target language use outside the language test situation. Performances on these tasks are then evaluated according to predetermined real-world criterion elements (i.e., task processes and outcomes) and criterion levels (i.e., authentic standards related to task success) (Brown & Hudson, 2002; Brown et al., 2002). In task-based performance assessment, the goals are generally to: (1) discuss a means whereby examinee performance on real-world language tasks can be validly assessed in terms of real-world criteria; (2) illustrate the potential for using task-based performance assessment to generalize about examinees' L2 abilities; and 3) facilitate a direct link between L2 classroom learning and real-world language use.

The ALP incorporated Skehan's condensation of prior definitions of task, in which he presents the following parameters as fundamental for a task activity:

a. Meaning is primary
b. Learners are not given other people's meanings to regurgitate
c. There is some sort of relationship to comparable real-world activities
d. Task completion has some priority
e. The assessment of the task is done in terms of outcome (Skehan, 1998, p. 147).

Additionally, the ALP addressed estimated task difficulty through adaptations to Skehan's *language code complexity*, *cognitive complexity*, and *communicative stress factors*. Tasks were selected and examined in relation to these variables to determine whether a task should be predicted to be more or less demanding for the examinees. For example, language code complexity in the following task could be adjusted as indicated.

> Task: *You would like to try out the fancy new Italian bistro "Il Gondoliero" tonight. Look up the phone number of the restaurant in the phone book and call to reserve a table for one at an appropriate time this evening.*

Low language code difficulty conditions could involve presenting the examinee with a simple telephone book layout with restaurants identified in the yellow pages format. The telephone message could involve standard formulaic expressions, simple single word responses to the telephone message. High difficulty code could involve a linguistically difficult message, low frequency vocabulary, or heavily accented speech with the telephone message delivered at a high rate of speech.

A number of test and item specifications, modeled after Popham (1981), specifying real-world task simulations and scales to assess examinee performance on each one, were developed to represent exemplars of the approach[3]. The examinees worked with a number of tasks which varied in complexity from fairly easy to very demanding. An example task in which an examinee must assist a friend who has injured his hand is shown in Table 7.

Table 7 Sample simulation task F05 (Source: Norris et al., 1998)

Situation: Your friend John has broken a bone in his hand. He cannot write (see photo of John). You told him that you would help him with writing. Now, he wants you to fill out a *change of address* form for him. Study the form provided. Be prepared to listen for the information requested on the form. John said he would leave the information on your answering machine.

Task: Play the message from John. Listen for the information from the *change of-address* form. Fill in the form for John. You may listen to the message as many times as you need to get the correct information.

Time: You have **10 minutes** to complete this task.

Product: Completed *change of address* form.

Such a task requires multiple modalities, both listening and writing. Table 8 presents a rating scale designed specifically for that task. Each task on the ALP had a separate task-dependent rating scale. Categories on these scales refer specifically to success of task requirements.

Additionally, a task-independent scale that reflected raters' evaluation to how the examinee performed across all of the tasks during the course of the test was developed. That is shown in Table 9. Both scales ranged from a designation of *inadequate* to *adept*. The task dependent scale related to categories of task success, an outcome that can only be realized if the examinee controls the language of both the input and the output.

Table 8 Example task-dependent rating scale for task F05

1	2	3	4	5
Inadequate		**Able**		**Adept**
Examinee incorrectly fills out change of address form such that any essential elements (listed in the *able* descriptor) are not processable by the post office (this might include illegibility, incorrect placement of information, absence of information, etc.	Examinee performance contains some elements from the *inadequate* descriptor and some elements from the *able* descriptor.	Examinee fills out change of address form according to information given by John, minimally including with correct spelling and correct locations (see form for details) —name —new address —old address —starting date —signature and printed name (either John Harris or examinee's own name).	Examinee performance contains some elements from the *able* descriptor and some elements from the *adept* descriptor	Examinee correctly fills out change of address form with ALL applicable information given by John on the answering machine message (see form for details).

Table 9 Example of task-independent rating scale across all task performances

1. *Inadequate:* A rating of insufficient indicates that the student seems generally incapable of coming to terms with the particular processing component (code, cognitive, communicative) on tasks like those found on the (test).

2. Student performance contains some elements from the *inadequate* descriptor and some elements from the *able* descriptor.

3. *Able*: A rating of able indicates that the student seems generally capable of coming to terms with the particular processing component on tasks like those found on the (test).

4. Student performance contains some elements from the *able* description and some elements from the *adept* descriptor.

5. *Adept*: A rating of adept indicates that the student seems quite capable of coming to terms with the particular processing component on tasks like those found on the (test); additionally, the student seems to have little or no difficulty in accomplishing such tasks in terms of the processing component.

In developing the task dependent scales, a criteria identification team was formed of three people familiar with the types of tasks on the test. These were a highly experienced ESL/EFL teacher, an advanced L2 user of English with much experience in accomplishing the types of tasks on the test, and a member of the university community with experience working with international students. Over a period of time, the members of the criteria team met and: (1) became familiar with the specific tasks; (2) produced drafts of what minimally sufficient, insufficient, and efficient task performances would look like; (3) worked with the drafts trying to rate actual performances; and, (4) jointly revised on agreed upon scoring rubrics for each item. Note that the task-independent descriptor does not actually mention the particular abilities that are to be sampled on the test. Rather, they refer the rater to the performance of the examinee across a range of tasks, and thus to a more global concept of language ability in context. Interestingly, correlations between the task-dependent scale and the task-independent scale turned out to be about .90. So, these two scales represent different approaches to language task performance scale development, although they do overlap a great deal in the actual rating variance they account for. Also, test results indicated high correlations between predicted difficulty and examinee performance.

Discussion and Conclusions

The topics addressed regarding performance and task based criterion-referenced scale development raise several issues. Three specific instances of scale development and performance assessment from different perspectives have been discussed. It is clear that there are very strong criticisms and questionings of such scales and task-based testing from a theoretical perspective that asks just what the goal of measurement is. In many ways, these reservations reflect the earlier mention of Bachman's criticism of behavioral scales. The association of language ability with authenticity of language use and setting raises real issues regarding the relationship of competence and performance, given that competence can only be inferred via some sample of performance (Shohamy, 1995). Further, a concern has grown about the extent to which successful task performance inherently involves nonlanguage abilities (Bachman, 1990; McNamara, 1996).

As noted, the difficulties in proceeding with behavioral scale application to task-based assessment need to be acknowledged, and it is certainly not appropriate for all language assessment to be task-based. However, also as noted earlier, not all language use is meaningfully interpretable as representing one of the traditional language skills. Rather, complex performances in social contexts require that they be interpreted with fidelity to what those performances mean in that context. Language traits interact with context, and a great deal of research has shown that identified research variables often show unpredicted and seemingly inexplicable interactions. These interactions can cause mischief as we try to identify the precise construct that we are measuring. However, there are ways we can try to remedy this indeterminacy. Those interactions may be partially dealt with using the statistical machinery available to us now. Multifaceted Rasch analysis and G-theory show a great deal of promise in finding and accounting for the relative effects of contextual features that we identify. In fact, if contextual features do affect how the particular language ability construct is engaged, then we should be purposefully seeking those features. Additionally, newer and emerging approaches such as the "evidence-centered design" model proposed by Mislevy et al., (2002a) that is aimed to design complex tasks, evaluate students' performances, and draw valid conclusions from them may be of assistance in the future.

Much more research needs to be done in several areas:

1. What are the relationships between task-dependent scales and task independent scales?
2. How do task specifications, task content, and scoring criteria interact?
3. How are examinee performances affected by task difficulty, task complexity,

task conditions, task characteristics, examinee's perceptions of task and raters?
4. To what extent can multifaceted Rasch model, G-theory, and the "evidence-centered assessment design" approach assist in disentangling factors that affect performance?

Certainly, the literature points out numerous disadvantages and problems with performance assessment in general. It has been observed that performance tests: (a) are difficult to create, (b) typically require more time and resources to administer and score than do other test types, (c) are accompanied by a variety of logistical problems (e.g., transporting and storing materials and realia), (d) may cause formidable reliability problems (because of both test administration and scoring inconsistencies), (e) may only lead to very restricted kinds of test-based interpretations, and (f) often face increased test security risks (Khattri, Reeve, & Kane, 1998).

Such disadvantages or problems notwithstanding, performance assessment of some sort seems essential to meet the kinds of assessment demands that are increasingly associated with L2 education contexts. Despite the difficulties, performance assessment is directly concerned with construct validity in its approach to finding tasks that can be generalized to real world language tasks. In contrast to the disadvantages just presented, several specific advantages often associated with language performance tests are that they: (a) can be designed to simulate authentic language use with high fidelity, (b) may compensate for negative effects often associated with traditional standardized testing, and (c) may initiate positive washback effects on language pedagogy and curriculum design. Those tasks in an educational setting can be directly linked to the curricular objectives that are increasingly communicatively oriented (Khattri, et al., 1998).

This discussion has attempted to show some of the different concerns that are addressed with the development of language proficiency scales and criterion-referenced task-based assessment. It has indicated how behavioral scales are an attempt to be explicit about what language learners are capable of doing with the language that they have. Clearly there are potential problems with this sort of endeavor. Finding descriptors that do actually relate to particular levels along the scale is difficult. However, the CLBA, CEF, and the ALP approaches are examples of attempts to do just that.

The concerns faced by language testers are very well illustrated by Mislevy,

Steinberg, and Almond in relation to contemporary measurement in general:

> Standard procedures for designing and carrying out assessments have worked satisfactorily for the assessments we have all become familiar with over the past half century. Their limits are sorely tested today. The field faces demands for more complex inferences about students, concerning finer grained and interrelated aspects of knowledge and the more complicated conditions under which this knowledge is brought to bear. (2002a, p. 126)

The literature presents some evidence that these demands may be addressed through more attention to the nature of our measurement scales and criterion-referenced behavior and task selection, as well as with more attention to the growing technology that may provide measurement tools.

Notes

1. It should be noted, however, that this is simply a short-hand reporting and record keeping scale. The original Wilds scale does have a separate set of descriptive and somewhat contextualized scale descriptions.

2. This discussion does not treat the FSI/ACTFL/ILR language scales. Those scales have been discussed in depth elsewhere (ACTFL, 1989; Bachman, 1988; FSI, n.d.; Lantolf & Frawley, 1985; Lee & Musumeci, 1988; Park, 1999). Additionally, although these scales have been claimed to be criterion-referenced, they are more properly seen as proficiency-referenced scales with the task criteria selected to reflect proficiency levels in a norm-referenced manner.

3. Note that the tasks developed here were intended to display a test development approach and methodology. They were not developed from a specific target language use needs analysis. We do argue that in any programmatic application of the approach, a comprehensive needs analysis is essential to fit the assessment to the appropriate context.

ANNOTATED BIBLIOGRAPHY

Brindley, G. (1998). Describing language development? Rating scales and SLA. In L. F. Bachman & A. D. Cohen (Eds.). *Interfaces between second language* acquisition and language testing research (pp. 112–140). Cambridge: Cambridge University Press.

A chapter that clearly presents many of the issues in the development and interpretation of scales that describe language ability. It presents the underlying differences between decontextualized scales and behavioral scales that describe performance.

Brown, J. D., Hudson, T., Norris, J., & Bonk, W. J. (2002). *An investigation of second language task-based performance assessments.* Honolulu: University of Hawai'i Press.

This book presents the follow-up results of the project initially described in Norris, et al. (1998). It describes the extent to which the ALP tasks demonstrated hierarchical orders of difficulty that were predicted. It also presents reliability and validity results for the study.

Brown, J. D., & Hudson, T. (2002). *Criterion-referenced language testing.* Cambridge: Cambridge University Press.

This text presents a systematic approach to the construction and analysis of criterion-referenced language testing. It comprehensively relates language criterion-referenced testing to criterion-referenced testing in other educational areas, discussing where the two are complementary and where they have differences.

Council of Europe. (2001). *Common European Framework of reference for languages: Learning, teaching, assessment.* Cambridge: Cambridge University Press.

This text is the definitive description of the Common European Framework scales, the uses for the scales, and the political context in which they were developed. It discusses the full scope of the scale use, including the language portfolio framework that is an extension of the language testing component of the program. It discusses how the framework provides a common basis for the elaboration of language syllabuses, curriculum guidelines, examinations, textbooks, and so on. across Europe.

North, B. (2000). *The development of a common framework scale of language proficiency.* New York: Peter Lang.

This study presents the development of the Common European Framework. It presents the rationale of the project, the scale development process, the piloting of the scales, through to the final process of which language features were included and which were not. Anyone interested in the detailed methodology of the Framework will profit from reading this text.

Pawlikowska-Smith, G. (2000). Canadian language benchmarks. English as a second language—adults. Retrieved March, 2003 from the Centre for Canadian Language Benchmarks www.language.ca/bench.html.

Pawlikowska-Smith, G. (2002). Canadian language benchmarks 2000: Theoretical framework. Retrieved March, 2003 from the Centre for Canadian Language Benchmarks www.language.ca/pdfs/final_theoreticalframeworks.pdf.

These two works present the benchmarks themselves as well as a comprehensive theoretical framework and rationale for the Canadian Language Benchmark Assessment. The works show how the benchmarks describe a learner's communicative proficiency as the skills of speaking, listening, reading, and writing over three stages of progression in the specific competency areas of social interaction, giving and receiving instructions, suasion, and information. They note that the benchmarks are considered to be directly observable and measurable performance outcomes.

OTHER REFERENCES

American Council on the Teaching of Foreign Languages (ACTFL). (1989). The ACTFL provisional proficiency guidelines. In T.V. Higgs (Ed.), *Teaching for proficiency, the organizing principle* (pp. 219–226). Lincolnwood, IL: National Textbook Company.

Alderson, J. C. (1991). Bands and scores. In J. C. Alderson & B. North. *Language testing in the 1990s* (pp. 71–86). London: Macmillan.

American Educational Research Association (AERA), American Psychological Association (APA), *and National Council on Measurement in Education* (NCME). (1999). *Standards for educational and psychological testing.* Washington, DC: American Educational Research Association.

Bachman, L. F. (1988). Problems in examining the validity of the ACTFL Oral Proficiency Interview. *Studies in Second Language Acquisition, 10*, 149–164.

Bachman, L. F. (1990). *Fundamental considerations in language testing.* Oxford: Oxford University Press.

Bachman, L. F. (2002). Alternative interpretations of alternative assessments: Some validity issues in educational performance assessments. *Educational Measurement: Issues and Practice, 2,* 5–18.

Bachman, L. F., & Palmer, A. S. (1983). *Oral interview test of communicative proficiency in English.* Urbana, IL: Photo-offset.

Bachman, L. F., & Palmer, A. S. (1996). *Language testing in practice.* Oxford: Oxford University Press.

Borman, W. C. (1986). Behavior-based rating scales. In R. A. Berk (Ed.), *Performance assessment: Methods & applications* (pp. 100–120). Baltimore: The Johns Hopkins University Press.

Canale, M., & Swain, M. (1980). Theoretical bases of communicative approaches to second language teaching and testing. *Applied Linguistics, 1,* 1–47.

Carson, J. (1993). Reading for writing: Cognitive perspectives. In J. G. Carson & I. Leki (Eds.), *Reading in the composition classroom* (pp. 85–104). Boston: Heinle and Heinle.

Education Week. (2002, January 10). Editorial projects in education, 17. Retrieved Septemeber 3, 2004, from http://nces.ed.gov/programs/digest/d02/tables/ dt153.asp.

Foreign Service Institute (FSI). (n.d.) Absolute language proficiency ratings. In M. L. Adams & J. R. Frith (Eds.), *Testing kit: French and Spanish* (pp. 13–17). Washington, D.C.: Department of State.

Glaser, R. (1963). Instructional technology and the measurement of learning outcomes: Some questions. *American Psychologist, 18,* 519–521.

Glaser, R. & Klaus, D. J. (1962). Proficiency measurement: Assessing human performance. In R. M. Gagne (Ed.), *Psychological principles in systems development* (pp. 419–474). New York: Holt, Rinehart, & Winston.

Khattri, N., Reeve, A., & Kane, M. (1998). *Principles and practices of performance assessment.* Mahwah, NJ: Erlbaum.

Lantolf, J. P. & Frawley, W. (1985). Oral proficiency testing: A critical analysis. The *Modern Language Journal, 69,* 337–345.

Lee, J. F. L., & Musumeci, D. (1988). On hierarchies of reading skills and text types. *The Modern Language Journal, 72,* 173–187.

Linacre, J. M. (1992). *Many-faceted Rasch Measurement.* Chicago: Mesa Press.

McNamara, T. (1996). *Measuring second language performance.* New York: Longman.

Mislevy, R. J., Steinberg, L. S., Breyer, F. J., Almond, R. G., & Johnson, L. (2002b). Making sense of data from complex assessments. *Applied Measurement in Education. 15,* 363–389.

Mislevy, R. J., Steinberg, L. S., & Almond, R. G. (2002b). On the roles of task model variables in assessment design. In S. H. Irvine & P. C. Kyllonen (Eds.), *Item generation for test development*, (pp. 97–128). Mahwah, N.J.: Erlbaum.

Norris, J., Brown, J. D., Hudson, T., & Yoshioka, J. (1998). *Designing second language performance assessments*. Honolulu: University of Hawai'i Press.

Norton, B., & Stewart, G. (1999). Accountability in language assessment of adult immigrants in Canada. *Canadian Modern Language Review, 56* (2), 223–244.

Park, S. (1999). *Testing the EFL skills and text hierarchy of the ACTFL reading guidelines.* Unpublished masters thesis, Department of English as a Second Language, University of Hawai'i.

Popham, W. J. (1981). *Criterion-referenced measurement.* Englewood Cliffs, NJ: Prentice-Hall.

Shohamy, E. (1995). Performance assessment in language testing. *Annual Review of Applied Linguistics, 15*, 188–211.

Skehan, P. (1998). *A cognitive approach to language learning.* Oxford: Oxford University Press.

Tukey, J. W. (1962). The future of data analysis. *The Annals of Mathematical Statistics, 33*(1), 1–67.

Wilds, C. P. (1975). The oral interview test. In, B. Spolsky & R. Jones (Eds.) *Testing language proficiency* (pp. 29–44). Washington, DC Center for Applied Linguistics.

12. TRENDS IN COMPUTER-BASED SECOND LANGUAGE ASSESSMENT

Joan Jamieson

In the last 20 years, several authors have described the possible changes that computers may effect in language testing. Since *ARAL*'s last review of general language testing trends (Clapham, 2000), authors in the *Cambridge Language Assessment Series* have offered various visions of how computer technology could alter the testing of second language skills. This chapter reflects these perspectives as it charts the paths recently taken in the field. Initial steps were made in the conversion of existing item types and constructs already known from paper-and-pencil testing into formats suitable for computer delivery. This conversion was closely followed by the introduction of computer-adaptive tests, which aim to make more, and perhaps, better, use of computer capabilities to tailor tests more closely to individual abilities and interests. Movement toward greater use of computers in assessment has been coupled with an assumption that computer-based tests should be better than their traditional predecessors, and some related steps have been taken. Corpus linguistics has provided tools to create more authentic assessments; the quest for authenticity has also motivated inclusion of more complex tasks and constructs. Both these innovations have begun to be incorporated into computer-based language tests. Natural language processing has also provided some tools for computerized scoring of essays, particularly relevant in large-scale language testing programs. Although computer use has not revolutionized all aspects of language testing, recent efforts have produced some of the research, technological advances, and improved pedagogical understanding needed to support progress.

Since 2000, six new books describing the assessment of reading, listening, language for special purposes, speaking, vocabulary, and writing have been published in the *Cambridge Language Assessment Series* edited by J. Charles Alderson and Lyle Bachman (Alderson, 2000; Buck, 2001; Douglas, 2000; Loumi, 2004; Read, 2000; Weigle, 2002). In the last chapter of every book (except for *Assessing Speaking*), the authors addressed the potential and the challenges of using the computer for assessment, following in the footsteps of Canale (1986) by alerting us to limitations while charting directions for the future. Each author mentioned some of the efficiency arguments that have, for many years now, been suggested for computer-based assessment such as less time needed for testing, faster score reporting, and provision of more convenient times for test-takers to take the test. Authors also mentioned the arguments that have been put forward for computer-adaptive assessment, such as more precise information about each individual's level of ability, which is thought to result in more challenging and more motivating experiences for test takers than traditional pencil-and-paper tests (e.g., Chalhoub-Deville & Deville, 1999; Madsen, 1986). The authors cautioned us that computer-based assessment is expensive, and that there is a danger in letting advances in both technology and in statistical procedures in psychometrics lead us down misguided paths of development. Most importantly, though, these experts articulated their visions of how computers may redirect second language assessment by providing us means to enhance the authenticity of our tests and to clarify our understanding of language abilities. In this chapter, I survey the field of computerized second language assessment mainly in terms of English as a second language (ESL), reflecting the directions of these commentators, looking at where we are, and, like the others, trying to foresee what lies ahead. For current reviews of widely used ESL tests, see Stoynoff and Chapelle (2005).

First Steps: Using Traditional Item Types and Constructs in Computerized Formats

The ease with which multiple choice or fill-in-the-blank items testing vocabulary, grammar, and reading comprehension can be adapted to a computerized environment is evident in the number of language tests on the Web. Glenn Fulcher maintains a very useful web site with links, as well as brief reviews, to many second language tests. Dave's ESL Cafe has a Quiz Center that provides students with a number of short tests which are immediately scored; these quizzes illustrate typical "low-tech" online assessments in which a hodgepodge of topics are grouped together in one site where a learner can answer a few questions, click on a button, and receive a percentage correct score. Somewhat more sophisticated examples offer quick checks of a learner's English level. There are many examples currently on the web; for the purpose of illustration, only a few examples are included here. ForumEducation.net offers learners two multiple choice vocabulary tests to estimate word knowledge as an indication of English proficiency. Wordskills.com offers visitors to its site three levels of tests (with 25 items each) which are said to approximate (disclaimer provided) the Cambridge First Certificate, Certificate in Advanced English, and the Certificate of Proficiency in English; the site has other tests including assessment of negotiation skills and e-commerce. Also, Churchill House offers online tests for students to check their level to prepare for the most appropriate test in the University of Cambridge Local Examination Syndicate (UCLES) suite of exams. All of the items are in multiple choice format. Netlanguages.com offers learners a two-part test to determine their level and appropriate placement in online courses. Learners initially select what they think their level of English is. The first section then tests grammar by having the test taker drag and drop a word into a sentence; if the test-taker's score is low after the first 10 items, for example, a message indicates that another level may be more appropriate. The second section consists of choosing a few questions from a larger set and then writing two or three sentences in response to them and submitting the responses to get scored by a human rater. Many of these tests are aligned with online learning programs. At study.com learners are provided with EFI (English for Internet) placements tests in listening, speaking, and writing in addition to vocabulary, reading, and grammar in preparation for free, online instruction.

In 2001, Irene Thompson edited a special issue of *Language Learning & Technology*, which was devoted to the topic of the theory and practice of computer-based language testing (Thompson, 2001). Several of the columns and reviews pointed out web resources (Leloup & Ponterio, 2001) and tools for web test development (Godwin-Jones, 2001; Polio, 2001; Winke & MacGregor, 2001). In his article on web-based testing in the same issue, Roever (2001) stated that these types of tests are most suitable for low-stakes decisions when the tests are used for checks on learning, test preparation, or research in which learners have little or no reason to cheat, and in situations in which test takers can take the test whenever they want, in the privacy of their own homes, and at their own pace.

In some cases, rather than creating a new set of items, a paper-and-pencil version of a test has been directly converted to a computerized format, which may be on the web or not. As in the examples given previously, language ability is often characterized in terms of performance on subtests such as vocabulary, grammar, reading comprehension, and/or listening comprehension; in other words, constructs that have been used in earlier tests are adapted to a new medium. In the case of the Test of English Proficiency at Seoul National University, new technology was used to measure English skills with accessible administration and fast score reporting (Choi, Sung Kim, & Boo, 2003). In the case of the Test of English as a Foreign Language (TOEFL) computer-based test, this was done for a research project to investigate the potential threat to validity caused by lack of computer familiarity (Taylor, Kirsch, Jamieson, & Eignor, 1999; also see ETS, 2000). Differences that may affect performance because of the ways computer-based tests and paper-and-pencil tests present tasks to test-takers are discussed briefly by both Alderson (2000) and Douglas (2000). In her comparison of paper-and-pencil and computerized reading tests, Sawaki (2001) provides us with a thorough review of many factors that need to be considered when the mode of delivery is changed.

Second Steps: "Added Value" to Computerized Assessments

Computer-Adaptive Tests

Because the cost of developing computer-based tests is much higher than that of traditional paper-and-pencil tests, Buck (2001) wrote that "there need to be significant advantages to make that worthwhile" (p. 255). In many language testing programs, a "value-added" approach to computerization of the paper-and-pencil format was the introduction of computer-adaptive sections. An added benefit of a computer-adaptive test is that theoretically test-takers are given items that are well-suited to their abilities, thus making the test both more interesting and a more accurate measure.

As described in Wainer et al. (2000) and Eignor (1999), information such as the content and difficulty of an item needs to be determined before it can be administered in a computer-adaptive test. Item function is characterized by item parameters—item difficulty, item discrimination, and guessing—and the measurement model used to estimate these parameters is Item Response Theory (IRT). Some computer-adaptive tests use only the first parameter, item difficulty; other tests use all three parameters. To get stable item parameters, items are typically pretested on what is considered a representative sample of test takers. Pretesting is a necessary, but expensive, condition for a computer-adaptive test. For example, the ACT ESL test used over 2,000 test-takers to estimate its item parameters (ACT, Inc., 2000).

The basic idea of computer adaptive tests is that a test taker will respond to an item with known item parameters. That response will be automatically scored by the computer so that a type of profile of the test taker can be initiated. As the test taker proceeds, his or her "profile" is continually updated, based on the correctness of response to items that are being selected as representative of a certain range of parameters. The necessity of automatic scoring for subsequent item selection was a relatively easy condition to meet for language tests using the traditional constructs of vocabulary, grammar, reading comprehension, and listening comprehension that were originally presented in a paper-and-pencil format with multiple choice items.

There are currently a number of computer-adaptive second language tests that reflect this trend. Examples range from the English Comprehension Level Test administered at the Defense Language Institute, the ACT ESL Placement Test (COMPASS/ESL), the Business Language Testing Service (BULATS), and the Structure and Written Expression section and the Listening Section of the computer-based TOEFL; the reading section was not computer-adaptive so that test takers could skip items and return to them later (ETS, 2000). Readers interested in issues related to computer-adaptive testing of reading are directed to the edited volume by Chalhoub-Deville (1999).

Because computer-adaptive tests for the most part rely on item response theory, a necessary assumption is that items must be conditionally independent. When several items are based on the same passage, in a reading comprehension test, for example, this situation can be handled by treating all of the items in a set as one "large" item, which is polytomously scored. In other words, instead of having six reading comprehension items each scored 0–1, there would just be one item, scored 0–6. Work reported in the mid-1990s found that polytomous IRT models could be used to combine scores from traditional, dichotomously scored items (correct/incorrect or 1/0) with these polytomously scored items (Tang, 1996; Tang & Eignor, 1997). However, the assumption cannot be met when a reading passage is not only used for reading comprehension items, but also as the content for a writing item.

"Adaptive" Tests in Different Guises

The idea of adapting test delivery and content to more closely match the test-taker's interests and/or ability level has been appealing to language test developers, whose tests, for one reason or another, do not meet the stringent requirements of traditional computer-adaptive tests. Consequently, there are a number of computerized language tests currently available or in the research and development stages that make adaptations from a format in which all test takers are given the same items in the same order. Two techniques which allow for the tailoring of tests to the individual are self-assessment and short screening tests.

There are cases in which computer-adaptive tests are not currently possible, such as speaking tests in which oral discourse is scored by human raters. Here, the condition of automatic scoring one item, or task, to aid in the selection of subsequent items cannot be met. Still, test developers are interested in incorporating some flexibility, or "adaptivity," into the selection of tasks. The COPI (Computerized Oral Proficiency Interview) is the latest development in assessing speaking from the Center for Applied Linguistics, following the SOPI (Simulated Oral Proficiency Interview—tape recorded) and the OPI (oral proficiency interview—humans). In the original COPI project, existing material from SOPIs formed a test bank. Test takers were asked to assess their speaking level, ranging from intermediate to superior. Seven speaking tasks were then generated from the pool—four at the level of self-assessment and three at the next level above that (Kenyon, Malabonga, & Carpenter, 2001). Contrasting test-takers' attitudes between the SOPI and the COPI, Kenyon and Malabonga (2001) reported that test-takers felt that the COPI was less difficult than the SOPI and that "the adaptive nature of the COPI allowed the difficulty level of the assessment task to be matched more appropriately to the proficiency level of the examinee" (p. 60) although, as Norris (2001) pointed out, this claim needs further investigation. The

Center for Applied Linguistics web site indicates that efforts are underway to create operational versions of the COPI in Arabic and Spanish which should be available on CD-ROM in 2006.

In other cases, items can be automatically scored, but the prerequisite pilot testing of items needed to estimate item parameters is not feasible. Still, test developers are interested in "adapting" the selection of items for each test taker. Two techniques have been used recently. One technique has test takers answer survey questions to select content of interest. The other has test takers respond to items in a screening test to estimate their ability level so that subsequent test sections can be selected at an appropriate level of difficulty. *Longman English Assessment* (Jamieson & Chapelle, 2002; Chapelle, Jamieson, & Hegelheimer, 2003) illustrates both of these techniques. This low-stakes test was designed to provide English language learners with an interesting experience that would give them feedback about their level of proficiency and recommendations for improving their English. This test begins with a fifteen minute "interest and ability finder." First, test-takers answer survey questions about why they want to learn English; responses are used to select business or more general content. Second, all test-takers are then administered a set of vocabulary and grammar questions; responses are used to recommend a level (i.e., beginning, intermediate, advanced) for the subsequent sections of the test. Because of the inability to pretest items in order to determine their difficulty empirically, the test developers relied on theory to create items and sections at different ability levels. For example, the vocabulary items were based on word frequency counts, the grammar items on developmental sequences, the written structures on textbook analysis, and the reading and listening comprehension items on a set of processing conditions (Rupp, Garcia, & Jamieson, 2002). The text passages were analyzed using corpus linguistic techniques together with the judgments of experienced teachers.

A final example in this section is DIALANG, which incorporates both self-assessment and a screening test to create an "adaptive" test for individual language learners. Like *Longman English Assessment*, DIALANG is a low-stakes test with which individual language learners can find out about their ability levels in vocabulary, grammar, writing, reading, and listening. It is currently available in 14 languages: Danish, Dutch, English, Finnish, French, German, Greek, Icelandic, Irish, Italian, Norwegian, Portuguese, Spanish and Swedish. The theoretical foundation for DIALANG is the Common European Framework. Test takers first select the language and the skill in which they want to be tested. Then, DIALANG begins with a vocabulary test which is used for initial screening; this is followed by a self-assessment section. These are followed by a test in whatever language skill was chosen, which is modified for the test taker based on information from the screening test and self-assessment. A pilot version can be downloaded from the DIALANG website.

In this section, I have illustrated language tests that are different from traditional tests mainly because they are administered on computer rather then with paper-and-pencil or with an interviewer, and because many of them make use of computer technology to branch test takers to different subsets of items or tasks. These tests can be adaptive or linear, and they can be administered via the web, CD, or network. Each method of delivery offers potential benefits and problems, as summarized by Brown (2004). However, many of these tests do not provide us with an alternate construct of language ability. So, although the tests are innovative in terms of technology, they are not particularly innovative in their operationalization of communicative language ability.

Next Steps: Innovation in How Language is Perceived

As Douglas wrote, "language testing that is driven by technology, rather than technology being employed in the service of language testing, is likely to lead us down a road best not traveled" (2000, p. 275). Moving beyond technical innovation and into the realm of how we perceive and measure language ability illustrates progress in our ability to make use of computers. In this section, I highlight innovations involved with language tasks and score reporting.

Language tasks

Considering both the nature of the input and the nature of the expected response as elements in a task, we can find examples of computerized tests that are trying to more closely replicate the target language use domain (TLU; Bachman & Palmer, 1996), addressing the test quality of authenticity and also enriching our understanding of language use in different situations. Read (2000) discussed how a broader social view of vocabulary in testing would take into account the concept of register, addressing questions such as what sort of vocabulary particular tasks require. Douglas (2000) pointed to the potential role of corpus linguistics investigating TLU contexts to increase our understanding of how grammar, vocabulary, and rhetorical structure are used in different contexts.

Informed by research in corpus linguistics, the development of the new TOEFL provides us with an example of how ideas such as these have been put into practice. Biber and his colleagues (2002) created a corpus of spoken and written academic language that was subsequently analyzed for lexical and syntactic characteristics. This corpus then served as a type of baseline for language used in different registers and genres. Spoken texts, for example, included lectures with different amounts of interaction, service encounters, and classroom management. Listening passages were developed following real-life examples. Biber et al. (2004) created tools which allowed the features of the created passages to be compared to the features of the texts analyzed in the corpus. Instead of incorporating this interactionist construct perspective, a trait perspective was used by Lanfer and her colleagues (2004a, 2004b) in their innovative vocabulary test of size and four degrees of strength of knowledge; the test was piloted in a computer-adaptive format.

Another innovation of the new TOEFL is that it includes tasks that resemble those performed by students in North American colleges and universities (Rosenfeld, Leung, & Oltman, 2001). These "integrated skills" tasks require test takers to use the information provided in the reading and listening passages in essay and/or spoken responses. The same passages also serve as the input for reading and listening comprehension questions. This use of more authentic tasks provides evidence for the representation inference in the validity argument for the new TOEFL, and it has also forced language testers to grapple with the traditional, yet conflicting, inferences of performance on language tests between underlying ability and task completion (Chapelle, Enright, & Jamieson, forthcoming). Moreover, this decision to include integrated tasks resulted in the violation of the assumption of IRT that tasks on a single scale be conditionally independent, and without IRT, the necessary psychometric base for calibrating items for computer-adaptive delivery was lost. The current need for human raters of speaking and writing tasks also precluded the use of computer-adaptive delivery (Jamieson, Eignor, Grabe, & Kunnan, forthcoming). The decision to develop computerized tasks that better represent authentic language use rather than to be constrained in task development by relying on known technology and psychometrics marks a new direction in large scale, high-stakes testing.

Another task factor that has been discussed in the literature is response type; associated with this is factor is whether or not the response can be scored by a computer. Up to this point, most of the examples discussed so far use multiple choice responses, which may appear as familiar types where test takers click on a circle before one of four choices, or as more novel drag and drop item types. These items share the essential quality of having one correct answer and being dichotomously scored as either correct or incorrect. More innovative item types require the test taker to identify several important points from a reading or listening passage, or to select sentences from a pool to form a paragraph. These items are often scored polytomously—on a scale from 0 to 3, for example. However, to date the rationales for associating the partial scores for each item have more to do with controlling for guessing (Enright, Bridgeman, Eignor, Lee, & Powers, forthcoming) than they have to do with the construct definition, as Chapelle illustrated in an example of decisions for partial correction in a c-test (2001). This is because the computer programs used to analyze responses in most current operational language tests are not based on analysis of linguistic output, but rather on matching the pattern of the correct response to the response given by the test-taker.

A test which stands in sharp contrast to this situation is the Spoken English Test, formerly known as PhonePass. SET-10 is administered over a telephone; it uses a speech recognition computer program to analyze and to score the phonological representation of responses to each item. "The system generates scores based on the exact words used in the spoken responses, as well as the pace, fluency, and pronunciation of the words... Base measures are derived from the linguistic units... based on statistical models of native speakers" (See ordinate website listed at the end of this chapter; Ordinate, 1999).

Score Reports

The desire to communicate meaningful interpretations of test scores is not limited only to computer-based assessment. However, recent language assessments delivered with computers have incorporated some innovations in the types of information about test-takers given to test score users.

"The possibility of recording response latencies and time on test or task opens up a whole new world of exploration of rates of reading or word recognition" (Alderson, 2000, p. 351). Although I think that Alderson was addressing a fundamental change in construct definition, the closest example of a large scale, standardized test which makes use of test takers' response times is ACT's COMPASS/ESL. ACT began development of this test in 1993, in consultation with ESL professionals. Its purpose is mainly placement of students in community colleges in the United States. Having chosen to deliver the test in an adaptive format, "students can proceed at their own pace on the computer, yet have their assessment time monitored automatically, allowing institutions to use the amount of time the student spends taking the test as an additional factor in placement decisions" (ACT, Inc., 2000, p. 132).

Each of the three tests in the ACT battery (grammar/usage, reading, and listening) includes a five-level score scale. The levels are mapped to the tests' specifications and proficiency descriptors are provided for each level. These proficiency descriptors were created by not only examining what was measured internally on the test, but by also examining external sources such as learning outcomes tied to college-level ESL curricula and well known benchmarks such as the ACTFL Guidelines. An example from the listening scale follows:

> Proficiency Level 2 (67-81): Students at Level 2 typically have the ability to understand brief questions and answers relating to personal information, the immediate setting, or predictable aspects of everyday need. They understand short conversations supported by context but usually require careful or slowed speech, repetitions, or rephrasing. Their comprehension of main ideas and details is still incomplete. They can distinguish time forms, some question forms (Wh-, yes/no, tag questions), most common word-order patterns, and most simple contractions, but the students may have difficulty with tense shifts and more complex sentence structures. (ACT, 2000, p. 45)

Proficiency scaling approaches assume that the abilities used to explain test scores are defined by task characteristics, which are hypothesized to be responsible for task difficulty. IRT, used as the psychometric model in the COMPASS/ESL test, allows items and person ability to be placed on the same scale. Similar proficiency scales were considered for test score reporting in the new TOEFL (Jamieson, Jones, Kirsch, Mosenthal, & Taylor, 2000). However, because IRT was not going to be used, other types of performance descriptors, for example, teacher assessments of what a person at a certain score level could probably be expected to do, were considered to accompany score reports (Powers, Roever, Huff, & Trapani, 2003).

Another way to make score reports meaningful to the test taker is to provide information on how to improve one's language ability. This type of feedback is provided by both DIALANG and *Longman English Assessment*. In the latter, the computer program generates a list of study strategies based on test takers responses to where they are studying English (in an English-speaking country or not), together with their level scores.

Future Steps: Computer Scoring of Constructed Responses, New Item Types

The authors in the *Cambridge Language Assessment Series* look forward to corpus-based vocabulary lists (Read, 2000) and corpora of field specific discourse (Douglas, 2001), realistic simulations, perhaps through virtual reality (Buck, 2001), and the capture of every detail of a learner's progress through a test (Alderson, 2000). All of these are possible, of course, yet it is the scoring of writing by computer (Weigle, 2002) that I think is the most probable advancement in technology that will occur in large scale language assessment in the near future.

Three computer scoring systems are clearly described by Weigle: Latent Semantic Analysis, Project Essay Grade (Tru-Judge, Inc.), and E-rater (Educational Testing Service, ETS). Another automatic scoring system is the IntelliMetric Essay Scoring Engine (Vantage Learning). Intelligent Essay Assessor uses Latent Semantic Analysis (formerly owned by Knowledge Assessment Technologies, its acquisition by Pearson Education was announced on June 29, 2004). According to Weigle (2002), Latent Semantic Analysis has the practical disadvantage of not taking word order into account. As described by Chodorow and Burstein (2004, p. 1), each system trains on essays that have been read by human raters who have assigned a holistic score. From the training examples, the system learns which features are the best predictors of the essay score. "The differences among the systems lie in the particular features that they extract and in the ways in which they combine the features in generating a score" (Chodorow & Burstein, 2004, p. 1). E-rater's particular features are based on four kinds of analysis: syntactic, discourse, topical, and lexical. In version 2.0, because essay length was found to be "the single most important objectively calculated variable in predicting human holistic scores" essay length as measured by number of words was included in e-rater's updated feature set (Attali & Burstein, 2004, p. 4). Although Weigle stated that this trend is controversial among writing teachers, these automated systems have none the less reported high correlations with human raters (Burstein & Chodorow, 1999).

COMPASS/ESL offers a writing section called COMPASS e-Write that is scored using IntelliMetric. An overall score ranging in value from 2–8 is given to each essay, along with feedback on content, style, organization, focus, and mechanics. This technology is available on the web; the instructional part of the software is available at MyAccess! Although not clear from the COMPASS/ESL website, MyAccess! is available for ESL students, and has been developed to score essays written by nonnative speakers of English. E-rater has been used by ETS for the Graduate Management Admissions Test Analytic Writing Assessment since 1999. Criterion Online Essay Evaluation is the instructional software using e-rater from ETS (Burstein, Chodorow, & Leacock, 2003). ETS currently uses automated scoring of essays, e-rater, in the Next Generation TOEFL Practice Test, as well as ScoreItNow. Research is underway to evaluate the feasibility of using e-rater operationally as second rater for new TOEFL independent writing samples. At present there are no plans for automated scoring of speech for new TOEFL (personal communication, M. K. Enright, October 27, 2004).

As research progresses, it will be interesting to watch for advances in computer scoring of constructed, or free, responses. Another ETS program, C-rater, has been developed to measure a student's understanding of specific content without regard for writing skills (Leacock, 2004). Also, the *Spoken English Test* has included a free response section on its Set-10 Form for many years. Information from this section has not been included in score reports, but rather has been included to collect data for research on automated scoring of spoken free responses. It was announced on September 29, 2004, that the company that developed *PhonePass*, Ordinate, was acquired by the large testing company, Harcourt Assessment, Inc.

Finally, to return to the topic of task types on language assessments, nothing has yet been mentioned about the use of video. Certainly this is one area in test development that seems natural to include in the creation of authentic language input. Multimedia computer-assisted language learning software such as *Longman English Interactive* (Rost & Fuchs, 2003) includes video in its quizzes and tests, but most stand-alone computer-based language tests do not. Why? It is expensive to develop, it requires high-end technology to transmit, and it is unclear how it affects the construct. Douglas (2000) commented that language testers have so far not made much progress in adapting multimedia to the goals of measurement; he cautions us that, although it is tempting to make use of video to provide authentic content and contextualization cues, we need to understand and control for test method effects associated with these technological resources. With this caution in mind, it is still intriguing to imagine new types of tasks to broaden our perspective of what is possible for language tests. (A good place to begin is at DIALANG's web site; click on "New item types.")

Summary

As we read in Burstein, Frase, Ginther, and Grant (1996), the role of computers in assessment is broad because computers have a number of functions essential for an operational testing program such as the TOEFL, including item creation and presentation; response collection and scoring; statistical analysis; and storage, transmission, and retrieval of information. This review has not gone into depth on many of these issues, but has rather highlighted a few recent trends mainly surveying the literature in which authors predict that technology will play a role in language assessment in the future. We can also see that the future envisioned by many of these commentators is the distant future. While discussing the advancement of applied linguistics through assessment, Chapelle (2004) referred to "the tunnel of efficiency" and "the panorama of theory." Although we may be mesmerized by panoramic visions, a journey begins on a path where we place one foot in front of the other, making what appears at first to be modest progress.

Web sites (Addresses functional as of December 8, 2004)

BULATS (http://www.bulats.org)
Churchill House (http://www.churchillhouse.com/english/exams.html)
COMPASS/ESL (http://www.act.org/compass/ or http://www.act.org/esl)
COMPASS e-Write (http://www.act.org/e-write/index.html)
COPI (http://www.cal.org/projects/copi/)
Dave Sperling's ESL Cafe Quiz Center (http://www.pacificnet.net/~sperling/quiz/)
DIALANG (http://www.dialang.org/)
DIALANG's experimental items http://www.lancs.ac.uk/fss/projects/linguistics/experimental/new/start.htm)
Educational Testing Service, Criterion, e-rater, and c-rater (http://www.ets.org/research/erater.html)
Educational Testing Service, Next Generation TOEFL (http://www.ets.org/toefl/nextgen/)
Elite Skills Ltd. (http://wordskills.com/level)
English Comprehension Level Test (http://www.dlielc.org/testing/ecl_test.html)
Forum Education (http://www.forumeducation.net/servlet/pages/vil/mat/index.htm)
Glenn Fulcher's web site (http://www.dundee.ac.uk/languagestudies/ltest/ltr.html)
Intelligent Essay Assessor (http://www.knowledge-technologies.com/)
Language projects supported by European Union (http://europa.eu.int/comm/education/programmes/socrates/lingua/index_en.html)
MyAccess! (http://www.vantagelearning.com/product_pages/myaccess.html)
Net Languages (http://www.netlanguages.com/home/courses/level_test.htm)
Ordinate, *Spoken English Tests* (http://www.ordinate.com/content/prod/prod-level1.shtml)
StudyCom English For Internet (http://study.com/tests.html)
Vantage Laboratories (http://www.vantage.com/)

REFERENCES

ACT, Inc. (2000). *COMPASS/ESL reference manual.* Iowa City, Iowa: Author.
Alderson, J. C. (2000). *Assessing reading.* New York: Cambridge University Press.
Attali, Y., & Burstein, J. (2004). Automated essay scoring with E-rater V.2.0. Available on-line at http://www.ets.org/research/erater.html

Bachman, L., & Palmer, A. (1996). *Language testing in practice*. New York: Oxford University Press.

Biber, D., Conrad, S., Reppen, R., Byrd, P., & Helt, M. (2002). Speaking and writing in the university: A multidimensional comparison. *TESOL Quarterly*, *36*, 9–48.

Biber, D., Conrad, S., Reppen, R., Byrd, P., Helt, M., Clark, V., Cortez, V., Csomay, E., Urzua, A. (2004). *Representing language use in the university: Analysis of the TOEFL 2000 Spoken and Written Academic Language Corpus*. TOEFL Monograph MS-25. Princeton, NJ: Educational Testing Service.

Brown, J. D. (2004). For computerized language tests, potential benefits outweigh problems. *Essential Teacher*, *1*, 4, 37–40.

Buck, G. (2001). *Assessing listening*. New York: Cambridge University Press.

Burstein, J., & Chodorow, M. (1999, June). Automated essay scoring for nonnative English speakers. In *Proceedings of the ACL99 Workshop on Computer-Mediated Language Assessment and Evaluation of Natural Language Processing*. College Park, MD. Available online at http://www.ets.org/research/dload/acl99rev.pdf

Burstein, J., Chodorow, M., & Leacock, C. (2003). Criterion online essay evaluation: An application for automated evaluation of student essays. Proceedings of the Fifteenth Annual Conference on Innovative Applications of Artificial Intelligence, Acapulco, Mexico. Available online at: http://www.ets.org/research/dload/iaai03bursteinj.pdf

Burstein, J., Frase, L., Ginther, A., & Grant, L. (1996). Technologies for language assessment. *Annual Review of Applied Linguistics*, *16*, 240–260.

Canale, M. (1986). The promise and threat of computerized adaptive assessment of reading comprehension. In C. Stansfield (Ed.), *Technology and language testing* (pp. 30–45). Washington, DC: TESOL Publications.

Chalhoub-Deville, M. (Ed.) (1999). *Issues in computer adaptive testing of reading proficiency*. Studies in Language Testing, 10. New York: Cambridge University Press.

Chalhoub-Deville, M., & Deville, C. (1999). Computer adaptive testing in second language contexts. *Annual Review of Applied Linguistics*, *19*, 273–299.

Chapelle, C. A. (2004). *English language learning and technology*. Philadelphia: John Benjamins.

Chapelle, C. A. (2001). *Computer applications in second language acquisition*. New York: Cambridge University Press.

Chapelle, C. A., Enright, M. K., & Jamieson, J. (forthcoming). Challenges in developing a test of academic English. In C. A. Chapelle, M. K. Enright, & J. Jamieson (Eds.), *Building a validity argument for TOEFL*. Mahwah, NJ: Erlbaum.

Chapelle, C. A., Jamieson, J., & Hegelheimer, V. (2003). Validation of a web-based ESL test. *Language Testing*, *20*, 409–439.

Chodorow, M., & Burstein, J. (2004). *Beyond essay length: Evaluating e-rater's performance on TOEFL essays.* TOEFL Research Reports, Report 73. Princeton, NJ: Educational Testing Service.

Choi, I-C., Sung Kim, K., & Boo, J. (2003). Comparability of a paper-based language test and a computer-based language test. *Language Testing, 20,* 295–320.

Clapham, C. (2000). Assessment and testing. *Annual Review of Applied Linguistics, 20,* 147–161.

Douglas, D. (2000). *Assessing languages for specific purposes.* New York: Cambridge University Press.

Educational Testing Service (ETS). (2000). *The computer-based TOEFL score user guide.* Princeton, NJ: Author.

Eignor, D. (1999). Selected technical issues in the creation of computer-adaptive tests of second language reading proficiency. In *Issues in computer adaptive testing of reading proficiency: Studies in Language Testing, 10* (pp. 167–181). New York: Cambridge University Press.

Enright, M. K., Bridgeman, B., Eignor, D., Lee, & Powers, D. E. (forthcoming). Designing measures of listening, reading, writing, and speaking. In C. A. Chapelle, M. K. Enright, & J. Jamieson (Eds.), *Building a validity argument for TOEFL.* Mahwah, NJ: Erlbaum.

Godwin-Jones, R. (2001). Emerging technologies. *Language Learning & Technology, 5*(2), 8–12.

Jamieson, J., & Chapelle, C. A. (2002). *Longman English Assessment.* New York: Pearson Longman.

Jamieson, J., Eignor, D., Grabe, W., & Kunnan, A. (forthcoming). The frameworks for reconceptualization of TOEFL. In C. A. Chapelle, M. K. Enright, & J. Jamieson (Eds.), *Building a validity argument for TOEFL.* Mahwah, NJ: Erlbaum.

Jamieson, J., Jones, S., Kirsch, I., Mosenthal, P., & Taylor, C. (2000). *TOEFL 2000 framework: A working paper.* TOEFL Monograph Series 16. Princeton, NJ: Educational Testing Service.

Kenyon, D., & Malabonga, V. (2001). Comparing examinee attitudes toward computer-assisted and other oral proficiency assessments. *Language Learning & Technology, 5*(2), 60–83.

Kenyon, D., Malabonga, V., & Carpenter, H. (2001). Response to the Norris commentary. *Language Learning & Technology, 5*(2), 106–108.

Lanfer, B., Elder, C., Hill, K., & Congdon, P. (2004a). Size and strength: Do we need both to measure vocabulary knowledge? *Language Testing, 21,* 202–226.

Lanfer, B., & Goldstein, Z. (2004b). Testing vocabulary knowledge: Size, strength, and computer adaptiveness. *Language Learning, 54,* 399–436.

Leacock, C. (2004). Scoring free-responses automatically: A case study of a large-scale assessment. Examens, 1, 3. English version available online at http://www.ets.org/research/erater.html

LeLoup, J., & Pontierio, R. (2001). On the net, language testing resources. *Language Learning & Technology*, 5(2), 4–7.

Loumi, S. (2004). *Assessing speaking*. New York: Cambridge University Press.

Madsen, H. (1986). Evaluating a computer-adaptive ESL placement test. *CALICO Journal*, 4(2), 41–50.

Norris, J. (2001). Concerns with computerized adaptive oral proficiency assessment. *Language Learning & Technology*, 5(2), 99–105.

Ordinate Corp. (1999). *PhonePass testing: Structure and content*. Ordinate Corporation Technical Report. Menlo Park, CA: Author.

Polio, C. (2001). Review of *Test Pilot*. *Language Learning & Technology*, 5(2), 34–37.

Powers, D. E., Roever, C., Huff, K. L., & Trapani, C. S. (2003). *Validating LanguEdge courseware scores against faculty ratings and student self-assessments*. (ETS Research Report 03–11). Princeton, NJ: Educational Testing Service.

Read, J. (2000). *Assessing vocabulary*. New York: Cambridge University Press.

Roever, C. (2001). Web-based language testing. *Language Learning & Technology*, 5(2), 84–94.

Rosenfeld, M., Leung, S., & Oltman, P. (2001). *The reading, writing, speaking, and listening tasks important for academic success at the undergraduate and graduate levels*. (TOEFL Monograph Series, MS-21). Princeton, NJ: Educational Testing Service.

Rost, M., & Fuchs, M. (2003). *Longman English Interactive*. New York: Pearson Education.

Rupp, A., Garcia, P., & Jamieson, J. (2002). Combining multiple regression and CART to understand difficulty in second language reading and listening comprehension test items. *International Journal of Language Testing*, 1, 185–216.

Sawaki, Y. (2001). Comparability of conventional and computerized tests of reading in a second language. *Language Learning & Technology*, 5(2), 38–59.

Stoynoff, S., & Chapelle, C. A. (2005). *ESOL tests and testing: A resource for teachers and administrators*. Alexandria, VA: Teachers of English to Speakers of Other Languages.

Tang, K. L. (1996). *Polytomous item response theory models and their applications in large-scale testing programs: Review of literature*. (TOEFL Monograph Series MS-2). Princeton, NJ: Educational Testing Service.

Tang, K. L., & Eignor, D. R. (1997). *Concurrent calibration of dichotomously and polytomously scored TOEFL items using IRT models*. (TOEFL Technical Report TR-13). Princeton, NJ: Educational Testing Service.

Taylor, C., Kirsch, I., Jamieson, J., & Eignor, D. (1999). Examining the relationship between computer familiarity and performance on computer-based language tasks. *Language Learning*, 49, 219–274.

Thompson, I. (2001). From the special issue editor (Introduction). *Language Learning &*

Technology, 5(2), 2–3.

Wainer, H., Dorans, N., Eignor, D., Flaugher, R., Green, B., Mislevy, R., Steinberg, L., & Thissen, D. (2000). *Computer adaptive testing: A primer* (2nd ed.). Mahwah, NJ: Erlbaum.

Weigle, S. C. (2002). *Assessing writing.* New York: Cambridge University Press.

Winke, P., & MacGregor, D. (2001). Review of Version 5, Hot Potatoes. *Language Learning & Technology, 5*(2), 28–33.

13. RESEARCH INTO THE ASSESSMENT OF SCHOOL-AGE LANGUAGE LEARNERS

Penny McKay

This chapter describes recent research into the assessment of school-age language learners in both second language and foreign language situations. The review is organized under five areas of research endeavor: the standards movement and its impact on second language learners in schools; large-scale content-based assessment and ways to counteract its negative impact on second language learners; investigations of academic language proficiency; explorations of classroom assessment; and young learner assessment. These areas of research are interrelated but sufficiently distinct to be addressed under separate headings. References to current research from various countries around the world are included, and suggested directions for further research are given.

This review of assessment research might be organized around assessment or curriculum themes. Broadfoot (1996) writes about assessment research under assessment for regulating competition, assessment for individual control, assessment for system control, and accountability. Coombe and Hubley (2003) refer to curriculum washback, in-program assessment, end-of-program assessment, and program evaluation. For this review of research into the assessment of school-age language learners, these themes are embedded within more broadly defined areas of research activity, first because there are at present, I believe, clearly distinguishable areas of research endeavor and interest in school-age language assessment, and second because these areas will be accessible and real to the many teachers and students, alongside researchers, who will read this review. The five main themes are the standards movement, large-scale, content-based assessment, academic language proficiency, classroom assessment, and assessment of young learners. Much of the research reported under the first three themes relates to the assessment of second language learners (those language learners learning a language in a minority language learning context); the remaining two themes include research into the assessment of foreign language learners (those learning a language in a situation where the language is seldom heard outside the classroom.).

Impact of the Standards Movement on L2 Learners and Teachers

Standards, also called outcomes-based curricula, attainment levels, and bandscales, are descriptions of curriculum outcomes, usually described in stages of progress. They may be content standards (describing what students should know and be able to do) or performance standards (describing how much, or at what level students need to perform to demonstrate achievement of the content standard). Many standards combine both purposes in the one document. Achievement on standards is often measured through external tests, although data are sometimes also collected on achievement through teachers' reports based on classroom assessment.

Use of large-scale standardized tests can bring a number of problems for second language learners and their teachers and schools, as I will outline next, especially when (as is usually the case) the reference group for the standards is mother-tongue speakers of the majority language. However, the results of assessment against standards can provide feedback to teachers, students, and parents about individual student learning in the established curriculum, and can give a common reference point for discussion of required pathways and whether they are being achieved.

The construction and implementation of standards by governments is driven by neo-liberal ideology, not simply by principles of educational philosophy. An understanding of this fact helps to make clear why governments employ standards, and why they are reluctant to address negative impact of those standards on minority groups. Briefly, governments are following business-world "managerialist" principles that seek to raise standards by (1) establishing competition between individuals, teachers, schools, and states; (2) commodifying the curriculum (making it measurable through standards); and (3) measuring, publishing, and then rewarding or punishing achievement. Standards are central to neo-liberal management of education and are closely tied to accountability. As noted by Katz, Low, Stack, and Tasang, "It is because of this accountability function that assessment serves a key role in the standards-reform effort" (2004, p. 5).

Researchers are investigating the impact of the standards-based movement on school-age minority learners, their parents, their teachers and their schools. The extent of concern is directly related to how high the stakes are; when children and subsequently their teachers and schools are labelled as failing, and suffer consequences for this, then the stakes are very high, for the children, their teachers, their school, their parents, and their community. Many studies in the United States have examined the equity of assessing ELL (English Language Learners) against states' standards through large-scale tests written with the expected language proficiency of mother-tongue speakers in mind (Katz et al., 2004; Liu, Anderson, & Thurlow, 1999; Swierzbin, Liu, & Thurlow, 2000). These studies are described further in the next section. In Australia, a national literacy standards test is administered to all elementary-age students regardless of English language proficiency (though new arrivals are exempt). Through their knowledge of second language development in the school context and analysis of students' language proficiency, Australian researchers have illustrated that the benchmarks fail to take sufficient account of minority learners who are in the process of developing their English language proficiency, and are bound not to show their progress in English in these tests, because the tests are focused on mother-tongue literacy (Davison & McKay, 2002; Davison & Williams, 2001a, 2001b; Hammond & Derewianka, 1999; McKay, 1998, 2000). A more recently discovered impact of literacy benchmarks testing in Australia is that, even as early as kindergarten, the more competitive elementary schools are checking their children for readiness for the benchmarks test in year 3. The result is a significant increase in children, especially ESL learners, being expected to repeat classes before year 3, as well as stress for teacher and children who are aware of this early monitoring process (McKay, 2004). As teachers point out to researchers in frustration, these procedures contrast with most principles of early childhood education that advocate individualized instruction and assessment to meet individual needs through the early years (e.g., Jalongo, 2000).

Many second language educators advocate the development and implementation of second language specific standards for second language learners to overcome these difficulties (Butler & Stevens, 2001; Davison & McKay, 2002; TESOL, 1997). The development of ESL-specific standards is discussed next. Breen et al. (1997) and Davison and Williams (2001a; 2001b) have investigated how teachers use ESL-specific standards (a number of which are available in Australia) in the classroom. Breen (1997) has observed that teachers go through stages of accommodation in the use of standards in their classrooms. Breen (1997) observed that genuine "accommodation" or take-up by teachers of external curriculum frameworks entails three phases: first, teachers need to recognize both conceptually and affectively the ultimate benefit to their own pedagogic priorities; second, they need to trial and adapt the framework to their established assessment procedures; third, they fully integrate the procedures into their practice. Davison and Williams (2001a; 2001b) also found that teachers differed in their use of the standards, depending on their experience and confidence and attitudes to the documents. In the United Kingdom, Leung and Teasdale (1997) investigated teacher assessment of speaking and listening of ESL learners at Key Stage 1 of the National Curriculum. They asked teachers to rate children's performance, and found that teachers did have some shared understanding about the general criteria for speaking and listening, but that there were also criteria used that were not specified in the National Curriculum. They suggest that some criteria were based on an understanding of an idealized native speaker norm rather than a model that reflects the language of ESL children.

All these researchers have noted the variability of interpretation of standards by teachers. Variability of interpretation is often because of the different experiences, understandings and attitudes of teachers, but not always. Arkoudis and O'Loughlin (2004) report on a secondary ESL situation where teachers came to understand that their inconsistent results were due to problems with the validity of the ESL standards themselves. When they tried to rewrite the standards to suit how they saw ESL development, the education authority was displeased and discounted their changes. One education department commentator presents his response:

> Without support from theory, teachers in a particular setting may produce a syllabus that reflects their shared understandings of a sequence in which to

introduce and practice new grammatical structures. However, this cannot be linked to authoritative statements about the order these structures are learned. (Ingamells, 2002, p. 3)

In an insight into teachers' roles in a standards-based education system, Arkoudis and O'Loughlin concluded "that teachers' knowledge and experience, which have informed the working of the [standards document], have been positioned as not really relevant to the bureaucracy" (p. 13). This study illustrates that teachers are not always the "culprits" in unreliable interpretations. It also demonstrates the negative impact on and disempowerment of teachers when standards descriptions are not valid.

The writing of performance standards (describing how much, or at what level, students need to perform to demonstrate achievement) can be a type of research in itself, depending on how this is done. Performance standards may be based on expected progress through curriculum content standards, often closely reflecting the outcomes described in the content standards; see, for example, the Illinois Foreign Language Learning Standards (Illinois State Board of Education, 2003) or they may be stand-alone descriptions of proficiency stages broadly situated in the known curriculum context, such as the National Languages and Literacy Institute of Australia (NLLIA) ESL Bandscales (McKay, Hudson, & Sapuppo, 1994); or the Common European Framework of Reference (Council of Europe, 2001). The latter type of performance standard usually involves research to ensure a degree of validity in the descriptions. Validity of proficiency-based performance standards can be attended to primarily as the standards are being developed (*a priori*) or after they have been developed (*a posteriori*; Sadler, 1987). North (1995) describes how the Common European Framework of Reference was developed in an *a priori* process. The Australian NLLIA ESL Bandscales, on the other hand, were written out of teachers' experiences, and are currently undergoing an *a posteriori* validation process, involving analyses of work samples and student performance, focus groups involving moderation, teacher interviews, and classroom observations of teacher assessment processes. Importantly, it is the final assessment decision on the quality of learners' performance that requires validation, therefore teachers' assessment processes are an important element in validation of standards. Brindley's (1998b; Brindley, 2001) articles on outcomes-based assessment are important references for researchers who require on overview of the issues in the development and implementation of standards.

To strengthen validity and reliability in standards, we need to know as much as possible about the proficiency development of language learners. Davison and Williams (2001a; 2001b) in Australia, and Cameron and Besser (2004) in the United Kingdom are researchers who have closely examined the nature of learners' developing proficiency in writing in English. Liddicoat (1997) has worked with teachers in a foreign language context to provide teachers with samples of work to help ensure reliable assessment of standards. Similarly, McKay (1999) provides an analysis of the effectiveness of language samples as aides to teacher assessment against standards. This kind of research is necessary to raise the likelihood that standards descriptors are valid, and that resulting assessment decisions are valid and reliable.

There is a need for continuing research into the validity of standards themselves, and into the validity of the tests, tasks, and decision-making processes used by teachers and assessors to identify children's levels on the standards. Much more research into the impact of standards is also needed, including research into the impact of standards on teacher assessment practices, discussed further in the following section.

Countering the Negative Impact of Large-scale Assessment on L2 Learners

Many standards are designed to assess students' content knowledge, that is, their knowledge and skills in a curriculum area, for example, in literacy, mathematics, and science. In these cases minority language learners in schools are being assessed, usually in large-scale tests, on their content knowledge in a language in which they are not yet proficient:

> While the rhetoric of content-area standards refers to their use for all students, the standards do not address such instructional issues as how to teach content material while students are still acquiring a second language, nor do they address assessment issues such as how English language learners can demonstrate knowledge of content material when tested in English. (Katz et al., 2004, p. 4)

Butler and Stevens (2001) provide a valuable overview of issues in the assessment of English language learners' (ELL) content knowledge in large-scale tests in the United States. Recent federal government acts have decreed that all students should be included in state and district assessment programs in order that comparable information about student progress can be obtained. The immediate questions for educators (including assessors) are the following:

1. When is it appropriate to give standardized content assessments to ELLs? That is, when are the inferences made about the performance of ELLs on standardized content assessments valid?
2. Until it is appropriate to give these assessments to ELLs, how do we provide accountability and assure equity?

(Butler & Stevens, 2001, p. 417)

Butler and Stevens list the following as strategies to include ELLs in assessment processes:

- Testing in the first language
- Using accommodations; there can be modifications of the test (such as assessment in the native language, modification of linguistic complexity, addition of visual supports) or modifications of the test procedures (extra assessment time, breaks during testing, oral directions in the native language)
- Measuring growth in English (through tests in English) as an alternative to inclusion in content-based tests

Results of research on whether accommodations make any significant difference in the performance of second language learners on content tests is mixed (Butler & Stevens, 1997; Gottlieb, 2003; Koenig & Bachman, 2004), and research is needed into the idea of tailoring accommodations to the nature of students' language proficiency and knowledge. Butler and Stevens (2001) also suggest that opportunity to learn (OTL) is an inherent problem with large-scale content assessments with ELLs. If ELLs are not receiving the content instruction that is covered on large-scale assessments, "then accountability data based on these assessments are neither valid nor reliable" (p. 421). Butler and Stevens, along with

Abedi, Courtney, Mirocha, Leon, and Goldberg (2000), recommend that classroom-based research is needed to determine whether ELLs are receiving the appropriate content instruction. They argue for the use of a multiple-assessment approach to evaluate school programs, with large-scale assessment being one approach. Gottlieb (2003) also advocates a multiassessment approach in which teacher-based assessment can be used "as a form of large-scale testing" when ELL students are at the beginning stages of language proficiency and when the following three conditions are met:

- Standard prompts (blueprints) appropriate for students' age and development are made available to teachers
- Content-related language samples are collected (a) in the fall to establish an initial baseline, (b) at midyear to monitor progress, and (c) at the end of the year to measure growth
- Samples of performance are collected and held in the students' records

Large-scale teacher-based assessment needs further research, but may provide some alternatives to facilitate inclusion for beginning ELL students before they can validly enter the testing system.

Analysis of the test results of ELL learners in state-wide content tests is quite commonly carried out by education departments. Liu, Anderson, and Thurlow (1999), for example, examine data trends in Minnesota's Basic Standards Tests (BST), statewide tests of reading and math, for the years 1996–1999 for LEP students. They made several observations, including the following:

- Participation for LEP students in the test remains high
- Performance of LEP students remains low, with a persistent although narrowing achievement gap of 20%–25% between LEP and non-LEP students taking reading texts than math tests, which suggests ESL teachers may be successful in teaching the reading skills needed on the BST.
- The relative number of Minnesota LEP students taking advantage of test accommodations (i.e., extended testing times, translation of directions, special test settings etc) is low. (Liu et al., 1999, p. 1)

Another report of this type is by Gonzalez for the Austin Independent School District (Gonzalez, 1999). These reports help researchers to gather layers of data about ELL performance and about the impact of testing on ELLs in content tests. Katz et al. (2004) analyzed student assessment data compiled by the San Francisco Unified School District to explore the relationship between content area testing and students' English language proficiency. They also reported on the results of classroom observations of ELLS to describe their academic performances, and conducted an auxiliary study of California's English Language Proficiency test. The researchers were particularly interested in determining at what point along the second language acquisition continuum educators "can regain confidence in the results of standardized tests conducted in English with ELLs" (p. 5). The researchers found that "more situated notions of English language proficiency are needed to enable educators to make reasoned decisions as to when students can move into English-only instruction and English-only assessment" (p. 69). They also found that testing results do not accurately reflect how ELL students function in classroom settings. They support the provision in the current No Child Left Behind legislation that allows ELLs to be exempted from testing for at least three years while being provided with appropriate language support.

Without research into the validity, reliability, and impact of large-scale content-based tests for ELL learners, we do not know the extent to which these tests limit or expand students' avenues for demonstrating competence and thus their life choices (Darling-Hammond, 1994). The use of large-scale tests is, after all, not necessarily to be accepted without question. Many educators have written about the advantages of alternative assessment over standardized assessment (Brown, 1998; Genishi & Brainard, 1995; Herman, Aschbacher, & Winters, 1992). Hasselgren (2000) describes how the alternative assessment conducted in Norway by the Norwegian Ministry of Education, in conjunction with the University of Bergen, yields valuable results for the Ministry, the children, and the teachers:

> In the absence of any tradition that smacks of grading in primary schools, both teachers and pupils are able to approach assessment without prejudice and put it to positive use. It seems that, in some ways, we have got it right. There are, so far, no "victims" of testing in the Norwegian primary school, and the principal challenge to those involving themselves in this area will be to ensure that the situation remains that way!
>
> (Hasselgren, 2000, p. 267)

Academic Language Proficiency Assessment in L2 Contexts

To assess the academic language proficiency needed for minority language learners, especially those in upper elementary and secondary schools, to succeed in content-based tests and mainstream classroom learning, a clear definition of the construct "academic language proficiency" is needed. A group of researchers at CRESST (National Center for Research on Evaluation, Standards, and Student Testing) in the United States, have been researching the nature of academic language proficiency for test development purposes (Bailey, in press; Bailey & Butler, 2003; Bailey, Butler, LaFramenta, & Ong, 2004; Butler & Bailey, 2002; Butler, Lord, Stevens, Borrego, & Bailey, 2004; Stevens, Butler, & Castellon-Wellington, 2000). In a recent report, Butler and colleagues (2004) describe how they have examined standards documents, textbooks, and classroom video samples to collect data about the type of language use required in upper elementary science and math classrooms. Their work has identified the grammatical features of language functions, the structural features of academic texts, the types of texts found in textbooks and the textual and linguistic features of the texts. Features of classroom discourse have also been identified. The researchers then used this information to write draft academic language proficiency test specifications and prototype tasks. This work is ongoing. Investigation into academic language proficiency is a high priority to ensure understanding of (a) what language is needed for successful participation in mainstream classes, (b) how test tasks should be constructed, and (c) what ELL students should be taught to be successful at school and in tests.

Classroom Assessment in School-Level Second and Foreign Language Learning

A cutting edge area of assessment research activity at present is research into classroom assessment. In recent years, a growing body of research has been conducted into formative assessment in generalist classrooms, that is, classrooms described without specific reference to language learners (Black & Wiliam, 1998; Hall, Webber, Varley, Young, & Dorman, 1997; McMillan, 2003; Smith, 2003). McMillan writes "What is needed is an understanding of how assessment and instruction are interwoven, with new conceptions about what assessment is and how it affects learning" (2003, p. 7).

McMillan's research has revealed, for example, that teachers make decisions about their classroom assessment based on achieving goals for students that include noncognitive outcomes (such as confidence and a sense of achievement) as well as those stated in the curriculum. Teachers "pull" for their students, in that they try to find ways that help their students succeed. They put great emphasis on promoting students' understanding and on accommodating individual differences, and they vary assessments to accommodate these differences. Teachers believe it is imperative for students to be actively engaged in learning, and for them to be motivated to do their best work.

In the context of formative assessment, then, McMillan suggests that there is validity in formative classroom assessment when an assessment decision has resulted in more student engagement, and when progress can be identified. Gipps (1994) had claimed earlier that teacher assessment is valid and reliable if carried out in a structured, repeated, and collegial way. Smith (2003) suggests that reliability should be deemphasized in formative assessment, because teachers are typically interested in how well the student does the task, rather than finding out how well the student has performed in relation to others (Smith, 2003, p. 5). Reliability, Smith suggests, can be checked through the collection of sufficient observation data over many tasks, and the impact of classroom assessment can be evaluated through a consideration of the intended and unintended consequences of teachers' decisions (2003, p. 9). These new ways of looking at validity, reliability, and impact demonstrate that new ways of thinking are emerging with regard to formative assessment. Leung (2004) and Leung and Teasdale (1997) have contemplated the implications of these new perspectives for second language assessment. Leung (forthcoming) has suggested that three kinds of questions require some immediate attention in the second language field:

- What do teachers do when they carry out formative assessment?
- What do teachers look for when they are assessing?
- What theory or "standards" do teachers use when they make judgments and decisions?

(Leung, forthcoming)

He questions whether teachers can assess

> the full range of pre-specified criteria which would cover all possible aspects of student learning, modes of participation and learning strategies, to name a few possible issues that can emerge in the teaching and learning process that might impact on teacher assessment; the fluid, socially dynamic and sometimes unpredictable nature of classroom activities would preclude this possibility.
>
> (Leung, forthcoming)

Language researchers have only recently undertaken investigations of teachers' formative assessment. Rea-Dickins and her colleagues (Gardner & Rea-Dickins, 2001; Rea-Dickins, 2001; Rea-Dickins & Gardner, 2000; Rea-Dickins & Rixon, 1999) have explored the nature of formative assessment in elementary classrooms, examining the range and quality of teacher assessment, the issues, and the assessment processes. Like Leung, Rea-Dickins has asked several questions about formative assessment:

- What constitutes 'quality' in formative assessment?
- Are these assessments creating opportunities for learning?
- What constitutes evidence of language learning?
- Are teachers in the EAL [English as additional language] context able to distinguish between a language learning need, a special education need, a curriculum content need?

(Rea-Dickins, 2001, pp. 457–458)

A current issue investigated by Rea-Dickins (2001) is the assessment processes followed by mainstream teachers in United Kingdom classrooms that include ESL students when teachers have to both formatively assess and also report on children's progress against externally-developed criteria or standards. She refers to the cycles of assessment described by Hall, Webber, Varley, Young, and Dorman (1997) and from her observations maps a cycle of assessment that involves planning (Stage 1); implementation, where scaffolding, self and peer assessment, and feedback to learners takes place (Stage 2); and monitoring, recording and dissemination (Stage 3). The fourth stage is where the teacher undertakes recording and dissemination work for accountability purposes.

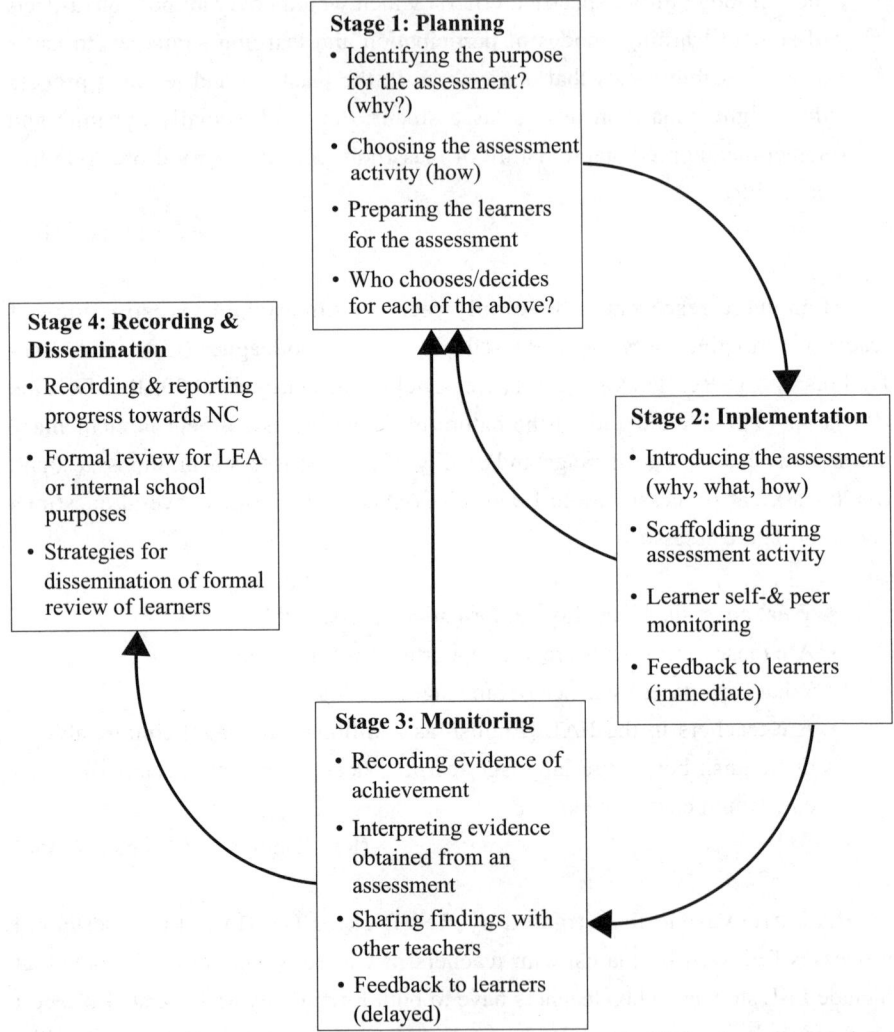

Figure 1. Processes and strategies in instruction-embedded classroom assessment. (from Rea-Dickins, 2001, p. 435)
(© Hodder Arnold. Permission to reproduce gratefully acknowledged.)

Because it is often the case that teachers' formative assessment and monitoring (in Stages 2 and 3) are translated into reporting (in Stage 4), Rea-Dickins warns that we need to remember that formative assessment may be more high-stakes than we usually acknowledge.

In the English as a foreign language (EFL) situation of Hong Kong, Morris, Lo, Chik, and Chan (2000) found that elementary schools high stakes assessment is a stark reality; such assessment is seen as a preparation for survival in a highly competitive society. After a new system of formative assessment against Bands of Performance had been introduced through the Hong Kong Target Oriented Curriculum, it was found that teachers were responding by formally assessing each outcome in the Bands, and noting each assessment result in detailed records. However, they said that they had little time to do follow-up work, and also that their workload was greatly increased. The lesson to be learned from this, according to the researchers, is that governments need to consider long-term and coherent strategies that address both the structural features of schooling and the prevailing beliefs about assessment. They suggest that the following conditions are needed if classroom, criterion-referenced assessment is to succeed:

- A clear linkage between external and school-based assessments
- The development of a system of recording and reporting assessment which stresses the role of teacher collaboration, the exercise of professional judgment and the provision of feedback designed to support learning
- Ongoing support for teacher professional development designed to promote their understanding of the roles and processes of assessment

(Morris et al., 2000, p. 207)

Also in Hong Kong, Davison is undertaking two projects into formative and summative school-based assessment (to be completed in 2006). One project is investigating the transition from norm-referenced to criterion-referenced, school-based assessment, and the other, alongside improvement of practices through action research, is aimed at "identifying and describing the factors which may facilitate and/or hinder the connection of formative assessment and feedback with learning and teaching in a range of different English language situations in Hong Kong" (Davison, personal communication). Gatullo (2000), in Italy, has reported on a two-year pilot study in which she found that teachers tended not to make productive use of information they had collected for formative purposes, and they made little or no use of some types of questioning and negotiations that could be fed into formative assessment and enhance the learning process.

To return to standards, there appears to be recognition, in both mainstream and language assessment research, of the tensions that exist for teachers required to operate in an accountability regime (preparing students for external tests, reporting on achievement to stakeholders) and at the same time conduct formative assessment (Black & Wiliam, 1998; Brindley, 1998a; McKay, 2004; McMillan, 2003; Rea-Dickins, 2001). The "managerialist" approach to education stands in direct opposition to the professionalism of teachers whose natural inclination is to work collaboratively to improve learning (Broadfoot, 1996; Clair, Adger, Short, & Millen, 1998; Hartley, 1997; McKay, 2004; Wiliam, 2001). Clair et al., (1998) have also mapped the extent of tensions between managerialist and professional perspectives in the introduction of standards and large-scale testing in California. McKay (2004) interviewed teachers of young learners in Australia who indicated changes in practice and stress for teachers with the introduction of performance indicators as early as grade 1. One teacher described the situation this way: "To get these indicators, instead of observing what children can do during activities, and planning for observing those, they're just teaching teaching teaching and testing, creating a test that tests each one of these" (Griffiths-Chandran interview in McKay, 2004). This teacher continued:

> It's the biggest talk at the moment, it's the biggest worry, assessment . . . the pressure on us from the administration, our reporting, our accountability, getting these students to those standards. You can't just get them [the learners] all there along the same phases because they're all different; it's actually going against the grain of inclusive education. (Griffiths-Chandran interview in McKay, 2004)

Breen and his colleagues (1997) also found these tensions exist for ESL specialists working with ESL learners in the mainstream:

> The tension between seeking to maintain a thorough check upon . . . students' progress and managing the teaching/learning process in the classroom emerged

again and again for many of the teachers who revealed exceptional commitment to the educational success of ESL children. (Breen et al., 1997 p. 104)

It is imperative to investigate ways in which teachers can meet the accountability requirements but at the same time successfully assess for formative purposes in the classroom. We also need to know more about the ways that ESL specialists coassess with mainstream teachers to monitor ESL students' progress over time, and through this, to coteach with mainstream teachers to improve learning of ESL students. Breen et al.'s (1997) study provides information of this kind.

Assessment of Young Language Learners

Much of what has gone before in this chapter relates to the assessment of both elementary and secondary age learners. Young learners are defined here as elementary age learners from around 5 to 12 years of age. Because there is relatively little in the literature on the assessment of young learners (Rea-Dickins & Rixon, 1997) it is worth highlighting existing research into this area to motivate further related efforts. A chapter summarizing research into the assessment of young language learners can be found in McKay (2005). There are several challenges for researchers in young learner assessment, not least because of the variability across programs, especially foreign language programs, and a lack of consensus about proficiency (Johnstone, 2000). There is general reporting, too, of variable teacher expertise in assessment. Teachers tend not to have assessment as a top priority (Hill, 2000; Jantscher & Landsiedler, 2000; Low, Brown, Johnstone, & Pirrie, 1995). In a survey in which British elementary teachers were asked about ways in which teaching English could be improved, teachers' responses did not mention assessment (Teasdale & Leung, 2000). In Hong Kong, too, teacher trainers' understanding of assessment was found to be somewhat "impoverished" (Morris et al., 2000).

The characteristics of young learners are highly relevant in the assessment process. Young learners are going through a period of *social, emotional, and cognitive growth*, they are *developing literacy*; and they are highly vulnerable (McKay, 2005). Researchers require specialist knowledge of young learners to investigate assessment issues. Such knowledge includes, for example, the characteristics of young learners and the characteristics of tasks (the setting, the input, the nature of the expected response, the relationship between the input and the response) likely to affect performance in assessment procedures. Carpenter, Fujii, and Kataoka (1995) present one of the few accounts of assessment task development and evaluation for young learners. In the Cambridge Young Learners English Test (University of Cambridge ESOL Examinations, 2003), we see a test development and implementation process that takes into account the characteristics of young learners, and follows implementation with ongoing research (Ball & Wilson, 2002; Marshall & Gutteridge, 2002; Taylor & Saville, 2002). Young learner assessment deserves to be established as a highly expert field of endeavor requiring, for example, knowledge of the social and cognitive development of young learners, knowledge of second language literacy development, and understanding of assessment principles and practices.

Conclusion

This chapter has reviewed research into the assessment of school-age language learners, taking areas of current research effort, rather than assessment theory, as its organizing principle. Some research appears in assessment journals like *Language Testing* (and in the future in the new journal *Language Assessment Quarterly*), in nonlanguage journals, and in government-sponsored and university reports. Other related research is published on web sites. A journal, or perhaps a section of an existing assessment journal dedicated to the assessment of school age language learners would help to provide an international meeting place for researchers, and stimulate further research. Broadly, at present, research is required in each of the areas of endeavor covered in this review. As research progresses, and governments change their approach to assessment, areas will change and new directions for research will be signaled.

ANNOTATED BIBLIOGRAPHY

Brindley, G. (1998b). Outcomes-based assessment and reporting in language learning progammes: A review of the issues. *Language Testing*, 15, 45–85.

Brindley covers outcomes-based assessment (or standards-based assessment) in adult and school sectors. The article provides comprehensive coverage of the issues in standards-based assessment, highlighting political as well as psychometric and teacher-based assessment issues. His references point readers to key theorists and researchers in the language assessment field. He provides suggestions to overcome challenges to validity and reliability for teacher assessment of standards, including professional development and teacher collaboration, and the collection of a task bank for teachers to draw on.

Butler, F. A., & Stevens, R. (2001). Standardised assessment of the content knowledge of English language learners K–12: Current trends and old dilemmas. *Language Testing, 18*(4), 409–427.

Butler and Stevens provide a valuable overview of the issues in large-scale, standardized, content-based testing for minority language learners. They articulate the current situation in the United States, set up through legislation, where states are required to include English language learners in their state-wide testing. They review possible ways to include English language learners more equitably: testing in the first language, accommodations, and measuring growth in English. They also offer alternative approaches to research into the use of standardized content assessment with English language learners.

Butler, F. A., Lord, C., Stevens, R., Borrego, M., & Bailey, A. L. (2004). *An approach to operationalizing academic language for language test development purposes: Evidence from fifth-grade science and math* (CSE Tech. Rep. No. 626). Los Angeles: University of California, National Center for Research on Evaluation, Standards, and Student Testing (CRESST).

This research report exemplifies the excellent and probably unparalleled work being carried out through CRESST into the assessment of school-age learners. The full report is available on the CRESST web site. The researchers describe how they are systematically analyzing the academic language requirements of science and math at upper elementary school level to inform the valid testing of English language learners. This report is one of a series of reports since the mid-1990s, and the authors signal that research will need to continue for some time to come.

Hasselgren, A. (2000). The assessment of the English ability of young learners in Norwegian schools: An innovative approach. *Language Testing*, *17*(2), 261–277.

This article is a report of a large-scale project carried out for the Norwegian Ministry of Education by the University of Bergen to systematically introduce formative assessment in English-as-a-foreign-language upper elementary classrooms. The report shows how large-scale classroom-based assessment can be carried out successfully, and that the system and its teachers can benefit greatly from innovative centrally-prepared assessment materials, and from opportunities for teachers to finetune their assessment procedures together.

McKay, P. (2005). *Assessing young language learners.* Cambridge: Cambridge University Press.

McKay provides a comprehensive overview of principles and practices in the assessment of young language learners, both second language and foreign language learners, from ages 5–12. Chapter 3 contains a detailed review of international research into young learner assessment.

McMillan, J. H. (2003). Understanding and improving teachers' classroom assessment decision making: Implications for theory and practice. *Educational Measurement: Issues and Practices*, *22*(4), 34–44.

McMillan's article provides a valuable overview of current mainstream thinking about teacher classroom assessment. Although not concerned with second or foreign language teachers specifically, this article gives language teachers access to some more recent perspectives in classroom assessment. (Teasdale and Leung's 2000 article presents a related discussion of teacher assessment in the language teaching field.)

OTHER REFERENCES

Abedi, J., Courtney, M., Mirocha, J., Leon, S., & Goldberg, J. (2000). *Language accommodation for large-scale assessment in science: assessing English language learners.* Draft deliverable to Office of Bilingual Education and Minority Language Affairs, OBEMLA, Contract No. R305B60002. Los Angeles, CA: University of California, National Center for Research on Evaluation, Standards, and Student Testing (CRESST).

Arkoudis, S., & O'Loughlin, K. (2004). Tensions between validity and outcomes: Teacher assessment of written work of recently arrived immigrant ESL students. *Language Assessment Quarterly*, *1*(3), 284–304.

Bailey, A. L. (in press). *From lambie to lambaste*: The conceptualization, operationalization and use of academic language in the assessment of ELL students. In T. Wiley & K. Rolstad (Eds.), *Rethinking school language*. Mahwah, NJ: Erlbaum.

Bailey, A. L., & Butler, F. A. (2003). *An evidentiary framework for operationalizing academic language for broad application to K–12 education: A design document* (CSE Tech. Rep. No. 611). Los Angeles: University of California, National Center for Research on Evaluation, Standards, and Student Testing (CRESST).

Bailey, A. L., Butler, F. A., LaFramenta, C., & Ong, C. (2004). T*owards the characterization of academic language in upper elementary science classrooms* (CSE Tech. Rep. No. 621). Los Angeles: University of California, National Center for Research on Evaluation, Standards, and Student Testing (CRESST).

Ball, F., & Wilson, J. (2002). Research projects relating to YLE speaking tests. In University of Cambridge Local Examinations Syndicate (Ed.), *Research Notes 7* (pp. 8–10). Cambridge: University of Cambridge Local Examinations Syndicate.

Black, P., & Wiliam, D. (1998). Assessment and classroom learning. *Assessment in Education*, *5*(1), 1–74.

Breen, M. P. (1997). The relationship between assessment frameworks and classroom pedagogy. In M. P. Breen, C. Barratt-Pugh, B. Derewianka, H. House, C. Hudson, T. Lumley, & M. Rohl (Eds.), *Profiling ESL children. How teachers interpret and use national and state assessment frameworks, Vol. 1* (pp. 91–128). Canberra: Department of Employment, Education, Training and Youth Affairs.

Breen, M. P., Barratt-Pugh, C., Derewianka, B., House, H., Hudson, C., Lumley, T., et al., (1997). *Profiling ESL children: How teachers interpret and use national and state assessment frameworks, Vol. 1*. Canberra: Department of Employment, Education, Training and Youth Affairs.

Brindley, G. (1998a). Assessing listening abilities. *Annual Review of Applied Linguistics*, *18*, 171–191.

Brindley, G. (2001). Outcomes-based assessment in practice: Some examples, and emerging insights. *Language Testing*, *18*(4), 393–408.

Broadfoot, P. M. (1996). *Education, assessment and society*. Buckingham: Open University Press.

Brown, J. D. (1998). *New ways of classroom assessment*. Alexandria, VA: Teachers of English to Speakers of Other Languages (TESOL).

Butler, F. A., & Bailey, A. L. (2002). Equity in the assessment of English language learners

K-12. *Idiom, 32*(1), 1–6.

Butler, F. A., & Stevens, R. (1997). *Accommodation strategies for English language learners on large-scale assessments: Student characteristics and other considerations* (CSE Tech. Rep. No. 448). Los Angeles: University of California, National Center for Research on Evaluation, Standards, and Student Testing (CRESST).

Cameron, L., & Besser, S. (2004). *Writing in English as an additional language at Key Stage 2.* Leeds: University of Leeds.

Carpenter, K., Fujii, N., & Kataoka, H. (1995). An oral interview procedure for assessing second language abilities in children. *Language Testing, 12*(2), 157–175.

Clair, N., Adger, C. T., Short, D., & Millen, E. (1998). *Implementing standards with English language learners: Initial findings from four middle schools.* Providence, RI: Northeast and Islands Regional Education Laboratory at Brown University.

Coombe, A. C., & Hubley, N. J. (2003). Themes in language assessment. In A. C. Coombe & N. J. Hubley (Eds.), *Assessment practices* (pp. 1–8). Alexandria, VA: TESOL.

Council of Europe. (2001). *Common European framework of reference for languages: Learning, teaching, assessment.* Cambridge: Cambridge University Press.

Darling-Hammond, L. (1994). Performance-based assessment and educational equity. *Harvard Educational Review, 64*(1), 5–30.

Davison, C., & McKay, P. (2002). Counting and dis-counting learner group variation: English language and literacy standards in Australia. In A. B. M. Tsui & S. Andrews (Eds.), *Journal of Asian Pacific Communication, 12*(1), 77–94 [Special issue on maintaining and setting standards and language variation].

Davison, C., & Williams, A. (2001a). *Learning from each other: Critical connections. Studies of English Language and Literacy Development, Volume 1.* Melbourne: Language Australia. Victorian Child Literacy and ESL Research Centre.

Davison, C., & Williams, A. (2001b). *Learning from each other: Literacy, labels and limitations. Studies of child English language and literacy development, K-12, Vol. 2.* Canberra: Language Australia.

Gardner, S., & Rea-Dickins, P. (2001). Conglomeration or chameleon? Teachers' representation of language in the assessment of learners with English as an additional language. *Language Awareness, 10*(2 & 3), 161–177.

Gatullo, F. (2000). Formative assessment in ELT primary (elementary) classrooms: An Italian case study. *Language Testing, 17*(2), 278–288.

Genishi, C., & Brainard, M. B. (1995). Assessment of bilingual children: Dilemma seeking solutions. In E. E. Garcia & B. McLaughlin (Eds.), *Meeting the challenge of linguistic and cultural diversity in early childhood education* (pp. 49–63). New York: Teachers College Press.

Gipps, C. V. (1994). *Beyond testing: Towards a theory of educational assessment.* London: Falmer Press.

Gonzalez, R. M. (1999). *Bilingual/ESL Programs Evaluation Report, 1999–2000.* Austin: Austin Independent School District, Texas.

Gottlieb, M. (2003). *Large-scale assessment of English language learners. Addressing educational accountability in K-12 settings.* Alexandria, VA: TESOL.

Hall, K., Webber, B., Varley, S., Young, V., & Dorman, P. (1997). A study of teacher assessment at Key Stage 1. *Cambridge Journal of Education, 27*(107–122).

Hammond, J., & Derewianka, B. (1999). ESL and literacy education: Revising the relationship. *Prospect, 14*(2), 26–41.

Hartley, D. (1997). The new managerialism in education: A mission impossible? *Journal of Education, 27*(1), 47–58.

Herman, J. L., Aschbacher, P. R., & Winters, L. (1992). *A practical guide to alternative assessment.* Alexandria, VA: Association for Supervision and Curriculum Development.

Hill, D. A. (2000). Adding foreign languages to the elementary school curriculum: The Italian experience. In J. Moon & M. Nikolov (Eds.), *Research into teaching English to young learners* (pp. 137–152). Pecs, Hungary: University Press, Pecs.

Illinois State Board of Education. (2003). *Foreign language standards.* Retrieved 15th August 2003, from http://www.isbe.net/ils/foreignlanguage/fog28.html

Ingamells, J. (2002). The ESL Companion-Let's move forward. *VATME (Victorian Association of TESOL and Multicultural Education) Newsletter* (4), 3.

Jalongo, M. R. (2000). *Early childhood language arts.* Boston: Allyn & Bacon.

Jantscher, E., & Landsiedler, I. (2000). Foreign language education at Austrian primary. In M. Nikolov & H. Curtain (Eds.), *An early start: Young learners and modern languages in Europe and beyond* (pp. 13–27). Strasbourg Cedex: Council of Europe.

Johnstone, R. (2000). Context-sensitive assessment of modern languages in primary (elementary) and early secondary education: Scotland and the European experience. *Language Testing, 17*(2), 123–143.

Katz, A., Low, P., Stack, J., & Tasang, S.-L. (2004). *A study of content area assessment for English language learners.* Final Report prepared for Office of English Language Acquisition and Academic Achievement for Limited English Proficient Students, U.S. Department of Education. (Contract No. T292B010001). Oakland, CA: ARC Associates.

Koenig, J. A., & Bachman, L. F. (2004). *Keeping score for all: the effects of inclusion and accommodation policies on large-scale educational assessment.* Washington, DC: National Research Council, National Academies Press.

Leung, C. (2004). Developing formative teacher assessment: Knowledge, practice and change. *Language Assessment Quarterly, 1*(1), 19–41.

Leung, C. (forthcoming). Classroom teacher assessment of second language development: construct as practice. In E. Hinkel (Ed.), *Handbook of research in second language learning and teaching*. Mahwah, NJ: Erlbaum.

Leung, C., & Teasdale, A. (1997). What do teachers mean by speaking and listening? A contextualised study of assessment in multilingual classrooms in the English National Curriculum. In A. Huhta, V. Kohonen, L. Kurki-Suonio, & S. Louma (Eds.), *New contexts, goals and alternatives in language assessment* (pp. 291–324). Jyvaskyla: University of Jyvaskyla.

Liddicoat, A. J. (1997). *Communicating in LOTE. Writing and oral interaction.* Canberra: Modern Language Teachers' Association of the Australian Capital Territory.

Liu, K., Anderson, M., & Thurlow, M. (1999). *Report on the participation and performance of limited English language proficiency students on Minnesota's Basic Standards Tests.* St. Paul: Minnesota State Department of Children, Families, and Learning.

Low, L., Brown, S., Johnstone, R., & Pirrie, A. (1995). *Foreign languages in primary schools.* Stirling: Scottish Centre for Information on Language Teaching and Research, University of Stirling.

Marshall, H., & Gutteridge, M. (2002). Candidate performance in the Young Learner English Tests in 2000. In University of Cambridge Local Examinations Syndicate(Ed.), *Research Notes 7* (pp. 5–8). Cambridge: University of Cambridge Local Examinations Syndicate.

McKay, P. (1998). Discriminatory features for ESL learners in the literacy benchmarks. In *Australian Language Matters Background Papers No. 2* (pp. 27–29). Melbourne: Australian Council of TESOL Associations.

McKay, P. (1999). The effectiveness of work samples as elaborations of profiles: Some comments based on the ACT LOTE Work Samples. *Babel, Journal of the Australian Federation of Modern Language Teachers Associations Inc, 34*(3), 21–25.

McKay, P. (2000). On ESL standards for school-age learners. *Language Testing, 17*(2), 185–214.

McKay, P. (2004, March). *Do standards have something to answer for? A pedagogic response to standards.* Plenary address TESOL Arabia. Dubai.

McKay, P., Hudson, C., & Sapuppo, M. (1994). NLLIA ESL Bandscales. In P. McKay (Ed.), *NLLIA ESL Development: Language and Literacy in Schools, Vol. 1.* (Sections A, B, and C). Canberra: National Languages and Literacy Institute of Australia.

Morris, P., Lo, M.-l., Chik, P.-m., & Chan, K.-k. (2000). One function, two systems-changing assessment in Hong Kong's primary schools. In B. Adamson, T. Kwan & K.-k. Chan (Eds.), *Changing the curriculum: The impact of reform on primary schooling in Hong Kong* (pp. 195–216). Hong Kong: Hong Kong University Press.

North, B. (1995). The development of a common framework scale of descriptors of language proficiency based on a theory of measurement. *System, 23*(4), 445–465.

Rea-Dickins, P. (2001). Mirror, mirror on the wall: Identifying processes of classroom assessment. *Language Testing, 18*(4), 429–462.

Rea-Dickins, P., & Gardner, S. (2000). Snares and silver bullets: Disentangling the construct of formative assessment. *Language Testing, 17*(2), 217–244.

Rea-Dickins, P., & Rixon, S. (1997). The assessment of young learners of English as a Foreign language. In C. Clapham & D. Corson (Eds.), *The encyclopaedia of language and education, Vol. 7: Language testing and assessment* (pp. 151–161). Netherlands: Kluwer Academic.

Rea-Dickins, P., & Rixon, S. (1999). Assessment of young learners' English: Reasons and means. In S. Rixon (Ed.), *Young learners of English: Some research perspectives* (pp. 89–101). Harlow, Essex: Longman.

Sadler, R. (1987). Specifying and promulgating achievement standards. *Oxford Review of Education, 13*(2), 191–209.

Smith, J. K. (2003). Reconsidering reliability in classroom assessment and grading. *Educational Measurement: Issues and Practices, 22*(4), 26–34.

Stevens, R. A., Butler, F. A., & Castellon-Wellington, M. (2000). *Academic language and content assessment: Measuring the progress of ELLs* (CSE Tech. Rep. No. 552). Los Angeles: University of Los Angeles, National Center for Research on Evaluation, Standards and Testing.

Swierzbin, B., Liu, K., & Thurlow, M. (2000). *Initial perceptions of English as a second language educators on including students with limited English proficiency in Minnesota's high standards: State assessment series.* St. Paul: Minnesota State Department of Children, Families and Learning.

Taylor, L., & Saville, N. (Eds.) (2002). Developing English language tests for young learners. In University of Cambridge Local Examinations Syndicate. *English as a Foreign Language (EFL), Research Notes 7*, (pp. 2–5). Cambridge: University of Cambridge Local Examinations Syndicate.

Teasdale, A., & Leung, C. (2000). Teacher assessment and psychometric theory: A case of paradigm crossing? *Language Testing, 17*(2), 163–184.

TESOL. (1997). *ESL standards for pre-K-12 students.* Alexandria, VA: Teachers of English to Speakers of Other Languages.

University of Cambridge ESOL Examinations. (2003). *Cambridge young learners handbook.* Cambridge: University of Cambridge ESOL Examinations.

Wiliam, D. (2001). An overview of the relationship between assessment and the curriculum. In D. Scott (Ed.), *Curriculum and assessment* (pp. 165–181). Westport, CT: Ablex.

CONTRIBUTOR BIODATA

Elizabeth B. Bernhardt (PhD, University of Minnesota) is Director of the Language Center and Professor of German Studies at Stanford University, Where she teaches undergraduate German language courses and offers graduate seminars on second-language learning and teaching and second language literacy. She has spoken and written on second language reading, teacher education, and policy and planning for foreign and second language programs. Her book *Reading Development in a second Language* won the Modern Language Association's Mildenburger Award as well as the Edward Fry Award from the National Reading Conference as an outstanding contribution to lieracy research. At Stanford, she is also the Warren Sheldon University Fellow in Undergraduate Education and is Dean of the South Row, an academic mentoring role for 19 undergraduate residences.
Contact information: ebernhar @ stanford. edu

Martha Bigelow is an Assistant Professor in the Second Languages and Cultures Education Program in the Department of Curriculum and Instruction at the University of Minnesota. Her work in SLA began with exploring the power written production and oral corrective feedback have for facilitating noticing of specific linguistic forms by literate adult learners. More recently she has become interested in SLA processes of ESL students with low literacy. Specifically, she has been studying how teen and adult learners with low literacy make use of oral feedback in English and has examined strengths and challenges such students bring to their oral language development process. This research informs her practice as a language teacher educator, especially with regard to teaching English language learners with low levels of literacy and limited formal schooling.
Contact information: mbigelow @ umn. edu

Anna Uhl Chamot is Professor of Secondary Education (ESL and Foreign Language Education) in the Graduate School of Education and Human Development at the George Washington University, Washington, DC, and codirector of the National Capital Language Resource Center (NCLRC), a partnership between George Washington and Georgetown Universities and the Center for Applied Linguistics. Holder of a Ph.D. in ESL and applied linguistics from the University of Texas at Austin, she has been principal investigator for many studies funded by the United States Department of Education on the language development of second and

foreign language learners. Her major research interests include language learning strategies, content-based second language instruction, and literacy development in adolescent immigrant students. She has published several related articles and books such as *The Learning Strategies Handbook* (Longman, 1999), *The CALLA Handbook:Implementing the Cognitive Academic Language Learning Approach* (Addison-Wesley, 1994), and *Learning Strategies in Second Language Acquisition* (Cambridge University Press, 1990).
Contact information: auchamot @ gwu. edu

Erica G. Davila is a graduate student at Portland State University. Prior to that, she taught ESL and adult literacy in Brooklyn, New York, where she also designed and implemented tutor training programs. She currently works at the National Labsite for Adult ESOL at Portland State University on a project that compiles and analyzes multimedia classroom data from low-level ESL learners. Her research interests include classrooms as communities of practice, dyadic classroom interaction around written texts, and computer assisted language learning.
Contact information: ericad @ pdx. edu

Thom Hudson is Associate Professor of Second Language Studies at the University of Hawai'i, where he has been on the faculty since 1989. A PhD in applied linguistics from UCLA, he has taught in Cairo, Egypt, Guadalajara, Mexico, and the United States, and has also spent a sabbatical year teaching in Japan. Research interests include second language testing, second language reading, English for specific purposes, and program development, with a long term focus on criterion-referenced testing in particular. His research has appeared in the journals *Annual Review of Applied Linguistics*, *Language and Communication*, *Language Learning*, *Language Testing*, *Studies in Second Language Acquisition*, and *TESOL Quarterly*. Coeditor of the journal *Reading in a Foreign Language*, he has authored or coauthored texts on measuring cross-cultural pragmatics, second language performance assessment, criterion-referenced language testing, and issues in language test development.
Contact information: tdh @ hawaii. edu

Gina Iberri-Shea is a doctoral student in the PhD Program in Applied Linguistics

in the English Departmenr at Northern Arizona University. Her reserach interests include second language acquisition and the role of oral communication activities in language development. Currently, she is working on a coauthored meta-analysis of the effects of task-based interaction on second language acquisition and studying the use of public speaking and debate activities in content-based instruction.
Contact information: gina. iberri-shea @ nau. edu

Joan Jamieson is Professor of English/Applied Linguistics at Northern Arizona University. Her research and teaching interests include second language testing, computer-assisted language learning (CALL), individual learner differences, and research design and statistics. In the last ten years, she has been involved in research and development projects with the Test of English as a Foreign Language and Pearson Longman. With a grant from the TESOL International Research Foundation, she is currently working with Carol Chapelle on the evaluation of CALL materials at six sites throughout the world to better understand the constraints of particular learning contexts and the robustness of CALL materials.
Contact information: joan. jamieson @ nau. edu

Mary McGroarty, Editor-in-Chief of ARAL, is Professor of English/Applied Linguistics Program in the English Department at Northern Arizona University and a past President of the American Association for Applied Linguistics (1997-98). A Woodrow Wilson Fellow, she has also received Fulbright and Mellon awards. Her articles have appeared in *Applied Linguistics*, *Canadian Modern Language Review*, *Language Learning*, *TESOL Quarterly*, and several anthologies. She has served on the editorial boards of *Applied Linguistics*, *ARAL*, *Journal of Language, Identity, and Education*, *Second Language Instruction and Acquisition Abstracts*, and *TESOL Quarterly*. Her research interests include theoretical and pedagogical aspects of language learning and teaching, bilingualism, language policy, and assessment of second language skills.
Contact information: mary. mcgroarty @ nau. edu

Penny McKay is Associate Professor at Queensland University of Technology, Brisbane, Australia, where she teaches in the M.Ed. program in TESOL. She moved into university teaching and research after having been a primary and secondary

mainstream and ESL teacher in Australia and working on a national curriculum effort, the Australian Language Levels Project. She has coordinated several large bilingual/ESL research projects, including *ESL Development: Language and Literacy in Schools*, a document that contains the National Language and Literacy Institute of Australia ESL bandscales (McKay, Hudson, & Sapuppo, 1994), and The Bilingual Interface Project (McKay et al., 1997). The author or editor of many papers on school ESL policy, teaching, and assessment, she has two 2005 books on related issues: *Assessing Young Learners* (Cambridge University Press), and *Planning and Teaching Creatively within a Required Curriculum for School-Age Learners in a new TESOL Curriculum series.*
Contact information: pa. mckay @ qut. edu. au

Brian Morgan is an Associate Professor in the Department of Languages, Literatures, and Linguistics and coordinator of the TESOL Certificate program at York University in Toronto, Ontario, where he teaches content-based English for Academic Purposes courses, a language teacher education course on the sociopolitics of TESOL, and a graduate course on language, culture, and ideology. Before coming to York, he spent ten years as a teacher, teacher educator, and curriculum consultant with the Toronto Catholic School Board, working exclusively in adult community-based ESL programs. Many of his publications and his first book, *The ESL Classroom: Teaching, Critical Practice, and Community Development* (University of Toronto Press, 1998) describe his efforts toward developing critical ESL programs for these settings.
Contact information: bmorgan @ yotku. ca

Denise E. Murray is Professor and Executive Director of the National Centre for English Language Teaching and Research (NCELTR) and also of the AMEP Research Centre at Macquarie University, Australia. A language teacher and teacher educator for over three decades in Australia, England, Thailand, and the United States, she was founding chair of Linguistics and Language Development at San José State University, California. She served on the TESOL Board of Directors for seven years and as president in 1996-1997. She has published widely on the use of computer technology in society and on language education in particular; her publications include *Knowledge Machines: Language and Information in*

a Technological Society (Longman, 1995); *Integrating Citizenship Content in Teaching Adult Immigrants English: An Evaluation of Let's Participate: A course in Australian citizenship* (NCELTR, 2003); *Communicating on the Net* (with P. McPherson; NCELTR, 2003); and "The Language of Cyberspace" in *Language in the USA* (Cambridge, 2004).
Contact information: denise. murray @ mq. edu.au

Terence Odlin is Associate Professor of English at Ohio State University. His research and teaching interests include the psycholinguistic issues involved in language transfer and contrastive analysis, pedagogical grammar, and sociohistorical factors in language contact, particularly in the Celtic lands, with related articles and reviews appearing in *Diachronica, Language, Language Awareness, The Modern Language Journal, Studies in Second Language Acquisition*, and *Second Language Research*. In addition to his book-length study *Language Transfer* (Cambridge University Press, 1989), his recent thinking on cross-linguistic influence includes articles in the *Concise Encyclopedia of Sciolinguistics*, the *Oxford Handbook of Applied Linguistics*, and the *Handbook of Second Language Acquisition*.
Contact information: odlin. 1 @ osu. edu

Lourdes Ortega is Assistant Professor of Applied Linguistics in the Department of Second Language Studies at the University of Hawai'i at Manoa. Her longstanding research interests include the longitudinal study of second language and literacy development, the fostering of explicit and implicit grammar learning through activities organized around "doing things with words" in the classroom (or so-called task-based language learning), second language writing, the relationship between language minority education and foreign language education, and the use of research methods in applied linguistics, particularly research synthesis and meta-analysis. Her ongoing projects are a special issue of *The Modern Language Journal* on values in instructed SLA research, a coedited John Benjamins volume on research synthesis, and a synthesis of longitudinal research funded by a National Academy of Education/Spencer Postdoctoral Fellowship.
Contact information: lortega @ hawaii. edu

Vaidehi Ramanathan is an Associate Professor in the Linguistics Department at the University of California, Davis. Her research and teaching interests include all social and political aspects of first and second language literacy and teacher education, especially as they pertain to dominant and vernacular languages. She has spent the last seven years working on issues related to English-and vernacualr-medium education in Gujarat, India. Her recent publications include *The English-Vernacular Divide: Postcolonial Language Politics and Practice* (Multilingual Matters, in press) and *The Politics of TESOL Education: Writing, Knowledge, Critical Pedagogy* (Routledge Falmer, 2002).
Contact information: vramanathan @ ucdavis. edu

Stephen Reder is University Professor and Chair of the Department of Applied Linguistics at Portland State University. His research and teaching interests, which he has pursued in a range of studies using both quantitative and qualitative methodologies, focus on literacy and language development during adulthood. As a graduate student he worked on the Vai literacy project with Sylvia Scribner and Michael Cole. He then conducted comparative studies of literacy and language development in communities having distinct sociohistorical contexts for literacy and language acquisition: an Eskimo village in Alaska; a highland Hmong community resettled in the northwest of the United States; and a partially settled community of agricultural workers in the migrant stream on the west coast. He is currently researching literacy, language, and education issues mooing high school dropouts in the Longitudinal Study of Adult Learning and among recent immigrants in the National Labsite for Adults ESOL.
Contact information: reders @ pdx. edu

Peter Robinson is Professor of Linguistics and Second Language Acquisition in the Department of English, Aoyama Gakuin University, Tokyo. His recent publications include *Cognition and Second Language Instruction* (Cambridge University Press, 2001); *Individual Differences and Instructed Second Language Learning* (John Benjamins, 2002); and (coauthored with D. Smith, S. Nobe, G. Strong, M. Tani, and H. Yoshiba) *Language and Comprehension: Perspectives from Linguistics and Language Education* (Kuroshio Publishing, 2004). He is editor of the book series *Cognitive Science and Second Language Acquisition* published by Lawrence

Erlbaum.
Contact information: peterr @ cl. aoyama. ac. jp

Elaine Tarone is Distinguished Teaching Professor in English as a Second Language, and Director of the Center for Advanced Research on Language Acquisition at the University of Minnesota. She has published research on second language acquisition since 1972 on topics such as interlanguage phonology, communication strategies in SLA, and language play in immersion classrooms, but is perhaps best knowm for her work on interlanguage variation and the influence of social context on SLA. Her current research focuses on the impact of literacy on the SLA of Somali adults residing in the Twin Cities of Minnesota. At present, along with Martha Bigelow and Kit Hansen, she is analyzing data gathered on the oral English language use of participants who differ in their degree of literacy in both Somali and English.
Contact information:etarone @ umn. edu

Gillian Wigglesworth is Associate Professor and Head of the School of Languages at the University of Melbourne, Australia. She has a wide range of research interests that include first and second language acquisition, language testing and assessment, and bilingualism. She has published widely in these areas and has recently completed a longitudinal study exploring the perceptions of learners of English about their language learning and the learning environment in Melbourne. At present she is working on a longitudinal study investigating the complex language input situation of Australian Aboriginal children in remote communities and its effect on the children's language acquisition.
Contact information: gillianw @ unimelb. edu.au

图书在版编目(CIP)数据

剑桥应用语言学年度评论.2005:应用语言学概述＝Annual Review of Applied Linguistics 2005·A Survey of Applied Linguistics:英文/(美)玛丽·麦克格罗蒂(Mary McGroarty)主编.—北京:商务印书馆,2016
(剑桥应用语言学年度评论)
ISBN 978－7－100－12465－2

Ⅰ.①剑… Ⅱ.①玛… Ⅲ.①应用语言学—研究—英文 Ⅳ.①H08

中国版本图书馆 CIP 数据核字(2016)第 187128 号

所有权利保留。
未经许可,不得以任何方式使用。

剑桥应用语言学年度评论 2005·应用语言学概述
Annual Review of Applied Linguistics 2005·
A Survey of Applied Linguistics
主编 〔美〕Mary McGroarty
导读 孙迎晖

商 务 印 书 馆 出 版
(北京王府井大街36号 邮政编码100710)
商 务 印 书 馆 发 行
北京市松源印刷有限公司印刷
ISBN 978－7－100－12465－2

2016年12月第1版　　开本 880×1230　1/32
2016年12月北京第1次印刷　印张 11⅜
定价:36.00元